Advancing Educational Equity in Computer Science

Computer Science Educational Justice Collective

Published by State University of New York Press, Albany

Advancing Educational Equity in Computer Science © 2025 by Computer Science Educational Justice Collective is licensed under CC BY-SA 4.0.

Printed in the United States of America

Links to third-party websites are provided as a convenience and for informational purposes only. They do not constitute an endorsement or an approval of any of the products, services, or opinions of the organization, companies, or individuals. SUNY Press bears no responsibility for the accuracy, legality, or content of a URL, the external website, or for that of subsequent websites.

EU GPSR Authorised Representative:
Logos Europe, 9 rue Nicolas Poussin, 17000, La Rochelle, France
contact@logoseurope.eu

For information, contact State University of New York Press, Albany, NY
www.sunypress.edu

Library of Congress Cataloging-in-Publication Data

Name: Computer Science Educational Justice Collective, author.
Title: Advancing educational equity in computer science
Description: Albany : State University of New York Press, [2025]. | Includes
  bibliographical references and index.
Identifiers: ISBN 9798855805437 (pbk. : alk. paper) | ISBN 9798855806083
  (ebook)
Further information is available at the Library of Congress.

*To everyone who ever thought
they don't belong in computer science:
You do.*

CONTENTS

Foreword	Beyond Access: Rethinking Equity, Language, and Identity in Computer Science Education	vi
Foreword	Making Computer Science Education What It Was Meant to Be: Computer Science for All	viii
Foreword	Computer Science Education: Overthrowing Fences and Uplifting Humanity	x
Preface		xii
Authors and Acknowledgments		xviii
Overview of the Book		xxiv
On Terminology		xxix
Chapter 1	Introduction: Getting Started with Equity in Computer Science and Computer Science Education	1
Chapter 2	Understanding Diversity in Computer Science and Computer Science Education	21
Chapter 3	Understanding Inequities in Computer Science and Computer Science Education	48
Chapter 4	Understanding Equity in Computer Science and Computer Science Education	68
Chapter 5	Busting Myths About Inequity: Theories for Computer Science Educators to Think With	92
Chapter 6	Building Your Computer Science Education Equity Toolkit	120
Chapter 7	Setting Your Computer Science Equity Commitments	146
Chapter 8	Getting Started with Digital Racial Literacy in Computer Science Education	166
Chapter 9	Applying Digital Racial Literacy in Computer Science Education	188

Chapter 10	Auditing Your Digital Racial Literacy Practice	207
Chapter 11	Language Injustice in Computer Science Education	221
Chapter 12	Translanguaging in Computer Science Education	239
Chapter 13	Literate Programming and Code as a Language Resource	261
Chapter 14	What Conversation Is This Code a Part of?	273
Chapter 15	Disability, Ableism, and You	288
Chapter 16	Unpacking the Universal Design for Learning Framework	317
Chapter 17	Universal Design for Learning in Computer Science Education	334
Glossary		358
Suggestions for Further Reading		371

FOREWORD

Beyond Access

Rethinking Equity, Language, and Identity in Computer Science Education

Yolanda Sealey-Ruiz, Ph.D.

> Sometimes respecting people means making sure your systems are inclusive.
>
> —Joy Buolamwini, Computer Scientist

When Christy Crawford[1] first invited me to be a part of New York City CS4All, I immediately knew I was stepping into a space of real transformation—a space where educators weren't just teaching computer science but actively reshaping who gets to participate, who gets to feel seen, and whose knowledge is valued. Christy is a visionary whose unwavering commitment to culturally responsive computing has left an undeniable impact on CS education. She and the extraordinary computer science educators and scholars of racial literacy, translanguaging, and disability in education who created this book understand something fundamental: access alone is not enough—representation, relevance, and justice must be at the center of how we teach computer science.

This book, *Advancing Educational Equity in Computer Science*, is a labor of love—curated by educators fighting for true equity in CS, working to redefine CS education as deeply reflective, culturally inclusive, and justice driven. At its core, this book reflects the very foundation of my work in racial literacy—developing the ability to read, discuss, and challenge systemic inequities in education. Just as I ask educators to excavate their own biases and histories through the Archaeology of Self™, this book asks educators to move beyond inclusion toward transformation—to not only invite more students into CS spaces but to interrogate and rebuild the very structures that have kept so many out.

---

1. See Preface for more information about Crawford's role.

One of the key frameworks discussed in this book—Universal Design for Learning (UDL) in Computer Science Education—challenges educators to think not just about who is in the room but how learning environments are designed to honor diverse ways of thinking, communicating, and problem solving. Language is a critical equity issue, and this book doesn't shy away from that truth. Translanguaging in Computer Science Education pushes us to recognize programming and code as languages of their own and exposes how monolingual, Eurocentric norms in computing marginalize multilingual learners. This book makes it clear: language itself is a site of exclusion—or liberation.

For too long, diversity in CS has been framed as simply broadening participation without questioning the structures that create the inequities in the first place. This book challenges that narrative. It pushes educators beyond surface-level inclusion toward meaningful, structural change in CS classrooms.

To the educators, scholars, and students engaging with this book—know that you are stepping into something that requires your imagination and belief that change in CS education can happen. Your reflections, actions, and willingness to challenge the status quo in CS education will help ensure that this field is not just a space for a select few—but a pathway to liberation for all.

Yolanda Sealey-Ruiz, Ph.D.
Professor of English Education
Teachers College, Columbia University
New York City, New York, 2025

FOREWORD

Making Computer Science Education What It Was Meant to Be

Computer Science for All

Mark Guzdial, Ph.D.

Teaching equitable computer science is about meeting the original purpose for the field. The first publication of the term "computer science" was by George Forsythe in 1961. He argued that all students in science and engineering would need computer science. (As did his wife, Alexandra, whose contributions weren't acknowledged by the field—see Chapter 3).

Alan Perlis, the first ACM Turing Award laureate, argued in 1961 that we should teach all students at all universities how to program because learning to program changes the way that you understand. He explicitly foresaw how the use of computational models and simulations would change the way that scientists and engineers would come to know.

When Forsythe and Perlis were making these claims, there was no Silicon Valley. Bill Gates and Steve Jobs were both six years old. No one had a job as a "software engineer." Computer science is such a powerful set of ideas that the inventors of the field thought it should be taught to *everyone*, long *before* it offered the lucrative opportunities that it does today.

The economic benefits of computer science have changed how we educate students. How can we *not* prepare students for those opportunities? For students from underprivileged backgrounds, the benefits of a successful computer science education can be life changing. Of course, we should give every student every opportunity to get a great job in computer science. To reference Jane Margolis and colleagues (2017), to do otherwise is to keep students stuck in the shallow end of the economic pool.[1]

---

1. Margolis, J., Estrella, R., Goode, J., Holme, J. J., & Nao, K. (2017) *Stuck in the shallow end: Education, race, and computing* (Updated edition). MIT Press.

But not every student is going to be a professional software developer. Not every student *wants* to be a professional software developer.

We also need scientists, artists, managers, and informed citizens of a technologically rich society who participate actively in the democratic process. We need *everyone* to know about computing, to use it in whatever career they choose, to make informed choices about computing, and to advocate for fair and just uses of computing.

This book offers insight into how to reach the broader goals for computer science laid out by the inventors of the field. The pioneers of the field meant computer science to be taught to *all* students, those who will program in the future and those who won't. Our world needs computer science teachers to embrace diverse methods of teaching to attract a diverse range of students who will use computing in a diverse range of careers.

Mark Guzdial, Ph.D.
Director, Program in Computing for the Arts and Sciences
Professor of Electrical Engineering and Computer Science
University of Michigan
Ann Arbor, Michigan, 2025

FOREWORD

Computer Science Education
Overthrowing Fences and Uplifting Humanity

Ofelia García, Ph.D.

Rarely does one read a book that expands one's view, brings into sharp clarity new understandings, and transforms one's world. This is what reading this book has done for me. With clarity of intent and with lucid writing, these authors have transformed the way that I see computer science (CS) education. As an older Latina, CS had always presented itself to me shrouded in mystery, the purview of white, young, well-to-do males. But this book has helped me understand that a fence—a socially constructed barrier—had kept me, and many educators like me, from getting a full and equitable vision of CS. This was especially brought home to me in Chapter 4 with the analysis of the popular social media images of equity depicted as people of different heights trying to see over the same fence. This book has given me understandings of why the fence exists but also a tool kit to overthrow fences and barriers that keep CS in the hands of the few.

As I write this, fences in and around CS have been rebuilt with more hardness than ever. Technology has become Elon Musk's weapon as he exerts power and control over others and in so doing, dehumanizes CS. But this book centers not technology but the teachers, students, and people who engage with CS in ways that can build back a human, generous, democratic world. Putting processes and ideologies surrounding race, language, disability, and gender at the center of teacher engagement with CS brings back a world and an education system in which we can *all* be equal participants.

To do so, myths in this book are debunked, images of who and what counts as CS transformed, and pedagogical tools identified. We are not presented with codes, algorithms, and static visions of separation. Instead, we are told stories of real teachers in real classrooms. Rather than projecting the usual image of CS as one lone person interacting with a machine, the process of *collaboration* among many teachers and students are described. *Equity is built by understanding relationship-building.*

Literacies are not separate; they are syncretic. Languages, including that of code, do not constitute different systems; they form one network of meaning-making. Our identities are intersectional.

This book is written with care and respect toward CS teachers and their students. Care is taken with words and images. Beyond describing the dynamic networks of signification in these CS classrooms, there is precise clarity in the writing. By giving CS teachers a clear path forward toward equity, this book disrupts the miasma of despair with which computing and technology are viewed today and renews our hope in its transformational potential.

Ofelia García, Ph.D.
Professor Emerita
City University of New York, Graduate Center
New York City, New York, 2025

PREFACE

Christopher Hoadley, Madison Allen Kuyenga, Christy Crawford, and the Computer Science Educational Justice Collective

WHAT IS THIS GUIDE AND WHERE DID IT COME FROM?

Welcome to all educators reading this! Whether you are new to computer science (CS), equity in education, or both, we hope that this guide will support you to advance equity in CS education (CS Ed) in your context. Before you embark on your journey into this resource, we'd like to share some background about the people who have contributed to it and how it came about.

This guide is the product of a community of educators and researchers committed to equity-focused work. We draw on the knowledge and experiences of educators and researchers who have laid the foundation for equity efforts in CS and in education. As a collective of educators, teachers, administrators, learners, and leaders, we are committed to engaging in critical reflection and practice with and around computing and computing education.

We were purposefully brought together to provide professional development to New York City Public School teachers as part of the district's CS Ed initiatives. The Director of Culturally Responsive-Sustaining Education, Christy Crawford, organized us as a group because of our range of professional experience and the diverse identities we hold around ability, class, gender and sexual orientation, language, nationality, race and ethnicity, religion, socioeconomic status, and more. Some of our many identities are reflected in Figure 1. We have spent time grappling with what these perspectives have offered as we have worked to better understand critical computing education.

Our story begins in 2015, when New York City made a commitment that within ten years, the city's public schools would provide meaningful CS instruction to all of its 1.1 million students. This effort was called "Computer Science for All," or CS4All. Through a public-private partnership with the Fund for Public Schools, New York City Public Schools (NYCPS) began developing a blueprint for CS education to meet this commitment.[1]

---

1. For more information, visit https://web.archive.org/web/20220706171912/https://www.fundforpublicschools.org/computerscienceforall and https://blueprint.cs4all.nyc/

Figure 1. Our Collective Identities. Word cloud created using https://www.jasondavies.com/wordcloud/; see full list of identities in Authors and Acknowledgments.

It quickly became clear that implementing the vision of meaningful CS for all in New York City involved two intertwined components. First, there was a need to increase teaching capacity for CS. Second, implementing meaningful CS instruction required meeting the needs of an increasingly diverse student population through relevant CS education.

Meeting the first goal found great success. When the CS4All initiative began, New York State did not have a CS teaching credential pathway. To ensure there were enough educators prepared to teach CS, NYCPS provided in-service teacher professional development, expanding the number of schools involved in the initiative.

However, progress toward achieving the second goal was more uneven. In examining the impact of the initiative, one study found that "schools not offering CS in New York City generally served higher-needs students, including English Language Learners, students with disabilities, low-income students, and students who were not proficient in math or English language arts" (Fancsali et al., 2022). Even as NYCPS mounted efforts to ensure that every school would have well-trained CS educators, it was clear that those educators and their collaborators needed tools to meet students' needs.

Given the diverse population of NYCPS students, CS teachers needed support to ensure that all students received a meaningful and relevant CS education. Since the project began, this diversity has only continued to grow. During the 2023–2024 school year, for example, across the city, 42.2% of students identified racially as Hispanic, 19.5% as Black,

18.7% as Asian, and 16.2% as white.[2] Of the district's students, 16.3% were classified as English Language Learners, with many more speaking a language other than English in the home, and 21.6% of students had district-documented disabilities (New York City Public Schools, 2024).

This diversity reinforced the need to prepare CS educators to teach CS in ways that interrogated how power dynamics like ableism, racism, and sexism have shaped technology and students' experiences with technology. The team leading the CS4All initiative recognized their role in contributing to social equity in technology through "attract[ing], engag[ing], and prepar[ing] the most diverse and socially aware generation of computer scientists and CS educators in the country" (Crawford et al., 2023, p. 3).

Experts from across New York City and the nation were brought together to consult, teach, and research how best to achieve this goal of equitably educating all NYCPS students in CS. These efforts aimed to ensure that all students had access to relevant CS coursework. But they also sought to go beyond access to CS education by preparing teachers who could disrupt—and help their students disrupt—the ways that people are marginalized in and by technology. To accomplish this goal, professional development offered by NYCPS was intentionally designed to support teachers in confronting and dismantling oppressions like ableism, racism, sexism, and xenophobia (Mirakhur et al., 2021). Computer science education was framed as an important contribution to a culturally responsive and sustaining education. This connection was bolstered in 2018 when New York State adopted a framework for culturally responsive-sustaining education.[3]

Crawford headed up efforts to ensure that equity was included in all city-provided teacher professional development (PD) programs for CS education. Under Crawford's leadership and in partnership with DiversFYI—a human and organizational development consultancy—the CS4All team launched a tiered, multi-year professional development program and learning ecosystem called "Exploring Equity in Computer Science" (EECS). EECS is guided by the following goals:

- Affirming students' sense of identities in CS by centering the genius and joy of students who identify as girls, Black, Latine, Southeast Asian, and other historically marginalized communities in CS.[4]

---

2. We preserve the terminology used in the original report. See the On Terminology section of this guide for an explanation on our use of different identity-related terms.

3. https://www.nysed.gov/sites/default/files/programs/crs/culturally-responsive-sustaining-education-framework.pdf

4. See the On Terminology section of this guide for an explanation on our use of different identity-related terms.

- Helping students acquire the skills they need to critically analyze attitudes, beliefs and systemic challenges related to ability, class, gender and sexual orientation, language, race and ethnicity, and the status quo in CS.

- Sharpening students' activism and advocacy capacities so that they are able to use CS knowledge and skills as a way to improve their CS classrooms, schools, and communities.

To accomplish these goals, EECS is structured to provide intensive summer sessions that focus on introductions to racial and equity literacy. The summer sessions scaffold teachers into year-long, curated PD activities as part of the journey work of equity. During successive school years, teachers progress from Level 1 to Level 4 (see Table 1) as part of the ongoing process required to work toward equity (Crawford et al., 2023).

The summer sessions were developed by three teams selected from many groups who had been involved with EECS. These teams included (1) DiversFYI, the consultancy who assisted with designing the EECS ecosystem as a whole; (2) the Creative Technology Research Lab (CTRL) of the University of Florida, which studies and supports techniques to aid in equitable CS education for students with disabilities; and (3) Participating in Literacies and Computer Science (PiLa-CS), a research-practice partnership focused on bi/multilingual learners and CS education.

Table 1. EECS Levels (see Crawford et al., 2023)

EECS Level	Level Description
Level 1	Level 1 works to help teachers build a foundation of shared knowledge and shared language for equity-focused CS work. As they enter inquiry work, teachers make new commitments to challenge inequity in CS and CS education.
Level 2	Level 2 moves beyond individual teachers and the social and emotional work required to engage in equity work. In Level 2, teachers consider systemic characteristics of oppression in CS. These "developing" teachers move beyond making individual commitments to "recogniz[ing] inequity in the systems in which they exist and teach" (Crawford et al., 2023, p. 10).
Level 3	Level 3 invites teachers to start addressing institutional and systemic challenges within their CS education contexts. These "advancing" teachers start to take up identities as "teacher advocates" or "teachers able to voice their own needs and the needs and rights of their students" (Crawford et al., 2023, p. 11).
Level 4	Level 4 teachers become members of the Ingenuity Team. They have "graduated" from EECS but "seek to continuously work with other CS4All alumni and staff to provide oversight to the NYC CS4All community and to implement the equity-focused skills they have gained. . . . [They] also provide leadership and mentoring for CS colleagues" (Crawford et al., 2023, p. 11).

In summer 2020, as the COVID-19 pandemic and protests galvanized by the police's murder of George Floyd blasted through NYC, Crawford assembled these three teams to provide online workshops on racial literacies, translanguaging pedagogies, and Universal Design for Learning for nearly 100 educators and administrators. As the teams repeated the summer PD annually, they gradually integrated the program and templates across these three areas to provide an interwoven foundation for equitable CS teaching.

In 2021, the teams came together to take what they had learned and create a new, integrated resource that could not only support the EECS courses in NYC but would also bring these approaches to a wider audience. With funding from the U.S. National Science Foundation (NSF), the teams began meeting and drafting the present guide. Additional collaborators adjacent to the three teams were brought in, and the name "Computer Science Educational Justice Collective" (CS-EJC) was chosen to describe the mission of the group.

The guide includes a variety of materials previously developed by the three individual projects described earlier as well as collaboratively created materials developed specifically for this guide. It is intended to be complementary to and supportive of the materials developed with NYCPS. The book is designed to grow over time and to be used in structured PD settings (with in- and pre-service educators) and as a tool for individual educators, administrators, or teacher trainers. It is a work in progress. It by no means covers every aspect of equitable teaching in CS, but it serves as a foundational resource for any educator beginning a journey toward advancing educational equity in CS.

We have used a combination of authorship designations to identify key lead authors of each chapter and the larger CS-EJC group as a source of inspiration and feedback. We also gratefully acknowledge feedback from a wide variety of educators and teacher PD experts whose ideas and insights informed and refined this guide. See Acknowledgments for full details and author biographies.

REFERENCES

Crawford, C., Kuyenga, M. A., Talley, L., Mirakhur, Z., & Clark, H. (2023). *Organizing for educational equity in computer science: Lessons from New York City's CS4All initiative.* New York City Department of Education. https://sites.google.com/schools.nyc.gov/cs4all-equity/about-us/impact-report?authuser=0

Fancsali, C., Lee, J., Hill, K., Adair, A., Rivera-Cash, E., & Clough, S. (2022). *CS4All: Examining equity in computer science access and participation in NYC schools.* NYU Research Alliance. https://steinhardt.nyu.edu/research-alliance/research/cs4all-examining-equity

Mirakhur, Z., Fancsali, C., & Hill, K. (2021). The potential of CR-SE for K-12 computer science education: Perspectives from two leaders. *Voices in Urban Education (VUE), 50*(1). https://doi.org/10.33682/3en3-cbgn

New York City Public Schools. (2024). *Demographic snapshot 2023–24: Visual guide.* https://infohub.nyced.org/docs/default-source/default-document-library/23-24-demographic-snapshot-summary—july-2024—web.pdf

AUTHORS AND ACKNOWLEDGMENTS

WHO WE ARE

This guide is a collective effort, and we wish to acknowledge those who made this book possible. We represent a range of professional experience, and we hold diverse identities around ability, class, gender and sexual orientation, language, nationality, race and ethnicity, religion, socioeconomic status, and more.

Some of the many ways we describe our identities include, but are not limited to:

able-bodied, African American, American, arts-based researcher, aunt, auntie, baby boomer, baker, beach-loving, bilingual, bilingual educator, bisexual, Black, Bronxite, Brooklynite, Buddhist, business owner, Caribbean, Caribbean American, Chicana who grew up in a mixed status family, Chinese-Taiwanese American, Christian, cis-gendered, classroom educator, Colombian-American, computer scientist, crafter, critical scholar, CS dabbler, CS education researcher, dancer, daughter, daughter of formerly undocumented Mexican immigrants, descendant of American Slaves, descended from immigrants, disability justice advocate, disabled, doctora, educator, eldest sibling, engineer, English, English-speaker, family genealogist, female, first-generation college graduate, former public school teacher, founder of the WOCArchive, friend, gamer, genderfluid, Georgian, godmother, grandma, heterosexual, hidden disabilities, immigrant, Jewish, language learner, Latinx, lifelong learner, male, mama, Mandarin, mentor, Midatlantic, middle class, middle-aged, millennial, mom, momma, monolingual, mother, multicultural, multilingual, nearsighted, neighbor, neurodivergent, New England, New Yorker, non-binary, parent, parent of a person with disabilities, partner, pastor's kid, Philadelphian, plant lady, profe, professor, queer, reader, researcher, scholar, scholar-activist, second-generation immigrant, senior citizen, sibling of a person with disabilities, sister, Southern, Spanish, Spanish-speaker, special education teacher, STEM education advocate, storyteller, straight, student, teacher, teacher educator, tech enthusiast, upper middle class, white, white Jewish, wife, woman, world traveler, writer, Xennial, 90s millennial

AUTHORS

The members of the Computer Science Educational Justice Collective are the primary authors of this book. We recognize these members for the time, expertise, writing, and labor that they contributed to the collective and to the writing of this guide. We include institutional affiliations for identification purposes only; any opinions, findings, conclusions, or recommendations expressed in this material are those of the author(s) and do not necessarily reflect the views of the institutions listed.

THE COMPUTER SCIENCE EDUCATIONAL JUSTICE COLLECTIVE

Laura Ascenzi-Moreno is a Professor of Bilingual Education and Bilingual Program Coordinator at Brooklyn College, City University of New York.

Madison Allen Kuyenga is an Assistant Professor of Learning, Design, and Technology at Pennsylvania State University, focusing on educational equity and culturally responsive-sustaining computer science education.

Wendy Barrales is a Postdoctoral Associate at New York University, former public school teacher, and founder of the WOCArchive, http://www.wocarchive.com, an intergenerational digital arts–based oral history project that documents, preserves, and amplifies the stories of matriarchs of color.

Joanne Barrett received her doctorate from the University of Florida and, after spending 25 years as a computer science middle and high school educator, joined the CS Everyone Center at the University of Florida.

Britty Cohen received her MA at New York University's Learning Technology Experience Design Program, focusing on the human-centered user experience and the importance of play and games through learning.

Christy Crawford, a former K-8 educator, is the Senior Director of Culturally Responsive-Sustaining Computer Science Education for New York City Public Schools.

Bethany Daniel is a Postdoctoral Associate at the University at Buffalo (SUNY). As a Learning Scientist and former K-16 French educator, her work focuses on teacher learning at the intersections of STEM and language education.

Christopher Hoadley is a Professor of Learning Sciences and Computer Science at the University at Buffalo (SUNY). He directs the UB Institute for Learning Sciences and broadly studies how technology, learning, and empowerment intersect.

Maya Israel is a former special education teacher. She is also a parent and sibling of persons with disabilities. She is an Associate Professor of Educational Technology and Computer Science Education at the University of Florida. She also serves as the Director of the CS Everyone Center for Computer Science Education, https://cseveryonecenter.org/.

Sarane James is a Research Assistant on the PiLa-CS project. She studied Creative Writing at the Macaulay Honors College at City University of New York Hunter College. Her interests lie in curriculum design and utilizing storytelling to illustrate both data and lived experience.

Nykema Lindsey is a STEM education training and content specialist, with an emphasis in computer science education. Her interests lie in using affordable, physically accessible edtech devices and tools to enrich learning environments.

Jasmine Y. Ma is an Associate Professor of Education at New York University.

Melissa Mejias Parker is the Associate Director of Equitable Practices at Computer Science for All NYC.

Spence J. Ray is Director of the K-12 Equity Lab at Cornell Tech and is pursuing doctoral studies in Educational Psychology and Educational Technology at Michigan State University.

Carla Strickland is a Digital Curriculum Developer at UChicago STEM Education. She is an experienced mathematics teacher and curriculum developer who brings an Afro-Caribbean perspective to her work helping elementary teachers integrate computer science into their mathematics instruction.

Lloyd M. Talley is a distinguished human development scholar and the founder of DiversFYI, Co. His work focuses on fostering inclusive and supportive environments that promote the holistic development of both children and adults. Learn more at www.Divers.FYI.

Sara Vogel is a born-and-raised Brooklynite, educator, and education researcher focusing on computing-integrated (teacher) learning environments and forms of education that center around bi/multilingual learners, their literacies, and communities. She currently works at the City University of New York.

Lauren Vogelstein is an Assistant Professor of Communications, Media, and Learning Technologies Design at Teachers College, Columbia University, where she researches the design and study of creative, expressive, and humanizing STEAM learning environments.

CHAPTER AUTHORS BUT NOT CS-EJC MEMBERS

Jenia Marquez is an undergraduate student at Princeton University in the Linguistics Department studying morphophonemics and language attrition in Occitan, with minors in French and conducting.

Felix Wu is a computer science and math teacher in New York City Public Schools and an Academy for Teachers Fellow.

Joyce Wu is an NYU Steinhardt alumna with degrees in mathematics education, computer science education, and special education, focusing on student-centered pedagogy. As a math learning specialist for New York City Public Schools, she is committed to equitable teaching practices and the empowerment of students who identify with historically marginalized groups.

EQUITY COHESION TEAM

Stephanie T. Jones is a scholar-educator-learner-auntie exploring, researching, and writing at the intersections of community and history, computing, race, and learning. Stephanie provided essential feedback at multiple points in the writing process to ensure that the content of the book reflected the CS-EJC's commitment to advancing equity in computer science education.

Edmund Adjapong is a dynamic educator, author, scholar, and community-based practitioner whose innovative approach to teaching leverages hip-hop culture as a transformative tool in educational spaces. As a STEM educator, Edmund has a deep commitment to addressing the racial disparities in STEM education and careers. His research and practice focus on exploring how hip-hop can be utilized to connect with students, foster positive educational outcomes, and challenge systemic inequities within K-12 schools and beyond.

COORDINATION TEAM

While the members of the CS-EJC collective are the primary authors of this work, we wish to acknowledge the efforts of **Christopher Hoadley**, **Sara Vogel**, and **Christy Crawford** who worked to ensure the production of this guide over four years (2021–2025). Chris proposed the initial conceptualization of the project and led the team in determining the appropriate form and format of the book. He served as the Principal Investigator of the grants that supported this work, including grant supplements that made funding for the creation of the guide possible. Sara offered intellectual and managerial leadership as she guided the CS-EJC through the process of conceptualizing, drafting, and revising the book's content. Christy was instrumental in navigating across various institutions, connecting authors to the NYCPS teachers and other consultants who provided feedback. **Maya Israel**, **Spence Ray**, and **Lloyd Talley** additionally formed part of the steering committee that shaped and led the work from 2021 to 2023. At various points, **Britty Cohen**, **Lauren Vogelstein**, and **Bethany Daniel** also helped manage the writing and editing process across authors.

EDITORIAL TEAM

We wish to acknowledge several editors who contributed to revising and editing the final version. **Bethany Daniel** prepared the book for publication including comprehensive copyediting and redrafting and facilitated multiple rounds of review and feedback on the book. **Edmund Adjapong** and **Chan Pham** provided editorial commentary on the book's foundational chapters, and **Warrick Balfour** provided pre-publication copyediting assistance.

ACKNOWLEDGMENTS

This material is based on work supported by the National Science Foundation (NSF) under Awards CNS-1738645, DRL-1837446, and DRL-2420361 and a grant from the George Lucas Educational Foundation (GLEF). The entire project was inspired by the EECS initiative developed for NYCPS with support from the FPS. Any opinions, findings, conclusions, or recommendations expressed in this material are those of the author(s) and do not necessarily reflect the views of NSF, GLEF, NYCPS, or FPS.

We wish to thank Anthony Wheeler and Christopher Hoadley for serving as faculty beta testers and facilitating pilots of this textbook in their computer science teacher education courses.

We wish to thank the students and educators who provided us with feedback on the content of this guide:

Alexis, Amanda Barelli, Nicole Berrios, Tarek Elabsy, Richard Gross, Carla Hannah, Melissa Hannon, Brandie Hayes, Peter Huu Tran, Kristi Jones, Jami Kowles, Yeidy Levels, Katy Liang,

Aaron Lober, Alicia Luna, Anjeliqe Martinez, Emily Martinez, Monique Maylor, D. Morales, Susan Murray, Lindsay Pinerio, Karime Robles, Jennifer Romeo, Christina Salters, Dawn Scalise, Sui King Dawn Shum, J. Lauren Soumilas, Ilka Stoessel, Anna Sun, Michelle Wiener, Rebecca Young, and four students and educators who remain anonymous.

We wish to thank participants of the PiLa-CS professional learning community and the 2019–2024 New York City CSforAll EECS participants, as well as the Asian American, Pacific Islander, Middle Eastern, North African; Black; Latinx; and White Anti-Racist CSforAll EECS affinity group members.

OVERVIEW OF THE BOOK

This guide is intended to support educators and others in their efforts toward advancing equity in computer science education (CS Ed). We ourselves are a collective of administrators, educators, leaders, learners, researchers, teachers, and technologists, and we hope that this book will help others like us and anyone else committed to equity in CS Ed.

Our goal is to make this guide accessible and useful to readers with different roles and commitments. Some readers may be K-12 educators teaching CS as a discipline, or they may be working to integrate CS into other content areas to make interdisciplinary connections. Some may teach CS or computing-integrated subjects in higher education or may be involved in teacher preparation. Some may be engaged in CS Ed policy or research; others may be in administration and leadership roles. Given this variation, we hope this guide will support many different needs. Here, we provide an overview of the book's content and organization as well as features of the book that might help different audiences find value in what this guide offers.

PURPOSES OF THIS GUIDE

We invite readers to personalize this guide for their contexts and communities. This guide might be used in many ways:

- as a primary or secondary text in CS teacher education programs,
- as a resource for in-service K-12 teachers' professional development,
- as a guide for individual educators or study groups of colleagues,
- as an introduction to equity issues in CS education for researchers, and more.

CONTENT OVERVIEW

We have intentionally designed the book to build across different topics, but each chapter also stands alone and can be read, assigned, or used individually.

The book begins with an **Introduction** (Chapter 1) that orients readers to the guide and serves as an entry point into considering issues related to equity in CS and CS Ed.

Chapters 2 through 4 explore key concepts related to exploring equity in CS:

- **Chapter 2** unpacks the notion of diversity.

- **Chapter 3** considers inequity in CS and CS Ed.

- **Chapter 4** offers different ways to think about equity, including the definitions we use in this book.

Each of these chapters illustrates their respective concepts through examples and concrete applications to CS and CS Ed. Together, Chapters 2 through 4 provide a foundation of shared understanding that we build on moving forward.

Chapters 5 through 7 build on this foundation by helping readers prepare a toolkit that they can use to explore equity issues in CS and CS Ed.

- **Chapter 5** offers several theoretical lenses that can be used to recognize how inequity manifests, both in society and in educational spaces. Chapter 5 also uses these theories to "bust" common myths that perpetuate inequity in CS and CS Ed.

Chapters 6 and 7 prepare readers to engage in equity work on a personal level. Because of the deep work involved in these types of reflection and commitment setting, it is highly recommended that readers engage in Chapters 6 and 7 in community with others.

- **Chapter 6** starts readers on their own personal journey of self-development, centering journaling and reflection as practices that support us to consider how our individual backgrounds and experiences shape our efforts to advance equity.

- **Chapter 7** invites readers to draw on their reflections to identify and set equity-related commitments that can guide their CS practice.

Following Chapter 7, the book considers what it looks like to advance equity in CS education with three specific focuses. Chapters 8 through 10 examine digital racial literacy in CS education, Chapters 11 through 14 take up language (in)justice in CS education, and Chapters 15 through 17 consider the Universal Design for Learning framework in CS education.

The first chapters of these three focuses provide foundational understandings of the topic, and later chapters apply the topic directly to CS Ed.

Chapters 8 through 10 examine digital racial literacy in CS Ed. Similar to Chapters 6 and 7, they are intentionally written to be read and engaged with in community. They invite readers to pause and reflect individually and with others and to identify steps to take action. Their structure makes them especially appropriate for settings like professional development, book clubs, or conversations with critical friends.

- **Chapter 8** offers digital racial literacy as a concept and way to engage with race as a social reality that impacts CS and CS Ed.

- **Chapter 9** focuses on how to apply digital racial literacy in CS Ed, including how to help students develop digital racial literacy.

- **Chapter 10** invites readers to actively apply what they have learned about digital racial literacy through auditing their CS Ed practices.

Chapters 11 through 14 consider the role of language in CS education.

- **Chapter 11** lays a foundation by exploring the issue of language injustice in computing and CS Ed.

- **Chapter 12** offers the theory of translanguaging as a way to disrupt language injustice and provides concrete examples of what translanguaging pedagogy can look like in CS Ed.

- **Chapter 13** introduces the idea of "literate programming" and invites readers to consider how code can be used as a form of expression in its own right.

- **Chapter 14** explores how code can become a part of social conversations that go beyond traditional school boundaries to support students in using computing to develop new forms of literacy.

Chapters 15 through 17 consider the Universal Design for Learning framework in the context of CS Ed.

- **Chapter 15** unpacks disability and the related inequity of ableism, exploring what these two topics mean for CS Ed.

- **Chapter 16** introduces the Universal Design for Learning framework as a tool that can help challenge ableism by intentionally designing instruction that removes barriers and meets all students' needs.

- **Chapter 17** applies the Universal Design for Learning framework to CS Ed contexts, illustrating ways to make CS Ed accessible for all learners.

TEXT FEATURES

Given the many potential purposes and audiences that this book could serve, we have worked to provide concrete, practical instructional strategies and the conceptual and theoretical foundations for those strategies, all grounded in research. Working toward this, we have included a number of different text features:

- **Chapter overviews** and **objectives** enable readers to quickly get a sense of what each chapter is about and can support using the book non-linearly.

- **Key terms** for each chapter and the corresponding **Glossary** work to make scholarly jargon more accessible and provide shared definitions for how we use terms that may be defined in multiple ways.

- **Teacher stories** and **examples** from real CS classes are incorporated into each chapter to illustrate how the concepts and principles can be applied in the real world of the classroom. Teachers' stories are used with permission.

- **Reflection questions** at the end of each chapter are intended to support readers to process the chapter content and consider how it might apply to their specific settings.

- **Takeaways for practice** offer action steps that classroom teachers can take to immediately apply what they have learned from the book to their work.

- **Reference** lists point to the scholarly and public sources that informed our work and allow us to contribute to scholarly conversations about equity in CS Ed.

- **Chapter resources** included at the end of some chapters provide extensions to the content. These resources include additional information to build on the chapter topic(s), extended examples of applications of the chapter content to CS classrooms, or additional activities to help readers process the chapter content. These resources may be especially useful to support conversations in classes or professional development settings or to support individual self-study.

- **Suggestions for further reading** are provided at the end of the book to share additional connections to those involved in work related to the topics discussed in the book. These suggestions may be of interest to readers who would like to delve deeper into a given topic.

THIS GUIDE AS A LIVING DOCUMENT

As a final note, we recognize that there are many issues and topics related to advancing equity in CS Ed that we did not address in this guide. We also know that our understanding of topics that are covered in this book will continue to grow. We see this guide as a living document and community resource. To facilitate ongoing conversations and learning, we have licensed the book under a Creative Commons copyright license. This means that you are free to share, adapt, and remix what you find here to further your own efforts in working toward equity in CS Ed. We just ask that you credit the authors of the guide, indicate any changes you make, and license your new contributions under the same Creative Commons license. We look forward to how this guide will be taken up and expanded by you!

ON TERMINOLOGY

Bethany Daniel, Sara Vogel, Jenia Marquez, Sarane James, Stephanie T. Jones, and the Computer Science Educational Justice Collective

Words matter. And words really matter when we use them to describe and talk about people. The words we choose can reaffirm identities and demonstrate respect for others. They can also alienate and reproduce stereotypes and harmful labels. Words are a part of language, and language is a living thing that changes over time. Language is influenced by society, culture, and the people who use it every day.

While there is not always a clear or simple answer to which words are the "right" ones to use, we can push ourselves to be thoughtful in the language we choose and the messages our words convey. Often, the ideal involves asking individuals what language they would prefer to use to describe themselves (American Psychological Association [APA], 2022; Mack & Palfrey, 2020). Because of the limits we faced in writing this book for a broad audience, we worked to be reflective in our choice of terms, consistent in their use throughout the guide, and transparent about our decisions.

We recognize that there are thoughtful arguments for using a variety of words. We also know that words change over time. What a word means at one point in time in one context may come to mean something very different at another time in another situation. The words we are choosing for this guide now may need to be revised in the future, as meanings change and as new words are offered that better capture what we want to express.

In the sections that follow, we outline some of our choices and our rationales for the terminology used throughout this guide. We provide references as resources and invite you as readers to consider which words may best capture and communicate meaning in your own settings and contexts. We hope that thinking about this will help you in your role as computer science (CS) educators to recognize how terms used in educational policy and practice may be exclusionary and to reflect on the language you use with and about your students.

LANGUAGE RELATED TO RACE AND ETHNICITY

We recognize that racial and ethnic identity labels are socially constructed and rooted in histories of racialized oppression. We also acknowledge that these labels are inconsistently applied and change over time (Harris, 1993). Furthermore, CS spaces often reproduce racialized inequity.

Often, an individual's racial and ethnic identities cannot be adequately captured by standardized categories or designations. For example, categories commonly used in educational research and policy (like Asian, Black, Hispanic, Latine, or white) may refer to people who have histories and ancestry from many different places, who have diverse phenotypic features, and who have a range of different lived experiences. Recognizing these complexities and the limitations of category labels, we have made the following decisions about race-related language, outlined in Table 1.

Table 1. Language Related to Race and Ethnicity

Issue	Explanation
Race and ethnicity as social constructs	Examples: *race-ethnicity* We consider race and ethnicity as social constructs that shape identities and lived experiences. Racial labels are frequently linked to physical features, while ethnic labels are often defined based on cultural group membership (Blake, 2016). Depending on the contexts and topics considered in this book, we highlight race, ethnicity, or both at different times. We recognize both race and ethnicity—and the conflicts that emerge related to them—as relevant to issues of inequity in CS and CS Ed. For example, Chapter 8 uses the term "race-ethnicity" to capture how both constructs need to be considered as part of developing racial and ethnic literacy. We also acknowledge that institutional categories do not always clearly distinguish between the two. For example, the U.S. Federal Census and the Advanced Placement exams have used terminology that conflate race and ethnicity and have adjusted the categories they have used over the years, highlighting how these categories are socially constructed (e.g., Brown & Thompson, 2020)
Language that indicates racialization as a social process	Examples: *racialized bilingual or racially minoritized students* We recognize that everyone is racialized through social processes. The terms above are examples of negative racialization, where being racialized is often linked to marginalization and oppression. However, white is also a race. Being racialized as white may afford individuals more privilege in many educational contexts. We strive to use language that emphasizes racialization as a social process and race and ethnicity labels as socially constructed terms.
Racial and ethnic category names	Examples: *Asian American, Black, Pacific Islander* We use racial and ethnic category names to acknowledge how they have become socially salient. We capitalize these names with one exception (white), discussed below. When we cite research or policy, we preserve the terminology, capitalization, and punctuation of the original source.
Capitalization of white	Example: *white students* We choose not to capitalize white to avoid recentering whiteness (Crenshaw, 1991; Harris, 1993; Laws, 2020) and to distinguish our use of the term from the white supremacist practice of capitalizing it (Daniszewski, 2020). However, we recognize that compelling arguments exist on both sides of this decision (e.g., Mack & Palfrey, 2020; Nguyên & Pendleton, 2020).

Issue	Explanation
Use of Latine	Example: *schools with large numbers of Black and Latine students*
	We use the term "Latine" instead of related terms like "Latino," "Latina," "Latinx," "Latin@," or "Hispanic." Latine is a gender-inclusive pronoun that follows existing Spanish language patterns (National Institutes of Health [NIH], 2024). The term was created by gender non-binary, queer, and feminist communities in Spanish-speaking countries (Cambio Center, n.d.; El Centro, n.d.).
Use of Indigenous	Example: *Indigenous students are less likely to have access to CS Ed*
	We use the term "Indigenous" collectively to refer to the descendants of those who lived in North America prior to European colonization. We recognize that this term collapses the diversity of Indigenous nations around the world. To avoid reinforcing static and monolithic interpretations, we try to use plural phrasing like "Indigenous peoples" or "Indigenous cultures" (APA, 2022; NIH, 2024).
Use of "people of color"	We avoid using the term "people of color" because of how it recenters whiteness by othering those who are racialized as non-white and because of how it collapses and essentializes racially marginalized groups (Kim, 2020). We do keep the term when it is used in direct citations.

LANGUAGE RELATED TO GENDER AND SEXUAL ORIENTATION

We recognize that individual gender identity, expression, and sexual orientation is varied. We also acknowledge that those who identify as lesbian, gay, bisexual, transgender and trans, queer and questioning, intersex, asexual or agender, two-spirit, and other related identities often face marginalization and exclusion from CS spaces. We work to attend to this reality by using inclusive language in the following ways outlined in Table 2.

Table 2. Language Related to Gender and Sexual Orientation

Issue	Explanation
Use of gender-affirming language	When referring to specific individuals, we use pronouns that affirm individuals' gender identities.
Avoiding use of gender-marked language	We avoid broad gender-marked language, including words like "mankind" or "seminal" (The Writing Center, n.d.).
Addressing the gender binary in CS and CS Ed	At times, we refer to gender categories in this guide in ways that reinforce a binary conception of gender (e.g., boys, girls). This is primarily done to emphasize how CS and CS Ed often reinforce these binaries, such as when reporting statistics that highlight gender-based inequities.
	We try to surface this reality and emphasize the need to think more expansively. To do this, we use terms like "non-binary," "gender non-conforming," or "LGBTQIA2S+" to indicate inclusion of individuals with a range of identities (The Gender and Sexuality Campus Center [GSCC], n.d.; GLAAD, n.d.).

LANGUAGE RELATED TO DISABILITY

We recognize that the idea of disability is socially constructed and shaped by legal definitions, social contexts, and medical diagnoses (Annamma et al., 2013). We also recognize that language often reinforces negative stereotypes about disability (National Center on Disability and Journalism [NCDJ], 2021). We try to use language that avoids reinforcing people without disabilities as the "norm" (National Education Association [NEA], n.d.). Our decisions about language related to disability are outlined in Table 3.

Table 3. Language Related to Disability

Issue	Explanation
Avoiding ableist language	Example: *make visible* We avoid ableist language and outdated and condescending terminology (Rahman, 2019). We also work to avoid metaphorical language related to disability, like "make visible" and phrases like "simple" and "simply" that imply a neurotypical norm.
Use of "common sense"	In everyday terms, "common sense" may reinforce ableist norms by implying that something should be easily understood or accepted by society. However, when we use the term, we do so in line with scholars who have challenged the term as being neither common nor sensical (e.g., Fairclough, 2014; Garfinkel, 1967). Our use of the term often seeks to examine how what we assume to be "common sense" actually serves to reproduce inequity.

LANGUAGE RELATED TO BI/MULTILINGUALISM

We recognize that dominant beliefs in the United States tend to reinforce English monolingualism as the norm. This results in educational policies and practices that identify students who are learning English as lacking in some way. We work to contest this reality by referring to people who speak multiple languages as outlined in Table 4.

Table 4. Language Related to Bi/Multilingualism

Issue	Explanation
Avoiding deficit-based terms	Examples: *English Learners, English Language Learners* We avoid using deficit-based terms for bi/multilingual students (Flores & García, 2020).
Use of asset-based terminology	Examples: *emergent bi/multilingual* We use terms that emphasize students' varied and dynamic linguistic resources. We use "multilingual" to highlight how we may not be able to assume that a learner only uses two languages and may have a broader linguistic repertoire (Holdway & Hitchcock, 2018).

REFERENCES

American Psychological Association. (2022, July). *Racial and ethnic identity*. https://apastyle.apa.org/style-grammar-guidelines/bias-free-language/racial-ethnic-minorities

Annamma, S. A., Connor, D., & Ferri, B. (2013). Dis/ability critical race studies (DisCrit): Theorizing at the intersections of race and dis/ability. *Race Ethnicity and Education, 16*(1), 1–31. https://doi.org/10.1080/13613324.2012.730511

Blake, R. (2016). Toward heterogeneity: A sociolinguistic perspective on the classification of Black people in the twenty-first century. In H. S. Alim, J. R. Rickford & A. F. Ball (Eds.), *Raciolinguistics: How language shapes our ideas about race* (pp. 153–169). Oxford University Press. https://doi.org/10.1093/acprof:oso/9780190625696.003.0009

Brown, A. V., & Thompson, G. L. (2020). How foreign are the Spanish advanced placement world language exams? The case of ethnicity, bilinguality, and heritage learner candidates. *Hispania, 103*(2), 181–198. https://doi.org/10.1353/hpn.2020.0031

Cambio Center (n.d.). *Hispanic, Latin@, Latinx or Latine?* Cambio Center, University of Missouri. https://cambio.missouri.edu/about/hispanic-latin-latinx-or-latine/

Crenshaw, K. (1991). Mapping the margins: Intersectionality, identity politics, and violence against women of color. *Stanford Law Review, 43*(6), 1241–1299. https://doi.org/10.2307/1229039

Daniszewski, J. (2020, July 20). Why we will lowercase white. *Associated Press*. https://blog.ap.org/announcements/why-we-will-lowercase-white#:~:text=But%20capitalizing%20the%20term%20white,that%20white%20is%20the%20default.

El Centro. (n.d.). *Why Latinx/é?* El Centro at Colorado State University. https://elcentro.colostate.edu/about/why-latinx/#:~:text=Language%20is%20complicated.,identify%20outside%20the%20gender%20binary.

Fairclough, N. (2014). *Language and power* (3rd ed.). Routledge. https://doi.org/10.4324/9781315838250

Flores, N., & García, E. S. (2020). Power, language, and bilingual learners. In N. S. Nasir, C. D. Lee, R. Pea, & M. McKinney de Royston (Eds.), *Handbook of the cultural foundations of learning* (pp. 178–191). Routledge. https://doi.org/10.4324/9780203774977-12

Garfinkel, H. (1967). *Studies in ethnomethodology*. Polity Press.

GLAAD. (n.d.). *An ally's guide to terminology: Talking about LGBT people & equality*. https://media.glaad.org/wp-content/uploads/2011/08/25203738/allys-guide-to-terminology_1-2c9.pdf

Harris, C. I. (1993). Whiteness as property. *Harvard Law Review, 106*(8), 1701–1791. https://doi.org/10.2307/1341787

Holdway, J., & Hitchcock, C. H. (2018, October). Exploring ideological becoming in professional development for teachers of multilingual learners: Perspectives on translanguaging in the classroom. *Teaching and Teacher Education, 75*, 60–70. https://doi.org/10.1016/j.tate.2018.05.015

Kim, E. T. (2020, July 29). The perils of "people of color." *The New Yorker*. https://www.newyorker.com/news/annals-of-activism/the-perils-of-people-of-color

Laws, M. (2020, June 16). Why we capitalize "Black" (and not "white"). *Columbia Journalism Review*. https://www.cjr.org/analysis/capital-b-black-styleguide.php

Mack, K., & Palfrey, J. (2020, August 26). *Capitalizing Black and White: Grammatical justice and equity.* MacArthur Foundation. https://www.macfound.org/press/perspectives/capitalizing-black-and-white-grammatical-justice-and-equity

National Center on Disability and Journalism. (2021, August). *Disability language style guide.* https://ncdj.org/style-guide/

National Education Association. (n.d.). *Words matter! Disability language etiquette.* https://www.nea.org/words-matter-disability-language-etiquette

National Institutes of Health. (2024, January 17). *Race and national origin*. https://www.nih.gov/nih-style-guide/race-national-origin

Nguyên, A. T., & Pendleton, M. (2020, March 23). *Recognizing race in language: Why we capitalize "Black" and "White."* Center for the Study of Social Policy. https://web.archive.org/web/20250318065619/https://cssp.org/2020/03/recognizing-race-in-language-why-we-capitalize-black-and-white/

Rahman, L. (2019, July). *Disability language guide.* Stanford Disability Initiative Board. https://disability.stanford.edu/sites/g/files/sbiybj26391/files/media/file/disability-language-guide-stanford_1.pdf

The Gender and Sexuality Campus Center, Michigan State University. (n.d.). *Glossary*. Michigan State University. https://gscc.msu.edu/education/glossary.html#:~:text=The%20GSCC%20primarily%20uses%20the,sign%20signifies%20additional%20identity%20terms.

The Writing Center, University of North Carolina Chapel Hill. (n.d.). *Gender-inclusive language.* https://web.archive.org/web/20240625060227/https://writingcenter.unc.edu/tips-and-tools/gender-inclusive-language/

1

Introduction

Getting Started with Equity in Computer Science and Computer Science Education

Sara Vogel, Christopher Hoadley, Lauren Vogelstein, Bethany Daniel, Stephanie T. Jones, and the Computer Science Educational Justice Collective

CHAPTER OVERVIEW

This introduction welcomes readers to the work of advancing equity in computer science education (CS Ed). It presents some of the inequities that CS students and teachers face, as well as some of the efforts that are underway to work toward equity in CS and CS Ed. It also describes the values and goals that are the foundation of this guide.

CHAPTER OBJECTIVES

After reading this introduction, I can:

- Describe recent efforts to work toward equity in CS and CS Ed.
- Identify inequities that continue in CS and CS Ed.
- Explain the values that shaped how the authors of this guide approached their work.

KEY TERMS

broadening participation; critical consciousness; culturally sustaining pedagogies; equity as access; equity as transformation; praxis

GETTING STARTED

Welcome! This guide focuses on advancing equity work in CS Ed. To begin, we wish to recognize how we as authors come to this work. We are a collective of CS educators and scholars who came together to work on a multi-year project focused on equity in CS Ed in New York City. We hold different identities at the intersections of disability, gender, language, and race among others. We have collaborated on many equity-related CS efforts, and this guide is a product of those collaborations. See the Preface for more details about our positionalities and the history of the guide.

We also acknowledge that you, our readers, come to this guide with different backgrounds and experiences that shape how you do this work. Some of the ideas presented here may resonate strongly with you. Some may make you pause or feel discomfort. We hope that as you explore these ideas, you'll feel compelled to process your responses, talk out what you're learning with colleagues, and importantly, try out something new in your settings. Equity work takes time, critical reflection, commitment, and individual and collective action. There's no one perfect way to do it. We hope this guide helps you take steps big and small to create more accessible, just, and ethical forms of CS Ed for your students.

To get started on our journey, let's meet Marilyn, a CS teacher who is asking some important questions about what equity looks and feels like in CS Ed.[1]

MARILYN'S STORY

It was a few minutes after the last bell on the last day of school at STEM Preparatory Academy, a diverse school in New York. Students had just cleared out of the building, and Marilyn, a sixth- and seventh-grade CS teacher, began to clean her classroom. On the walls were posters of "giants" in computing, people like Katherine Johnson, Jerry Lawson, and Alan Turing, whose racial, ethnic, and gender identities reflected the diverse student body at her school.[2] Marilyn had hung them up after attending a professional development (PD) workshop about representation in CS Ed earlier in the year. As she took down the posters, she sighed. A math

---

1. Marilyn is a composite character based on New York City public school teacher Susan Murray and the collective experiences of the authors, teachers, and collaborators of this guide.

2. See Resource 1 at the end of the chapter and this calendar of leaders in CS for more resources: https://sites.google.com/schools.nyc.gov/cs4all-equity/pioneer-calendar?authuser=0

teacher for fifteen years, this was Marilyn's first year tentatively entering the world of CS. She found the PD trainings intellectually interesting and the mission to bring CS to all students a compelling one. But she couldn't deny that her entry into CS this year had left her with many questions.

Marilyn's PD trainings had shared troubling statistics about how young women and girls are often excluded from CS Ed and careers. Inspired to change this, Marilyn adopted a curriculum from the Girls Who Code organization and convinced her principal to fund an after-school club.[3] Marilyn reflected on her experience:

> You know, everyone says "do Girls Who Code." And I have that after school, you know. And you say, "Oh, it's open to everyone." But it doesn't mean anyone feels comfortable. 'Cause the boys don't want to go if it says, "Girls Who Code."
>
> But now I'm working with my girls, right? And I'm adding more girls, and they're doing more coding projects. But what about my Black boys? My Brown boys? My Arab students? Those are kids who are still underrepresented in code. Am I doing a disservice by focusing on a single group? Should I focus on my girls one year and my Black kids the next year? My Arab kids the next year?[4]
>
> How do I equitably do equity? Who do I leave out? Can I leave out somebody? Should I focus on everybody all at once? How do you build equity without being inequitable?

Marilyn's questions point to complex issues. On the one hand, programs like Girls Who Code are designed to address the fieldwide issues that Marilyn learned about at her PD by helping girls spark an interest in computing. This interest might lead more girls to major in CS-related fields, create innovative tech tools, found tech companies, experience economic mobility, and have an impact on society. On the other hand, Marilyn recognized that programs like Girls Who Code might not feel welcoming or relevant to all of her students. Marilyn acknowledged how the diverse groups of boys at her school were not always interested in a coding club framed for girls. And we would add that non-binary and gender non-conforming students might also not feel comfortable in a program called Girls Who Code.

Marilyn's questions might also prompt us to reflect on the girls at her school. They were alike in some ways, but they also had varying abilities, racial and ethnic identities, language practices, and lived experiences.

---

3. To learn more about Girls Who Code, visit https://www.girlswhocode.com/
4. We preserve the terms used by Marilyn. See the On Terminology section of this guide for an explanation on our use of different identity-related terms.

What kinds of CS learning opportunities might help her reach girls with disabilities? Black and Latine girls? Black and Latine girls with disabilities? Girls who are bi/multilingual? The questions that Marilyn asked about recognizing the diverse identities and needs of her students are thought provoking, especially when teachers, including Marilyn, have limited time, resources, and capacity. Where is the best place to put that energy?

There are also issues related to equity in CS that Marilyn didn't touch on in her quote. She was inspired to bring CS Ed to her school in response to statistics about a lack of gender diversity in technology industries. Is that the core reason to do CS Ed? Are there other purposes for learning and doing computing that might resonate more deeply with students? Or that might serve students' communities? Or that might push toward social change?

Marilyn's ultimate goal is to support her students to realize their potential and thrive, and she thinks that CS Ed is a part of reaching that goal. But she wonders what kinds of changes in policy, curricula, and pedagogy would be needed—not just in her club, but in her school, her district, and even her state—to engage all students and their diverse identities in meaningful and equity-oriented computing education.

CS FOR *ALL*?

Marilyn isn't the only one with questions about equity in CS Ed. The initial movement to provide CS Ed for all students in the United States, known as Computer Science for All (CSforAll), took off in the 2010s. More than a decade later, educators and policy makers are still grappling with how to make CS Ed more equitable. For years, those working toward equity in CS Ed have focused on providing "access" to the kind of CS Ed that will "make them job-ready on day one," a goal that President Barack Obama identified at a 2016 Hour of Code event at the White House (Smith, 2016). To meet those and similar goals, hundreds of millions of dollars from the government, private foundations, and industry were committed to **broadening participation** in computing. This vision worked to help young people from a range of backgrounds learn the kinds of CS skills that would help them join fast-growing and exciting industries.

Responding to these national initiatives, educators across the nation worked hard. They expanded CS course offerings, recruited students to take new courses, and built up after-school programs like Girls Who Code. They spent hours in professional development learning new CS skills, worked to keep up with emergent professional standards, taught new courses like Advanced Placement Computer Science Principles (AP CSP) from the College Board AP program, and integrated CS concepts and skills into other subject areas. They created new CS departments and industry partnerships and

broadening participation
A way of thinking about equity, similar to access, that seeks to increase the participation of members of underrepresented and/or marginalized groups in CS and CS Ed. These groups have historically been excluded from computing fields.

advocated for CS graduation mandates. These efforts have made progress toward the broadening participation vision: **access** to CS classes increased from approximately half a million students in 2013 to 46 million students in 2019, and booming enrollments continue in CS departments across the United States (Code.org, 2020). There is also increased infrastructure for CS Ed and a greater awareness of the importance of CS Ed.

However, CS Ed equity has not yet been fully realized. CS Ed still disproportionately benefits the students who have historically been centered in education: white students, male students, students from affluent backgrounds, and students who attend high-resourced schools. Inequities related to CS Ed, industry, and technology continue to abound. A recent report documented how students with marginalized gender and racial and ethnic identities, multilingual learners, low-income youth, and students with disabilities continue to be excluded at nearly all levels of CS Ed, from K-12 to higher education (100Kin10, 2021). A similar report specifically about New York City Public Schools found that the schools who made the most progress toward CSforAll initiatives were schools who served fewer Black and Latine students (Fancsali et al., 2022).

Some argue that these disparities persist because those working to promote CS for all students simply haven't found the right combination of funding, courses, policies, and curriculum to truly broaden participation. But the causes of inequity in CS Ed are complicated and multilayered, and they reflect deeper social and structural realities. Schools and districts serving higher proportions of bi/multilingual learners, low-income students, and racially marginalized students are often under resourced. Implementing equitable instruction in content areas like math and literacy in these settings is a struggle in its own right, which often means that CS Ed gets further sidelined. When CS is offered to marginalized groups, it is often presented in culturally irrelevant ways or delivered with negative assumptions about students' computing abilities.

Cultures of exclusion also exist in higher education settings and tech companies, centering white, middle class, male, nondisabled cultural norms. These settings become unwelcoming and marginalizing for well-trained and qualified CS experts who have identities that are not centered in the CS industry. Even tools produced by the tech industry disproportionately harm marginalized groups through biases embedded in the tools' algorithms, interfaces, and systems (Benjamin, 2019). Tech industries also negatively impact society at large by polluting our environments, promoting misinformation and labor exploitation, and enabling mass surveillance and new ways to wage war (see Ko et al., 2020; Philip & Sengupta, 2021; Vossoughi & Vakil, 2018). As with tech tools, these industrial impacts also disproportionately affect those from marginalized groups.

Focusing on broadening participation alone can't address issues of inequity that are deeply rooted in our educational systems, in computing

---

equity as access
Giving all students the opportunities and support they need to participate in CS. Equity as access emphasizes giving everyone what they need to participate in mainstream CS. This approach recognizes that members of marginalized groups may not have the same opportunities to participate in CS, leading to a focus on broadening participation in CS and CS Ed.

industries, and in wider society. As one CS teacher, Anna, pointed out, it's often "implicitly assumed that creating better CS education programs [is] the same thing as getting more kids to participate in said programs." However, getting students to participate in unjust CS programs doesn't achieve the visions many of us have for a more just world. We argue that access to *and* **transformation** of CS industries, CS Ed, and society are needed if we are to advance equity in CS Ed.

WHAT CAN EDUCATORS DO?

In the face of these challenges and our students' needs, what can educators do to advance equity in CS Ed?

This question is at the center of this guide. For five years, the authors of this work—a collective of educators, district leaders, educational researchers, students, and other stakeholders in CS Ed—have collaborated to support public school teachers, preparing them to provide K-12 students with meaningful CS learning experiences. (See our Preface and Crawford et al., 2023, for more about us.)

As we've engaged in this work, we've connected with some incredible agents of change. These include educators who have been named Equity Fellows by the U.S. Computer Science Teachers Association (CSTA) and members of the CSforAll Ingenuity Team in New York City Public Schools.[5] We've also met many educators making quiet changes in small and practical ways in their classrooms on a daily basis. These educators vary just as their students do. They hold different identities around disability, gender and sexual orientation, and race and ethnicity. They work in urban, suburban, and rural settings with different student populations. They use many languages, teach different content areas, and have different backgrounds in CS.

What all of these teachers have in common is a commitment to advancing equity in CS Ed. They are working to build on the strengths of the students and communities who have been marginalized in computing and in education. They advocate for and promote expansive, just, and ethical kinds of CS and CS Ed. They recognize that equity work requires self-examination and self-awareness and involves building community and coalitions. And these teachers understand that advancing equity in CS Ed is a long-term effort and an ongoing process that is never done—a marathon, not a sprint. It's hard work, but through learning, action, and

---

5. To learn more about the CSTA Equity Fellows, visit https://csteachers.org/pd-opportunities/equity/. To learn more about the NYCPS Ingenuity Team, visit https://sites.google.com/schools.nyc.gov/cs4all-equity/ig-team/ig-team

connecting with others, these educators have found joy and purpose in their efforts. Recognizing the transformational work that educators across the nation are doing, we highlight a few real stories from their classrooms in Table 1.

Table 1. Meet Some Equity-Focused CS Teachers

CS Teacher	Equity-Focused Examples
Ethan Brown	Ethan taught middle school CS, and now he works as a technology instructional coach for his school district. He has developed lessons to engage his students in thinking about ethics in CS and the role of artificial intelligence (AI) in learning. For example, in one of his lessons, students discussed issues that exist with chatbots as they learned about the history of hip-hop and rappers in their local communities.
Melissa Hannon	Melissa studied industrial design before coming to education as a Library Media Specialist. In that role, Melissa integrated CS into her time with students, helping them make natural connections between CS, literacy, and libraries. For example, when teaching how to code using the Scratch website, one of her students connected CS terms in Scratch (like "sprite" or "stage") to literacy examples (like "character" or "setting"). These parallels helped make CS more accessible to all of Melissa's students, including her multilingual learners. After eight years as a Library Media Specialist, Melissa is now part of her district's CS Ed team, designing and facilitating professional learning series to support the dedicated and talented teachers she works with as they deliver impactful and engaging CS content to their students.
Kristi Jones	Kristi is a high school CS teacher. She took a culturally responsive approach to her AP Computer Science Principles curriculum by creating a Barbershop Computing event. Her students learned about the history of barbering, designed haircut styles using code, and had barbers come in to cut the winning styles. In coordinating with families to plan the event, Kristi worked to meet the different needs of her students' families. For example, Kristi sent messages home as texts to a student with a parent who was deaf instead of making phone calls and leaving voicemails that might be incorrectly auto-transcribed.
Katy Liang	Katy is a high school math teacher. She integrates CS into her Algebra 2 and Pre-Calculus classes. Her students used mathematical modeling to figure out how a water footprint calculator was determining its results. They collaborated with industry partners and created new models for water footprint calculators available in multiple languages that more accurately reflected their local community.
Aaron Lober	Aaron seized the opportunity to become a middle school STEM teacher. He refined his craft by learning various coding languages and pursuing a second master's degree in CS Ed. He spearheaded the establishment of a STEM department at his school and works to craft STEM curriculum for his district. Aaron prioritizes student-centered education, social-emotional learning, and experiential learning. In his CS classes, he has students explore the history of coding through a project that investigates stereotypes and historical narratives.
Ilka Stoessel	Ilka is an educational technology integration coach and CS teacher with more than two decades of experience in education. She transitioned from corporate America to teaching and is deeply committed to helping marginalized students (particularly racially marginalized students and girls) see CS as a viable and exciting career path. She continues to deepen her understanding of equity in CS and shares this passion with colleagues. For example, she regularly leads professional learning sessions like Leveraging Technology for Educational Equity, exploring AI's implications for teaching and learning.

Our work with teachers has shown us that educators, working together in community, can and are making a huge difference. Because inequities have been created by humans over time, they can be dismantled by people too. Resource 2, Historical Efforts to Advance Educational Equity, describes some of these examples, which include the 1960s New York City School Boycott, efforts in the 1970s to address the needs of bilingual students and those with disabilities, and contemporary efforts against gun violence in schools. People are also working to bring about change in CS industries. Joy Buolamwini is one contemporary example of someone working to dismantle inequities in technology. Read more about Buolamwini below.

JOY BUOLAMWINI: DISMANTLING INEQUITIES IN THE TECH INDUSTRY

Joy Buolamwini stands as a contemporary example of how people can challenge inequity in CS.[6] While completing her doctoral degree at the Massachusetts Institute of Technology, Buolamwini discovered that facial recognition software was incapable of detecting her face as a Black woman. However, that same software recognized a white Halloween mask. Buolamwini founded the Algorithmic Justice League to call attention to these biases embedded in software algorithms and to hold industries accountable for the impacts of these biases (Buolamwini, 2023).[7] The documentary film *Coded Bias* explores Buolamwini's discovery.[8] It also shares stories of technologists, scholars, and community groups who have organized to resist the harmful effects of tech tools and to create their own tools that embed values like community and justice. Chapter 3 further explores how these tools have been weaponized against marginalized and minoritized groups.

---

6. Photo credit: Niccolò Caranti; *CC BY-SA 4.0*
7. To learn more about the Algorithmic Justice League, visit https://ajl.org
8. To learn more about the film *Coded Bias*, visit https://codedbias.com/about

Following the examples of these change agents and others, we too can work to make change in CS Ed and computing fields. Promoting equitable change requires tenacity and nerve. It calls for the stirring up of what Congressman and civil rights activist John Lewis called "good trouble" (see Hayden, 2020). It requires collective action and people who are "coconspirators" against inequity, using their privilege to challenge and undo inequitable status quos (Love, 2019).[9] As U.S. state and federal legislation prohibit attention to diversity, equity, and inclusion in schools (Betts, 2024; Gross, 2022), our collective efforts as CS educators to work toward equity and justice are needed now more than ever.

OUR GUIDE AND VALUES

This guide is designed to support educators who want to advance equity in CS Ed for themselves, their students, and their communities. It will provide you with a foundation and tools to develop a **praxis**, or mindsets and theory put into action, that can advance equity in CS Ed.

What do we mean by advancing equity in CS Ed? This is a question that we will explore throughout the chapters of this guide. However, the authors of this guide share core values that are important to highlight at the outset. As a collective, we believe that advancing equity begins by acknowledging that inequities in education, in CS, and in CS Ed exist and persist. We recognize that the inequities we live with today are a result of choices made by individuals, groups, and institutions historically. We also acknowledge that injustices are continually reproduced today through systems of oppression, or socially organized patterns of mistreatment, and not solely through the actions of individual people or "bad actors." These systems create inequities based on social categories like race and ethnicity, class, disability, gender and sexual orientation, religion, and more. Inequities are reproduced by individuals, groups, and institutions in ways that contribute to unjust conditions and outcomes for marginalized individuals and groups. Because these systems are woven into our social life, how we understand ourselves and our students, how we interact, and how we learn are all influenced by inequities, shaping what happens in our schools and classrooms.

We also recognize that we as individuals and groups have the power to resist and change social patterns and norms. For equity to become a sustained reality, we need to think of it not as an object or thing that can be acquired. Instead, equity is an ongoing effort to disrupt inequitable systems and to create dynamic structures that reinforce and replicate

praxis The combination of teaching practices and theory. This guide supports praxis by providing theories about equity that help teachers develop mindsets to take transformative action toward equitable CS education.

---

9. Love spells this word without a hyphen.

equitable ideas, habits, resources, distribution of power, and outcomes. Working toward equity in CS Ed doesn't happen in isolation. It's part of a conversation about educational equity more broadly. There's also not one perfect way to do this work. The work will naturally look different in different communities that have different histories and interests. We may make mistakes along the way, but we can take responsibility for them, learn from them, and move forward. As we know better, we can do better. And what is better or right may look a little different for each teacher, classroom, school, and community.

Many educators, researchers, and scholars are making significant contributions to these efforts. In our own work, we were particularly influenced by the ideas of Zaretta Hammond (2014), Gloria Ladson-Billings (1994, 2021), Gholdy Muhammed (2020, 2023), and Django Paris and H. Sami Alim (2017). Their scholarship centers teaching that honors and incorporates students' histories, identities, and experiences into instruction to create **culturally sustaining pedagogical** practices.

We have drawn on the work of these equity-oriented scholars as we have thought about what it means to promote equitable changes in CS Ed. Their ideas have helped us define the futures we want to see, futures that include:

- **Access** to relevant computing tools and literacies so that learners whose identities have been marginalized in society have what they need to learn and thrive and to contribute to and sustain their communities' cultural and language practices.

- Equipping all learners with **critical consciousness** about computing tools, cultures, and industries so that they can work toward the ethical and just **transformation** of those tools, cultures, and industries.

We also share some principles that guide how we act in service of these goals that might also inspire educators to act. We hope you will notice the following principles in action in the coming chapters:

1. We critically <u>examine</u> our own identities and relationships to CS Ed and industry.

2. We <u>exercise</u> creative courage to disrupt the status quo. We invite our students to do the same (Anaissie et al., 2021).

3. We actively <u>elevate</u> multiple ways of knowing, being, and computing, especially those ways that have been marginalized in and by our systems.

Culturally sustaining pedagogies Ways and approaches to teaching that value and center students' cultural identities, practices, and ways of knowing as resources for learning, rather than excluding or eradicating students' cultures from the classroom (see Ladson-Billings, 2021; Paris & Alim, 2017).

Critical consciousness A social and political awareness that allows for a critique of how cultural norms, values, and institutions reproduce social inequities (Ladson-Billings, 1995).

equity as transformation A way of thinking about equity that recognizes that because the status quo tends to reproduce inequity, it needs to be transformed. Equity as transformation works to disrupt what is considered "normal" in CS disciplines and industries by valuing and centering marginalized knowledge systems, tools, and people.

4. We <u>support</u> multiple goals, cultural and language practices, and pathways for success, including those not always valued or accepted by our systems.

5. We <u>promote</u> all learners' agency to tinker with, create, and modify computing tools for purposes that matter to them.

6. We <u>create</u> supportive CS learning environments where each student has what they need to participate meaningfully.

7. We <u>cultivate</u> collaboration within and outside of institutions and together with marginalized communities to dismantle oppressive systems in education, computing, and CS Ed.

We share these values and principles with you as the foundation of this guide. The guide is intended to help you examine and reimagine how you understand yourself, your students, and your teaching. With those new perspectives, you can identify concrete ways to transform what happens in your contexts every day. You will find ways to support *all* of your students to use computing to meet their personal goals, to reach their potential, and to become change agents for their communities and the CS field.

REVISITING MARILYN'S STORY

In reflecting on her efforts as a CS educator, Marilyn expressed very real concerns about how to "build equity without being inequitable" given her students' diverse backgrounds, identities, interests, and needs. Marilyn's questions point to the complexity of doing equity work. Marilyn discussed these challenges with her colleagues several times during the summer. During their conversations, Marilyn and her fellow teachers realized that there wasn't a quick solution. They recognized that these conversations were just the start and that they needed more time to figure out how to "do equity equitably." They worked to plan time and space for collaboration into the coming school year. They look forward to getting to know their students and making concrete changes that will benefit their classrooms as the new year begins. We'll follow their thinking about how to best support their students' needs and work toward equitable outcomes in CS in the chapters that follow. We hope that this book will inspire you to engage in your own conversations about equity in CS like Marilyn and her colleagues.

REFLECTION QUESTIONS

1. Which pieces of Marilyn's story resonated with you? What challenges do you face or anticipate facing in your work as a CS educator?

2. What kinds of inequities are you aware of in your teaching settings? In the communities where you and your students live?

3. What values and principles currently shape your work as an educator generally? As an educator in CS specifically? As an equity-oriented educator? How do these align with, differ from, or build on the values and principles that shape this guide?

TAKEAWAYS FOR PRACTICE

- Review the current state of CS Ed in your setting. Inventory who has access to CS Ed currently, what assets you have to support CS teaching and learning, and what resources you need to work toward equitable CS Ed in your setting.

- Consider which of the seven CS equity principles listed above you would prioritize in your own teaching in the near and long term and how you might center those principles.

- Learn more about some of the diverse leaders in CS and CS Ed by exploring Resource 1. Consider integrating these individuals into your existing lessons to help students recognize themselves in CS.

GLOSSARY

Term	Definition
broadening participation	A way of thinking about equity, similar to access, that seeks to increase the participation of members of underrepresented and/or marginalized groups in CS and CS Ed. These groups have historically been excluded from computing fields.
critical consciousness	A social and political awareness that allows for a critique of how cultural norms, values, and institutions reproduce social inequities (Ladson-Billings, 1995).

culturally sustaining pedagogies	Ways and approaches to teaching that value and center students' cultural identities, practices, and ways of knowing as resources for learning, rather than excluding or eradicating students' cultures from the classroom (see Ladson-Billings, 2021; Paris & Alim, 2017).
equity as access	Giving all students the opportunities and support they need to participate in CS. Equity as access emphasizes giving everyone what they need to participate in mainstream CS. This approach recognizes that members of marginalized groups may not have the same opportunities to participate in CS, leading to a focus on broadening participation in CS and CS Ed.
equity as transformation	A way of thinking about equity that recognizes that because the status quo tends to reproduce inequity, it needs to be transformed. Equity as transformation works to disrupt what is considered "normal" in CS disciplines and industries by valuing and centering marginalized knowledge systems, tools, and people.
praxis	The combination of teaching practices and theory. This guide supports praxis by providing theories about equity that help teachers develop mindsets to take transformative action toward equitable CS education.

REFERENCES

100Kin10. (2021). *unCommission research summary on the communities most excluded from STEM learning*. 100Kin10. https://docs.google.com/document/d/1xOgL3AvDkYjyjVTxgxaDUfpUIEC7c0czPUsDSfLhYzE/edit

Anaissie, T., Cary, V., Clifford, D., Malarkey, T., & Wise, S. (2021). *Liberatory design: Mindsets and modes to design for equity*. Liberatory Design. https://static1.squarespace.com/static/60380011d63f16013f7cc4c2/t/60b698f388fe142f91f6b345/1622579446226/Liberatory+Design+Deck_June_2021.pdf

Benjamin, R. (2019). *Race after technology: Abolitionist tools for the new Jim code* (1st ed.). Polity. https://doi.org/10.1093/sf/soz162

Betts, A. (2024, May 23). *What to know about state laws that limit or ban D.E.I efforts at colleges*. New York Times. https://www.nytimes.com/2024/04/21/us/dei-education-state-laws.html

Buolamwini, J. (2023). *Unmasking AI: My mission to protect what is human in a world of machines* (1st ed.). Random House.

Code.org. (2020, Feb 20). *Code.org 2019 annual report: The state of K-12 computer science*. Code.org. https://code.org/files/Code.org-Annual-Report-2019.pdf

Crawford, C., Kuyenga, M. A., Talley, L., Mirakhur, Z., & Clark, H. (2023). *Organizing for educational equity in computer science: Lessons from New York City's CS4All initiative*. New York City Public Schools.

Fancsali, C., Lee, J., Adair, A., Hill, K., Rivera-Cash, E., & Clough, S. (2022). *CS4All: Examining equity in computer science access and participation in NYC schools*. NYU Research Alliance. https://steinhardt.nyu.edu/research-alliance/research/cs4all-examining-equity

Gross, T. (2022, Feb 3). *From slavery to socialism, new legislation restricts what teachers can discuss*. NPR. https://www.npr.org/2022/02/03/1077878538/legislation-restricts-what-teachers-can-discuss

Hammond, Z. L. (2014). *Culturally responsive teaching and the brain: Promoting authentic engagement and rigor among culturally and linguistically diverse students*. Corwin.

Hayden, C. D. (2020, July 19). *Remembering John Lewis: The power of "good trouble."* Library of Congress. https://blogs.loc.gov/loc/2020/07/remembering-john-lewis-the-power-of-good-trouble/

Ko, A. J., Oleson, A., Ryan, N., Register, Y., Xie, B., Tari, M., . . . & Loksa, D. (2020). It is time for more critical CS education. *Communications of the ACM, 63*(11), 31–33. 4:01. https://doi.org/10.1145/3424000

Ladson-Billings, G. (1994). *The dreamkeepers: Successful teachers of African American children*. Jossey-Bass.

Ladson-Billings, G. (1995). But that's just good teaching! The case for culturally relevant pedagogy. *Theory Into Practice, 34*(3), 159–165. https://doi.org/10.1080/00405849509543675

Ladson-Billings, G. (2021). *Culturally relevant pedagogy: Asking a different question*. Teachers College Press.

Love, B. L. (2019). *We want to do more than survive: Abolitionist teaching and the pursuit of educational freedom*. Beacon Press.

Muhammad, G. (2020). *Cultivating genius: An equity framework for culturally and historically responsive literacy*. Scholastic.

Muhammad, G. (2023). *Unearthing joy: A guide to culturally and historically responsive curriculum and instruction*. Scholastic.

Paris, D., & Alim, H. S. (2017). *Culturally sustaining pedagogies: Teaching and learning for justice in a changing world*. Teachers College Press.

Philip, T. M., & Sengupta, P. (2021). Theories of learning as theories of society: A contrapuntal approach to expanding disciplinary authenticity in computing. *Journal of the Learning Sciences, 30*(2), 330–349. https://doi.org/10.1080/10508406.2020.1828089

Smith, M. (2016, Jan 30). *Computer science for all*. The White House. https://www.obamawhitehouse.archives.gov/blog/2016/01/30/computer-science-all

Vossoughi, S., & Vakil, S. (2018). Toward what ends? A critical analysis of militarism, equity, and STEM education. In A. I. Ali & T. L. Buenavista (Eds.), *Education at war: The fight for students of color in America's public schools* (1st ed., pp. 117–140). Fordham University Press. https://doi.org/10.2307/j.ctt2204pqp

RESOURCE 1: HISTORICAL GIANTS IN COMPUTING

Anyone can be a computer scientist! Here are some examples of historical leaders who changed the field of computing and who also held diverse racial, ethnic, gender, and sexual identities.

Computer Scientist	Contribution
Fair Use	**Anita Borg** (1949–2003) was an American computer scientist who advocated for and worked to expand opportunities for women and non-binary people in the CS industry. https://www.britannica.com/biography/Anita-Borg https://en.wikipedia.org/wiki/Anita_Borg
CC BY-SA 2.5 *Photo by Charles Rogers*	**Lynn Ann Conway** (1938–2024) was an inventor, computer scientist, electrical engineer, and transgender rights advocate. Her work helped develop new integrated circuits that revolutionized computer chip design. https://computerhistory.org/blog/in-memoriam-lynn-conway-1938-2024/ https://en.wikipedia.org/wiki/Lynn_Conway
	Clarence "Skip" Ellis (1943–2014) was the first African-American to earn a Ph.D. in CS. He was a pioneer in designing groupware and computer-supported collaborative technology. https://siebelschool.illinois.edu/about/awards/alumni-awards/alumni-awards-past-recipients/clarence-ellis https://en.wikipedia.org/wiki/Clarence_Ellis_\(computer_scientist\)

Computer Scientist	Contribution
 *Public Domain*	**Grace Hopper** (1906–1992) was an American computer scientist who also served in the United States Navy. She was the first to develop a programming language based on English instead of assembly languages based on binary code. https://president.yale.edu/biography-grace-murray-hopper https://en.wikipedia.org/wiki/Grace_Hopper
 *Public Domain*	**Mary Jackson** (1921–2005) was NASA's first Black female aerospace engineer. She conducted experiments studying high-speed flight and was an advocate for female mathematicians, engineers, and scientists at NASA. https://www.nasa.gov/people/mary-w-jackson-biography/ https://en.wikipedia.org/wiki/Mary_Jackson_(engineer)
 *Public Domain*	**Katherine Johnson** (1918–2020) was one of the first Black graduate students at West Virginia University. She later became a NASA mathematician. Her contributions helped successfully land John Glenn on the moon. https://www.nasa.gov/centers-and-facilities/langley/katherine-johnson-biography/ https://en.wikipedia.org/wiki/Katherine_Johnson
 *Fair Use*	**Jerry Lawson** (1940–2011) was an African-American engineer who was a video game pioneer. He created the first interchangeable cartridge game console. https://www.iamhistory.co.uk/home/2023/8/31/jerry-lawson-the-engineer-who-changed-the-game https://en.wikipedia.org/wiki/Jerry_Lawson_(engineer)

Computer Scientist	Contribution
 *CC BY-SA 4.0* *By Antoine Claudet*	**Ada Lovelace** (1815–1852) was an English mathematician who wrote the first published computer algorithm. She recognized that computing machines had the potential to go far beyond number crunching. https://www.britannica.com/biography/Ada-Lovelace https://en.wikipedia.org/wiki/Ada_Lovelace
 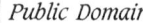 *Public Domain*	**Alan Turing** (1912–1954) was an English mathematician and computer scientist. He worked as a codebreaker for Great Britain during World War II and is often credited as a founder of theoretical CS. He also faced criminal charges and unjust treatment because of his sexual orientation. https://www.nytimes.com/2019/06/05/obituaries/alan-turing-overlooked.html https://en.wikipedia.org/wiki/Alan_Turing
 *Public Domain*	**Dorothy Vaughan** (1910–2008) was NASA's first African American manager. She led the segregated West Area Computing unit, whose female employees contributed widely to NASA's research. https://www.nasa.gov/people/dorothy-vaughan/ https://en.wikipedia.org/wiki/Dorothy_Vaughan

RESOURCE 2: HISTORICAL EFFORTS TO ADVANCE EDUCATIONAL EQUITY

These historical examples represent some of the many efforts people have been involved in to advance educational equity. This is by no means an exhaustive list but highlights some of the efforts related to the equity issues that we focus on throughout this guide.

Year	Historical Effort
1960s	**New York City School Boycott:** Most curricula about school desegregation following the 1954 *Brown v. Board of Education* Supreme Court decision focus on the Civil Rights Movement in the southern United States. However, one of the largest boycotts was led by New York City students and parents. Although the city's schools were not legally segregated, schools that served predominately African American and Puerto Rican populations were in poor condition. Parents and students protested these substandard conditions as a form of de facto segregation, advocating for fully integrated and better resourced schools for all students. https://rethinkingschools.org/articles/the-largest-civil-rights-protest-you-ve-never-heard-of/ https://www.zinnedproject.org/news/tdih/nyc-school-children-boycott-school/ https://themetropole.blog/2017/11/29/the-new-york-times-and-the-movement-for-integrated-education-in-new-york-city/
1960s	**Bilingual Student Education in New York City:** After World War II, many Puerto Ricans migrated to New York City. Advocate Antonia Pantoja created an organization for Puerto Rican youth called ASPIRA. This group fought for linguistic justice in education, successfully suing the New York City Board of Education and gaining the right to educate bilingual students in their home languages. https://pbslearningmedia.org/resource/87537891-1a6d-41c6-9662-b09db4c17201/antonia-pantoja-presente/
1970s	**Bilingual Student Education Nationally:** Chinese parent groups in San Francisco in the 1970s called attention to linguistic injustice through organizing efforts that led to the Supreme Court case *Lau v. Nichols*. This case ruled that if schools did not provide supplemental language instruction for students learning English, they were in violation of the Civil Rights Act of 1964. These parents' advocacy was foundational to providing meaningful access to education for bi/multilingual learners in schools today. https://www.justice.gov/opa/blog/celebrating-50th-anniversary-lau-v-nichols

Year	Historical Effort
1970s	**Disability Needs in Public Schools:** Judy Heumann is often called the "mother of the disability rights movement." She used a wheelchair after contracting polio as a child. Heumann was originally kept from attending school because her wheelchair was considered a fire hazard. After completing her education, Heumann was denied a teaching license because of her disability. She sued the New York City Board of Education in 1970 for discrimination based on disability. Heumann won and began teaching. She remained a disability activist throughout her life. https://harvardlawreview.org/blog/2023/03/remembering-judy-heumann/ https://judithheumann.com/ https://www.nytimes.com/1970/05/27/archives/woman-in-wheelchair-sues-to-become-teacher.html
2000s	**Student Efforts to End Gun Violence in Schools:** The United States has seen a sobering increase in mass school shootings in recent years. Students and educators across the nation have led efforts to advocate for gun control and school safety. For example, the group Students Demand Action organized a school walkout in Nashville, Tennessee, after three children and three adults were killed in a school shooting in 2023. https://www.usatoday.com/story/news/nation/2023/04/05/nashville-shooting-nationwide-student-walkout-gun-safety/11608207002/

2

Understanding Diversity in Computer Science and Computer Science Education

Lauren Vogelstein, Christopher Hoadley, Carla Strickland, Joanne Barrett, Sara Vogel, Bethany Daniel, Stephanie T. Jones, and the Computer Science Educational Justice Collective

CHAPTER OVERVIEW

This chapter considers the idea of diversity and why it matters for computer science (CS) industries and CS education (CS Ed). It defines what diversity is and then explores how diversity (or a lack of diversity) impacts CS industries and CS Ed. The chapter concludes with some implications for what diversity means for CS teachers' everyday practices in their classrooms with their students.

CHAPTER OBJECTIVES

After reading this chapter, I can:

- Define what diversity is and what diversity is not.
- Explain how diversity is related to (in)equity in CS and CS Ed.
- Recognize why diversity is important in CS and CS Ed.
- Identify strategies to recognize and draw on diversity as a resource in my classroom.

KEY TERMS

ableism; culturally sustaining pedagogies, diversity; essentialization; funds of knowledge; gatekeeping; intersectionality; invisible disabilities; marginalized/minoritized identities; opportunity hoarding; othering; tokenism; xenophobia

MARILYN'S STORY

In Chapter 1, we met Marilyn, a CS teacher who was grappling with how to equitably include all of her students from different backgrounds in her after-school coding club.[1] Marilyn shared her thoughts:

> You know, everyone says "do Girls Who Code."[2] And I have that after school, you know. And you say, "Oh, it's open to everyone." But it doesn't mean anyone feels comfortable. 'Cause the boys don't want to go if it says "Girls Who Code."
>
> But now I'm working with my girls, right? And I'm adding more girls, and they're doing more coding projects. But what about my Black boys? My Brown boys? My Arab students? Those are kids who are still underrepresented in code. Am I doing a disservice by focusing on a single group? Should I focus on my girls one year and my Black kids the next year? My Arab kids the next year?[3]
>
> How do I equitably do equity? Who do I leave out? Can I leave out somebody? Should I focus on everybody all at once? How do you build equity without being inequitable?

Marilyn raised real concerns, asking questions that don't have easy answers. However, Marilyn's description surfaces something foundational to understanding and working toward equity: the notion of **diversity**.

Marilyn recognized that her students were different from one another. They had different identities, backgrounds and experiences, interests, talents, and abilities. Marilyn also recognized that because of the "-isms" that shape society (like ableism, classism, racism, etc.), her students

---

diversity Collectives of individuals with different identities, perspectives, experiences, and backgrounds. Diversity is often described in terms of social categories like age, disability, gender identity and sexual orientation, educational background, language, national origin, race and ethnicity, religion, and socioeconomic status.

---

1. Marilyn is a composite character based on New York City public school teacher Susan Murray and the collective experiences of the authors, teachers, and collaborators of this guide.
2. Girls Who Code is a nonprofit organization that offers after-school clubs to increase the number of girls, women, and non-binary people in computer science. To learn more, visit https://www.girlswhocode.com
3. We preserve the terms used by Marilyn. See the On Terminology section of this guide for an explanation on our use of different identity-related terms.

could be centered or marginalized in school and in computing based on their differing traits. For example, she acknowledged that her students differed around gender, and girls have been historically underrepresented in computing fields. This reality motivated Marilyn to start her after-school coding club in the first place.

But Marilyn was also aware that if she focused only on girls in her program, not everyone, including boys and gender non-conforming students, would feel comfortable or like they belonged in that space. She wondered about how to reach other students whose identities are underrepresented in computing, like Black and Arab students. Marilyn was aware of the diversity that existed in her classes and her students. And Marilyn recognized how limiting students' identities to only one or two labels, like gender or race, or grouping them into buckets based on labels and trying to focus on different groups didn't seem to be an ideal solution. She wondered how she could recognize the diversity of her students in ways that would meet all of their needs.

WHAT IS DIVERSITY?

Diversity comes from recognizing a simple fact: people are different from one another. We define diversity as differences in people's identities, backgrounds, and perspectives. Most often, diversity is described in terms of social categories like age, disability, gender identity and sexual orientation, educational background, language, national origin, race and ethnicity, religion, and socioeconomic status. All individuals have varied physical features, lived experiences, physical, emotional, and intellectual abilities, language and cultural practices, and so forth. Given this reality, no one person in isolation can be diverse. Instead, diversity describes variation in collectives of individuals with differing identities and backgrounds. We emphasize this definition of diversity as something that applies to a group.

People often think that committing to diversity means making a special effort to reach diverse populations or people, where the term "diverse" stands in for members of **marginalized** groups, or groups whose social categories are devalued by society. For example, committing to "racial diversity" in CS often involves the unstated reality that most people in CS are racialized as white and implies a focus on recruiting individuals who are racialized in ways that are marginalized by society (e.g., Asian, Black, Latine). Representing a diversity of perspectives and experiences matters, as we will see throughout this chapter. However, when "diversity" is used as a stand-in or euphemism for members of marginalized groups, it becomes a harmful way to suggest that a person deviates from

marginalized/minoritized identities Identity categories that are devalued by society, often because they are different from what society has established as the "ideal" norm. Those with marginalized/minoritized identities often face oppression and exclusion from mainstream society.

We use both marginalized and minoritized as adjectives to emphasize how social processes actively construct inequity (Black et al., 2023). The term "minoritized" emphasizes historical systematic oppression and may be used regardless of whether an identity group actually represents a numerical minority in a context (see Black et al., 2023; Flores & Rosa, 2015).

the implicit white, male, English-speaking, nondisabled norm that society has deemed "acceptable." CS teacher Brandie expanded on this idea:

> Diversity is such a general term that can mean different things to different people. [It is important to] address the **"othering"** quality that . . . the concept of diversity often has. Diversity doesn't equate to any particular group of people. Diversity is inclusive of all the ways that people are and can be different from each other.

othering The process of treating a group of people (often those with minoritized or marginalized identities) as intrinsically different from the dominant social norm.

Rather than using the term as a stand-in for marginalized groups, we can use the word diversity to acknowledge variation among the people in a collective. We should also recognize that within diverse groups, there are people whose identities, backgrounds, and practices are implicitly valued and catered to in learning, professional, and disciplinary spaces more than others. This way of defining diversity helps us avoid treating some groups as "other" and can help us recognize which perspectives might be overrepresented (e.g., white males in CS) and which perspectives are missing.

Valuing diversity also helps us ask questions about the systemic and structural factors that create barriers to a group's participation (see Chapter 5 for more on how to do this). For example, teachers can reflect on how policies that privilege the use of English in classrooms might create barriers for multilingual students' participation in CS Ed. They can examine their own implicit biases that lead them to perceive multilingual learners as "less capable" of doing computing. They might design an activity that leverages multilingual learners' expertise to help students critique the usability of an English-only computing tool. Actions like these help educators intentionally create spaces that elevate marginalized voices into positions with power.

HOW IS DIVERSITY RELATED TO INEQUITY?

That we differ from one another along many dimensions is a fact about humanity. However, when those differences get filtered through society's power hierarchies, diversity becomes closely intertwined with inequity. Hierarchies have been created over time through human activities—historical and cultural processes such as slavery and colonialism—and have become embedded in society's institutions and structures. These activities transform human differences into markers and labels that are still being used by people and institutions to organize and implicitly "rank" people. These rankings systematically privilege some human characteristics and marginalize others. In education, those with socially privileged traits are often afforded more power because learning spaces and teaching practices tend to be designed for them and have their experiences, goals, languages, and interests in mind. By contrast, those with identities that are marginalized by society often experience learning spaces where their identities and cultural practices are not always welcomed, recognized, or valued.

The relationship between diversity and inequity is evident in many of the "-isms" that pervade society. For every dimension of human difference, there is an associated way that biases tend to reinforce inequity. Differences in ability are filtered through **ableism**, or an implicit or explicit preference for bodies and minds that are socially constructed as nondisabled, creating prejudice for disability and the oppression of disabled people. Differences in physical appearance and place of origin are filtered through racism and **xenophobia**, or fear or prejudice against foreigners, which impacts how people move through society. How society perceives one's age, gender, sexual orientation, linguistic background, socioeconomic class, and the many other facets of our identities and experiences shape how people are included (or not) in different spaces, including CS spaces. At the same time, the identity markers people claim and are assigned are not static, and they do not predetermine people's experiences. There are many factors that shape whether and how people experience oppression or privilege based on their differences across different contexts.

For example, the collective group of school children in the United States is very linguistically diverse (National Center for Education Statistics, 2024). However, power hierarchies around language filter those differences in different ways. In U.S. schools, speaking English is a privileged trait. Children who speak "standard" English as a home language tend to have more access to social privilege and educational resources. Those who speak other varieties of English like African American Vernacular English or those who speak languages other than English must often adapt and learn the "idealized" version of English to access the same opportunities (Chang-Bacon, 2020). Students' linguistic expertise in language varieties other than "standard" English gets overlooked or even penalized in school spaces (Flores & Rosa, 2015). Filtering based on linguistic hierarchies creates inequities that benefit English speakers over speakers of other languages. While these trends manifest at the level of most social institutions and structures (e.g., the medical system, the criminal justice system, the education system), whether or not and how an individual experiences linguistic injustice also depends on their own particular identities, circumstances, experiences, and contexts.

Because everyone has many different identities, the concept of **intersectionality** is also important in understanding diversity. Intersectionality captures the reality that people experience inequities in ways that are unique to how their identities intersect and overlap. For example, Marcos,

ableism Implicit or explicit social preference for nondisabled bodies and minds that creates prejudice and oppression of disability and disabled people (Shew, 2020).

xenophobia A system of prejudice and discrimination against foreigners.

intersectionality A theory that recognizes how people's different identities (e.g., disability, gender, race) overlap and intersect, creating access to privilege or resulting in oppression in ways that cannot be understood or addressed by considering each identity separately (Crenshaw, 1991; Collins, 2019).

a Latine, bilingual English/Spanish-speaking child with a disability would experience oppression related to disability differently than his peer Ethan, a white, monolingual, English-speaking child. Marcos may experience disability as it intersects with racial and linguistic oppression, while Ethan's experiences with disability may be shaped by racial and linguistic privilege. We examine the role of intersectionality further in Chapter 5.

As we'll see in future chapters, the drastic inequities that exist in CS and CS Ed often mirror the broader institutionalized and systematic ways that people can be oppressed or privileged based on their differences. How people experience inequities in CS are shaped by the identity markers society has assigned them in different settings and how those markers have been filtered through the social power hierarchies operating in those settings. These realities significantly impact the CS field and students' experiences in CS classrooms.

WHY DOES DIVERSITY MATTER IN CS INDUSTRIES?

Working toward equity in CS Ed requires understanding why diversity matters. In this section, we consider why diversity is important to the CS industry. We critically examine diversity in the CS industry because many students will be interested in applying their skills and knowledge there and because tech companies play an outsized role in funding and supporting CS Ed. As a result, the industry's values and track record on diversity matter. We also recognize that promoting diversity in CS industries is not the only reason to care about diversity in CS Ed, and we consider other reasons in the sections that follow.

DIVERSITY IN COMPUTING INDUSTRIES

Although people vary widely, there is a consistent pattern of homogeneity, or sameness, in the CS industry with respect to demographics like class, disability, gender, language, and race. For example, 78% of CS bachelor's degrees awarded in the United States in 2021 went to men. Of non-international CS degree earners, 81% were white or Asian American (Zweben & Bizot, 2022). These statistics highlight how the CS industry tends to be homogenous in terms of gender and race.

Similarly, privileged communities who hold identities that society has constructed as "normative" (e.g., white, English-speaking, upper class) have historically been afforded preferential access to the tools, capital, and knowledge needed to create computational technologies and to use them for their own ends (see Patitsas et al., 2014, for a gendered example). These groups' preferential access and power has been maintained in many ways, including through practices like **gatekeeping** (policies and structures that limit participation in computing for marginalized groups) and **opportunity hoarding** (processes through which privileged groups control and prevent access to resources for marginalized groups; see Ko, 2024, for a fuller discussion).

The history of CS has translated into the contemporary perception of a "bro" culture in coding and computing: white male coders in jeans and hoodies sitting alone at their computers for long stretches of time. When presented with this description, CS teacher Anjeliqe noted that it was "*the exact description that students give you when you ask them what a computer scientist looks like.*" Media reflect this perception back to us in ways that emphasize the lack of diversity in the CS field as normal. For example, HBO's television show *Silicon Valley* represents CS professionals as stereotypically white, male, college dropouts whose computing expertise will allow them to get rich. These representations subtly broadcast the idea that those who do not look or act like a stereotypical coder do not belong in CS and would find it difficult to fit in and be happy in the CS industry. CS teacher Karime identified how this reality "*make[s] the field unwelcoming . . . [and] extremely unappealing for anyone that doesn't fit this description.*"

gatekeeping Institutional policies and structures that control who gets to participate in opportunities and who has access to resources in ways that limit the participation of marginalized groups.

opportunity hoarding Processes through which privileged groups control and prevent access to resources for marginalized groups.

THE IMPACT OF A LACK OF DIVERSITY ON TECHNOLOGY

Diversity matters in the CS industry because people vary—so our tech tools and ways of doing computing should too. The sameness in the CS industry, whether real or perceived, shapes which technologies get developed and their impacts on society. The lack of diversity also influences which problems technologies are designed to solve, which communities technologies are developed for, and who sees or wants a future in the CS community. When CS professional communities are homogenous, technological development tends to focus on the needs and concerns of those communities, overlooking the needs, interests, and desires that underrepresented groups have for themselves and their members. Biases associated with the shared identities of computer scientists get embedded into technology, whether by design or inadvertently, adversely impacting communities not represented among creators.

The development of facial recognition technology is an example that illustrates the impact that a lack of diversity has on computing. Computer scientists who developed facial recognition technology often boast about its accuracy, averaging about 90% overall (Najibi, 2020). However, when that data is broken down into different categories based on identity markers, a different story emerges. Facial recognition algorithms are much less accurate at recognizing women and people with darker skin tones. As a result, women of color are recognized even less accurately (Najibi, 2020). The algorithms are most accurate when identifying white male faces—faces most similar to those who created them.

The consequences of these biased algorithms are significant, affecting more than just unlocking your phone (or someone else's) or getting ahead in airport lines. Facial recognition technology is used by law enforcement to apprehend suspects (Algorithmic Justice League, n.d.). This means that being mistaken for someone else can lead to an unwarranted interaction with police, which could become a permanent part of someone's criminal record, regardless of whether they're innocent or not.

Similarly, judges use artificial intelligence (AI)–based recidivism algorithms to determine sentence length for convicted individuals. Recidivism algorithms make inferences based on data from sources like arrest records and demographic information. They are used to predict whether someone charged with a crime may be at "high risk" of committing another crime in the future (Larson et al., 2016; Lee et al., 2019). Researchers have found that these algorithms—and the data they draw on—are racially biased. This bias results in longer sentences for racially **minoritized** suspects (Angwin et al., 2016). A lack of diversity in those designing technological tools can result in highly consequential and inequitable outcomes for marginalized groups.

The lack of diversity in the tech industry is not the only explanation for these dynamics. They are also influenced by historical and cultural processes that have worked to eliminate diversity and reinforce sameness. For example, some recidivist algorithms may weigh the zip code of where a person lives as part of calculating the probability that they will be a repeat criminal offender. The contemporary racial demographics of zip codes reflect historical redlining policies and current real estate biases that restrict and shape where racially minoritized people live. Many of these realities were established in the United States during the Jim Crow era, after the end of the Civil War, when state and local laws reinforced racial segregation. Scholar Ruha Benjamin names these data points that carry embedded biases as the "outputs of Jim Crow." She argues how the outputs of Jim Crow become the "inputs of New Jim Code," creating technologies that continue to perpetuate racist outcomes in the present day (Benjamin, 2019).

While inequitable impacts of technology are complex, a lack of diversity only contributes to these problems. Limited diversity in CS fields means that there are missing and underrepresented perspectives.

Centering diversity can bring in perspectives that lead to new ideas, better solutions, and technology that helps everyone. Diversity in CS fields can result in people questioning the technologies that are created, what their purposes are, whom they might help, and why.

At the same time, promoting a diverse workforce within CS fields can only go so far. Many technology companies report diverse hiring practices, but when individuals attempt to raise critical questions or change inequitable company practices, they may be ignored or even fired. In one case, technologist Timnit Gebru was fired from Google because of her work that critiqued how large language models used in AI (including Google's AI) can spread disinformation (Allyn, 2020; Perrigo, 2022). In another instance, Meta founder Mark Zuckerberg ended certain company practices related to fact checking misinformation and moderating hate speech on products like Facebook, Whatsapp, and Instagram, ignoring the protests from a global community of fact checkers they had hired. The policy change is expected to have adverse impacts especially for LGBTQ+ people, women, and culturally and racially minoritized groups around the world (International Fact-Checking Network, 2025). Not only must CS industry workers and leaders reflect the diversity of the nation and world, but companies whose products shape the lives of so many must be held accountable to values that reflect the safety, desires, and interests of the diverse collectives who are impacted by them.

Despite these issues, there has been incremental progress that we can celebrate and take inspiration from. Many diverse CS teams have already succeeded in creating more inclusive products, such as voice recognition software that understands speech patterns of people with disabilities, accents, and language varieties (e.g., fluent.ai, n.d.; voiceitt.com, n.d.). Benjamin (2019) provided examples of ways that people have drawn on their unique perspectives and experiences to create tools that resist embedded biases and challenge tech norms. One example is Hyphen-Labs, a team of racially diverse women who work "at the intersection of technology, art, science, and the future" (MIT Open Documentary Lab, n.d.).[4] They developed designs for jewelry and clothing that can record police interactions and prevent facial recognition, counteracting some of the tools that disproportionately harm racially minoritized people. Another development team, Brian Clifton, Sam Lavigne, and Francis Tseng, created a White Collar Crime Risk Zones tool to counteracts the anti-Black technology used in crime tracking (Clifton et al., n.d.).[5] Using machine learning, the tool flags city blocks where financial crimes are likely to occur and

---

4. Learn more about Hyphen-Labs at https://hyphen-labs.com/
5. Learn more about White Collar Crime Risk Zones at https://whitecollar.the newinquiry.com/

provides facial recognition programs to identify likely perpetrators (in this case, generally white and male). Their tool flips the script on algorithms used to track crime and surfaces the biases embedded in those systems.

These examples illustrate how technology can be used to actively contest the inequities it often reproduces. However, making this resistance happen requires the industry and the governments that regulate it to not just promote diversity but to empower marginalized people and perspectives. Making space for diverse backgrounds, perspectives, and experiences in CS fields can generate new imaginings that allow us to reform existing systems and to transform inequities into new possibilities and futures (Benjamin, 2024).

WHY DOES DIVERSITY MATTER IN CS ED?

To have diversity in CS industries, we must support diverse groups of students who can see futures for themselves in CS fields. Many students whose identities have been marginalized and who have been excluded from CS Ed have important ideas and perspectives that could empower them and bring essential change to CS. CS educator Tarek captured this connection:

> Diversity in the CS classroom is so much more than just having different faces in the room. It's about embracing and valuing the unique experiences and perspectives those faces represent. It's about understanding how things like race, gender, and even where you're from have shaped the history of computer science and continue to affect who gets to participate and what kinds of technologies are created. When we [recognize that past and embrace diversity], we can create a more inclusive and innovative future for tech. By understanding and using kids' backgrounds and interests, we can make computer science a field where everyone feels like they belong and can contribute meaningfully.

LACK OF STUDENT DIVERSITY IN CS ED

Achieving a vision of full and meaningful participation in CS Ed requires addressing barriers to diversity that exist in CS Ed. The homogeneity or sameness that exists in the CS industry is mirrored in CS Ed. Research has shown that students taking CS courses in their K-12 education is a predictor of choosing a STEM major in college (Lee, 2015). However, students do not all have the same access to CS courses. Marginalized students are less likely to attend schools with CS course offerings (Code.

org et al., 2022), and not all students see CS as a place where they belong. Marilyn's concerns at the beginning of this chapter reflect this reality. Marginalized students often experience CS learning environments as unsupportive or irrelevant (Margolis et al., 2017; Ryoo et al., 2020). Research also shows that even when students are good at STEM-related subjects, they may opt out of those course pathways because of social stigma or prejudice (Eccles et al., 2020). The cost-benefit analysis of their choices and interests leads them away from STEM and CS-related paths (DiSalvo et al., 2014; Eccles et al., 2020). These patterns all contribute to limited diversity in CS Ed.

While these statistics and research point to the challenges we face, we can also acknowledge the incremental progress that has been made. In 2017, when the AP CSP exam was first offered, 26.4% of test takers identified as female, and 47.7% identified as Asian, Black, Indigenous, Latine, or Pacific Islander. In 2023, those percentages had increased to 30.9% and 56%, respectively, illustrating progress in increasing participation in CS for students who have historically been marginalized based on gender and race (Code.org, 2025). In 2016, Chicago Public Schools was the first U.S. school district to make CS a graduation requirement, an example of structural and systemic changes that increase access to CS Ed for all students (Chicago Public Schools, 2020).

LACK OF DIVERSITY IN CS ED CURRICULUM

We might also understand the lack of diversity in CS Ed in terms of the topics covered in CS courses and curriculum. Because CS Ed tends to mirror CS industries, the focus of CS Ed also mirrors priorities of CS industries—programming examples used in textbooks may overemphasize commercial applications over public sector, civic, or recreational types of software development. This approach erases the computational practices embedded in non-Western societies (e.g., Indigenous beadwork, hair braiding patterns).

Mainstream CS curricula tend to center white, male, or English-speaking norms. For example, a typical programming assignment might require students to create a program that asks users to input their first and last names and add them to a list or array. However, budding programmers might not recognize the diversity embedded in names as a cultural practice. They might fail to consider things like accents and scripts beyond the Roman alphabet to write names, a need to include maternal and paternal family names, and cultures where family names precede given names in their designs. Without explicitly exploring this diversity as part of the assignment, students may create exclusionary input options. Similarly, textbooks often overlook teaching novice programmers how to use or program multilingual or accessibility features in computing environments, despite the fact that this skill is critical for developing software for broad adoption. A lack of diversity in curriculum topics impacts the kinds of tools that students use, the kinds of CS tools they create, and their understanding of what CS is, who it is for, and what "counts" as successful computing.

Many educators have worked to change this state of affairs by incorporating computing practices and tools grounded in histories and practices of different communities into CS Ed curricula. One resource is the set of Culturally Situated Design Tools (CSDT) developed by CS educators to connect STEM and computing principles to cultural practices like African fractals, Appalachian quilting algorithm, and Native and Indigenous beadwork.[6] There are also many resources that explore the diversity of the CS field that existed historically and continues to exist today but that often gets erased or excluded from CS curriculum (see Chapter 3 for more on erasure). Jean Ryoo, Jane Margolis, and Charis JB's 2022 graphic novel *Power On!* is one resource.[7] This book emphasizes how diverse computer scientists' identities and perspectives shaped their work and commitments, leading them to contribute to computing in transformative ways. Teachers can also include examples of historical and contemporary CS creatives who come from backgrounds that reflect their students' identities. Resource 1 in Chapter 1 provides some historical examples to get started. Other contemporary examples that some of our teachers have used to represent their own students include people like the winners of the Ada Lovelace Award,[8] Ayanna Howard,[9] Joshua Miele,[10] Angelica Ross,[11] and Erin Spiceland.[12] Chapter 4 also highlights several activist groups who are using CS to work toward social justice for marginalized groups. These examples offer ways to incorporate reasons for computing into CS curricula that go beyond the commercial purposes that are often prioritized.

---

6. Learn more about Culturally Situated Design Tools at https://csdt.org

7. Learn more about *Power On!* at https://www.poweronbook.com

8. Learn more about the Ada Lovelace Award at https://awc-hq.org/ada-lovelace-awards.html

9. Learn more about Ayanna Howard at https://engineering.osu.edu/about/office-dean/about-dean-ayanna-howard

10. Learn more about Joshua Miele at https://www.macfound.org/fellows/class-of-2021/joshua-miele

11. Learn more about Angelica Ross at https://time.com/collection/closers/6564908/angelica-ross-tech/

12. Learn more about Erin Spiceland at https://github.blog/developer-skills/career-growth/leader-spotlight-erin-spiceland/

CS educator Tarek shared some strategies that he has used to address the lack of diversity in CS curricula:

> The world sends messages that tell certain groups they don't belong in tech. I've seen it happen with some girls and students of color in my class. They feel like they don't fit in because they've heard the message that tech is a white, male-dominated field. I remember one super smart girl who was hesitant about CS because she didn't see many women in the field. It's heartbreaking to see them hold themselves back.
>
> To fight against those stereotypes, I try to show my students that there are tons of amazing women and people of color who are killing it in tech. I also try to build a classroom culture where everyone feels like their contributions matter. I use inclusive language, I make sure there are diverse faces in examples and stories, and I encourage teamwork over competition. I want my students to feel empowered to own their place in tech.

Through his efforts, Tarek has worked to resist stereotypes of who does (not) belong in CS and to help students see themselves reflected in his CS classroom. Given the importance of diversity for both CS industries and CS Ed, CS educators can work to center diversity as a resource for learning in their classrooms.

HOW CAN CS EDUCATORS CENTER DIVERSITY?

Centering diversity can involve (1) welcoming students who may be excluded from CS spaces; (2) recognizing students' diversity; and (3) building on and affirming student diversity.

WELCOMING DIVERSITY

To welcome students whose identities have been marginalized in CS Ed classrooms, it is important for teachers to investigate why particular groups of students might not be participating in CS learning opportunities and to create welcoming spaces. Marilyn's dilemma around her Girls Who Code club illustrates the need to create spaces that center cultural practices and values that are not always included in mainstream CS Ed settings. There are several approaches that can help address this need. One approach is to create spaces that prioritize historically marginalized groups. This might look like creating affinity groups where those with an affinity or

culturally sustaining pedagogies Ways and approaches to teaching that value and center students' cultural identities, practices, and ways of knowing as resources for learning rather than excluding or eradicating students' cultures from the classroom (see Ladson-Billings, 2021; Paris & Alim, 2017).

shared set of values can come together and center their cultural practices, ways of knowing, and experiences. Another way to create welcoming spaces is to center plurality within mainstream spaces using approaches like **culturally responsive and sustaining pedagogies**. A third approach blends the first two, creating spaces that foster syncretism, or combining different traditions, perspectives, and practices to create something new (see Chapter 14 for more on syncretism in CS Ed).

As an example of what it might look like to welcome diversity in practice, let's consider Sophie, a fictional teacher of AP CS. Sophie recognized that most of the students in her class were typically white and male. She asked herself why more of her school's growing population of West African immigrant students weren't enrolled in the course. Was it a language issue? Were students not satisfying gatekeeping prerequisites? Were competing courses happening at the same time? Were students unaware of the course as an option? Did they feel that they wouldn't belong or be interested in the course? Many of these reasons could be overlapping and contributing to Sophie's enrollment patterns. Sophie resolved to stay curious as she worked to understand the issues by talking to the school guidance counselor and students about enrollment.

RECOGNIZING DIVERSITY

Educators can learn to recognize students' backgrounds and experiences across a range of dimensions and use that understanding to plan and facilitate CS learning activities. Recognizing diversity is harder than it might seem. Even with the best intentions, as we seek to notice variation and difference, we can inadvertently perpetuate assumptions about groups of people, causing harm to students. One way this happens is when we act on incomplete knowledge of how our students differ from ourselves and from each other.

invisible disabilities Disabilities that are not readily perceived by society.

For example, Sophie needed to be careful not to assume that because most of her current students were male and white, they were all the same. Her students had varied motivations for participating in CS and different prior experiences with technology. Sophie couldn't immediately recognize students who had hidden or undocumented barriers to CS learning. These challenges included things like **invisible disabilities**, varying language backgrounds, family income, and Internet access at home. Similarly, Sophie did not immediately notice the personal resources or cultural assets her students and their families could contribute to the CS classroom. One of Sophie's white male students had a reading disability that was exacerbated by the way a particular programming environment displays text on the screen. That same student had a family member with a disability that motivated his participation in CS. As Sophie got to know this student, his goal to develop tools with and for his loved one became a valuable asset for his CS class. Creating diverse and inclusive CS Ed environments requires gathering information about students' experiences and questioning assumptions about sameness.

Our ability to recognize diversity might be constrained by the categories we use to describe students. Not all differences can be reduced to demographic categories. For example, the identity categories commonly used in U.S. education to label students along racial and ethnic (e.g., Asian American, Black, Latine/Hispanic, Native American or Indigenous) or gender lines (e.g., male, female, non-binary) may be helpful in the aggregate to provide a high-level overview. However, these labels can quickly collapse individual students' backgrounds, experiences, and interests. We need to be careful not to **essentialize**, or assume or imply sameness within a group, especially within minoritized and marginalized groups.

Instead of relying on demographic categories to recognize diversity, a teacher like Sophie might seek to understand and build on students' **funds of knowledge**, or the bodies of knowledge and experience that students bring with them from their home lives and cultural communities (González et al., 2005). Understanding students' funds of knowledge requires deeply learning about students' family and community practices rather than making assumptions about or essentializing students based on demographic labels. For example, one student in Sophie's school, Dee, shared that their family had funds of knowledge related to hair styling. At home, they were responsible for doing their siblings' hair, and they spent time learning and observing at the barber shop where their parents worked. Sophie took time to learn more about Dee and their family's funds of knowledge. She considered the relationship that these caretaking and hairstyling practices had to CS. Sophie also reflected on how everyone in the classroom could learn from the knowledge that Dee brought from their home and family.

BUILDING ON AND AFFIRMING DIVERSITY

Equipped with knowledge about students and their communities' differences and strengths, teachers can affirm this diversity through their CS instruction. There are many ways to do this, which will be explored in the chapters that follow (e.g., Chapters 8–17). In this chapter, we'll focus on Sophie's attempt to build on Dee's family's funds of knowledge in her planning.

A popular resource on the CSDT website has students explore African and African diasporic cornrow braiding patterns in hair and use a block-

---

essentialization Reducing the complexity inherent in people or groups and portraying them in stereotypical ways.

funds of knowledge Funds of knowledge describe the bodies of knowledge, cultural practices, and ways of interacting that students bring into classrooms from their home communities and cultures. Funds of knowledge may include students' academic and personal background knowledge, lived experiences, skills to navigate everyday social contexts, and world views based on broader historical and cultural influences (González et al., 2005; Washington Office of Superintendent of Public Instruction, 2023).

based coding interface to design their own cornrow patterns.[13] Braiding as a cultural practice inherently requires sophisticated computational thinking and is related to Dee's home practices and funds of knowledge. Sophie reasoned that these activities might help Dee explore CS in the context of their interests while providing opportunities for others to learn about the practices of groups who are different from them and see computing in a new light.

In the process of planning this activity, Sophie needed to take care not to appropriate or oversimplify cornrow braiding, instead treating the practice with respect and care. She first worked to understand her own relationship to cornrow braiding, considering if and how it was something practiced in her own communities and culture. She also identified where cornrow braiding practices originated and researched who practiced them in the past and who practices them today by learning from (and compensating or reciprocating) local experts, reading, and watching media created by and for cornrow braiders. Sophie also considered how different households have different practices related to braiding. Rather than assume that any of her students who were a part of the African diaspora had braiding as a household practice, Sophie explored how different households have different relationships with cornrow braiding and how and why the practice might have been (or might not have been) handed down over generations. She also considered how these practices came about, what they mean in different contexts, and how they are related to computation. She reflected on how these practices play a role in the everyday lives of students whose families carry this expertise and how they demonstrate, share, and pass along braiding as a relational and caregiving practice.

Sophie brought some of the examples she discovered through her research to the classroom for her students to explore. She also asked Dee and Dee's family members to share their histories and practices related to haircare and cornrow braiding. As students were given opportunities to get inspired by those examples, they were able to experience mirrors of people who reflected back to them aspects of their own identities or experience windows into practices that let them experience other ways of computing (Bishop, 1990). Windows and mirrors can create a new vision of what CS is, who practices it, and for what purposes, promoting cultural awareness and cultural competence for all students, whether or not they are members of groups who have been marginalized in computing.

As she facilitated discussions about the topic, Sophie also worked to avoid **tokenizing** students. Tokenizing occurs when a single individual is

tokenism Treating a single individual as representative of an entire group or allowing the presence of a few people with marginalized identities give an illusion of representation and inclusion.

---

13. See the activity at https://csdt.org/culture/cornrowcurves/index.html

treated as representative of an entire group, such as asking a student with disabilities to speak for all people with disabilities instead of only from their own experience. Because everyone has different funds of knowledge and lived experiences, no single person can speak for an entire group. Teachers may be more likely to inadvertently tokenize students when they ask learners to share expertise that they assume students have based on perceived identities. Instead, teachers can get to know individual students, understand how those students identify themselves, and learn about their personal backgrounds and experiences.

This meant that Sophie avoided singling Dee out to explain cornrow braiding in general as a broad cultural practice. Instead, all students were invited to share specific hair care practices from their families, and Dee shared one example of cornrow braiding. Reflecting on Sophie's story, CS teacher Christina shared her insights:

> It made me think about how to go beyond simply labeling students based on their race or gender and instead understand their individual stories and how those stories shape their learning. For example, a classroom activity focused on cornrow braiding might not be relevant or engaging for all Black girls. This makes me think about how we need to be really careful about assuming that everyone in a certain group shares the same interests and experiences.

As we work to avoid assumptions of sameness, essentialization, and tokenization, we can ensure that the diversity in our classrooms is a resource that truly benefits all.

REVISITING MARILYN'S STORY

Diversity is central to the questions Marilyn raised about her after-school coding program. She recognized that her students were different and that while social labels are one way to name those differences, they don't always help capture the power of diversity. Marilyn ended up using Girls Who Code as her after-school program and acknowledged its limitations as she worked to better center her students' diverse backgrounds. Her colleague Rebecca described how she navigated this tension in her own context:

> I personally had the same issue when I wanted to join Girls Who Code. The organization name didn't sound right for my diverse

students, so we didn't do it. Instead, we created our own after-school club to accommodate boys, girls, non-binary, multilingual, and special ed students. We exposed diverse groups of students to various CS activities. Some students gained confidence through the CS club. . . . Their confidence later boosted their desire to do more and do well in other subject areas. It was also helpful when I took them to a [CS-related] event outside of school. They otherwise wouldn't have had any chance to be invited to such an event. Students were excited and wanted to learn more about CS.

Marilyn and Rebecca worked to recognize diversity by deliberately lifting it up in their after-school spaces to make all students feel welcome. This approach can help foster inclusive learning environments in diverse CS classrooms and schools. At the same time, as we'll see with other teachers throughout the book, sometimes promoting diversity is best achieved through creating affinity spaces specifically for historically marginalized groups so that their experiences can be centered. Both approaches can help navigate the tensions that Marilyn raised and promote equitable teaching and learning.

As we hope this chapter has shown, diversity applies to everyone. We can learn to recognize diversity even in groups that may appear to seem the same on the surface. At the same time, because diversity is often intertwined with inequity, we need to be thoughtful about how we cultivate diversity in ways that make space for and center the perspectives and experiences of those who hold marginalized and minoritized identities. Diversity can become a powerful resource for learning in more equitable and transformational ways.

REFLECTION QUESTIONS

1. After reading this chapter, what does diversity mean to you? How would you define it? How would you explain the role that diversity plays in CS Ed to someone else?

2. What barriers to diversity have you observed in your own experiences with CS and CS Ed? How might you advocate or work to change some of those barriers in your own setting?

3. What kinds of diversity are present in your CS Ed setting? What aspects of diversity do your students bring that might you not have initially recognized? How do you support all of your heterogeneous students and provide them with opportunities to learn?

TAKEAWAYS FOR PRACTICE

- Consider the diversity that exists in a CS Ed setting that you are in or will be in. Think about diversity that may be readily apparent and diversity that might be harder to recognize. Create a representation (e.g., collage, mindmap, word cloud) that helps you capture the different kinds of diversity that exist in this setting. Consider how you might be able to use these different perspectives as resources for learning.

- Reflect on how the concept of "funds of knowledge" might apply to your CS Ed setting. Consider the funds of knowledge that students already use and how you could learn more about other practices that students have. Explore ways to incorporate these practices into CS learning experiences.

GLOSSARY

Term	Definition
ableism	Implicit or explicit social preference for nondisabled bodies and minds that creates prejudice and oppression of disability and disabled people (Shew, 2020).
culturally sustaining pedagogies	Ways and approaches to teaching that value and center students' cultural identities, practices, and ways of knowing as resources for learning rather than excluding or eradicating students' cultures from the classroom (see Ladson-Billings, 2021; Paris & Alim, 2017).
diversity	Collectives of individuals with different identities, perspectives, experiences, and backgrounds. Diversity is often described in terms of social categories like age, disability, gender identity and sexual orientation, educational background, language, national origin, race and ethnicity, religion, and socioeconomic status.
essentialization	Reducing the complexity inherent in people or groups and portraying them in stereotypical ways.
funds of knowledge	Funds of knowledge describe the bodies of knowledge, cultural practices, and ways of interacting that students bring into classrooms from their home communities and cultures. Funds of knowledge

	may include students' academic and personal background knowledge, lived experiences, skills to navigate everyday social contexts, and world views based on broader historical and cultural influences (González et al., 2005; Washington Office of Superintendent of Public Instruction, 2023).
gatekeeping	Institutional policies and structures that control who gets to participate in opportunities and who has access to resources in ways that limit the participation of marginalized groups.
intersectionality	A theory that recognizes how people's different identities (e.g., disability, gender, race) overlap and intersect, creating access to privilege or resulting in oppression in ways that cannot be understood or addressed by considering each identity separately (Crenshaw, 1991; Collins, 2019).
invisible diabilities	Disabilities that are not readily perceived by society.
marginalized/ minoritized identities	Identity categories that are devalued by society, often because they are different from what society has established as the "ideal" norm. Those with marginalized/minoritized identities often face oppression and exclusion from mainstream society. We use both marginalized and minoritized as adjectives to emphasize how social processes actively construct inequity (Black et al., 2023). The term "minoritized" emphasizes historical systematic oppression and may be used regardless of whether an identity group actually represents a numerical minority in a context (see Black et al., 2023; Flores & Rosa, 2015).
opportunity hoarding	Processes through which privileged groups control and prevent access to resources for marginalized groups.
othering	The process of treating a group of people (often those with minoritized or marginalized identities) as intrinsically different from the dominant social norm.
tokenism	Treating a single individual as representative of an entire group or allowing the presence of a few

	people with marginalized identities give an illusion of representation and inclusion.
xenophobia	A system of prejudice and discrimination against foreigners.

REFERENCES

Algorithmic Justice League. (n.d.). *What is facial recognition?* Algorithmic Justice League. https://www.ajl.org/facial-recognition-technology

Allyn, B. (2020, Dec 17). *Ousted Black Google researcher: "They wanted to have my presence, but not me exactly."* NPR. https://www.npr.org/2020/12/17/947719354/ousted-black-google-researcher-they-wanted-to-have-my-presence-but-not-me-exactl

Angwin, J., Larson, J., Mattu, S., & Kirchner, L. (2016, May 23). *Machine bias.* ProPublica. https://www.propublica.org/article/machine-bias-risk-assessments-in-criminal-sentencing

Benjamin, R. (2019). *Race after technology: Abolitionist tools for the new Jim code.* Polity.

Benjamin, R. (2024). *Imagination: A manifesto.* W. W. Norton & Company.

Bishop, R. S. (1990). Windows and mirrors: Children's books and parallel cultures. In M. Atwell & A. Klein (Eds.), *Celebrating literacy: Proceedings of the 14th Annual California State University, San Bernardino Reading Conference* (pp. 3–12).

Black, C., Cerdeña, J. P., & Spearman-McCarthy, E. V. (2023). I am not your minority. *Lancet Regional Health Americas, 19.* https://doi.org/10.1016/j.lana.2023.100464

Chang-Bacon, C. K. (2020). Monolingual language ideologies and the idealized speaker: The "new bilingualism" meets the "old" educational inequities. *Teachers College Record, 123*(1), 1–19. https://doi.org/10.1177/016146812112300106

Chicago Public Schools. (2020, Mar 3). *Cracking the code: Expanding computer science opportunities for CPS students through an equity lens.* Chicago Public Schools. https://www.cps.edu/sites/blog/search/2020/march/cracking-the-code/

Clifton, B., Lavigne, S., & Tseng, F. (n.d.). Predicting financial crime: Augmenting the predictive policing arsenal. *The New Inquiry* [White paper]. https://whitecollar.thenewinquiry.com/assets/whitepaper.pdf

Code.org. (2025). *Dig deeper into AP computer science.* Code.org. https://code.org/promote/ap

Code.org, CSTA, & ECEP Alliance (2022). *2022 State of Computer Science Education: Understanding Our National Imperative.* Retrieved from https://advocacy.code.org/stateofcs

Collins, P. H. (2019). *Intersectionality as critical social theory.* Duke University Press. https://doi.org/10.1215/9781478007098

Crenshaw, K. (1991). Mapping the margins: Intersectionality, identity politics, and violence against women of color. *Stanford Law Review, 43*(6), 1241–1299. https://doi.org/10.2307/1229039

Culturally Situated Design Tools. (n.d.). *Culturally situated design tools.* National Science Foundation. https://csdt.org

DiSalvo, B., Guzdial, M., Bruckman, A., & McKlin, T. (2014). Saving face while geeking out: Video game testing as a justification for learning computer science. *Journal of the Learning Sciences, 23*(3), 272–315. https://doi.org/10.1080/10508406.2014.893434

Eccles, J. S., & Wigfield, A. (2020). From expectancy-value theory to situated expectancy-value theory: A developmental, social cognitive, and sociocultural perspective on motivation. *Contemporary Educational Psychology, 61*, 101859. https://doi.org/10.1016/j.cedpsych.2020.101859

Flores, N., & Rosa, J. (2015). Undoing appropriateness: Raciolinguistic ideologies and language diversity in education. *Harvard Educational Review, 85*(2), 149–171. https://doi.org/10.17763/0017-8055.85.2.149

fluent.ai. (n.d.) *Our mission, our team.* https://fluent.ai/about/

González, N., Moll, L. C., & Amanti, C. (2005). *Funds of knowledge: Theorizing practices in households, communities, and classrooms.* Lawrence Erlbaum Associates.

The International Fact-Checking Network. (2025, Jan 9). *An open letter to Mark Zuckerberg from the world's fact-checkers, nine years later.* Poynter. https://www.poynter.org/ifcn/2025/an-open-letter-to-mark-zuckerberg-from-the-worlds-fact-checkers-nine-years-later/

Ko, A. J. (2024). Critical CS education history. In A. J. Ko, A. Beitlers, B. Wortzman, M. Davidson, A. Oleson, M. Kirdani-Ryan, S. Druga, & J. Everson (Eds.), *Critically conscious computing: Methods for secondary education.* https://criticallyconsciouscomputing.org/

Ladson-Billings, G. (2021). *Culturally relevant pedagogy: Asking a different question.* Teachers College Press.

Larson, J., Mattu, S., Kirchner, L., & Angwin, J. (2016, May 23). *How we analyzed the COMPAS recidivism algorithm.* ProPublica. https://www.propublica.org/article/how-we-analyzed-the-compas-recidivism-algorithm

Lee, A. (2015). Determining the effects of computer science education at the secondary level on STEM major choices in postsecondary institutions in the United States. *Computers & Education, 88*, 241–255. https://doi.org/10.1016/j.compedu.2015.04.019

Lee, N. T., Resnick, P., & Barton, G. (2019, May 22). *Algorithmic bias detection and mitigation: Best practices and policies to reduce consumer harms.* Brookings. https://www.brookings.edu/articles/algorithmic-bias-detection-and-mitigation-best-practices-and-policies-to-reduce-consumer-harms/

Margolis, J., Estrella, R., Goode, J., Holme, J. J., & Nao, K. (2017). *Stuck in the shallow end, updated edition: Education, race, and computing.* MIT Press.

MIT Open Documentary Lab. (n.d.). *Hyphen-labs.* MIT Open Documentary Lab. https://opendoclab.mit.edu/presents/hyphen-labs/

Najibi, A. (2020). Racial discrimination in face recognition technology. *Harvard Online: Science Policy and Social Justice, 24.* https://web.archive.org/web/20240730143205/https://projects.iq.harvard.edu/sciencepolicy/blog/racial-discrimination-face-recognition-technology

National Center for Education Statistics. (2024). English Learners in Public Schools. In U.S. Department of Education (Ed.), *Condition of Education.* U.S. Department of Education, Institute of Education Sciences. https://nces.ed.gov/programs/coe/indicator/cgf/english-learners

Paris, D., & Alim, H. S. (2017). *Culturally sustaining pedagogies: Teaching and learning for justice in a changing world.* Teachers College Press.

Patitsas, E., Craig, M., & Easterbrook, S. (2014). A historical examination of the social factors affecting female participation in computing. *Proceedings of the 2014 conference of innovation & technology in computer science education* (pp. 111–116). https://doi.org/10.1145/2591708.2591731

Perrigo, B. (2022, Jan 18). Why Timnit Gebru isn't waiting for big tech to fix AI's problems. *Time.* https://time.com/6132399/timnit-gebru-ai-google/

Ryoo, J. J., Margolis, J., JB, C. (2022). *Power on!* MIT Press. https://doi.org/10.7551/mitpress/14166.001.0001

Ryoo, J. J., Tanksley, T., Estrada, C., & Margolis, J. (2020). Take space, make space: How students use computer science to disrupt and resist marginalization in schools. *Computer Science Education, 30*(3), 337–361. https://doi.org/10.1080/08993408.2020.1805284

Shew, A. (2020). Ableism, technoableism, and future AI. *IEEE Xplore, 39*(1), 40–85. https://doi.org/10.1109/MTS.2020.2967492

Straub, E. O. (2024, Mar 5). *Roundup on research: The myth of "learning styles."* University of Michigan Online Teaching. https://onlineteaching.umich.edu/articles/the-myth-of-learning-styles/

voiceitt.com. (n.d.) *Inclusive voice AI.* voiceitt. https://www.voiceitt.com/#accessible

Washington Office of Superintendent of Public Instruction. (2023). *Funds of knowledge toolkit.* https://ospi.k12.wa.us/sites/default/files/2023-10/funds_of_knowledge_toolkit.pdf

Zweben, S., & Bizot, B. (2022). *2021 Taulbee survey: CS enrollment grows at all degree levels, with increased gender diversity.* Computing Research Association. https://cra.org/wp-content/uploads/2022/05/2021-Taulbee-Survey.pdf

RESOURCE 1: RECOGNIZING DIVERSITY IN CS CLASSROOMS

This resource dives deeper into the story of Brandie, a CS educator who has worked to recognize and center diversity in her classrooms. We provide commentary throughout to highlight how Brandie took up the ideas presented in this chapter. Her story concludes with implications for recognizing diversity in your practice.

BRANDIE'S STORY: "DIVERSITY . . . HELPS BROADEN THEIR UNDERSTANDING OF THE WORLD"

Brandie is an elementary CS teacher. Her story illustrates the importance of teachers being aware of their own and their students' identities as a key aspect of centering diversity as a resource for learning. Brandie's story also highlights how diversity can disrupt dominant norms.

Brandie began with a reflection on her own identities and what that meant in her CS Ed context:

> Thinking about and addressing racial and cultural diversity is not something that I thought was appropriate to address at school in the beginning of my career. . . . [S]chool was about teaching academics. However . . . I've grown to realize the importance that race and culture play at school.
>
> I have come a long way in realizing the importance of me being a Black teacher in a predominately white school and investigating what that means for me, my students, families, and other staff members.
>
> I am a role model, an example, a non-example, a therapist, an advocate, an enigma.
>
> I am active in roles that seek to center diversity, and I care deeply about creating positive, affirming, and fulfilling experiences for my students, their families, myself, and my colleagues.

Like many educators, as an early career teacher, Brandie was initially hesitant about addressing issues like race and culture at school. As we'll see in later chapters, in the United States in particular, we are socially conditioned to avoid talking about racial topics. Brandie came to recognize that race and culture shape schooling regardless of whether we explicitly name their role or not. Her awareness demonstrates her growth in becoming an equity-oriented teacher.

Building on that realization, Brandie engaged in careful reflection about how her own identity and her students' identities shape her work. She recognized that the diversity she brings to the collective of her school influences the many roles she plays in that space. She has chosen to lean into those roles and center diversity as a resource for everyone in her school community.

Brandie elaborated on why and how diversity supports learning in her school context:

> My school is predominantly white, upper-class, and academically high performing, so for me, attention to diversity is really important. It's important for the students who do not fit into those categories to feel seen and valued, because it can be challenging to exist in a space where you may not feel like you belong or where your differences make you feel uncertain, unconfident, or unable to connect enough to feel comfortable enough to be yourself.
>
> Attention to diversity is also important for the students who are white, upper-class, and academically well performing. Having opportunities where they and/or their culture is not centered, and where they are learning about different experiences than their own, helps broaden their understanding of the world [can keep them from perpetuating the status quo], and hopefully increases their open-mindedness, respect for difference, and dedication to equity.

Brandie's description illustrates several key points from this chapter. Diversity involves bringing in students who may feel excluded from CS spaces and ensuring that those students and their contributions are welcomed and valued. It also includes disrupting patterns of sameness for those who hold privileged identities. Brandie's commitment to diversity helps students who differ from the majority in her school to feel a sense of belonging. Brandie also recognized how her efforts offer new perspectives and opportunities for learning to her students who are in the majority in her school.

Although Brandie recognized how diversity could benefit different groups of students in her school, she was also aware that not everyone within a group was the same. Brandie explained how she worked to avoid essentializing her students:

> It is very important to stay grounded in the fact that there is a broad range of individual experiences within any group, regardless of their similarities. There is undoubtedly diversity within a group

that is culturally homogeneous in some way. Girls might want to start a coding group, or we might create a Black student affinity group in my mostly white school. The shared identity marker is the impetus for the creation of the group because of the assumption that there is some experience or interest that they all share.

[Although] everyone in that group is similar [in some way], . . . the reality [is] that they might be very different. . . . [G]etting to know students helps with considering what experiences to choose for students and what the goals of those experiences are (e.g., a mirror v. a window or a sliding door).

Brandie acknowledged that a single (or several) shared interests or identity traits might be a reason to create a group to meet students' needs. However, she also clearly recognized the diversity that continues to exist within any group. She named how getting to know students is an important way to understand the diversity within a group. Brandie's reference to mirrors, windows, and sliding doors draws on the popular analogy that exploring diversity can allow students to experience mirrors reflecting people who are similar to them, windows that let them learn about other ways of being, or sliding glass doors that allow them to walk into new worlds and possibilities (Bishop, 1990).

Brandie concluded her story with a concrete example of how she incorporated diversity into one CS lesson, highlighting a Black computer scientist, Jerry Lawson. (See Resource 1 in Chapter 1 to learn more about Jerry Lawson.)

In our CS units this past school year, my classes in grades 2–5 were learning about what makes a computer and [how] computers work. I centered CS pioneer Jerry Lawson because his work with creating the first video game cartridge revolutionized how data can be stored in computers.

Some of the students got to experience Jerry Lawson's Google Doodle, which featured the opportunity to play several mini-games, edit those games, and create your own game. I made sure to name the game developers who created the games in the Doodle, show their pictures, and create a link to each game developer's website. Not only were all the game developers young and Black, but two of the three developers were female.

I invited students to visit the game developers' websites to learn more about who they are and how their interests and experiences so clearly live in the games they create. To see each game developer tell their story of how their personality, passions, and interests are central to the game they create is so cool, and I think inspiring for kids.[14]

Brandie centered diversity in her activity by representing individuals whose identities are often marginalized in CS and CS Ed (e.g., Black and Black female game developers). She made this connection explicit for students by showing pictures of the developers, and she also avoided tokenizing or essentializing the people in her unit by inviting students to explore the individual stories of each developer. Given Brandie's diverse school community, this unit may have served as a mirror for her racially marginalized students and a window for her white students, disrupting stereotypes about who belongs in CS.

IMPLICATIONS FOR PRACTICE

- Consider your identity and the different identities in your classroom and school communities. In what ways do they align and differ? What roles might your identity lead you to take on in your context? (Chapters 6 and 7 include specific prompts and support to engage in a deeper reflection of your identity and its role in teaching, similar to the process Brandie describes here.)

- Consider who might feel pushed out or excluded in your classroom and school communities. How can diversity serve as a resource to support these students' learning?

- Consider who might often have their experiences and cultures centered in your school communities. How can diversity serve as a resource to support these students' learning?

- Think of a CS lesson you have taught or experienced. How (if at all) did it provide students with *mirrors*, *windows*, or *sliding glass doors* (Bishop, 1990)? How could you revise the lesson to incorporate diversity in ways that make space for these possibilities?

---

14. Visit Jerry Lawson's Google Doodle at https://doodles.google/doodle/gerald-jerry-lawsons-82nd-birthday/

3

Understanding Inequities in Computer Science and Computer Science Education

Sara Vogel, Christopher Hoadley, Lauren Vogelstein, Bethany Daniel, Stephanie T. Jones, and the Computer Science Educational Justice Collective

CHAPTER OVERVIEW

This chapter considers how inequities created by social beliefs, structures, and interactions influence computer science (CS) and CS education (CS Ed). It explores some of the historical and contemporary inequities that shape CS and CS Ed. The chapter focuses specifically on inequities that happen through the unjust distribution of CS resources and CS Ed learning opportunities, exclusion from CS and CS Ed, deficit narratives about marginalized groups in CS and CS Ed, erasure and a narrowing of what "counts" as CS and CS Ed, and embedded bias and the unjust impacts of technology on marginalized groups.

CHAPTER OBJECTIVES

After reading this chapter, I can:

- Describe inequities that shape CS and CS Ed.
- Identify how inequities impact CS students and CS teaching and learning.

KEY TERMS

bias(es); deficit narratives; dysgraphia; erasure; exclusion; gatekeeping; inequity; intersectionality; marginalized/minoritized identities

MS. MORALES' STORY

Working toward equity in CS and CS Ed requires an understanding of the challenges created by the **inequities** that exist and persist in the industry and in classrooms, influencing what happens from day to day. Ms. Morales, an elementary CS teacher, recognizes some of the inequities that she and her students face and is working hard to change them.[1]

Ms. Morales is a New York City–based K-8 public school teacher involved in an equity-focused CS professional development (PD) community. Different experiences and aspects of Ms. Morales' identity have shaped how she engages in equity work. When asked to describe herself during an interview with the authors of this guide, Ms. Morales named some of the identities she holds, including that of CS teacher, artist, and stepmother. She shared that she has Puerto Rican and Chinese heritage and speaks English and conversational Spanish with her family. She also described how "when I was younger, I was dealing with mild **dysgraphia** in school and helping my brother who has hearing impairments." Ms. Morales' background shaped her desire to teach, and an early interest in technology eventually led her to become a CS teacher.

Ms. Morales also shared some of the issues that she needs to address as a CS teacher. Those challenges include things like:

- meeting the needs of her students from different cultural and linguistic backgrounds,
- supporting her students with disabilities,
- helping students feel like they belong in CS Ed,
- developing her own CS skills to support her students,
- making sure that all of the students she services have CS learning opportunities, and
- having access to the technology (working computers, wireless internet access, etc.) needed to teach CS.

inequity Injustice or unfairness that is created and reproduced by social forces. It is important to remember that "fairness" does not mean "sameness," so working to right unfairness and inequity does not mean just giving everyone the same thing.

dysgraphia A learning disability that may affect a person's physical ability to write and/or impact their ability to express their thoughts through writing.

---

1. Ms. Morales' experiences are shared with permission.

Ms. Morales can address some of these problems within her own classroom and in collaboration with educators at her school. Other problems are more complex and tied to broader systems of inequity. These problems require us to organize collectives and build power and resources to work toward change.

INEQUITIES IN CS INDUSTRY AND CS ED

Ms. Morales' concerns represent inequities that impact CS students and teachers across the country. Many of them fall into five categories: (1) the unjust distribution of CS resources and learning opportunities; (2) **exclusion** from CS; (3) **deficit narratives** about **marginalized** groups; (4) **erasure** and a narrowing of what "counts" as valuable knowledge and practices; and (5) embedded **biases** and unjust impacts of technology. We look at the historical roots of these inequities and how they continue in CS industry and CS Ed today. While we break them out into separate groups, it's important to recognize that inequities are intertwined and often overlap, as the examples that follow illustrate.

UNJUST DISTRIBUTION OF RESOURCES

One foundational inequity is the reality that access to resources that facilitate CS learning are not equitably distributed in U.S. society or across U.S. schools. Resources include things like technological tools, rigorous CS instruction, and well-qualified teachers. Not all students have the same access to the resources needed to learn CS.

Schools with large populations of racially marginalized and low-income students tend to have more limited access to technology (like computers, tablets, and modems) and the programs and infrastructure needed to do computing (like websites and apps, software, internet connections, and power; Blikstein, 2018). Historically, only school districts that served high-income students had the resources to spend on new technology. School districts serving low-income and racially marginalized students could not afford the high costs of computers (Sutton, 1991). Today, while most households and schools have access to devices, many groups lack access to broadband internet connectivity (King et al., 2022). Students might be "smartphone-only" internet users, because these tools tend to be less expensive than other computing devices (Pew Research Center, 2024). Smartphones lend themselves well to entertainment, information seeking, taking and sharing photos and videos, and communication. However, many tasks valued in school, like extended research and writing

---

marginalized/minoritized identities Identity categories that are devalued in society, often because they are different from what society has established as the "ideal" norm. Those with marginalized/minoritized identities often face oppression and exclusion from mainstream society. We use both "marginalized" and "minoritized" as adjectives to emphasize how social processes actively construct inequity (Black et al., 2023). The term "minoritized" emphasizes historical systematic oppression and may be used regardless of whether an identity group actually represents a numerical minority in a context (see Black et al., 2023; Flores & Rosa, 2015).

tasks, web publishing, and coding and programming are more difficult to accomplish on a smartphone. These realities demonstrate how societal hierarchies contribute to an unjust and inequitable distribution of and access to the technological resources needed to engage in computing.

Resources related to rigorous CS instruction are also inequitably distributed. When computers started appearing in classrooms in the 1980s and 1990s, their use was often tied to racially constructed norms of behavior that favored students racialized as white. These students were perceived as "better behaved" and had more opportunities to use computers (Arias, 1990; Sutton, 1991). This trend continues today. Students who are perceived as "struggling" or as "troublemakers" may end up being tracked on remediation pathways, giving them fewer chances to take electives like CS. Even in schools where all students have opportunities to take courses related to technology, middle- and upper-class white students are more likely to use computers for activities like programming. By contrast, lower-income and racially marginalized students are more likely to use computers for drill and practice (Margolis et al., 2008). This distinction is important, as it highlights the difference between simply using computers and actually engaging in practices of computing.

Lack of access to well-prepared CS educators is another example of inequitable distribution of resources. Students from historically marginalized groups are more likely to attend elementary schools with fewer CS Ed opportunities, and a recent study found that only 8% of low-income schools offered the AP Computer Science course compared to 37% of high-income schools (Code.org et al., 2022). This could be in part from a lack of teachers who are qualified to teach CS. STEM teacher J. Lauren reflected on the impact that the unjust distribution of resources has on CS education:

> There are countless students in underfunded schools across the country who may very well be incredible contributors to CS fields, but if they don't have access to a computer for most of their education, or if their tech use is limited to a narrow suite of apps on an outdated school-owned iPad or Chromebook, they won't even know that computer science and technology is a passion that they can have!

CS teachers need to be aware of the different ways that unjust distribution of resources can impact students. Educators may perpetuate inequity if they assume that all students have access to things like a computer or internet. Karime, a CS teacher, shared an example of how this plays out at school:

Low-income students are being denied the agency of working when and where they want to and are expected to give up their free time. I have students who were [enrolled] in CS [courses] against their wishes and do not have computers at home, so they are made to use the computer lab during lunch and after school. Instead of giving them computers (which [the school is] supposed to do), the CS teacher is being asked to rewrite the curriculum so that it can be completed on a phone. The inconvenience is enough to alienate someone from the field.

These examples illustrate how the unjust distribution of resources, including access to hardware and software, rigorous CS learning experiences, and well-qualified CS teachers, contributes to inequities in CS Ed.

EXCLUSION

At Ms. Morales' school, CS learning experiences were offered mostly to 6th through 8th graders because of scheduling issues and misconceptions about what Computer Science for All was. How to structure things to achieve the "for all" goal was a challenge. Ms. Morales was often assigned more middle school classes than elementary classes and did not have enough time in her schedule to reach all the grades. These factors contributed to students in younger grades not consistently receiving CS instruction and feeling excluded from CS. The situation at Ms. Morales' school shows how inequity often persists because of constraints that limit what is possible in a given space and time in tangible ways. It takes collective and intentional efforts to find creative solutions to overcome these challenges.

Nevertheless, in many cases, **exclusion** as a form of inequity is and has been built into the social fabric of CS. Exclusion can often be recognized by a lack of diversity and representation in CS Ed and CS fields. For example, those with certain identities may have easier access to CS courses, labs, and jobs than others who are excluded from those opportunities. Exclusion operates at two levels: an external level of oppression, where individuals may be kept from opportunities to participate in CS; and a psychological or emotional level of internalized oppression, where individuals may feel excluded and unwelcome in a space even though they are physically present.

External exclusion is often reproduced through practices like **gatekeeping**, or institutional systems and policies that control who gets to participate in opportunities and who has access to resources. For example, course policies in U.S. school systems may push students with

exclusion Processes and efforts that limit the presence and participation of marginalized and oppressed groups in a space.

gatekeeping Institutional policies and structures that control who gets to participate in opportunities and who has access to resources in ways that limit the participation of marginalized groups.

marginalized identities onto an academic track that prevents them from enrolling in CS courses (Margolis et al., 2008). This gatekeeping in CS Ed also impacts the field. Keeping high schoolers from exploring CS in K-12 schooling may prevent them from choosing CS-related college majors or pursuing CS careers.

Exclusion also happens implicitly. Society and its institutions have invisibilized norms, policies, and practices that send messages about who can or should be involved in computing. For example, Ms. Morales' teaching schedule seemed to be aimed toward the upper elementary and middle school grades, which, whether intentional or not, perpetuated a notion of not needing to provide coding or technology opportunities to younger students. This form of gatekeeping limits young children's CS opportunities despite research that shows the benefits of teaching coding skills and CS concepts as a form of literacy through both "unplugged" activities and age-friendly tech tools (e.g., Bers, 2019; Wohl et al., 2015). Advocating for other teachers to integrate CS into their practice and have access to CS resources that they could use within their existing curriculum were some of the ways that Ms. Morales worked to include young children in CS at her school.

Exclusion and gatekeeping have persisted since the earliest days of the field of CS.[2] Backus (1980) described how early on, the CS field developed a culture of "priesthood," where access to the power of digital computers was restricted to a chosen few. He described this priesthood as a fraternity of members selected because of "a colorful personality [or] . . . an extraordinary feat of coding . . . [instead of] for intellectual insight" (Backus, 1980, p. 127). These original programmers, generally white males who held social power and privilege, prided themselves on being a part of this select group. They resisted efforts to "make programming so easy that anyone could do it" (Backus, 1980, p. 128).

This resistance led to exclusion and the discrediting of work done by individuals who held marginalized identities. The differences between how early computer scientists Alexandra Forsythe and her husband George were treated illustrate this. Both Alexandra and George made significant contributions to the CS field. Alexandra wrote the first CS textbook (Forsythe et al., 1969), and George coined the term "computer science" and helped found the Department of Computer Science at Stanford University. Alexandra and George both began as Ph.D. students at Brown University. While George graduated with his Ph.D., a dean canceled Alexandra's fellowship because, as Alexandra explained, "he [the dean] didn't think I properly stayed on the sidelines like a woman should do" (Forsythe,

---

2. To learn more about the history of CS, see the book *Critically Conscious Computing* (Ko et al., 2024); https://criticallyconsciouscomputing.org/

1979, p. 9). Despite the gatekeeping that prevented Alexandra from earning her doctoral degree, she went on to teach at Vassar College and eventually at Stanford alongside her husband.

Unfortunately, exclusion persists in CS industries and CS Ed today. Recent statistics illustrate how exclusion in CS impacts marginalized groups (100Kin10.org, 2021):

- **Women** face **greater exclusion from CS careers** than women in STEM broadly.
- Only **19%** of **CS bachelor's degrees** are awarded to women, even though they earn **85%** of **health-related bachelor's degrees** as a STEM field.
- **74%** of **women** in CS careers report **workplace gender discrimination**.
- Only **3.4%** of all **CS doctorates** in recent years were awarded to **Black** people.
- Only **7%** of those in **computer occupations** are **Black** although Black people make up 11% of the overall workforce.
- **Native American/Alaskan Native** students are the **least likely** of all racially minoritized students to attend **schools with CS courses**.[3]
- Only **5.6%** of the 11.2% of students labeled as **English learners** and **7.6%** of the 12.9% of **students with disabilities participated in CS** in recent years.

intersectionality A theory that recognizes how people's different identities (e.g., disability, gender, race) overlap and intersect, creating access to privilege or resulting in oppression in ways that cannot be understood or addressed by considering each identity separately (Crenshaw, 1991; Collins, 2019).

These statistics highlight how exclusion in CS and CS Ed occurs for those with socially marginalized identities around class, disability, gender, language, and race. But the data in the report did not look at how individuals who hold overlapping marginalized identities are excluded. **Intersectionality** (explored further in Chapter 5) helps us understand how those with multiply marginalized identities experience inequity at the intersections of their exclusion. While the data identify Black people and women as being excluded from CS, it does not consider how Black women are uniquely impacted because their identities lie at the intersections of being Black and being female. Similarly, the report noted that data often wasn't even available to understand many groups' participation in CS. For example, there was no data on non-binary students and employees,

---

3. We use Native American/Alaskan Native here to match the term used in the original research report. See On Terminology for a full discussion of terms used in the guide.

limited data on those with disabilities, and no data on multilingual learners and employees beyond the PK-12 school system. The fact that data for these groups were not collected emphasizes how exclusion continues to persist in CS and CS Ed.

DEFICIT NARRATIVES ABOUT MARGINALIZED GROUPS

Ms. Morales observed that many of the adults around her had a "mindset that kids can't grasp computing at a young age." But Ms. Morales resisted this story about her students. She knew it wasn't true from her own experience. Observing her students after the COVID-19 experience, Ms. Morales recognized that even students in kindergarten and first grade "had experiences navigating websites and gaining new [computing] skills." In identifying the incorrect assumptions she was hearing about her students, Ms. Morales was noticing another common inequity in CS and CS Ed: **deficit narratives**. In this case, those narratives were myths about young learners' potential to do CS that created inequitable access to CS learning opportunities at her school.

Deficit narratives are broadly held beliefs, including stereotypes, that position groups of people as deficient or lacking in some way (Louie et al., 2021; Steele, 2011). In Ms. Morales' school, young children were positioned as lacking the skills or ability to engage meaningfully in computing. Deficit narratives often show up as "common sense" statements like "kids can't grasp computing at a young age."[4] These statements make assumptions about the abilities of a group or blame individuals instead of the systems around them that reproduce inequities (Philip, 2011).

Deficit narratives might sound like, "Women just aren't naturally as good at math as men," or, "Students of color just aren't interested in CS."[5] What makes deficit narratives problematic is that they aren't based in truth. Women can be just as successful in math as men (Steele, 2011), and studies have found that Black and Hispanic students are more likely to be interested in CS coursework than their white peers (Gallup, 2020).[6] Deficit narratives come out of assumptions about groups of people who

deficit narratives Broadly held beliefs, including stereotypes, that identify groups of people as lacking or deficient in some way (Louie et al., 2021; Steele, 2011).

---

4. When naming something as "common sense," we align with scholars who have pointed out that what is often considered common sense is neither common nor sensical (Fairclough, 2014; Garfinkel, 1967).

5. This deficit narrative is also problematic because it collapses the different experiences of racially marginalized people into an overly broad category of "students of color" and fails to consider individual experiences.

6. We use Hispanic here to match the term used in the original source. See On Terminology for a full discussion of terms used in the guide.

differ in some way from what has been constructed as normal (and implicitly, the "ideal") by society, not out of what is true. In the United States, society positions identities like white, male, upper-middle class, English-speaking, cis-gender, and heterosexual, among others as the "norm." Individuals and groups who differ from these norms are positioned by society as lacking in some way, and the narratives told about them reproduce the social hierarchies that perpetuate inequity.

Deficit narratives about marginalized groups are embedded into the policies and practices of U.S. education in general. Historically, schooling was used as a tool to assimilate immigrant groups, to "civilize" Indigenous peoples, and to segregate Black people.[7] Deficit thinking about Black, Latine, low-income, immigrant, and other minoritized children persists in education today. Educators often offer deficit beliefs as rationales for how schools fail racially marginalized youth. These narratives include statements like, "the parents just don't care, these children don't have enough exposure/experiences, these children aren't ready for school, their families don't value education" and so on (Ladson-Billings, 2007, p. 318). Again, these narratives are not based in reality. Recent research shows that Black and Hispanic caregivers are actually more likely to value CS Ed and to recognize the need for CS in future careers than white caregivers (Gallup, 2020). However, deficit-based explanations can lead educators and institutions to lower expectations for marginalized youth, blaming students and families rather than the systems that underserve them.

Those lowered expectations often result in limited meaningful CS learning opportunities for low-income youth and students with marginalized identities. An examination of three different schools in Los Angeles showed how the forces that reproduced inequity went beyond the availability of technology and CS courses (Margolis et al., 2008). Low expectations were set for racially marginalized students regardless of whether they attended a school where a majority of the student body held racially marginalized identities or a school where they were integrated with white, upper-middle class students. School tracking policies funneled low-income and racially minoritized students into basic computing classes, while students who came from the most prepared, technologically equipped households were encouraged to take advanced CS coursework. The researchers concluded that "technology has not been the great equalizer because schools are providing different learning opportunities, and these opportunities vary according to the racial and socioeconomic demographics of the students"

---

7. U.S. public schooling was first founded by African Americans following their emancipation from enslavement and reflected their deep commitment to education. Segregation policies then worked to maintain underfunding in schools for Black and other marginalized students. See Anderson (1988) for a full discussion.

(Margolis et al., 2008, p. 134). More than a decade after that research, concerns still exist about "the unequal presence of CS in public schools, the quality of instruction, and the educators' and counselors' unconscious bias regarding who is 'suited' to take CS classes" (Blikstein, 2018, p. 34).

Ms. Morales appreciated arguments about the need for young children to get off screens and into settings where they play and interact with each other. But she had also read about the benefits of having students explore computational thinking through "unplugged activities" that don't use technology, having young learners code digital stories using age-appropriate tools like Scratch Jr. and even having them engage in critical conversations about tech tools in their own lives (Bers, 2019; Wohl et al., 2015). Ms. Morales recognized that having moments of offline activities that reinforce key skills are important in all core subjects, including CS. She hoped to resist the deficit narratives that framed her young students as less capable at computing.

ERASURE AND NARROWING WHAT "COUNTS" AS VALUABLE

Another concern that Ms. Morales identified in her work as a CS educator was how to best include her students' different backgrounds and meet their different needs. Ms. Morales' students typically come from many different countries: Albania, Georgia, Honduras, Mexico, Russia, Turkey, and Uzbekistan, among others. Her students speak a range of languages, bring with them a variety of cultural experiences and practices, and have diverse abilities. Ms. Morales described how she wants her students to "be very comfortable" sharing and participating in class so that they feel like they belong. One challenge for Ms. Morales was that only a few coding websites (e.g., code.org and Scratch) provide multiple languages for students to learn from.[8] Given her students' diverse language abilities, this meant that many resources that Ms. Morales might use presented challenges for her students from the very beginning. She recognized that the CS curriculum doesn't always center or make space for her students' different languages, experiences, and interests.

The lack of relevant curriculum for Ms. Morales' diverse students is part of a broader inequity that comes from a narrowing within CS and CS Ed of what kinds of knowledge and computing "count" as valuable. The computational knowledge that is valued has typically been determined by people who hold socially powerful and privileged identities. Yet those who have historically been excluded also have rich knowledge that can

---

8. Visit https://code.org and https://scratch.mit.edu/ to learn more.

erasure Processes and efforts that render invisible the presence and labor of marginalized and oppressed groups.

contribute to and (re)shape the CS industry and CS Ed. Gaskins (2021) emphasized that although many creative "innovations [are] produced by ethnic groups," these contributions "are often overlooked" (p. 5). The limited recognition of the knowledge, practices, and contributions of marginalized and minoritized people often remains unacknowledged through a process known as **erasure**. Erasure refers to efforts that render invisible the presence and labor of minoritized and oppressed groups, contributing to a narrow view of what is valued in CS and CS Ed. Below, we share some examples of creative innovations that people marginalized based on their race and gender identities have contributed to the field, despite efforts to erase their contributions.

One historical example appears in the experiences of Katherine Johnson,[9] Dorothy Vaughan,[10] and Mary Jackson,[11] often known as the "Hidden Figures."[12] These three Black women worked as human computers for NASA in the 1960s (see Shetterly, 2016). Their mathematical and computing expertise were central to supporting major innovations in space exploration and rocketry. Yet the women faced workplace discrimination and racial segregation throughout their employment. Their intellectual contributions were discredited and ignored for many years until they were finally recognized as mathematicians by NASA. Similar histories shaped the development of artificial intelligence (AI). Six women (Frances Bilas, Betty Jean Jennings, Ruth Lichterman, Kathleen McNulty, Elizabeth Snyder, and Marlyn Wescoff) were trained as human programmers for one of the first electronic digital computers. Despite their mathematical expertise and the computational skills needed for the job, the women's work was framed as "clerical" work, and they received little credit (Schwartz, 2019).

Another stark example of erasure comes from the early days of CS. The Fairchild Semiconductor company was an important early influence in Silicon Valley. The company established a manufacturing plant in Shiprock, New Mexico, to utilize the skills of Navajo women. These women's traditional knowledge of weaving and their handiwork skills proved essential to laying out computer circuitry. However, the Navajo women's labor and expertise were never treated as an important intellectual contribution to

---

9. Learn more about Katherine Johnson at: https://www.nasa.gov/centers-and-facilities/langley/katherine-johnson-biography/

10. Learn more about Dorothy Vaughan at: https://www.nasa.gov/people/dorothy-vaughan/

11. Learn more about Mary Jackson at: https://www.nasa.gov/people/mary-w-jackson-biography/

12. Their story was told in Margot Lee Shetterly's 2016 book, *Hidden Figures: The American Dream and the Untold Story of the Black Women Mathematicians Who Helped Win the Space Race*, and the 2016 film based on Shetterly's book.

CS. Instead, their work was labeled as a "labor of love" that reinforced Western stereotypes of Indigenous women as docile and their skills were reduced to simply having "nimble fingers" (Nakamura, 2014). The Fairchild company eventually called their Navajo collaboration a failure, although they continued to use techniques perfected by the Navajo women. Their decisions illustrate processes of erasure: they extracted the Indigenous knowledge held by the Navajo women; disconnected that knowledge from those women, their labor, and their cultural practices; and then erased the history of the Navajo influence on circuitry entirely.

Erasure and the narrowing of what counts as valuable in CS continue in CS Ed today. As Ms. Morales noticed, many CS curricula are narrow, focusing on specific sets of skills like knowing the syntax of particular programming languages or, for younger students, doing coding puzzles. This emphasis means that CS courses tend to be taught as if the code on screens, the people behind the screens, and the screens themselves were politically neutral, which is never the case (Benjamin, 2019). As a result, CS courses fail to engage students in exploring biases that are embedded in technology (Noble, 2018). CS Ed can also continue the history of erasure when curricula exclude people like the Hidden Figures or the Navajo women described above. Students often have limited opportunities to deeply engage with the worlds around their technology or the worlds they create through their tech. When students are rarely asked to confront injustices and be agents of change, disrupting inequity by broadening what might count as valuable computing is limited.

EMBEDDED BIAS AND UNJUST IMPACTS OF TECHNOLOGY

As Ms. Morales was talking to her colleague Ms. Kors, they named another inequity they deal with as CS teachers—recognizing biases embedded in technology. Ms. Kors shared an experience from her middle school class that illustrated this problem. She had asked her students to produce a Scratch project that shared a family story. One of her students, John, had lived most of his life in eastern Africa and was a recent arrival to the United States. He decided that he wanted to add a picture to his project to represent his mother—a Black woman who wears traditional Eritrean dress. John used Google Images to search for a picture. When he typed "woman" into the search bar, John and Ms. Kors noticed that almost all of the women in the images that came up were young, white, and wearing Western outfits. Ms. Kors shared this example with Ms. Morales to illustrate how the **biases** (prejudice in favor of or against a

bias(es) Attitudes, beliefs, or actions for or against an idea or group when compared with another; may be conscious or unconscious.

group) embedded in technologies and the negative impacts of technology can disproportionately affect minoritized and marginalized groups, including their CS students (see Vogel, 2020, for more on John and Ms. Kors' experience).

There are many reasons to do CS, and these reasons differ across cultures. In many instances in the United States, CS has been used to advance military and law enforcement goals and has been linked to consumer capitalist purposes. Computing industries tend to focus on solving problems faced by white, male, middle-class/wealthy people (Vossoughi & Vakil, 2018). As a result, the interests of those groups become embedded as biases in algorithms, interfaces, and systems that make up the computing tools in our world, causing harm to marginalized groups.

Biases have been embedded into technology since the development of the CS field began. The early "priesthood" of male computer scientists programmed in binary, a language of 0s and 1s that is compatible with the on/off switches of circuit boards. As the field grew, computer scientists continued to code in binary as a way to keep computing knowledge in the hands of a few (Backus, 1980). Over time, fluency in binary faded and other forms of in-group/out-group boundaries evolved. For example, students at many schools with computing programs developed "hacker" cultures and worked to create codes of ethics that sought to counter traditional militaristic and capitalistic objectives, including making software open to freely share and modify (Vadén & Stallman, 2002). Yet, even though this hacker culture was intended to open up access to computing, it often created new ways to exclude people, notably women (Steinmetz et al., 2019).

Many efforts to disrupt these embedded biases came from people marginalized in the CS field. Women like Kathleen Booth and Grace Hopper tried to create more accessible ways to program. Booth invented early assembly language (programs composed of mnemonic letters and digital numbers) that humans could read more easily than machine language (strings of binary digits). Hopper invented the first programming language that used elements of English grammar and vocabulary to further simplify programming. While these efforts still reproduced embedded biases that favor English as a dominant computing language, Booth, Hopper, and others shaped the trajectory of CS in ways that led to the creation of high-level, more user-friendly programming languages.

Many of the tools and tech created and used today are treated as neutral and benign, despite biases that are embedded into their designs that make them anything but neutral. Scholar Ruha Benjamin named the racism that is embedded into digital technologies the "New Jim Code," referencing the Jim Crow segregation policies that existed in the United States from 1877 through the 1950s (Benjamin, 2019). Ms. Kors and John discovered these racial biases in the search algorithms and data sets they used trying to find a picture to represent John's mother. Their experience echoes similar research by scholar Safiya Noble (2018) who found that biases in Google search engine algorithms perpetuated the hypervisibility and hypersexualization of Black women that have been historical realities in the United States. Other examples of embedded biases in technology that lead to harm of individuals and communities include the following:

- Social media algorithms that signal-boost racist and sexist ideologies in advance of elections (Guess et al., 2023).

- Voice recognition software that frequently incorrectly processes language from people who speak with accents that deviate from a standard (Paul, 2017).

- Cryptocurrency mining operations that emit carbon dioxide at the same rate as entire countries. This results in environmental impacts that especially harm low-income and racialized communities (Mahoney, 2024; United Nations University, 2023).

- Body scanners used by airport security that have disproportionately flagged trans individuals for additional screening (Costanza-Chock, 2020).

- Police departments that have used and mis-used facial recognition software in ways that have surfaced major privacy violations and racial profiling errors. These violations have in turn led to police violence against innocent people and false imprisonment (Najibi, 2020).

- Content moderation to develop AI that has come at the expense of underpaid and exploitative labor (Data Workers Inquiry, 2024; Perrigo, 2023).

These realities make it clear that to work toward equitable outcomes in CS and CS Ed, we need definitions of equity that prepare us to resist or dismantle unjust technology. We need definitions that reimagine the purposes of technology and how it is created and ensure that the impacts of technology are more just.

REVISITING MS. MORALES' STORY

In their PD community, Ms. Morales and her colleagues grappled with the different inequities that we've considered here: the unjust distribution of CS resources; exclusion from CS; deficit narratives about marginalized groups in CS; erasure and a narrowing of what counts as CS; and embedded biases and the unjust impacts of technology. Recognizing the weight of what they and their students faced in their CS classrooms felt heavy. Yet Ms. Morales and her colleagues took strength from their relationships with each other. They were creative and dedicated teachers, and while they would not be able to solve all of these issues at once, they were committed to doing something to bring about changes within their communities. In Chapter 4, we'll dive deeper into the work of their equity-focused PD community and explore how they developed definitions of equity that could help resist the inequities they were seeing.

REFLECTION QUESTIONS

1. Which inequities discussed in this chapter exist in your settings? The inequities considered here are an incomplete list. Are there other patterns of inequity that are apparent in your CS spaces?

2. What have you noticed about the relationship between equity and inequity in your work? How do the ways that people define equity impact the problems and inequities they are working to solve?

TAKEAWAYS FOR PRACTICE

Analyze your CS Ed context through the lenses of the inequities discussed in this chapter:

- *Unjust Distribution of Resources:* Evaluate the CS resources that are available. What do students have access to (or not)? How are they invited to engage in computing instead of simply "using computers"? What access to well-prepared CS educators do they have?

- *Exclusion:* Evaluate the CS opportunities that are available. Who is included? Who is not present? How welcoming are those spaces to students with different marginalized and minoritized identities?

- *Deficit Narratives:* Listen to the conversations around you. What do you notice about how students are discussed? Is the focus on students' strengths and contributions or on what students are missing and lack? You may also want to analyze a school or district policy to see if/how deficit narratives are institutionalized in your setting.

- *Erasure:* Evaluate your curriculum. Are there perspectives, voices, or identities that have been erased? Consider some ways you might include them and expand what counts as valuable in your space. The resource Historical Giants in Computing from Chapter 1 may be a helpful starting point.

- *Embedded Bias:* Think about the different tech tools you use in your classroom. What kinds of biases might be embedded in these tools? How could you help students recognize these biases? What can you do as a CS Ed instructor to help students navigate the biases and create tools that challenge them?

GLOSSARY

Term	Definition
bias(es)	Attitudes, beliefs, or actions for or against an idea or group when compared with another; may be conscious or unconscious.
deficit narratives	Broadly held beliefs, including stereotypes, that identify groups of people as lacking or deficient in some way (Louie et al., 2021; Steele, 2011).
dysgraphia	A learning disability that may affect a person's physical ability to write and/or impact their ability to express their thoughts through writing.
erasure	Processes and efforts that render invisible the presence and labor of marginalized and oppressed groups.
exclusion	Processes and efforts that limit the presence and participation of marginalized and oppressed groups in a space.

gatekeeping	Institutional policies and structures that control who gets to participate in opportunities and who has access to resources in ways that limit the participation of marginalized groups.
intersectionality	A theory that recognizes how people's different identities (e.g., disability, gender, race) overlap and intersect, creating access to privilege or resulting in oppression in ways that cannot be understood or addressed by considering each identity separately (Crenshaw, 1991; Collins, 2019).
inequity	Injustice or unfairness that is created and reproduced by social forces. It is important to remember that "fairness" does not mean "sameness," so working to right unfairness and inequity does not mean just giving everyone the same thing.
marginalized/ minoritized identities	Identity categories that are devalued in society, often because they are different from what society has established as the "ideal" norm. Those with marginalized/minoritized identities often face oppression and exclusion from mainstream society. We use both "marginalized" and "minoritized" as adjectives to emphasize how social processes actively construct inequity (Black et al., 2023). The term "minoritized" emphasizes historical systematic oppression and may be used regardless of whether an identity group actually represents a numerical minority in a context (see Black et al., 2023; Flores & Rosa, 2015).

REFERENCES

100Kin10. (2021). *unCommission research summary on the communities most excluded from STEM learning.* 100Kin10. https://docs.google.com/document/d/1xOgL3AvDkYjyjVTxgxaDUfpUIEC7c0czPUsDSfLhYzE/edit

Anderson, J. D. (1988). *The education of Blacks in the South, 1860–1935.* University of North Carolina Press.

Arias, M. B. (1990). Computer access for Hispanic secondary students. In C. J. Faltis & R. A. DeVillar (Eds.), *Language minority students and computers* (pp. 243–256). The Haworth. https://doi.org/10.1300/J025v07n01_12

Backus, J. (1980). Programming in America in the 1950s—Some personal impressions. In N. Metropolis, J. Howlett, & G. C. Rota (Eds.), *A History of*

Computing in the Twentieth Century (pp. 125–135). Academic Press. https://doi.org/10.1016/B978-0-12-491650-0.50017-4

Benjamin, R. (2019). *Race after technology: Abolitionist tools for the new Jim code* (1st ed.). Polity.

Bers, M. U. (2019). Coding as another language: A pedagogical approach for teaching computer science in early childhood. *Journal of Computers in Education, 6*, 499–528. https://doi.org/10.1007/s40692-019-00147-3

Black, C., Cerdeña, J. P., & Spearman-McCarthy, E. V. (2023). I am not your minority. *Lancet Regional Health Americas, 19*. https://doi.org/10.1016/j.lana.2023.100464

Blikstein, P. (2018). *Pre-college computer science education: A survey of the field.* Google LLC. https://services.google.com/fh/files/misc/pre-college-computer-science-education-report.pdf

Code.org, CSTA, & ECEP Alliance (2022). *2022 State of Computer Science Education: Understanding Our National Imperative.* Retrieved from https://advocacy.code.org/stateofcs

Collins, P. H. (2019). *Intersectionality as critical social theory.* Duke University Press.

Costanza-Chock, S. (2020). *Design justice: Community-led practices to build the worlds we need.* MIT Press. https://doi.org/10.7551/mitpress/12255.001.0001

Crenshaw, K. (1991). Mapping the margins: Intersectionality, identity politics, and violence against women of color. *Stanford Law Review, 43*(6), 1241–1299. https://doi.org/10.2307/1229039

Data Workers Inquiry. (2024). https://data-workers.org/

Fairclough, N. (2014). *Language and power* (3rd ed.). Routledge. https://doi.org/10.4324/9781315838250

Flores, N., & Rosa, J. (2015). Undoing appropriateness: Raciolinguistic ideologies and language diversity in education. *Harvard Educational Review, 85*(2), 149–171. https://doi.org/10.17763/0017-8055.85.2.149

Forsythe, A. (1979, 16 May). *An interview with Alexandra Forsythe* [Interview]. Charles Babbage Institute, University of Minnesota. https://conservancy.umn.edu/server/api/core/bitstreams/563c9e36-1ecd-47a8-abfe-4204ec0ea11d/content

Forsythe, A. I., Keenan, T., Organic, E., Sternberg, W. (1969). *Computer science: A first course* (1st ed.). Wiley.

Gallup, Inc. (2020). *Current perspectives and continuing challenges in computer science education in U.S. K-12 schools.* Gallup, Inc. https://services.google.com/fh/files/misc/computer-science-education-in-us-k12schools-2020-report.pdf

Gaskins, N. R. (2021). *Techno-vernacular creativity and innovation: Culturally relevant making inside and outside of the classroom.* MIT Press. https://doi.org/10.7551/mitpress/12379.001.0001

Garfinkel, H. (1967). *Studies in ethnomethodology.* Polity Press.

Guess, A. M., Malhotra, N., Pan, J., Barberá, P., Alcott, H., Brown, T., Crespo-Tenorio, A., Dimmery, D., Freelon, D., Gentzkow, M., González-Bailón, S., Kennedy, E., Kim, Y. M., Lazer, D., Moehler, D., Nyhan, B., Rivera, C. V., Thomas, D. R., Thorson, E., . . . Tucker, J. A. (2023). How do social media feed algorithms affect attitudes and behavior in an election campaign. *Science, 381*(6656), 398–404. http://doi.org/10.1126/science.abp9364

King, H., Martin, M., McArdle, S., Goldberg, R., & DeSalvo, B. (2022, May 13). *New digital equity act population viewer shows broadband access and demographic characteristics.* United States Census Bureau. https://www.census.gov/library/stories/2022/05/mapping-digital-equity-in-every-state.html

Ko, A. J., Beitlers, A., Wortzman, B., Davidson, M., Oleson, A., Kirdani-Ryan, M., Druga, S., & Everson, J. (2024). *Critically conscious computing: Methods for secondary education.* https://criticallyconsciouscomputing.org

Ko, A. J., Oleson, A., Ryan, N., Register, Y., Xie, B., Tari, M., Davidson, M., Druga, S., & Loksa, D. (2020). It is time for more critical CS education. *Communications of the ACM, 63*(11), 31–33. 4:01 https://doi.org/10.1145/3424000

Ladson-Billings, G. (2007). Pushing past the achievement gap: An essay on the language of deficit. *Journal of Negro Education, 76*(3), 316–323.

Louie, N., Adiredja, A. P., & Jessup, N. (2021). Teacher noticing from a sociopolitical perspective: The FAIR framework for anti-deficit noticing. *ZDM-Mathematics Education, 53*, 95–107. https://doi.org/10.1007/s11858-021-01229-2

Mahoney, A. (2024, July 9). *Crypto-mining creates new environmental injustices for Black Texans.* Capital B News. https://capitalbnews.org/crypto-mining-natural-gas-black-communities/

Margolis, J., Estrella, R., Goode, J., Holme, J. J., & Nao, K. (2008). *Stuck in the shallow end: Education, race, and computing.* MIT Press.

Najibi, A. (2020, Oct 4). Racial discrimination in face recognition technology. *Science in the News, Harvard Graduate School of Arts and Sciences.* https://web.archive.org/web/20240730143205/https://projects.iq.harvard.edu/sciencepolicy/blog/racial-discrimination-face-recognition-technology

Nakamura, L. (2014). Indigenous circuits: Navajo women and the racialization of early electronic manufacture. *American Quarterly, 66*(4), 919–941. https://doi.org/10.1353/aq.2014.0070

Noble, S. U. (2018). Conclusion: Algorithms of oppression. In *Algorithms of oppression,* pp. 171–182. New York University Press. https://doi.org/10.2307/j.ctt1pwt9w5.11

Paul, S. (2017, Mar 20). Voice is the next big platform, unless you have an accent. *Wired.* https://www.wired.com/2017/03/voice-is-the-next-big-platform-unless-you-have-an-accent/

Perrigo, B. (2023, Jan 18). Exclusive: OpenAI used Kenyan workers on less than $2 per hour to make ChatGPT less toxic. *Time.* https://time.com/6247678/openai-chatgpt-kenya-workers/

Pew Research Center. (2024, Nov 13). *Internet, broadband fact sheet.* https://www.pewresearch.org/internet/fact-sheet/internet-broadband/

Philip, T. M. (2011). An "ideology in pieces" approach to studying change in teachers' sensemaking about race, racism, and racial justice. *Cognition and Instruction, 29*(3), 297–329. https://doi.org/10.1080/07370008.2011.583369

Schwartz, O. (2019, Mar 25). Untold history of AI: Invisible women programmed America's first electronic computer. *IEEE Spectrum.* https://spectrum.ieee.

org/untold-history-of-ai-invisible-woman-programmed-americas-first-electronic-computer

Shetterly, M. L. (2016). *Hidden figures: The American dream and the untold story of the Black women mathematicians who helped win the space race.* William Morrow.

Steele, C. M. (2011). *Whistling Vivaldi: How stereotypes affect us and what we can do.* W. W. Norton.

Steinmetz, K. F., Holt, T. J., & Holt, K. M. (2019). Decoding the binary: Reconsidering the hacker subculture through a gendered lens. *Deviant Behavior, 41*(8), 936–948. https://doi.org/10.1080/01639625.2019.1596460

Sutton, R. E. (1991). Equity and computers in the schools: A decade of research. *Review of Educational Research, 61*(4), 475–503. https://doi.org/10.3102/00346543061004475

United Nations University. (2023, Oct 24). *UN study reveals the hidden environmental impacts of Bitcoin: Carbon is not the only harmful by-product.* https://unu.edu/press-release/un-study-reveals-hidden-environmental-impacts-bitcoin-carbon-not-only-harmful-product

Vadén, T., & Stallman, R. (2002). *The hacker community and ethics* [Interview]. GNU Operating System. https://www.gnu.org/philosophy/rms-hack.html

Vogel, S. (2020). *Translanguaging about, with, and through code and computing: Emergent bi/multilingual middle schoolers forging computational literacies.* [Doctoral Dissertation], City University of New York. https://academicworks.cuny.edu/cgi/viewcontent.cgi?article=5015&context=gc_etds

Vossoughi, S., & Vakil, S. (2018). Toward what ends? A critical analysis of militarism, equity, and STEM education. In A. I. Ali & T. L. Buenavista (Eds.), *Education at war: The fight for students of color in America's public schools* (1st ed., pp. 117–140). Fordham University Press. https://doi.org/10.2307/j.ctt2204pqp

Wohl, B., Porter, B., & Clinch, S. (2015). Teaching computer science to 5–7 year-olds: An initial study with Scratch, Cubelets, and unplugged computing. In J. Gal-Ezer, S. Sentance, & J. Vahrenhold (Eds.), *WiPSCE '15: Proceedings of the Workshop in Primary and Secondary Computing Education* (pp. 55–60). Association for Computer Machinery. http://doi.org/10.1145/2818314.2818340

4

Understanding Equity in Computer Science and Computer Science Education

Sara Vogel, Christopher Hoadley, Lauren Vogelstein, Bethany Daniel, Stephanie T. Jones, and the Computer Science Educational Justice Collective

CHAPTER OVERVIEW

This chapter unpacks what we mean by the term "equity" broadly and within the contexts of computer science (CS) and CS education (CS Ed) specifically. Given that equity is the central focus of this guide, it is important to understand what we mean by the term. However, in many contexts, equity is not well defined. This chapter explores how different definitions of equity are connected to the inequities that CS educators want to work to address. The chapter also considers how working toward equity in CS Ed may require multiple ways of thinking about equity.

CHAPTER OBJECTIVES

After reading this chapter, I can:

- Explain the relationship between inequity and equity.
- Define equity as it applies to CS and CS Ed in different ways.
- Recognize the advantages and limitations of different definitions of equity in relation to CS and CS Ed.

KEY TERMS

assimilation; broadening participation; equality; equity as access; equity as transformation; ethnocomputing; generative computing; inequity; language agnostic; marginalized/minoritized identities; social justice; underrepresentation

MS. MORALES' STORY

As shared in Chapter 3, K-8 public school teacher Ms. Morales and her colleagues attended professional development (PD) sessions where they learned about many of the inequities embedded in CS fields and CS Ed. After these PD sessions, the teachers clearly recognized how inequities were shaping their work as educators and their students' experiences in CS Ed. Less clear to them, however, was what exactly "equity" meant. The term was clearly being set up as a counterpoint to inequity, but it still seemed like a buzzword. As they reflected together, they hoped to better understand both equity in general and how specific definitions of equity could shape their work as CS educators.

THE RELATIONSHIP BETWEEN EQUITY AND INEQUITY

Ms. Morales and her colleagues' efforts to understand equity demonstrates an important point: equity is not an easy word to define or unpack. It gets used by policy makers in the media, by educators in schools, and by people in society generally. It can be defined in many ways, but people are often not clear about how they are using it and may not share the same definition. People may use "equity" interchangeably with **"equality"** (giving everyone the same thing) or as an empty buzzword, like Ms. Morales and her colleagues noticed. Although it can be hard to define, how we think about equity matters, because our definitions of the term guide how we understand policies and programs and the actions we take to work toward more equitable outcomes in CS and CS Ed.

People's approaches to equity often grow out of how they think about **inequity**. When we identify inequities, we point to problems that we think we need to solve. Then, we define equity in ways that work toward solutions to those problems. For example, one problem that has been identified in CS is that people with **marginalized identities** (e.g., racially and gender minoritized individuals, people with disabilities) are underrepresented in the computing workforce. When the field frames the limited presence of marginalized people in the workforce as a problem

---

equality An approach to addressing inequity that focuses on giving everyone the same resources and opportunities.

inequity Injustice or unfairness that is created and reproduced by social forces. It is important to remember that "fairness" does not mean "sameness," so working to right unfairness and inequity does not mean just giving everyone the same thing.

marginalized/ minoritized identities Identity categories that are devalued in society, often because they are different from what society has established as the "ideal" norm. Those with marginalized/ minoritized identities often face oppression and exclusion from mainstream society. We use both "marginalized" and "minoritized" as adjectives to emphasize how social processes actively construct inequity (Black et al., 2023). The term "minoritized" emphasizes historical systematic oppression and may be used regardless of whether an identity group actually represents a numerical minority in a context (see Black et al., 2023; Flores & Rosa, 2015).

underrepresentation A group of people who are not represented within a context or setting proportionate to their overall representation within the general population.

broadening participation A way of thinking about equity, similar to access, that seeks to increase the participation of members of underrepresented and/or marginalized groups in CS and CS Ed. These groups have historically been excluded from computing fields.

of **underrepresentation**, they often define equity as broadening participation. Working toward equity as **broadening participation** looks like creating opportunities for marginalized people to participate in CS and CS Ed. Those focused on working toward equity in this way might measure the success of their efforts based on the diversity of students taking CS Ed courses or on the number of employees in the CS industry who hold marginalized identities.

While these efforts help address the problem of underrepresentation, they don't necessarily consider whether those who hold marginalized identities feel welcome in CS and CS Ed spaces. Similarly, a broadening participation approach to equity might not examine whether the products that workers design and program are having just and ethical impacts. These are different inequities that generate different understandings of equity and lead us to take different actions. Most approaches to equity are limited in some way, which means it is often helpful to draw on different perspectives of equity at different times for different purposes, or even to use multiple understandings of equity together (National Academies of Sciences, Engineering, and Medicine [NASEM], 2022). Taking a multifaceted approach can enable us to work toward equity in different ways and address different levels of inequity in tandem.

EXPLORING DEFINITIONS OF EQUITY

As Chapter 3 showed, there are many inequities that society and our students face related to computing and CS Ed. This means that defining equity to address those problems is complex. Exploring this complexity, Ms. Morales and her colleagues worked to refine their understanding of equity. They hoped that having a clearer definition would allow them to better respond to the challenges they faced, better support their diverse students, and work toward more equitable outcomes in their classrooms. Ms. Morales' personal experiences with her students and the topics that her PD community focused on (like disability, language, and race) made her an important voice as she and her colleagues reflected together on what equity means.

The PD community began by looking at a set of images about equity that often circulates around social media (Figure 1). Each of the three images in the series shows three young people of different heights trying to watch a baseball game from behind a tall fence. The first image is meant to show "reality." It illustrates the tallest person standing on a set of seven boxes. The next tallest person stands on a single box, and the shortest person stands in a pit underground. This image suggests that some individuals disproportionately receive the social resources they need

Figure 1. Illustrations of Reality, Equality, and Equity. Equality vs. Equity © 2016 by *Angus Maguire and the Interaction Institute for Social Change* is licensed under *CC BY-SA 4.0*

to be successful, but others have to deal with extra disadvantages. The second image represents "equality." All three people stand on one box each, and the pit is gone. Although they all received the same resources, the shortest person still cannot see over the fence. In the final image, all three people receive the appropriate amount of boxes that they individually need to see over the fence to view the game. This image is meant to show "equity."

The "reality" image resonated with Ms. Morales and her colleagues. They agreed that we don't all start from the same place or with the same resources. Similarly, our students don't all start with the same experience with or access to CS Ed. The teachers also found the images useful in helping them distinguish between "equity" (the third image) and "equality" (the second image) or giving everyone the same thing (like the same type of education, jobs, money, healthcare).

The image representing equality illustrates that while giving everyone the same thing might seem "fair" on the surface, it only gets us so far in meeting students' needs. In a classroom based on equality, all students would get an identical computer, compatible with English, but with the "r" keyboard letter key missing. When students needed to type out their names, even though everyone has the same computer, not everyone would be able to accomplish the task. Students who had an "r" in their name, or students whose names were written in other writing systems (like the Arabic alphabet or Chinese characters), or students who needed assistive technologies to type because of disabilities would not be able to use their computers to type their name. Giving everyone the *same* opportunities and resources doesn't necessarily result in equal outcomes.

The concept of equity offers an alternative to equality. The National Equity Project defines equity as providing "each child . . . [with] *what they need* to develop their full academic and social potential" (National Equity Project, n.d., emphasis added). A key phrase in this definition is "what they need." In a classroom based on equity, each student would receive a personalized laptop with a keyboard and settings in their desired language and any accessibility tools they needed. This tailored approach would support students to successfully complete the assigned task of typing their name.

The CS teachers in Ms. Morales' PD community appreciated the distinction between equity and equality. But as they sat with that definition of equity—that it is about providing people with what they need to thrive—more questions surfaced. Ms. Morales shared how she had "a love-hate" relationship with the images:

> Why have the fence there at all? Why do we have these obstacles in the forefront already? I tend to think equity is . . . not only giving the tools that students need, but then also taking away those barriers that are always around. . . . Let's get rid of those things.

Recognizing Ms. Morales' point, many people add a fourth panel to Figure 1. This last image shows all three people watching the game, but the fence has been removed entirely. The removal of the fence symbolizes **"social justice,"** or the dismantling of oppressive conditions and systems that act as barriers to opportunities and resources.

social justice A view that wealth, opportunities, and privileges should be equitably distributed to all members of society.

Ms. Morales and her colleagues agreed that these four images together (see Figure 2) provided a metaphor for giving students what they need and breaking down barriers to access (in this case, access to a baseball game).

But the teachers still had questions about different parts of the metaphor and places where the analogy seemed to break down and fall short. Specifically, they asked questions about the three individuals in the picture, the fence, and the game itself:

- Individuals
  - Why are the people in the picture all seemingly of male gender presentation?
  - Why are they all dark-skinned?

Figure 2. Illustrations of Versions of (In)Equity. Equality vs. Equity © 2016 by *Angus Maguire and the Interaction Institute for Social Change* is licensed under *CC BY-SA 4.0*

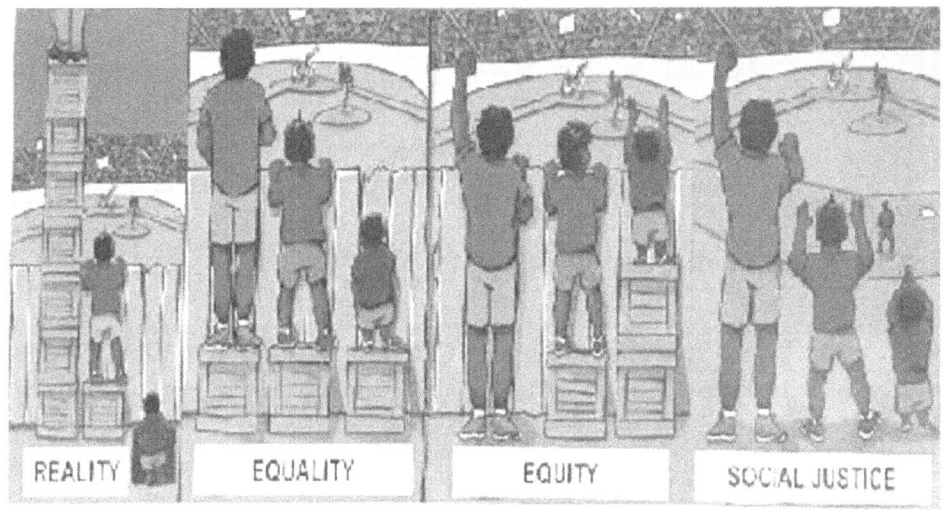

- Why are these people watching outside of the stands? Why aren't they ticketed spectators with a seat?

- Is height being used to symbolize disability? Privileges/deficiencies? What would this symbol mean, because we know that people come in all shapes and sizes and that disabilities are shaped as much by social norms and designs as by individual traits? (Annamma et al., 2013; McDermott, 1993)

• The Fence

- The barrier shown in these images is a physical one, but many of the barriers that marginalized students and communities aren't physical. They are social and political and are embedded in interactions, policies, institutions, and structures. How do you dismantle barriers that aren't solely physical?

- What about dismantling barriers built from histories of injustices that have been produced through the actions of individuals, groups, and institutions over time?

• The Game

- Why is a baseball game used to represent what the three people want access to?

- Would any of these people rather play the game than have to observe from the outside?

- Would any of these people rather watch or play a different game?

The thought-provoking questions that Ms. Morales and her colleagues raised show how complex it is to define and understand equity in ways that can lead to potential solutions for the inequities discussed in Chapter 3. Making sense of equity requires understanding and dismantling historical and present-day barriers, being clear about what the purposes of equity work are and who the beneficiaries are, and recognizing those communities' goals, aspirations, and needs.

EXPLORING TENSIONS IN DEFINING EQUITY

One core question that the teachers considered as they viewed the images above centered around using the game of baseball as a metaphor. They wondered why baseball was drawn as the activity that the individuals in the images were attempting to gain access to. They figured it might have something to do with baseball's traditional reputation as the "great American pastime." Applying this to education, the teachers related the baseball game to the kinds of schooling that equity initiatives often seek to provide students access to. Those ways of schooling tend to center the speaking, reading, writing, and computing practices of those with more power in society (e.g., white, English-speaking, middle class, college-educated, male, nondisabled). Yet there are so many ways to be, speak, read, write, and compute. Ms. Morales highlighted this reality:

> We need to go beyond and not assume that everyone wants to even watch a baseball game in the first place. Not every CS student will see themselves coding a website or a video game. There may be other paths that involve the computational skills that CS helps teach students.

Inequities like those discussed in Chapter 3 exist because many diverse ways of being are not perceived as legitimate in society's institutions, including schooling. Teachers wondered what would shift if they changed the game in the picture, centering the interests, cultures, and aspirations of those often considered "on the margins" in their teaching.

As teachers discussed these possibilities, one teacher raised her hand to ask a question: Would teaching students to achieve goals outside the mainstream purposes of schooling mean that students wouldn't get a chance to learn the knowledge, skills, and programming languages they'd need to pass a test or succeed during a job interview? The group acknowledged that to an extent, they did have a professional responsibility to prepare their students for the world around them. They grappled with the desire to "change the game" (e.g., "baseball") to something more relevant to their students and communities and to prepare their students with the knowledge they would need to succeed in the game that was already being played.

These tensions are captured in two common ways of conceptualizing or thinking about equity (see Table 1).

These conceptions of equity can work together and be complementary, or they might be in opposition. There are also many other ways to think about equity. Along with understandings about access and transformation, the field of CS Ed has developed different frameworks that lay out multiple dimensions of equity in CS Ed. Some of these frameworks are summarized in Table 2. You may find that one or more of these frameworks is useful to help you think about equity in your own context.

Table 1. Conceptualizing Equity (see Grapin et al., 2023; Philip & Azevedo, 2017; NASEM, 2022)

Concept	Definition
Equity as access	Focusing on making sure that everyone—including members of marginalized groups—has what they need to participate in and access mainstream STEM and CS disciplines, expertise, and tools as they currently stand. This notion encompasses efforts toward "broadening participation" in the field.
Equity as transformation	Focusing on disrupting the status quo of disciplines, fields, and industries; valuing and centering marginalized knowledge bases, tools, and people.

Table 2. Some Equity Frameworks in Computer Science Education

Framework	Description
The CAPE Framework* (Capacity, Access, Participation, and Experience) (Fletcher & Warner, 2021)	This framework centers students' experiences as meaningful resources for CS learning while also addressing the need to develop capacity in the systems around students to support their access and participation.
The Culturally Responsive-Sustaining Computer Science Education Framework** (Kapor Center; Davis et al., 2021)	This framework provides a shared definition of culturally responsive-sustaining CS Ed and identifies six components to implement culturally responsive-sustaining approaches. The components center anti-racism, sociopolitical critique, student voice and agency, and community and cultural assets as resources for learning.

continued on next page

Table 2. Continued.

Framework	Description
The Inclusive Teaching Pedagogies Framework† (Computer Science Teachers Association; [CSTA], n.d.)	This framework integrates Universal Design for Learning (UDL) and translanguaging as teaching practices that attend to the needs of students with disabilities and multilingual learners in CS. Implementing these pedagogies can create more inclusive CS learning environments.
The Culturally Responsive Computing Framework‡ (Scott et al., 2015)	This framework attends to CS learners' intersectional identities, culminating in students engaging in activism for more equitable computing and technology.

*View the CAPE Framework at https://cacm.acm.org/opinion/cape/

**View the Kapon Center's Framework at https://www.kaporcenter.org/wp-content/uploads/2021/07/KC21004_ECS-Framework-Report_final.pdf

†View the Inclusive Teaching Pedagogies Framework at https://csteachers.org/inclusive-teaching-pedagogies/

‡Read about the Culturally Responsive Computing Framework at https://www.tandfonline.com/doi/full/10.1080/17439884.2014.924966

Regardless of how we frame it, unpacking different notions of equity is important to ensure that our definitions address the problems that we, our students, and our communities care about. In the next sections, we explore what equity as access and equity as transformation mean and consider limitations of these definitions as well.

EQUITY AS ACCESS TO MAINSTREAM WAYS OF DOING CS: PLAYING THE GAME

As teachers pointed out during the PD session, there are benefits to being able to achieve success within mainstream systems of schooling. Because certain practices and knowledge are privileged by society, efforts toward equity as access support marginalized students to engage in the practices and learn the knowledge that afford power in society (Delpit, 1988). This is sometimes referred to as helping students learn to "play the game" (Gutiérrez, 2009). In other words, if U.S. educational systems have decided that baseball is the game that should be played, then ensuring that all students have access to the skills and tools they need to play baseball is one way to engage in equity work.

What does it mean to "play the game" in CS Ed? CS benefits from being a subject that is not required or tested in many states. This means that the rules of the CS "game" are still being written. At the same time, there are ways of doing CS that teachers and schools might perceive as "mainstream" or particularly powerful because they support entry into CS careers. These ways of computing are often aligned with expectations of beginning-level CS courses in college (e.g., CS 101) that prioritize using programming languages like Java to code applications that solve decontextualized problems. Over the years, courses like AP Computer Science A have worked to teach students this code. Similarly, efforts like Code.org's Hour of Code have worked to broaden participation by encouraging students around the country, including those who have been historically marginalized from CS Ed, to get early exposure to programming.[1] As Ms. Morales pointed out, "Opening the door to CS is the first step, ensuring that it doesn't lead to another closed door requiring many keys to open. Students should be able to continue to progress with CS skills and have multiple opportunities from elementary school on."

Early exposure to computing and related efforts can increase the "pipeline" of **underrepresented** groups who enter CS careers, becoming a first step toward some equity goals. However, this approach may fall short of meeting other equity goals (Perez & Garcia, 2023). Equity as access doesn't guarantee a sense of relevance, belonging, or power in the CS field for those who enter. Even marginalized learners who work to speak, read, write, and compute in ways that align with mainstream cultural expectations still experience racism, sexism, and linguistic injustice in educational spaces (Flores & Rosa, 2015). Furthermore, broadening participation arguments don't address the negative environmental, social, and political impacts of computing described in Chapter 3. Those issues prompt us to ask the question: What kind of CS do we want to broaden participation into?

We propose that advancing equity in CS might mean not just providing learners with *access* to the CS knowledge valued in industry but also *transforming and expanding* the valued reasons for doing CS and what counts as CS knowledge. We consider below what equity as transformation might encompass.

underrepresentation A group of people who are not represented within a context or setting proportionate to their overall representation within the general population.

EQUITY AS TRANSFORMATION OF THE STATUS QUO: CHANGING THE GAME

Our students do not code in a vacuum. They are computing in a complex world that often tries to assimilate them, erase them, surveil them, and label them. But they also code and compute in a world that they are actively participating in and find joy in. They may have ideas about

---

1. To learn more about Hour of Code, visit https://code.org/hourofcode

how to remake and transform their world, too. We are inspired by scholar Zaretta Hammond, who defines equity as ensuring that all students have the ability to be "powerful learners," engaged in "deep learning," who are full of "intellectual curiosity and engagement" (Hammond, as quoted in Rebora, 2021, pp. 14–15).

This way of thinking about equity resonated with Ms. Morales. She wondered:

> What type of things are we putting out there for children? Do we have their end goal in mind? How do we provide the tools so that kids can get access to them . . . and not only just access, but then, being able to share their own background and their history and their culture involved with it too?

Equity as transformation pushes us to think beyond giving students access to mainstream ways of computing, to question what lies beyond the status quo, and to consider alternative possibilities. Equity-as-transformation perspectives move us closer to alternatives to playing "baseball." Instead of merely providing students with access to play the game that society has already established, we can consider what it might look like to "change the game" and transform it into something new (Gutiérrez, 2009).

A first step toward changing the game in CS involves interrogating what the purposes of CS are. Mainstream purposes for CS often seek to reproduce militaristic and industrial ends (Vossoughi & Vakil, 2018; Jones & melo, 2021). A common purpose for CS education is **assimilation** into the dominant status quo. At best, assimilation ignores, and at worse it violently suppresses, the cultural expertise and experiences, the goals and aspirations, and the language and cultural practices of students with diverse gender, racial and ethnic, and linguistic and cultural identities, as well as students with different abilities (González et al., 2005).

Equity as transformation involves recognizing that there are a range of benefits that learners and their communities want to and already gain from computing. Transformative ways of computing include **ethnocomputing**, or studying the computational practices that are entwined in minoritized communities' cultural practices (Eglash et al., 2006; Lachney et al., 2021; New York City Public Schools, n.d.), and **generative computing**, or connecting computing practices to local community practices in culturally responsive ways (Lachney et al., 2021). Transformative computing also mobilizes traditions and histories from feminist, Black, Latine, Asian, and Indigenous perspectives.[2] Lewis et al. (2018), for example, employs aspects of Indigenous ways of knowing to unpack artificial intelligence.

---

2. See the On Terminology section of this guide for an explanation on our use of different identity-related terms.

---

assimilation Processes through which minoritized and marginalized groups are encouraged or forced to adopt dominant norms and practices.

ethnocomputing The study of computational practices that are entwined in marginalized/minoritized communities' cultural practices (Eglash et al., 2006).

generative computing Computing approaches that connect computational thinking and computing practices to local community practices in culturally responsive ways (Lachney et al., 2021).

In CS Ed, transformation might include mobilizing computing to promote project-based and inquiry models of learning; to innovate and solve local and global problems of interest; to participate in civic life; to promote joy and creativity; and to work toward social justice through critique, organizing, activism, and holding power to account (Vogel et al., 2017). If our schools only define equity as "broadening participation" for industry, they miss these other purposes and rationales for equitable computing that benefit everyone. CS teacher Karime reflected on students' varied values and interests and how those might drive them to do CS for different purposes:

> Students may have different motivations for wanting to learn [CS]. Especially in their earliest introduction to the field, I think it is really important to present students with all of the rationales [for computing], so that every student—the one who is there because of their genuine love of problem-solving, the one taking the class for college credit, or the one who just wants job security (and any student in between)—feels validated.

In some classrooms, teachers are guiding students to reckon with the tensions between dominant ways of developing technology and more "justice-centered" CS approaches. Tarek, a New York City-based CS educator, shared an example of how he did this by asking his students to "design an app to solve a problem in their community." Tarek explained that "at first, they all focused on things in their own neighborhoods. But when I encouraged them to think about problems faced by other communities, their ideas exploded!" Tarek described some of the apps his students created:

- One group created an app called *Parking Superhero* to help teachers find parking.[3] They really understood the challenges teachers face.

- Another group made an app called *Confusing Words* to help English Language Learners learn new vocabulary.[4]

- There was a group who noticed all the stress their friends were feeling, so they built *Calm It Down* to help them manage daily challenges.[5]

---

3. View the *Parking Superhero* app at: https://www.figma.com/proto/Rw9Whgny rpdJLyoryYDg58/Parking-SuperHero-(Copy)?node-id=813-9\&starting-point-node -id=237%3A848\&t=qBrvFkBfDpG5C2iV-1

4. View the *Confusing Words* app at: https://www.figma.com/proto/OYm2wQIP nDuBHlmD9RSIs4/Confusing-Words?node-id=15-11\&starting-point-node-id= 15%3A11\&t=42X4BiI2UNIvlSh7-1

5. View the *Calm It Down* app at: https://www.figma.com/proto/O0k4tysppZND lJegEfj4uE/Calm-It-Down-2?node-id=1-2\&starting-point-node-id=1%3A2\&t=dlfL jiD99dqIxuic-1

Other educators begin to move toward equity-as-transformation orientations by exploring the contributions of diverse groups and their active efforts to resist the unjust impacts of technology. Some examples of those using technology for social action appear in Table 3. These organizations and others like them actively resist inequity and work to transform computing that supports a more equitable world.

Inspired by students and the diverse computing practices of people in the world, CS educators have created new kinds of curriculum and opportunities for students who have been traditionally excluded from CS Ed. One core effort has been the creation of culturally relevant and culturally responsive computing curricula that is rooted in theories of culturally relevant and culturally responsive pedagogy and teaching (Gay, 2018; Hammond, 2014; Ladson-Billings, 1995; Madkins et al., 2020; Scott et al., 2015). For example, Margolis and colleagues (2015) shared their popular Exploring Computer Science (ECS) curriculum. This curriculum is meant to introduce students—especially those from underrepresented backgrounds—to CS concepts and practices through the lens of project-based

Table 3. Computing to Promote Social Justice

Group Name	Description
Data for Black Lives	This group works to "challenge discriminatory uses of data and algorithms across systems" to resist the ways that Black communities are impacted by embedded biases in technology.
	Website: https://d4bl.org/
Surveillance Technology Oversight Project (S.T.O.P.)	This group works to end mass surveillance that discriminates against groups like Muslim Americans, immigrants, Indigenous peoples, communities of color, and the LGBTQIA2S+ community.
	Website: https://stopspying.org
WITNESS	This group provides resources to "[help] people use video and technology to protect and defend human rights."
	Website: https://witness.org
XFR Collective	This group works to preserve "at-risk audiovisual media — especially unseen, unheard, or marginalized works."
	Website: https://linktr.ee/xfrcollective

and inquiry-driven units. These approaches benefit all students by centering their voices and perspectives as students use computing to address social issues that they personally care about.

EQUITY IN THE EVERYDAY

Thus far, we've presented equity as access and equity as transformation as separate and in tension. Yet these ideas are also interrelated and overlapping. Doing equity work in the day-to-day often requires drawing on both notions in tandem.

The AP CS Principles course provides one example of this reality. Historically, high schools with CS courses mostly offered AP Computer Science A to prepare students for beginning-level CS courses in college. These AP courses, however, lost female, Black, and Latine test takers over the years (Apraci-Dusseau et al., 2013). Acknowledging this reality, the College Board and other stakeholders came together to design and introduce the AP CS Principles (AP CSP) course and exam. Instead of focusing on teaching a particular programming language, the new AP CSP exam is **language agnostic**, focusing on core skills that can be applied across different programming languages. The AP course and exam center big ideas about computing and computational thinking practices.[6] In AP CSP, students are asked to use computing for real-world problem solving. The course has proven popular and has led to an increase in students taking the AP CSP exam, making modest gains in promoting more diversity among test takers.

While still aiming to provide "access" to college credit and skills needed for success in higher education and industry spaces, the AP CSP revision has had some modest transformational impacts as well. It expanded what "counted" as valuable CS knowledge to include skills beyond programming, like collaboration and creativity. It also engaged students in exploring the impacts of computing technology (Blikstein, 2018, p. 17). Equity-oriented CS teachers may not need permission to incorporate this content into their CS instruction. However, by explicitly including those topics in the AP CSP course design, it is less risky for all teachers to move in those directions.

At the same time, these modest efforts toward transformation are not guaranteed. The same AP CSP course taught by a less equity-oriented teacher could reproduce narratives of computing that support industrial and militaristic ends and fail to adequately meet marginalized learners'

language agnostic
Computing approaches that focus on core computing skills that can be applied across different programming languages.

---

6. The AP CSP big ideas and computational thinking practices can be found at https://apcentral.collegeboard.org/media/pdf/ap-computer-science-principles-course-overview.pdf

needs and experiences. AP CS teachers will also navigate situations where working toward equity as access and equity as transformation might clash, such as needing to balance time spent discussing issues related to social justice and computing with time spent preparing students for the AP exam. These tensions show how complex equity work can be, how we often need to think about equity in multiple ways at the same time, and how educators play a critical role in working toward equity in all kinds of CS Ed spaces. See Resource 1 at the end of the chapter for another example of how teachers can identify inequities in their classrooms and work to further multiple definitions of equity.

OUR VISION OF EQUITY

In defining equity for this guide, we echo academic Scott Grapin and colleagues who argue that efforts should "attend to equity as access while pushing toward equity as transformation" (Grapin et al., 2023, p. 1018). This notion is core to this book's mission. Thinking of equity in these terms, we hope to work toward a future where:

- learners whose identities have been marginalized in CS and in society have what they need—including *access to* relevant computing tools and literacies—to learn, to thrive, and to sustain and contribute to the evolution of their communities' cultural and language practices; and

- all learners are equipped with critical consciousness about computing tools, cultures, and industries so they might work toward *transforming* those tools, cultures, and industries to become ethical and just.

We emphasize our focus on access to *relevant* computing that is meaningful for our students—not just access to the kinds of CS that have been mainstreamed. We want our students to thrive by supporting their *critical* awareness of the sociopolitical games embedded in society, technology fields, and education and empowering them to choose how they want to play. We also want educators and students to practice changing the game.

Scholars Alim, Paris, and Wong (2020) provide us with one more vision of what it would be like to change the game:

> What would our pedagogies look like if these hegemonic gazes weren't the dominant ones? What if, indeed, the goal of teaching

and learning with young people of color was not ultimately to see how closely they could perform white middle-class norms, but rather was to explore, honor, extend and, at times, problematize their cultural practices and investments? What would our educational contexts look like in a world where we owed no explanations, to anyone, about the value of our children's culture, language and learning potential? (p. 262)[7]

Educators play a key role in their classrooms to enact pedagogies that value and honor students' cultures and experiences. However, administrators, policy makers, and industry leaders are also responsible for engaging in this transformational work. Collective efforts will change the game not only within individual classrooms but also through more lasting structural and system-wide changes.

REVISITING MS. MORALES' STORY

Ms. Morales is on the path toward that vision in her own CS classroom. She shared an example of one project that she developed as an introduction to CS. Recognizing the cultural and linguistic diversity of her students, Ms. Morales focused on computing tools as a form of self-expression to support social-emotional learning. She wanted students to share their identities: "what makes them unique, special and how we represent ourselves." Drawing on students' experiences in their communities (e.g., language, culture, hobbies), her students created projects in Scratch that blended computing with other forms of expression, like poetry, illustrations, and song in multiple languages to share about themselves and make connections to each other and to CS as a resource to support understanding. Ms. Morales described her students' reactions to this experience:

> This project has become a favorite for my CS students, from third to eighth grade now. Students are able to express themselves in their native languages and it also allows a sense of community in my classroom. It allows students to feel successful in developing coding skills, all while representing their interests.

---

7. By White, middle-class norms, the authors refer to cultural practices such as how people comport themselves and language practices like using "standard" English (see Delpit, 1988). The specific norms and practices might be different based on geography, population and so on but are associated with power and status that confirm a certain type of success within a given local context.

Ms. Morales' project used multiple strategies to give all her students access to participating but also worked toward transforming CS from a decontextualized discipline for a few to a powerful way for her students to express themselves in ways that "value[d] . . . [their] culture, language and learning potential" (Alim et al., 2020, p. 262).

In the chapters that follow, you'll continue to think about equity in terms of access and transformation and their overlaps. You'll be invited to reflect on the purposes of CS Ed in your settings and will consider concrete suggestions for pedagogical strategies and approaches that can help you enact changes toward transforming what CS looks like in your classrooms and schools. We also recognize, as we noted earlier, that no single definition of equity is enough (NASEM, 2022). We invite you to consider the inequities you notice around you and develop your own definitions of equity that help you address those inequities in your local contexts and spaces. As you do so, you can become change agents for your colleagues, your students, and the field of CS Ed.

REFLECTION QUESTIONS

1. Based on what you have read in this chapter, how would you personally define equity? What is your own vision of equity?

2. In your contexts, what efforts are being made to help students "play the game"? To help students "transform the game"?

3. How have you seen tensions related to different equity efforts play out in the settings where you work?

TAKEAWAYS FOR PRACTICE

- Analyze the computing spaces you work in through the framings of equity we explored in this chapter. Are definitions of equity clearly stated in these spaces? Where and how do you recognize efforts to work toward equity as access? Where and how do you recognize efforts to work toward equity as transformation?

- Identify one small change you can make in your personal CS Ed context that can work toward your definition of equity from Reflection Question 1 above.

GLOSSARY

Term	Definition
assimilation	Processes through which minoritized and marginalized groups are encouraged or forced to adopt dominant norms and practices.
broadening participation	A way of thinking about equity, similar to access, that seeks to increase the participation of members of underrepresented and/or marginalized groups in CS and CS Ed. These groups have historically been excluded from computing fields.
equality	An approach to addressing inequity that focuses on giving everyone the same resources and opportunities.
ethnocomputing	The study of computational practices that are entwined in marginalized/minoritized communities' cultural practices (Eglash et al., 2006).
generative computing	Computing approaches that connect computational thinking and computing practices to local community practices in culturally responsive ways (Lachney et al., 2021).
inequity	Injustice or unfairness that is created and reproduced by social forces. It is important to remember that "fairness" does not mean "sameness," so working to right unfairness and inequity does not mean just giving everyone the same thing.
language agnostic	Computing approaches that focus on core computing skills that can be applied across different programming languages.
marginalized/ minoritized identities	Identity categories that are devalued in society, often because they are different from what society has established as the "ideal" norm. Those with marginalized/minoritized identities often face oppression and exclusion from mainstream society. We use both "marginalized" and "minoritized" as adjectives to emphasize how social processes actively construct inequity (Black et al., 2023). The term "minoritized" emphasizes historical systematic

	oppression and may be used regardless of whether an identity group actually represents a numerical minority in a context (see Black et al., 2023; Flores & Rosa, 2015).
social justice	A view that wealth, opportunities, and privileges should be equitably distributed to all members of society.
underrepresentation	A group of people who are not represented within a context or setting proportionate to their overall representation within the general population.

REFERENCES

Alim, H. S., Paris, D., & Wong, C. P. (2020). Culturally sustaining pedagogy: A critical framework for centering communities. In N. S. Nasir, C. D. Lee, R. Pea, & M. McKinney de Royston (Eds.), *Handbook of the cultural foundations of learning* (pp. 261–276). Routledge. https://doi.org/10.4324/9780203774977-18

Annamma, S. A., Connor, D., & Ferri, B. (2013). Dis/ability critical race studies (DisCrit): Theorizing at the intersections of race and dis/ability. *Race Ethnicity and Education, 16*(1), 1–31. https://doi.org/10.1080/13613324.2012.730511

Apraci-Dusseau, A., Astrachan, O., Barnett, D., Bauer, M., Carrell, M., Dovi, R., Franke, B., Gardner, C., Gray, J., Griffin, J., Kick, R., Kuemmel, A., Morelli, R., Muralidhar, D., Osborne, R. B., & Uche, C. (2013). Computer science principles: Analysis of a proposed advanced placement course. In T. Camp, P. Tymann, J. D. Dougherty, & K. Nagel (Eds.), *SIGCSE '13: Proceeding of the 44th ACM technical symposium on computer science education* (pp. 251–256). ACM Special Interest Group on Computer Science Education (SIGCSE). https://doi.org/10.1145/2445196.2445273

Black, C., Cerdeña, J. P., & Spearman-McCarthy, E. V. (2023). I am not your minority. *Lancet Regional Health Americas, 19.* https://doi.org/10.1016/j.lana.2023.100464

Blikstein, P. (2018). *Pre-college computer science education: A survey of the field.* Google LLC. https://services.google.com/fh/files/misc/pre-college-computer-science-education-report.pdf

Collins, P. H. (2019). *Intersectionality as critical social theory.* Duke University Press. https://doi.org/10.1215/9781478007098

Computer Science Teachers Association [CSTA]. (n.d.). *Inclusive teaching pedagogies.* https://csteachers.org/inclusive-teaching-pedagogies/

Crenshaw, K. (1991). Mapping the margins: Intersectionality, identity politics, and violence against women of color. *Stanford Law Review, 43*(6), 1241–1299. https://doi.org/10.2307/1229039

Davis, K., White, S. V., Becton-Consuegra, D., & Scott, A. (2021). *Culturally responsive-sustaining computer science education: A framework.* Kapor Center. https://www.kaporcenter.org/wp-content/uploads/2021/07/KC21004_ECS-Framework-Report_final.pdf

Delpit, L. D. (1988). The silenced dialogue: Power and pedagogy in educating other people's children. *Harvard Educational Review, 58*(3), 280–299. https://doi.org/10.17763/haer.58.3.c43481778r528qw4

Eglash, R., Bennett, A., O'Donnell, C., Jennings, S., & Cintorino, M. (2006). Culturally situated design tools: Ethnocomputing from field site to classroom. *American Anthropologist, 108*(2), 347–362. https://doi.org/10.1525/aa.2006.108.2.347

Fletcher, C. L., & Warner, J. R. (2021). CAPE: A framework for assessing equity throughout the computer science education ecosystem. *Communications of the ACM, 64*(2), 23–25. https://doi.org/10.1145/3442373

Flores, N., & Rosa, J. (2015). Undoing appropriateness: Raciolinguistic ideologies and language diversity in education. *Harvard Educational Review, 85*(2), 149–171. https://doi.org/10.17763/0017-8055.85.2.149

Gay, G. (2018). *Culturally responsive teaching: Theory, research, and practice* (3rd ed.). Teachers College Press.

González, N., Moll, L., & Amanti, C. (2005). *Funds of knowledge: Theorizing practices in households, communities, and classrooms.* Lawrence Erlbaum Associates.

Grapin, S. E., Pierson, A., González-Howard, M., Ryu, M., Fine, C., & Vogel, S. (2023). Science education with multilingual learners: Equity as access and equity as transformation. *Science Education, 107,* 999–1032. https://doi.org/10.1002/sce.21791

Gutiérrez, R. (2009). Framing equity: Helping students "play the game" and "change the game." *Teaching for Excellence and Equity in Mathematics, 1*(1), 4–8. https://www.todos-math.org/assets/documents/TEEMv1n1excerpt.pdf

Hammond, Z. L. (2015). *Culturally responsive teaching and the brain: Promoting authentic engagement and rigor among culturally and linguistically diverse students.* Corwin.

Jones, S. T. & melo, n. a. (2021). We tell these stories to survive: Towards abolition in computer science education. *Canadian Journal of Science, Mathematics and Technology Education, 21,* 290–308. https://doi.org/10.1007/s42330-021-00158-2

Lachney, M., Babbitt, W., Bennett, A., & Eglash, R. (2021). Generative computing: African-American cosmetology as a link between computing education and community wealth. *Interactive Learning Environments, 29*(7), 1115–1135. https://doi.org/10.1080/10494820.2019.1636087

Ladson-Billings, G. (1995). Toward a theory of culturally relevant pedagogy. *American Education Research Journal, 32*(3), 465–491. https://doi.org/10.3102/00028312032003465

Lewis, J. E., Arista, N., Pechawis, A., & Kite, S. (2018). Making kin with the machines. *Journal of Design and Science.* https://doi.org/10.21428/bfafd97b

Madkins, T. C., Howard, N. R., & Freed, N. (2020). Engaging equity pedagogies in computer science learning environments. *Journal of Computer Science Integration, 3*(2), 1–27. https://doi.org/10.26716/jcsi.2020.03.2.1

Margolis, J., Goode, J., & Chapman, G. (2015). An equity lens for scaling: A critical juncture for exploring computer science. *ACM Inroads, 6*(3), 58–66. https://doi.org/10.1145/2794294

McDermott, R. P. (1993). The acquisition of a child by a learning disability. In S. Chaiklin & J. Lave (Eds.), *Understanding practice* (pp. 269–305). Cambridge University Press. https://doi.org/10.1017/CBO9780511625510.011

National Academies of Sciences, Engineering, and Medicine. (2022). *Science and engineering in preschool through elementary grades: The brilliance of children and the strengths of educators.* National Academies Press. https://nap.nationalacademies.org/catalog/26215/science-and-engineering-in-preschool-through-elementary-grades-thebrilliance

National Equity Project (NEP). (n.d.). *Educational equity definition.* https://www.nationalequityproject.org/education-equity-definition

New York City Public Schools. (n.d.). *Ethnocomputing: Computational thinking of indigenous and vernacular cultural designs.* New York City Public Schools CS4All. https://sites.google.com/schools.nyc.gov/cs4all-equity/eecs/ethnocomputing

Perez, M., & Garcia, P. (2023). Tracing participation beyond computing careers: How women reflect on their experiences in computing programs. *ACM Transactions on Computing Education, 23*(2), 1–23. https://doi.org/10.1145/3582564

Philip, T. M., & Azevedo, F. S. (2017). Everyday science learning and equity: Mapping the contested terrain. *Science Education, 101*(4), 526–532. https://doi.org/10.1002/sce.21286

Rebora, A. (2021). Zaretta Hammond on equity and student engagement. *Educational Leadership, 79*(4), 14–18. https://www.ascd.org/el/articles/zaretta-hammond-on-equity-and-student-engagement

Scott, K. A., Sheridan, K. M., & Clark, K. (2015). Culturally responsive computing: A theory revisited. *Learning, Media and Technology, 40*(4), 412–436. https://doi.org/10.1080/17439884.2014.924966

Vogel, S., Santo, R., & Ching, D. (2017). Visions of computer science education: Unpacking arguments for and projected impacts of CS4All initiatives. In M. E. Caspersen, S. H. Edwards, T. Barnes, & D. D. Garcia (Eds.), *Proceedings of the 2017 ACM SIGCSE Technical Symposium on Computing Education* (pp. 609–614). ACM Special Interest Group on Computer Science Education. http://doi.org/10.1145/3017680.3017755

Vossoughi, S., & Vakil, S. (2018). Toward what ends? A critical analysis of militarism, equity, and STEM education. In A. I. Ali & T. L. Buenavista (Eds.), *Education at war: The fight for students of color in America's public schools* (1st ed., pp. 117–140). Fordham University Press. https://doi.org/10.2307/j.ctt2204pqp

RESOURCE 1: WORKING TOWARD EQUITY IN CS CLASSROOMS

This resource explores one example of how CS educators might work toward equity in different ways in their classrooms. We share Aaron's story and provide commentary throughout to highlight how Aaron identified inequities in his setting and changed his practices and curriculum to further multiple forms of equity. The story concludes with some reflection questions to support you in working toward equity in your practice.

AARON'S STORY: "HOW YOU SUPPORT YOUR STUDENTS REFLECTS YOUR UNDERSTANDING OF EQUITY"

Aaron is a public middle school STEM teacher. His story shows how working toward equity is an ongoing process but one that can lead to better outcomes for all students.

Aaron began by emphasizing how his efforts to promote equity and meet students' needs have developed over time. He described:

> Equity [in my classroom] has definitely evolved to be more individualized over time. For me personally, it came in stages because it is an overwhelming thought to give every student an individualized experience that suits them best. As a teacher who has 300+ students every school year, it is always a struggle to make sure that each student is getting a personalized, authentic experience.

Aaron acknowledged the realities of teaching that can contribute to practices that may reproduce inequity. The sheer number of students that Aaron has each year makes it difficult for him to tailor his teaching to meet everyone's different needs. He explained how over time, he has changed his thinking and practices to become more individualized:

> I started by thinking, "Oh, this class is behind. I should review this lesson with them." Then, it evolved to, "Only three or four students in this class truly need time to review. We can work together in a focus group while other students work autonomously on another project."

Aaron was committed to ensuring that all his students had equitable access to his CS curriculum. At first, his approach was to give everyone in a class a review if anyone in the class was struggling. This "equality" approach of giving everyone the same thing is often a reality given large numbers of students, time constraints, and pressure to cover curricular material. However, over time, Aaron realized that this approach was not ideal because it didn't give students what they individually needed and inequitably distributed the resources of time and his support.

He shifted his approach by adjusting his practice. Instead of a whole group lesson, he implemented small focus groups for students who needed a review and gave them tailored support. For students who did not need his focused attention, he gave them time to work independently in ways that would continue to expand their skills. This shift allowed Aaron to promote greater equity in his classroom by giving his students greater access to time and support in ways that would promote their individual CS learning.

Aaron described how his approach continued to change:

> Present day, I evaluate. "Why are these students having a harder time? Are they getting equitable access to language through my instruction? Do they feel the content is not relevant to their future, community, and culture? Are they not engaged because of socioeconomic factors happening in their personal life?" The process of how you support students reflects your understanding of equity, because I see time and time again students being brushed off when a teacher "teaches to the middle." Naturally, there will be students who are not in that middle.

Aaron acknowledged that the common approach to "teaching to the middle" is not one that promotes equity as access. Instead, Aaron worked to promote equity as access by working to remove barriers like language or socioeconomic factors that might prevent students from accessing his CS instruction. He also analyzed his curriculum and considered how students might respond to it, because he recognized that CS curricula are not always relevant to students' different backgrounds. Through this strategy, Aaron worked toward equity as transformation by expanding what counts as CS and ensuring that his content was meaningful for students.

Aaron concluded with an example of a unit he teaches with students that helps students "play the game" but also pushes toward equity as transformation by reimagining what counts as CS.

> If students have an interest in the content or skills being practiced [in a unit], I outline what kinds of fields and careers are involved in these areas. I also detail what it takes to get to these places to accomplish their goal. For example, in my Hydroponics Unit (Sustainable Farming), I discuss what a career in agriculture looks

like and what a career as a data analyst who works in agriculture looks like. This is to help students understand that there are many pathways to getting into the field of their choice with a skillset they are familiar with.

In Aaron's unit, he worked toward helping students "play the game" by helping them identify their interests and preparing them with skills that can allow them to access multiple careers across different fields. He is also transforming CS by connecting it to fields like farming and expanding what is valued by centering environmental sustainability as an important goal of computing. Aaron's story highlights how reflecting and adjusting practices as a CS educator can further multiple forms of equity.

REFLECTION QUESTIONS

- A key takeaway from Aaron's story is how the changes he made to his practice were part of an ongoing process. What inequities have you already recognized in your context? What changes have you made to address them? What are your next steps to continue addressing inequities in your space?

- Aaron faced a number of challenges that might have constrained his efforts to work toward equity (e.g., limited time, large numbers of students). What challenges do you face? What changes can you make that account for these challenges and provide your students with more equitable access to CS instruction?

- Aaron worked to balance providing students with access to CS instruction while also transforming his instruction to ensure that it was relevant and responsive to his students. What changes can you make to ensure that CS instruction in your context sustains students' interests and backgrounds? How can you help students transform what, how, and why they engage in computing?

5

Busting Myths About Inequity

Theories for Computer Science Educators to Think With

Sara Vogel, Lauren Vogelstein, Madison Allen Kuyenga, Lloyd Talley, Nykema Lindsey, Christy Crawford, Melissa Parker, Bethany Daniel, Stephanie T. Jones, and the Computer Science Educational Justice Collective

CHAPTER OVERVIEW

This chapter offers some theoretical tools to think with as educators engage in equity-focused work. Specifically, the chapter examines the idea of intersectionality and a framework called "the Four I's" that illuminates how inequity can be reproduced through systems of oppression at ideological, institutional, interpersonal, and internalized levels. The chapter uses these theories as lenses to bust myths that are often given as explanations for why inequity exists in computer science (CS) and CS education (CS Ed).

CHAPTER OBJECTIVES

After reading this chapter, I can:

- Identify common myths in CS Ed and explain how these myths reproduce inequities.
- Apply the theory of intersectionality to make sense of inequities in CS and CS Ed.

- Apply the theory of the Four I's of Oppression and Advantage to make sense of inequities in CS and CS Ed.

KEY TERMS

ableism; classism; the Four I's of Oppression and Advantage; ideological oppression; ideologies; imposter syndrome; institutional oppression; internalized oppression; interpersonal oppression; intersectionality; marginalization; matrix of domination; microaggression; racism; sexism; structural oppression; theory; tokenism; xenophobia

EMILY'S STORY

Emily is an elementary teacher who is concerned about equity at her school.[1] She has heard several myths about students and recognizes how those myths contribute to the inequity she sees. Emily shared:

> 65% of the population of students at my school are multilingual learners. I have heard countless times from teachers that "multilingual learners can't even read or write. How can they do CS?"[2]

Emily noticed that when teachers believe this myth, they often don't expose their students to CS in their classrooms, which "widens the inequity for these students as they go through their education." Emily finds it "very frustrating to hear these sentiments" and wants to learn how she can speak back to these myths to support more equitable instruction at her school.

THEORIES AS TOOLS TO THINK WITH

Understanding why and how inequities persist is an important part of working toward educational equity. People offer many different explanations for why there are inequities in CS and CS Ed. Some of these explanations may sound like the following:

---

1. Emily's experiences are shared with permission.
2. See the On Terminology section of this guide for an explanation on our use of different identity-related terms.

- Computer science is for "techies." It's a hard, technical field, so not everyone is cut out for it, which is why you don't see a lot of diversity.

- If tech companies could find enough women and racially minoritized coders with the right skills, they'd hire them. It's not about bias, it's about qualifications.

- Since CS tends to attract certain types of students, like male students, there's no need to spend extra time or resources supporting them. They already have an advantage.

While these explanations may make sense on the surface, there are a lot of false assumptions embedded in them. For example, the explanations suggest that participating in computing requires a certain set of abilities or identities but overlook the fact that anyone with interest and support can thrive in CS. They collapse differences between individuals, assuming that everyone from a certain group is the same, and they place blame on individuals without acknowledging systemic patterns that contribute to inequity.

Despite the fact that these statements are all actually myths based on incomplete information, these and other stories about inequity in CS have become second nature in CS educational spaces. There are many pitfalls, traps, tropes, and detours that people working toward equitable outcomes can fall into when they make assumptions like those described above (Dugan, 2021). To reach our goal of equity-centered CS Ed, we need to constantly examine the assumptions we are making about our students, CS as a discipline, and our classrooms.

Theories are one tool we can use to examine our assumptions. Developed by scholars, educators, activists, and people in their everyday lives, **theories** offer explanations for phenomena that can help us interpret what is happening around us so we can more effectively take action. In this chapter, we consider two theories: **intersectionality** and the **Four I's of Oppression and Advantage** (ideological, institutional, interpersonal, and internalized).

Sometimes, the writing that describes theories from academic disciplines like sociology, law, and education can use dense language. We attempt to provide examples and explanations to make the theories presented in this chapter more relevant to CS educators and provide a glossary for support. Engaging with theoretical ideas and lingo, even though it can be challenging, can be an important way to support equity-focused growth, because it helps us take up new perspectives outside of our own experiences.

---

theory A set of ideas based on scholarship and practice that are used to explain and interpret how society works.

intersectionality A theory that recognizes how people's different identities (e.g., disability, gender, race) overlap and intersect, creating access to privilege or resulting in oppression in ways that cannot be understood or addressed by considering each identity separately (Crenshaw, 1991; Collins, 2019).

Four I's of Oppression and Advantage A theory that illustrates how systems of oppression and advantage (like ableism, classism, or racism) are produced across multiple layers of society. The Four I's are ideological, institutional, interpersonal, and internalized. (See Bell, 2013; Chan & Coney, 2020; Chinook Fund, n.d.; Kuttner, 2016.)

As we explore the theories of intersectionality and the Four I's in this chapter, we use them to challenge common myths you might hear in the media, from administrators and colleagues, or even from students themselves. By using theory and facts to demystify these myths, we can't promise that working toward equitable changes in CS Ed will get easier. However, if we better understand the systems that have led to pervasive issues and challenges in the field, we can better understand how to work to change those systems and guide our students to be change agents too. Hopefully, by thinking with us about these theories and myths, you'll be prepared with a powerful response the next time you hear a myth being perpetuated.

INTERSECTIONALITY

Intersectionality starts with a recognition of the fact that people's identities are multifaceted and complex. It also draws on the idea that identities are socially constructed and that people can experience oppression and **marginalization** related to particular identities, while other identities afford access to social power and privilege. Building on these two principles, intersectionality as a theory argues that different aspects of people's identity (e.g., disability, gender, race) overlap and intersect in ways that result in forms of oppression that cannot be understood or addressed by focusing on each identity separately (Crenshaw, 1991; Collins, 2019).

marginalization The social process of excluding or oppressing individuals who hold identities that are devalued or differ from society's "ideal" norm.

The concept of intersectionality has long been used in efforts to work toward social justice—even before legal scholar Kimberlé Crenshaw coined the term in the late 1980s. For example, Sojourner Truth was a formerly enslaved Black abolitionist who lived in the United States in the mid-1800s. During her life, emancipation efforts gave Black men the right to vote and suffrage movements worked to grant the right to vote to white women. Truth named how her identity as a Black woman left her overlooked by both of these movements (The Sojourner Truth Project, 1851; Collins, 2019).

Truth's experience illustrates how social dynamics marginalize Black women in unique ways that cannot be described or understood by paying attention to just race or gender in isolation. Scholars have shown how intersectionality is important when working for social justice because everyone has different overlapping identities that are perceived in different ways by society. Kimberlé Crenshaw (1989) used this analogy to explain why intersectionality matters:

> Consider an analogy for traffic in an intersection, coming and going in all four directions. Discrimination, like traffic through an intersection, may flow in one direction, and it may flow in another. If an accident happened in an intersection, it can be caused by cars traveling from any number of directions and, sometimes, from all of them. Similarly, if a Black woman is harmed because she is in the intersection, her injury could result from sex discrimination or race discrimination. (p. 149)

Sociologist Patricia Hill Collins calls these intersecting systems of power the **matrix of domination** (Combahee River Collective, 1977; Collins, 2019). The matrix of domination creates dynamics that produce distinct and interlocking forms of oppression based on identities like gender and race. Those who hold multiple marginalized identities experience domination and oppression at the intersections of their identities.

Intersectionality can help educators recognize why equity-based initiatives might fall short. Often, equity initiatives consider the marginalization a student might face in an "additive" way. For example, an initiative might assume that by addressing issues of racial discrimination, gender discrimination, and class discrimination separately, they will have helped a student who faces all three issues. But intersectionality emphasizes how our identities don't just get added on top of each other. Instead, our identities intersect and overlap to result in distinct lived experiences, oppression, biases, and access or lack of access to power and privilege (Esposito & Evans-Winters, 2021).

Sometimes, the intersectional nature of identity gets obscured. For example, a Computer Science for All (CSforAll) initiative might consider statistics about girls' pass rates for the AP CS Principles (AP CSP) course to measure progress toward broadening participation in CS. In 2022, 61% of girls and 64% of boys passed the AP CSP exam (Ericson, 2023). These numbers make it seem like the gender gap is closing. However, looking at the statistics in terms of gender *and* race highlights how large disparities still exist. In 2022, 70% of white girls passed the exam, but only 32% of Black girls, 38% of Hispanic girls, and 34% of Pacific Islander girls who took the exam passed.[3] Looking at the data only through gender or only through race obscures how racially minoritized girls continue to be marginalized in CS at the intersections of their racial and gender identities.

---

matrix of domination
Intersecting systems of power that produce distinct and interlocking forms of oppression (Combahee River Collective, 1977; Collins, 2019).

---

3. We use the racial and gender categories that were used on the exam. We acknowledge that these categories do not fully capture students' diverse racial and gender identities.

MYTHBUSTING TIME!

Myth: Because CS Ed tends to attract males, we don't need to spend time and energy supporting male students.

Wrong! Even in initiatives and programs that have high rates of male participation, we need to understand how males with different combinations of identities might be experiencing CS Ed. Males also have intersecting racial, gender and sexual, religious, socioeconomic, disability, and linguistic identities that shape barriers they might face in CS Ed. Intersectionality helps us see that focusing on the single identity marker of gender hides the unique experiences of those with identities at particular intersections.

For example, Carey (2024) used the theory of intersectionality to show how an urban charter school reinforced the criminalization of Black boys and the stigmatization of Latine boys through school norms, disciplinary policies, and daily interactions. Schooling practices treat boys at the intersections of gender and race in unique ways, which shape how these students participate in CS Ed.

This myth also ignores the fact that students whose identities afford them more privilege (like males) benefit from learning about the experiences of marginalized groups in CS. If a goal of CS Ed is to achieve equitable outcomes and resist systems of oppression, then everyone plays a role. We and our students can work to ensure that people of all genders are respected in CS spaces, that products are designed with different genders in mind, and so on. Disrupting systems of oppression requires the work of many people, including those who are typically centered in CS and those who have been pushed to the margins of CS.

THE FOUR I'S OF OPPRESSION AND ADVANTAGE

One myth about education in general is that just having "bad actors" or individuals change their behaviors would fix inequities. But the reality is more complicated than that. Inequities are shaped by interlocking systems of oppression and advantage like **ableism**, **classism**, **racism**, or **sexism**. These cultural, economic, and political systems were established during periods of slavery, colonialism, and imperialism and continue to shape society today (Tatum, 2003). They reproduce different forms of

---

ableism Implicit or explicit social preference for nondisabled bodies and minds that creates prejudice and oppression of disability and disabled people (Shew, 2020).

classism A system of prejudice and discrimination in favor of people with higher socioeconomic status (e.g., upper middle-class) and against people with lower socioeconomic status (e.g., lower class).

racism A system of prejudice and discrimination based on race that privileges individuals racialized as white and oppresses racially minoritized individuals.

sexism A system of prejudice and discrimination based on gender and gender identity that privileges men and oppresses women, non-binary, and gender-fluid individuals.

identity-based discrimination and exclusion through a combination of individual prejudiced action and power embedded in institutional structures (Bell, 2013). They are systems of oppression *and* advantage because some identities are afforded a more dominant status in society and provide people with those identities with power and privilege.

This differential distribution of power creates social hierarchies (Wilkerson, 2020). For example, in the United States, racial hierarchies afford people racialized as white with access to particular social privileges while racially marginalized people face discrimination, exclusion, and oppression around their racial identities. Members of groups who are granted more privileged status may be socialized not to talk about or even notice these -isms, while members of marginalized groups may experience their direct consequences frequently (Tatum, 2003). How hierarchies are structured and how individuals experience injustice as a lived reality vary across cultures and countries. However, because benefits and privileges are embedded in social structures, inequities get (re)produced across social contexts.

The Four I's of Oppression and Advantage (Four I's) is a theory that helps us understand how systems of oppression and advantage are produced across multiple layers of society: ideological, institutional, interpersonal, and internalized (Chinook Fund, n.d.). Table 1 summarizes the Four I's and their application to CS and CS Ed.

Dynamics at all four levels of oppression shape CS education and computing professions. This means that working toward equitable outcomes in CS Ed requires more than just having people change by taking up equity-minded behaviors and mindsets. Real change also requires disrupting what we assume to be common sense, changing the policies and practices of institutions, and attending to how resources and benefits get distributed across society. The Four I's are not exhaustive, but they can offer us a way to think about the interconnected systems that support

Table 1. The Four I's of Oppression and Advantage

Dimension	Definition	Computer Science Application	CS Industry Example
Ideological Oppression	Dominant sets of beliefs and values that justify and maintain systems of oppression; often disguised as "common sense"	The myth of meritocracy in tech suggests that anyone can succeed if they work hard enough. This ignores systemic barriers faced by marginalized groups.	The myth of the solo "genius" tech-company founder can influence who is considered a strong leader and discount the contributions and leadership styles of those who don't fit the Steve Jobs/Mark Zuckerberg Silicon Valley mold.

Dimension	Definition	Computer Science Application	CS Industry Example
Institutional Oppression	Structures and policies within institutions that disadvantage certain groups and benefit others	Algorithmic bias in facial recognition software leads to higher misidentification rates for racially minoritized people.	A 2019 study found that facial recognition software from Amazon, Rekognition, had a 53% higher error rate for identifying racially minoritized women when compared to white men (Buolamwini, 2019).
Interpersonal Oppression	Prejudice and discrimination experienced by individuals or small groups in interpersonal interactions	Colleagues who question the programming expertise of a gender-marginalized coworker enact microaggressions in tech workspaces.	A venture capitalist is influenced by societal messages about racially minoritized women as less savvy and refuses to invest in a startup led by young Latine women, attributing it to a lack of "market potential."
Internalized Oppression	Acceptance of negative stereotypes about one's own group, leading to self-doubt and discouragement	Marginalized groups underestimate their coding abilities due to stereotypes about their lack of aptitude in STEM fields.	A study found that college women felt less confident in their coding skills than college men, even when their actual skill levels were comparable (Beyer, 2014).

oppression and advantage in society. Looking at each one individually, we can use them to debunk common myths in CS Ed.

IDEOLOGICAL OPPRESSION AND INEQUITY

One important way that inequity is maintained is through **ideologies**, or systems of ideas that circulate in society. Dominant ideologies that reproduce inequity are harmful because they perpetuate ideas that reinforce the supremacy of certain groups over others and contribute to ideological oppression. Ideologies are often hard to recognize because they get embedded in narratives and myths that are accepted as "common sense" by society.[4]

ideologies Systems of ideas that circulate in society. Dominant ideologies perpetuate ideas that reinforce the supremacy of certain groups over others.

---

4. We use the term "common sense" in line with scholars who have noted that what society names as common sense is generally neither common nor sensical (Fairclough, 2014; Garfinkel, 1967).

For example, in many CS classrooms, solving problems quickly and without asking questions is associated with intelligence. Valuing the ability to solve problems quickly may at first seem like "common sense." But it actually draws on several ideologies that reproduce inequities. This unspoken value is rooted in Western cultural ideologies that equate time with money as part of a capitalist system. Valuing quick problem solving also promotes ableist ideologies that discriminate against neurodivergent students who process information differently and at different speeds. It may also marginalize bi/multilingual learners who draw on their full linguistic repertoires to complete a task. Prioritizing this value in CS classrooms can create inhospitable conditions for learners, creating competitive environments that reproduce other ideologies like individualism, which values individual achievement over collective growth.

Amanda, an elementary CS teacher, shared an example of **ideological oppression** in her context. She explained: "In my school, a well-spoken student is automatically thought of as 'smarter.' People assume that they must have 'a well-educated family.' " Amanda named narratives that draw on language ideologies that equate intelligence and education with certain, privileged language practices. People often equate being "well-spoken" to using "standard" or "academic" English, and "well-educated" with having attended college, despite there being many ways of communicating and learning. Amanda challenged this ideological influence as she reflected that "I don't think enough time is spent thinking about [how] we can call people into these spaces and make our teaching more culturally responsive and relevant to families." Amanda's call to think about how to create learning environments that value and center students' language and cultural practices could be one way to contest ideological oppression in her space.

ideological oppression
Dominant sets of beliefs and values that justify and maintain systems of oppression; often disguised as "common sense."

MYTHBUSTING TIME!

Myth: Inequities in CS exist because CS is a "hard," "logical," and "technical" field. It's for "techies," not for humanities types.

Wrong! Gone unchecked, this myth can prevent people from entering CS fields because they feel like their motivations and interests don't align with stereotypical "techie" profiles. This contributes to inequity by narrowing the kinds of problems that CS works to solve and the ways of solving those problems.

This myth has two big ideological assumptions embedded in it that are important to tease out. First is the assumption that CS as a field and the products it produces are objective and logical and thus politically and culturally neutral. The second assumption is that CS is incompatible with concerns of the humanities, like expression, social issues, language, and culture.

CS as a field is defined as "the study of computers and algorithmic processes, including their principles, their hardware and software designs, their applications, and their impact on society" (Tucker et al., 2003, p. 6). CS activities like programming software and creating algorithms do involve using precise syntax and logic that allows hardware to process coded tasks.

However, humans write code, frame problems, design programming languages, and create interfaces and platforms to solve problems. Whenever humans are involved, social life and politics are also involved. As we've explored in earlier chapters, mainstream technologies have the values and biases of their creators embedded into them. If developers do not carefully think through the ethics of their creations, tools can easily reinforce the default -isms that already characterize our societies.

Ways of thinking about the world that come from the humanities and other fields may actually help computer scientists better examine the impact that technologies have on people's lives. Techniques from CS can also offer people in the humanities new ways to do their work. For example, computing may help people analyze text or data, create art, and express and share their work with varied audiences.

If CS is deeply connected to the social and political human experience, then why does CS have a reputation of being "politically neutral"? Because CS has the word "science" in its name, it often gets linked to dominant ideologies that establish science as an objective way of learning about the world. While scientific methods have made significant contributions to our understanding of the world, the Western practices most often associated with "science" are not neutral. Western scientific disciplines were developed as part of European colonization of Asia, Africa, the Americas, and the Pacific. Europeans used "science" to classify, codify, and organize the natural world and the peoples they had "discovered." As part of their colonizing efforts, they distinguished their practices as "hard science" and dismissed non-Western and Indigenous ways of knowing that viewed humans as an inextricable part of the natural world as lesser, "folk" traditions (Bang et al., 2012).

Framing CS as a hard science divorced from other ways of knowing creates narrow pathways into the discipline. These visions may not align with students from marginalized backgrounds, who may have interests and definitions of success that differ from what is currently accepted (McGee & Bentley, 2017). Influenced by ideologies of science as objective and separate from social life, in the United States, STEM subjects are traditionally taught in decontextualized and mechanical ways (Boaler & Greeno, 2000). This results in a focus on "unbiased," objective observations that discount the ideas and concerns that children and youth bring to CS learning.

One way to counteract this myth is to intentionally take up students' experiences as resources for learning. For example, one middle school teacher, Lucy, planned to use computational modeling with her students to consider the relationship between natural disasters and immigration. She originally planned to focus on using statistics to reason about immigration data. Her students, however, focused their initial ideas on the social and political reasons that would prompt families to immigrate to a new country. Instead of worrying that her students' ideas would derail the class from the intended STEM content goals, Lucy recognized that both perspectives were needed. Putting the computational thinking in conversation with students' social and political concerns allowed the class to create richer models of immigration. (For more on this example, see Radke et al., 2022.)

INSTITUTIONAL OPPRESSION AND INEQUITY

institutional oppression
Structures and policies within institutions that dis- advantage certain groups and benefit others.

structural oppression
Historically maintained structures and policies across institutions (e.g., the CS industry, education) that disadvantage certain groups and benefit others over time.

Ideologies that contribute to inequity often become embedded into policies and routines in social structures. These practices create inequitable opportunities and outcomes for different groups of people. Oppression can be **institutionalized** (reproduced at individual institutions like a single school or a single tech company) or **structural** (present across similar institutions over time, like schooling in general or the technology industry).

Institutional and structural oppression in the tech industry can be seen in how African American, Native American, and Latine women may become stuck in low-level positions in tech companies. Despite well-intended recruitment and retention policies, structural barriers may prevent racially marginalized people from advancing in their careers (McKinsey & Company, 2024; Smith, 2022).

In CS Ed, institutionalized inequity may appear in recruitment policies for CS Ed programs. For example, a school might have a policy that requires students to have received high grades, completed prerequisite courses, and have a "squeaky clean" disciplinary record to participate in CS classes. This kind of policy is advantageous for students who have been able to afford tutoring and support to succeed in courses—often those from more affluent households. However, it disadvantages students who did not have the same opportunities and who may have been disciplined more frequently. This kind of policy that institutionalizes inequity at one school becomes structural if similar practices occur at schools across the country and over time.

In fact, these kinds of structural systems of disadvantage and oppression do exist and work to exclude racially minoritized students, bi/multilingual students, and students with disabilities from CS learning opportunities. Across schools in the United States, Black and Latine students are disciplined at higher rates than their white peers (Losen, 2011; Noguera, 2003). This means that policies requiring a squeaky-clean record to participate in CS may exclude Black and Latine students who would otherwise be interested in and successful at CS. Similarly, bi/multilingual students and racially minoritized students are overrepresented in special education programs (Annamma et al., 2013). Structural policies that situate CS as an enrichment course may mean that students in special education programs are excluded from CS opportunities as well (Wille et al., 2017). These institutionalized and structural layers of oppression create a situation where CS courses come to be treated as clubhouses, reserved for students who meet particular standards for what an average or typical CS student looks, sounds, and acts like (Margolis & Fisher, 2003). As a result, inequitable access to CS educational opportunities continues.

Dawn, another elementary CS teacher, described how institutional oppression reproduced inequity at her school. She shared:

> CS at my school was originally offered to all children equally. Due to budget cuts, that program no longer exists. Now, the expectation is for classroom teachers to teach it as part of the STREAM [science, technology, reading, engineering, arts, and math] curriculum. Most classroom teachers do not feel comfortable teaching the CS unit, so only a few trained teachers do.

Dawn identified several institutional factors at play in her context: the budget cuts that eliminated the CS program, the expectation for teachers to incorporate CS into an already full curriculum with limited time, and the lack of training for teachers to feel confident teaching CS. All of these institutional factors have contributed to inequitable access to CS at Dawn's school, despite the fact that at one time, all children did have CS opportunities.

MYTHBUSTING TIME!

Myth: There's not enough time in the school day as it is for English Language Learners to learn English, let alone time for them to do CS. They need to prioritize fundamental skills like learning English and cannot be in CS classes.

Wrong! This myth is similar to the ones that Emily has heard in her school. Statements like these may be expressed by educators and school administrators with the best of intentions. Because they recognize the dominant role that English plays in the United States, educators might want to prepare their students with skills that can give them access to the power that comes from English proficiency. Whole school systems may institutionalize this sentiment through policies that include English prerequisites for CS classes or that schedule required English classes at the same time as CS "enrichment" courses. But withholding access to CS Ed for students who are already marginalized only exacerbates inequities.

It's important to question what is at the root of statements like these. In the United States, one dominant ideology is that using "standard" English is a sign of intelligence and capability. Other languages and ways of communication are perceived as less valid. These beliefs come from histories of colonization, **xenophobia** toward immigrants, and racism toward linguistically and culturally marginalized groups. They have been institutionalized in policies that label bi/multilingual children as "English Language Learners." This term focuses on students' potential to learn "standard" English instead of taking into account the vast language competencies that they already have.

xenophobia A system of prejudice and discrimination against foreigners.

These ideologies are also institutionalized in the computing industry through conventions that use English-based programming language and code documentation. Thinking about language in this way hides the reality that people can express themselves and demonstrate their capabilities in many ways. Multilingual, verbal, written, symbolic, artistic, and embodied forms of language and expression can be used to communicate with those around us. While it may feel counterintuitive or like it is asking too much of students, CS educators can support all learners, including bi/multilinguals, to leverage all the language they know to learn computing. We explore this idea more fully in Chapters 11 through 14.

Many teachers have shared that instead of being a challenge, CS has actually been a resource and support for multilingual learners. Computing can allow students to express themselves in new ways and share their experiences with their teachers and peers. Visual programming languages and environments like the Scratch platform link code to multiple communication methods like written language and multimedia. This offers multiple entry points for students, regardless of their language backgrounds.

Ms. Kors, one of the teachers we met in Chapter 3, used this approach in her English as a New Language classroom. She asked her middle school students to tell family stories using Scratch. As they created and shared their stories, students used code alongside images, sounds, and languages they used at home and at school to represent and describe things like their stories' settings and the personalities of their family members. This project supported Ms. Kors' students in developing their coding and language skills, but it also supported Ms. Kors to learn more about her students' lives and their complex language competencies (see Vogel, 2020, for more).

INTERPERSONAL OPPRESSION AND INEQUITY

Inequities that are based in ideologies and embedded in institutional and structural policies are often felt most oppressively in individual and group interactions as a form of **interpersonal oppression**. People may assume that interpersonal issues are simply "bad people" acting on their prejudices and biases, but interpersonal oppression goes deeper than that. Interpersonal layers of inequity are reproduced in everyday actions when people make racist or sexist jokes or share comments that perpetuate stereotypes about groups of people. It also occurs in interactions like harassment, threats, violence, and police brutality against marginalized groups. Interpersonal forms of advantage can happen when someone privileges a member of a particular group over others in interactions like hiring and promoting decisions or when approving a loan. Ideologies and

interpersonal oppression Prejudice and discrimination experienced by individuals or small groups in interpersonal interactions.

institutional and structural policies shape people's interpersonal interactions and vice versa, creating a continual feedback loop.

Interpersonal oppression is shaped by power. While all people can act on prejudiced ideas that harmfully assert the supremacy of some groups over others, not all people's actions are socially powerful in the same way (Kendi, 2019; Leonardo, 2007). When individuals with social and institutional power act on prejudice in ways that draw on power, they contribute to the harmful reproduction of society's -isms in a way that is not possible for those who lack social or institutional power. For example, in 2020, a white woman called the police on a Black man in New York City's Central Park for doing nothing more than "birding while Black" (Gross, 2023). She could marshall and rely on the power of law enforcement in ways that marginalized individuals may not feel safe doing, even when reporting actual hate crimes (Devine et al., 2018).

Interpersonal forms of oppression occur in CS Ed too. CS educators may wittingly or unwittingly hold lower expectations for their racially minoritized students, their students with disabilities, or their bi/multilingual students learning English. These expectations may be revealed in their interactions with or about students. For example:

- A teacher might comment to another teacher, "Oh that Spanish-speaking student is so well spoken," reproducing the assumption that this student is an exception to a norm.

- A teacher might give the benefit of the doubt to a student who has a missing homework assignment because they perceive them as coming from a "good" family (e.g., with two professional, college-educated parents or caregivers).

- A teacher might want to raise awareness about ableism and unwittingly **tokenizes** a student with a disability by asking them to "represent" people with disabilities during class discussions.

- Male students might exclude their female and non-binary peers from contributing to a group project and question their capabilities.

tokenism Treating a single individual as representative of an entire group or allowing the presence of a few people with marginalized identities to give an illusion of representation and inclusion.

While our interpersonal interactions can convey negative biases that reproduce inequitable power dynamics, they can also be used to contest inequities. As CS educators, we can work to understand our negative biases. We can strive to have interactions with students and families that are driven by a spirit of curiosity and openness rather than by stereotypes we might have been socialized into. When appropriate, we can call our colleagues in when we see interpersonal oppression happening around us and invite them to reflect on their own actions as a step toward disrupting inequity.

Amanda, the elementary CS teacher who shared about the ideological oppression she saw in her school, also recognized interpersonal oppression in her experiences with her students that resulted in lowering expectations for her bi/multilingual learners. She described:

> I struggled the last couple years with my third and fourth grade ENL [English as a New Language] classes. I had a hard time communicating with them at the beginning of the school year. I felt frustrated and the students did too. The more I tried to break things down, I realized that I lowered expectations and the work was too easy for them. Through PD [professional development] and lots of reflection, I realized that challenging them and giving them choice in the work was the recipe for success. I made things more personal and I challenged them with projects they could personalize, and they made so much more progress.

By adjusting her interpersonal interactions with her students to center their expertise and challenge them, Amanda was able to disrupt some of the inequities in her space and transform her students' experiences with CS.

MYTHBUSTING TIME!

Myth: Tech companies would hire more women and Black and Latine coders if there were enough of them out there with the requisite skills.

> Wrong! This statement needs more context. There are many more Black and Latine students of all gender identities graduating with CS degrees than there are working in tech jobs. As one article reported, "At the top 25 undergraduate programs, nearly 9% of graduates are underrepresented minorities. . . . But technical workers at Google, Microsoft, Facebook, and Twitter, according to the companies' diversity reports, are on average 56% white, 37% Asian, 3% Hispanic, and 1% Black" (Bui & Miller, 2016).
>
> Applying the interpersonal lens from the Four I's can help us uncover some reasons why these statistics exist. First, hiring managers at tech companies may be acting on implicit or explicit biases. They may look more favorably on candidates who have

traits and life experiences that are associated with the white, Ivy League–educated males that predominate the industry. Many talented STEM graduates earn degrees from Historically Black Colleges and Universities, but employers often erroneously assume that these programs are not as rigorous as those at predominately white institutions (Tiku, 2021).

Hiring managers might also draw on ideologies like the "model minority" myth in their decision making. This myth perpetuates the stereotype that members of Asian and Asian American groups are better suited to STEM fields than other minoritized groups (Jin, 2021). Making hiring decisions based on this myth glosses over the racism that members of "model minority" groups experience in the field and pits marginalized groups against each other, furthering inequity (Chen & Buell, 2018; McGee, 2018; Shah, 2021).

A second contributing factor relates to the interpersonal dynamics within the CS industry. The people who make up a company establish the culture there, including the in-jokes and ways of talking, dressing, and behaving. Members of tech industry communities may perpetuate cultures of exclusion through their interpersonal interactions as they maintain their tech culture. This might happen through privileging the experiences and cultural references of dominant groups, through **microaggressions**; through overt acts of racism, classism, or sexism; or through tokenizing. (See Daniels et al., 2019, for a racial analysis of the tech industry; Margolis & Fisher, 2003, for a gender analysis; and Noble & Roberts, 2019, for an analysis that considers race, class, and gender.)

microaggression
Common, everyday slights (verbal or behavioral) toward socially marginalized groups or individuals; microaggressions may be intentional or unintentional, but they still significantly impact those receiving them.

While the other Four I's can shed additional light on issues that contribute to a lack of diversity in the tech industry, it's important to recognize how interpersonal forms of oppression play a key role.

INTERNALIZED OPPRESSION AND INEQUITY

internalized oppression
Acceptance of negative stereotypes about one's own group, leading to self-doubt and discouragement.

Systems of oppression can also include **internalized oppression** felt by individuals. Individuals who hold identities that are marginalized are often socialized, sometimes harshly, into the idea that they have no place in CS and related fields. Similarly, those who hold identities that are afforded power and privilege are socialized to the idea that they do belong in CS and "others" don't.

How do students develop and internalize these deficit views of themselves? The other three I's can contribute to the internalized layer of oppression. The ideological myth of meritocracy positions success as solely linked to skill or effort, so if students struggle in CS courses, they might internalize their difficulties as a personal weakness. This interpretation can create doubt in their abilities and erode confidence. Interpersonal interactions may also contribute to internalized oppression as students may hear messages from peers, family members, educators, and even guidance counselors about what they would or would not be good at, leading them to avoid CS courses. Institutionalized policies like those that require prerequisites for CS courses (e.g., calculus or algebra) can lead a student to second-guess their abilities even though skills from the prerequisite courses may not be required to succeed in the CS course.

Internalized oppression is often based on harmful stereotypes and assumptions (McGarr et al., 2023). The effects of negative stereotypes are often addressed, but expecting students to live up to positive stereotypes like the model minority myth described earlier can be just as damaging to students' sense of belonging, self-efficacy, and agency (McGee, 2018). Research has shown that just knowing that a stereotype exists and being afraid of confirming that stereotype can interfere with learning and performance (Steele & Aronson, 1995). Anything that makes stereotypes more apparent in a setting, like asking students to identify their race or ethnicity on an exam, makes learners more likely to respond in ways that reinforce the stereotype (Steele, 2011). Introductory "weed out" courses that are intentionally designed to push out students who are considered less likely to succeed in CS are one example. Historically, students who are "weeded out" have been disproportionately Black, Indigenous, Latine, and female (Weston et al., 2019).

While internalized forms of oppression can be particularly harmful and pervasive, educators can also have a great deal of influence when it comes to students' mindsets. We can support our students to think critically about and resist messages that frame them and their communities in deficit ways. We can also expose them to role models that represent where they come from and advocate for policies that foster their budding interests in CS fields.

CS teacher Nicole described how reflecting on her own biases helped her recognize how interpersonal and internalized oppression might be connected in her work. Nicole noticed that she might be making assumptions that contribute to inequitable interpersonal interactions. Nicole shared:

> As the CS teacher in my school, trying to build my CS team is so difficult. Older teachers are always hesitant to learn CS Ed. . . . Often younger teachers are more willing. Am I making

this stereotype about older teachers? Are their own views of internalized oppression making them doubt themselves and lack confidence or interest? This made me think about how to approach them differently. At the beginning of the year, I am going to sit down and ask them different questions to see if I can spark a new interest in CS, change their internalized beliefs that cause them to avoid CS, and get more teachers involved in CS Ed.

Nicole recognized how rather than stereotyping teachers, she could address her own assumptions and biases. Then, she could intentionally plan for interactions that might explore and potentially alleviate some of the teachers' concerns that could come from internalized negative views about CS.

MYTHBUSTING TIME!

Myth: Internalized oppression is just that—internal. It often comes out as self-talk and might sound like students telling themselves myths like, "Only guys do well in the AP CSP class. I don't want to be the only woman and student with a disability in the class. There's no way I can succeed."

Wrong! As with many instances of internalized oppression, the myth is based on assumptions and stereotypes that are false. The AP CSP course was designed to be an introductory course and to welcome all learners with interest.

Unfortunately, self-talk like this happens when students absorb false messages from society about how their identity and their experiences are negatively linked to their potential. Students experiencing internalized oppression based on this myth may be reacting to past experiences in unsupportive learning environments that made them feel less than capable.

For example, many schools do not serve students with disabilities well and may even track students with disabilities away from AP courses. Students with identities at the intersection of disability and other marginalized identities may experience this oppression in distinct ways. A white student with a disability may be more likely to receive adequate special education services than a Black or Latine student, an affluent student would be more likely to receive adequate services than a low-income student, a monolingual English-speaking student may be more likely to receive services than a multilingual student labeled as an English Language Learner. An Asian student with a disability might experience undue pressure to perform well in an AP course because of the "model-minority stereotype" that assumes that students from Asian backgrounds are educationally and economically successful (McGee, 2018). Students with multiple marginalized identities are uniquely impacted by internalized oppression.

Similarly, high school AP CS teachers may not be prepared to support students with disabilities or to teach computing in ways that are relevant to students' interests, cultures, and identities. It is easy to interpret deficiencies in a learning environment as deficiencies in oneself. This primes students to internalize oppression felt through a lack of belonging or **imposter syndrome**.

> **imposter syndrome**
> Feelings and beliefs of intellectual and professional inferiority or incompetence; "a perceived self-doubt in one's abilities and accomplishments compared with others, despite evidence to the contrary" (Walker & Saklofske, 2023, n.p.).

REVISITING EMILY'S STORY

As Emily learned about the theories discussed in this chapter, she recognized that the myth about multilingual students at her school not being able to do CS was connected in part to an institutionalized layer of inequity. Thankfully, the administration at Emily's school also recognized this. Emily described how the admin "are very adamant about students receiving CS education and have now tied parent events to the CS courses. Parents are invited a few times a year to see what their child has worked on and the events are very well attended." Connecting CS learning to a schoolwide event helped disrupt institutional inequity because the teachers at Emily's school have become more diligent in implementing CS for all students. Emily concluded that "the students LOVE showing off their work and the parents are really thankful for the CS education their children are receiving." Emily's experience shows how using theories can help us recognize how inequities are being reproduced in our environments so that we can work to disrupt them.

REFLECTION QUESTIONS

1. How does applying the theories of intersectionality and the Four I's of Oppression and Advantage help you make sense of inequities in CS Ed? How might you apply these theories in your contexts?

2. What myths exist in the spaces you work in? How can you use the theories in this chapter to understand and combat those myths?

TAKEAWAYS FOR PRACTICE

- Reflect on how intersectionality applies to you and how your intersectional identities influence your work as an educator. Consider changes you might make in your setting to better attend to the intersectional identities of students.

- Identify one myth in this chapter that is relevant to your work. Apply the Four I's to determine whether that myth is influenced by ideological, institutional/structural, interpersonal, or internalized oppression (or some combination of the four). Create an action plan to start addressing this myth in your setting.

GLOSSARY

Term	Definition
ableism	Implicit or explicit social preference for nondisabled bodies and minds that creates prejudice and oppression of disability and disabled people (Shew, 2020).
classism	A system of prejudice and discrimination in favor of people with higher socioeconomic status (e.g., upper middle-class) and against people with lower socioeconomic status (e.g., lower class).
Four I's of Oppression and Advantage	A theory that illustrates how systems of oppression and advantage (like ableism, classism, or racism) are produced across multiple layers of society. The Four I's are ideological, institutional, interpersonal, and internalized. (See Bell, 2013; Chan & Coney, 2020; Chinook Fund, n.d.; Kuttner, 2016.)
ideological oppression	Dominant sets of beliefs and values that justify and maintain systems of oppression; often disguised as "common sense."
ideologies	Systems of ideas that circulate in society. Dominant ideologies perpetuate ideas that reinforce the supremacy of certain groups over others.

imposter syndrome	Feelings and beliefs of intellectual and professional inferiority or incompetence; "a perceived self-doubt in one's abilities and accomplishments compared with others, despite evidence to the contrary" (Walker & Saklofske, 2023, n.p.).
institutional oppression	Structures and policies within institutions that disadvantage certain groups and benefit others.
internalized oppression	Acceptance of negative stereotypes about one's own group, leading to self-doubt and discouragement.
interpersonal oppression	Prejudice and discrimination experienced by individuals or small groups in interpersonal interactions.
intersectionality	A theory that recognizes how people's different identities (e.g., disability, gender, race) overlap and intersect, creating access to privilege or resulting in oppression in ways that cannot be understood or addressed by considering each identity separately (Crenshaw, 1991; Collins, 2019).
marginalization	The social process of excluding or oppressing individuals who hold identities that are devalued or differ from society's "ideal" norm.
matrix of domination	Intersecting systems of power that produce distinct and interlocking forms of oppression (Combahee River Collective, 1977; Collins, 2019).
microaggression	Common, everyday slights (verbal or behavioral) toward socially marginalized groups or individuals; microaggressions may be intentional or unintentional, but they still significantly impact those receiving them.
racism	A system of prejudice and discrimination based on race that privileges individuals racialized as white and oppresses racially minoritized individuals.
sexism	A system of prejudice and discrimination based on gender and gender identity that privileges men and oppresses women, non-binary, and gender-fluid individuals.
structural oppression	Historically maintained structures and policies across institutions (e.g., the CS industry, education) that disadvantage certain groups and benefit others over time.

theory	A set of ideas based on scholarship and practice that are used to explain and interpret how society works.
tokenism	Treating a single individual as representative of an entire group or allowing the presence of a few people with marginalized identities to give an illusion of representation and inclusion.
xenophobia	A system of prejudice and discrimination against foreigners.

REFERENCES

Annamma, S. A., Connor, D., & Ferri, B. (2013). Dis/ability critical race studies (DisCrit): Theorizing at the intersections of race and dis/ability. *Race Ethnicity and Education, 16*(1), 1–31. https://doi.org/10.1080/13613324.2012.730511

Bang, M., Warren, B., Rosebery, A. S., & Medin, D. (2012). Desettling expectations in science education. *Human Development, 55*(5–6), 302–318. https://doi.org/10.1159/000345322

Bell, J. (2013). *The four "I's" of oppression*. Begin Within. https://beginwithin.info/articles-2/

Beyer, S. (2014). Why are women underrepresented in Computer Science? Gender differences in stereotypes, self-efficacy, values, and interests and predictors of future CS course-taking and grades. *Computer Science Education, 24*(2–3), 153–192. https://doi.org/10.1080/08993408.2014.963363

Boaler, J., & Greeno, J. G. (2000). Identity, agency, and knowing in mathematics worlds. In J. Boaler (Ed.), *Multiple perspectives on mathematics teaching and learning* (pp. 171–200). Ablex Publishing. https://doi.org/10.5040/9798400688362.0011

Bui, Q., & Miller, C. C. (2016, Feb 25). Why tech degrees are not putting more Blacks and Hispanics into tech jobs. *New York Times*. https://www.nytimes.com/2016/02/26/upshot/dont-blame-recruiting-pipeline-for-lack-of-diversity-in-tech.html

Buolamwini, J. (2019, Jan 25). Response: Racial and gender bias in Amazon Rekognition—Commercial AI system for analyzing faces. *Medium*. https://medium.com/@Joy.Buolamwini/response-racial-and-gender-bias-in-amazon-rekognition-commercial-ai-system-for-analyzing-faces-a289222eeced

Carey, R. L. (2024). Criminalized or stigmatized? An intersectional power analysis of the charter school treatment of Black and Latino boys. *Urban Education*, 00420859241227947. https://doi.org/10.1177/00420859241227947

Chan, E. L., & Coney, L. (2020). Moving TESOL forward: Increasing educators' critical consciousness through a racial lens. *TESOL Journal, 11*(4), 1–13. https://doi.org/10.1002/tesj.550

Chen, G. A., & Buell, J. Y. (2018). Of models and myths: Asian (Americans) in STEM and the neoliberal racial project. *Race Ethnicity and Education, 21*(5), 607–625. https://doi.org/10.1080/13613324.2017.1377170

Chinook Fund. (n.d.) *4 I's of oppression.* https://chinookfund.org/wp-content/uploads/2015/10/Supplemental-Information-for-Funding-Guidelines.pdf

Collins, P. H. (2019). *Intersectionality as critical social theory.* Duke University Press. https://doi.org/10.1515/9781478007098

Combahee River Collective. (1977). *The Combahee River Collective statement.* BlackPast. https://www.blackpast.org/african-american-history/combahee-river-collective-statement-1977/

Crenshaw, K. (1989). Demarginalizing the intersection of race and sex: A Black feminist critique of antidiscrimination doctrine, feminist theory and antiracist politics. *University of Chicago Legal Forum, 1*(8), 139–167.

Crenshaw, K. (1991). Mapping the margins: Intersectionality, identity politics, and violence against women of color. *Stanford Law Review, 43*(6), 1241–1299. https://doi.org/10.2307/1229039

Daniels, J., Nkonde, M., & Mir, D. (2019). *Advancing racial literacy in tech: Why ethics, diversity in hiring & implicit bias trainings aren't enough.* Data and Society Fellowships Program. https://datasociety.net/wp-content/uploads/2019/05/Racial_Literacy_Tech_Final_0522.pdf

Devine, C., Byington, L., & News21 Staff. (2018, Aug 16). *Millions are victims of hate crimes, though many never report them.* Center for Public Integrity. https://publicintegrity.org/politics/millions-are-victims-of-hate-crimes-though-many-never-report-them/

Dugan, J. (2021). Beware of equity traps and tropes. *Educational Leadership, 78*(6), 35–40.

Ericson, B. (2023, Apr 10). *AP CS data for 2022.* Computing for Everyone. https://cs4all.home.blog/

Esposito, J., & Evans-Winters, V. (2021). *Introduction to intersectional qualitative research* (1st ed.). SAGE Publications.

Fairclough, N. (2014). *Language and power* (3rd ed.). Routledge. https://doi.org/10.4324/9781315838250

Garfinkel, H. (1967). *Studies in ethnomethodology.* Polity Press.

Gross, T. (2023, June 12). *Central Park birder Christian Cooper on being "a Black man in the natural world."* NPR. https://www.npr.org/2023/06/12/1181314626/central-park-birder-christian-cooper-on-being-a-black-man-in-the-natural-world

Jin, C. H. (2021, May 25). *6 charts that dismantle the trope of Asian Americans as a model minority.* NPR. https://www.npr.org/2021/05/25/999874296/6-charts-that-dismantle-the-trope-of-asian-americans-as-a-model-minority

Kendi, I. X. (2019). *How to be an antiracist.* One World.

Kuttner, P. J. (2016). Hip-hop citizens: Arts-based, culturally sustaining civic engagement pedagogy. *Harvard Educational Review, 86*(4), 527–555. https://doi.org/10.17763/1943-5045-86.4.527

Leonardo, Z. (2007). *Teaching whiteness in a multicultural context and color-blind era* [Video-stream]. University of British Columbia Centre for Culture, Identity and Education. https://www.youtube.com/watch?v=Lma988cWi5A

Losen, D. J. (2011). *Discipline policies, successful schools, and racial justice*. National Education Policy Center. http://nepc.colorado.edu/publication/discipline-policies

Margolis, J. & Fisher, A. (2003). *Unlocking the clubhouse: Women in computing*. MIT Press.

McGarr, O., Exton, C., Power, J., & McInerney, C. (2023). What about the gatekeepers? School principals and school guidance counselors attitudes towards computer science in secondary schools. *Computer Science Education, 33*(2), 168–185. https://doi.org/10.1080/08993408.2021.1953296

McGee, E. (2018). Black genius, Asian fail: The detriment of stereotype lift and stereotype threat in high-achieving Asian and Black STEM students. *AERA Open, 4*(4). https://doi.org/10.1177/2332858418816658

McGee, E. O., & Bentley, L. (2017). The equity ethic: Black and Latinx college students reengineering their STEM careers toward justice. *American Journal of Education, 124*, 1–36. https://doi.org/10.1086/693954

McKinsey & Company. (2024, Sep 17). Women in the workplace 2024: The 10th-anniversary report. https://www.mckinsey.com/featured-insights/diversity-and-inclusion/women-in-the-workplace

Noble, S. U., & Roberts, S. T. (2019). Technological elites, the meritocracy, and postracial myths in Silicon Valley. In R. Mukherjee, S. Banet-Weiser, & H. Gray (Eds.), *Racism Postrace* (pp. 113–129). Duke University Press. https://doi.org/10.1515/9781478003250-007

Noguera, P. A. (2003). Schools, prisons, and social implications of punishment: Rethinking disciplinary practices. *Theory into Practice, 42*(4), 341–350. https://doi.org/10.1207/s15430421tip4204_12

Radke, S. C., Vogel, S. E., Ma, J. Y., Hoadley, C., & Ascenzi-Moreno, L. (2022). Emergent bilingual middle schoolers syncretic reasoning in statistical modeling. *Teachers College Record, 124*(5), 206–228. https://doi.org/10.1177/01614681221104141

Rankin, Y. A., Thomas, J. O., & Erete, S. (2021). Black Women Speak: Examining Power, Privilege, and Identity in CS Education. *ACM Transactions on Computing Education, 21*(4), 1–31. https://doi.org/10.1145/3451344

Shah, N. (2021, Mar 19). *Asians are good at math? Why dressing up racism as a compliment just doesn't add up.* The Conversation. https://theconversation.com/asians-are-good-at-math-why-dressing-up-racism-as-a-compliment-just-doesnt-add-up-128731

Shew, A. (2020). Ableism, technoableism, and future AI. *IEEE Xplore, 39*(1), 40–85. https://doi.org/10.1109/MTS.2020.2967492

Smith, R. A. (2022, July 31). Black and Hispanic employees often get stuck at the lowest rung of the workplace. *The Wall Street Journal*. https://www.wsj.com/articles/black-hispanic-employees-stuck-lowest-rung-workplace-11659131490

Steele, C. M. (2011). *Whistling Vivaldi: How stereotypes affect us and what we can do*. W. W. Norton & Company.

Steele, C. M., & Aronson, J. (1995). Stereotype threat and the intellectual test performance of African Americans. *Journal of Personality and Social Psychology, 69*(5), 797–811. https://doi.org/10.1037/0022-3514.69.5.797

Tatum, B. D. (2003). *Why are all the Black kids sitting together in the cafeteria? And other conversations about race.* Basic Books.

The Sojourner Truth Project. (1851). *The Sojourner Truth project.* https://www.thesojournertruthproject.com/

Tiku, N. (2021, Mar 4). Google's approach to historically Black schools helps explain why there are few Black engineers in Big Tech. *Washington Post.* https://www.washingtonpost.com/technology/2021/03/04/google-hbcu-recruiting/

Tucker, A. (2003). *A model curriculum for K–12 computer science: Final report of the ACM K–12 task force curriculum committee.* Association for Computing Machinery (ACM). https://dl.acm.org/doi/pdf/10.1145/2593247

Vogel, S. (2020). *Translanguaging about, with, and through code and computing: Emergent bi/multilingual middle schoolers forging computational literacies.* [Doctoral Dissertation, City University of New York]. https://academicworks.cuny.edu/cgi/viewcontent.cgi?article=5015&context=gc_etds

Walker, D. L., & Saklofske, D. H. (2023). Development, factor structure, and psychometric validation of the impostor phenomenon assessment: A novel assessment of imposter phenomenon. *Assessment, 30*(7), 2162–2183. https://doi.org/10.1177/10731911221141870

Weston, T. J., Seymour, E., Koch, A. K., & Drake, B. M. (2019). Weed-out classes and their consequences. In E. Seymour & A. Hunter (Eds.), *Talking about leaving revisited: Persistence, relocation and loss in undergraduate STEM education* (pp. 197–243). Springer. https://doi.org/10.1007/978-3-030-25304-2_7

Wilkerson, I. (2020). *Caste: The origins of our discontents.* Random House.

Wille, S., Century, J., & Pike, M. (2017). Exploratory research to expand opportunities in computer science for students with learning differences. *Computing in Science and Engineering, 19*(3), 40–50. https://doi.org/10.1109/MCSE.2017.43

RESOURCE 1: APPLYING THE THEORIES IN ACTION

Intersectionality and the Four I's of Oppression and Advantage provide tools that CS educators can use to make sense of what happens in CS classrooms. These theories also work well when combined together. Let's use them to unpack an experience shared by Jade, a Black woman graduate student interviewed as part of a study done by Rankin and colleagues (2021).

As you read Jade's story, try to apply the theories discussed in this chapter. The reflection questions can help with this. When you're ready, read some of the ways that the theories could apply to Jade's experience. There may also be other applications you recognize that aren't described here!

JADE'S STORY

Jade was a Black woman and graduate student enrolled in an undergraduate programming class with a group project assignment. Because there were only a few women enrolled in the course, Jade ended up in a group with three white males. As the group brainstormed how to solve the assigned programming problem, Jade offered several ideas for finding a solution, but her suggestions were rejected by her peers. Jade went along with what the group decided even though she suspected that the direction they were going in wouldn't work. Jade described how she followed her group's lead because she "wanted to be a team player" (Rankin et al., 2021, p. 17). As the project deadline approached without a solution, Jade ended up solving the problem on her own at home. The next day, because her group was still struggling, Jade showed them her solution. Her peer tried to take credit for the solution as something he had suggested earlier, but Jade refused to let her solution and her contribution go unacknowledged.

REFLECTION QUESTIONS

- How does the theory of intersectionality help us understand Jade's story?
- Where can you identify each of the four I's of oppression and advantage (ideological, institutional, interpersonal, and internalized) in Jade's experiences?

POSSIBLE APPLICATIONS OF THE THEORIES

INTERSECTIONALITY

Rankin and colleagues analyzed Jade's experience through the lens of intersectionality. Jade emphasized in her interview with them how her intersectional identity as a Black woman shaped how she was positioned in her group. Jade was not valued as an equal contributor to her group, given credit for her work or invited to fully collaborate with her peers. Jade described being unsure if her peers' treatment of her during the project was "because of her race or her gender" (Rankin et al., 2021, p. 17).

Intersectionality helps us understand how it may not really matter whether Jade can untangle which parts of her experience were influenced by her racial identity or by her gender identity. Instead, her experience unfolded how it did because of how her racial and gender identities intertwined. The authors emphasized this point: "Black women deal with these kinds of microaggressions on a routine basis and can never discern if it is their gender or their race that causes their White male peers to dismiss them as being incompetent computer scientists" (Rankin et al., 2021, p. 17).

THE FOUR I'S OF OPPRESSION AND ADVANTAGE

The Four I's of Oppression and Advantage also provide insights into Jade's experience. The *interpersonal* oppression is especially clear in this story. The peers in her group, all white males, rejected and excluded Jade's contributions as a Black woman throughout their group interactions. The group's response to Jade may be influenced by *ideological* oppression that perpetuates ideas of women and racially marginalized individuals as being less capable at programming and computing than white males. We can also recognize *institutional* oppression in the structural patterns that resulted in Jade being one of only a few women enrolled in her programming course. However, Jade's story provides a counterexample to *internalized* oppression. Rather than accepting the devaluing of her work, Jade instead refused to allow her peers to take credit for her work.

6

Building Your Computer Science Education Equity Toolkit

Lloyd Talley, Sara Vogel, Sarane James, Spence J. Ray, Christy Crawford, Lauren Vogelstein, Christopher Hoadley, Wendy Barrales, Stephanie T. Jones, and the Computer Science Educational Justice Collective

Acknowledgements: Melissa Parker

CHAPTER OVERVIEW

This chapter lays a foundation for developing an equity-oriented praxis, or engaging in reflection and learning to take action to transform computer science education (CS Ed). The chapter offers guidance to support educators in journaling and dialogue practices to develop self-awareness. There are six reflection topics with prompts that invite teachers to consider their own identities and what that means for talking about topics like race, identity, and power with students; their past experiences with schooling and CS; and their motivations as CS educators. Journaling and reflection as part of developing self-awareness are important practices that are part of building an equity toolkit.

CHAPTER OBJECTIVES

After reading this chapter, I can:

- Explore my identities, past experiences, and motivations and how they shape my work as a CS educator.

- Journal and dialogue with critical friends to practice self-awareness and educate myself about historical and contemporary issues of (in)equity in CS Ed as part of personal development.

- Identify actions that I can take to work toward equity in CS Ed that are based on my reflections.

KEY TERMS

ableism; affinity group; antisemitism; archaeology of self; classism; critical friend; dead angle; gatekeeping; homophobia; intersectionality; praxis; racism; self-efficacy; sexism; transmisia/transphobia; trigger

AMANDA AND YEIDY'S STORIES

One of the most important steps you can take in your journey toward equity-centered CS Ed is to deepen your self-awareness and continue your learning about equity. These ongoing efforts will help you strengthen the skills you'll need to notice, process, and respond to issues of inequity. As CS educator Karime noted, "There is no script that you can follow to respond to equity issues. This type of preparation is essential to be able to think on your feet and respond appropriately without creating further issues yourself."

Given the intensity of an average school day, it can be difficult for teachers to stop and notice when their practices or when policies and wider systems are causing inequitable outcomes or harms. It can also be a challenge to find space and time to work toward interrupting inequitable patterns and resolving situations in an equitable manner. This chapter provides supports to hold space for this work. It will help you better understand yourself and your own role in systems that create just or unjust outcomes (Stevenson, 2014). Critical and continuous learning about your own identities and about historical and current power dynamics is a key part of this work (Price-Dennis & Sealey-Ruiz, 2021). Teachers in CS should pay special attention to the dynamics that shape CS fields, education, and broader society.

Most of this chapter is dedicated to providing you with resources so that you can learn through journaling and self-reflection. We wish to begin the chapter with an important note. Some of the topics and prompts invite you to dig deeply into your past and may be connected to challenging or traumatic past experiences that surface difficult emotions (e.g., fear, overwhelm, shame). Grappling with strong emotions can be an important part of this learning. However, we encourage you to prioritize caring for yourself—mentally, physically, and emotionally—as you do this work.

Caring for yourself will look different for everyone. We provide some suggested social-emotional supports in Resource 2 that can help as you engage in the activities in this chapter. We also invite you to draw on additional resources as needed.

With this caution in mind, to begin this journey, we share stories from two teachers, Amanda and Yeidy, who described their personal growth as they have engaged in practices to support self-awareness and become more equity-minded CS educators.

Amanda shared:

> When I first started my equity journey, I learned a lot more than I thought I would. I thought, "I work in a diverse environment. I love all of my students, and I do not have any biases." I believed I was someone who knew myself and did not need to do so much of this work. However, I found that I was wrong.
>
> Digging deep into family experiences and my culture and thinking about how marginalized individuals may have felt at different times gave me real perspective. I thought more deeply about how my students felt during times of unrest and how they saw people who looked like them being brutalized by police and seen as "others" in this country.

Yeidy described her experiences as well:

affinity group A group of people with shared identities who come together to connect around a common goal.

> One thing that I found very helpful for me to engage in critical and continuous learning was joining my **affinity group**. I had never unpacked my own identity before, so it was very powerful to read *For Brown Girls with Sharp Edges and Tender Hearts* in a book club-style format with other Latinx people.
>
> My family is from Puerto Rico, so my experiences as a Latina woman here in New York City are very different from those immigrating from another country. I was able to read about and experience life through the eyes of a Latinx immigrant. My school's demographics show we have 79% Hispanic, and the majority of those students are recent immigrants from South American countries. Reading this book helps me see things through some of those students' perspectives.[1]

---

1. *For Brown Girls with Sharp Edges and Tender Hearts: A Love Letter to Women of Color* is a non-fiction book written by Prisca Dorcas Mojica Rodríguez. We also note that we preserve Yeidy's original terminology; see the On Terminology section of this guide for an explanation on our use of different identity-related terms.

These stories show how equity work is personal work. Amanda and Yeidy described unique journeys deeply linked to their own identities. Engaging in the practices outlined in this chapter supported both of them to expand their perspectives and grow to become CS teachers working toward equity in powerful ways.

THE ROLE OF SELF-AWARENESS IN BUILDING AN EQUITY TOOLKIT

As we recognize the complex inequities in CS and CS Ed (see Chapter 3), getting started doing equity work can feel daunting. But avoiding equity work because of its nuance and complexity only reinforces the status quo. At the same time, addressing equity issues is a long-term process. It isn't a "quick fix" that you can easily add to your existing teaching practices. It's something more fundamental and transformational, requiring committed work every day. It requires self-examination and learning that lead to intervening in and changing harmful policies, practices, and systems. It also requires accepting that there is no way to do this work perfectly. Everyone will make mistakes and can learn from them and do better. What works for one teacher may not work well for another because we all have different backgrounds, serve different groups of students, and face different situations. What is most important is to continue our efforts as part of an ongoing journey.

A key foundational step of this work is self-awareness, or being able to "read, discuss, and write about situations that address . . . inequity and . . . bias as part of the norm of the schooling process" (Price-Dennis & Sealey-Ruiz, 2021, p. 22). Self-awareness goes beyond learning one-off techniques to use with students. Instead, it involves committing yourself to lifelong, continuous learning that leads to individual and collective action. Self-awareness is a key component of an equity-oriented **praxis**.

We experience the world through our own perspectives and angles. As teachers, we bring our whole selves into the classroom—our bodies, our experiences, our beliefs and values. All of these shape what we notice and prioritize and whether and how we feel empowered to act (Rodgers & Scott, 2008). Our personal perspectives can support us to promote equitable change. We can influence practice by being positively biased toward values like social justice and affirming diversity. At the same time, we may also have **dead angles**, or areas related to equity work that we can't see from our current perspectives, that keep us from promoting equitable classroom changes (Copur-Gencturk et al., 2020). These dead angles may come simply because we lack awareness or experience with a given topic.

praxis The combination of teaching practices and theory. This guide supports praxis by providing theories about equity that help teachers develop mindsets to take transformative action toward equitable CS education.

dead angles An issue or topic related to equity that a person lacks awareness of or experience with or holds negative biases in ways that prevent equitable change. It also avoids ableism implicit in terms like "blind spot."

When this is the case, learning more about an issue can help us expand our perspectives and make changes. Other times, our dead angles may be based in negative biases about groups of people. In these instances, we may need to engage in deep self-reflection to shift our mindsets and beliefs. Learning to recognize and work on both types of dead angles is an important part of self-awareness as part of our equity toolkit. CS teacher Christina shared how she recognized a dead angle that she was previously unaware of as she heard students share their experiences and made changes to her classroom practice as a result:

> A time that I found a "dead angle" was when I found out about something that I would describe as "invisible disabilities." As a teacher, we are taught to manage the disabilities that we can see. I was doing a PD [professional development] about disabilities and there were students talking about how they have disabilities, and I would never have guessed. . . . Students deal with some internal struggles that might not present like we are used to. . . . These students may or may not "look normal."
>
> Since experiencing this, I am more sensitive to students who appear distressed with tasks or activities that I deem simple. I try to create a "stress-free" environment for my classroom, so that all students know that it is never a problem for however they want to interact. I worry about those students who suffer in silence and try to help.

trigger A topic or conversation that surfaces strong emotions or memories; triggers can motivate equitable action or reproduce inequitable patterns.

self-efficacy A belief in one's ability to accomplish a task or achieve a goal.

As we noted in the beginning of the chapter, given our past experiences and backgrounds, particular conversations about power and oppression in society might be difficult. Everyone has topics that are challenging for them to engage with. These topics might **trigger** us, or surface strong emotions or memories. Triggers can motivate us to take actions that promote equitable practice, or they can lead us to reproduce patterns that limit equitable changes. It is important to be aware of our triggers and develop coping strategies to manage our emotional responses to these topics. (See Resource 2 for ideas.) Stronger **self-efficacy**, or confidence in discussing topics related to identity, can help us better notice and respond to equity issues in our settings. Proactive coping strategies in the moment can also help groups address conflicts that may arise or tensions that prevail when dialoguing about equity issues. As we develop these strategies for ourselves as individuals, we are better able to create classroom cultures that can support students when they face triggers of their own. Although addressing equity issues out loud can be challenging, it is necessary. Silence often contributes to inequity and marginalization.

While this chapter centers on self-awareness, it is important to recognize that promoting equitable CS Ed is the work of collectives, not just individuals. Equity work can be emotionally stressful and taxing when taken on by just a few. This can lead to burn-out, which doesn't advance equitable changes at all! People whose identities have been marginalized in CS Ed often end up doing a disproportionate amount of equity work because they can't as easily ignore inequity. But people who are afforded privilege based on their identities also have a responsibility to learn for themselves about equity issues and to use their privilege to work toward changes for educational justice (Love, 2019).

JOURNALING AND DIALOGUE TO DEVELOP SELF-AWARENESS

Being willing to probe deeply into your experiences, beliefs, values, and motivations is key to developing self-awareness on your journey to becoming a CS Ed equity leader. Scholars like Sealey-Ruiz call this work an **archaeology of self**, or the "deep excavation and exploration of beliefs, biases, and ideas that shape how we engage in the work [of equity]" (Sealey-Ruiz, 2022, p. 22).

There are many ways to engage in this reflection toward self-awareness. In this chapter, we focus on journaling and dialogue as activities that can deepen your understanding of equity and lead to meaningful action. Journaling involves reflecting and recording your thoughts in words, images, mapping, or another format that resonates with you. Dialoguing involves sharing some of those thoughts and reflections with critical friends and engaging in open conversation about the topics. (See Resource 3 for more on finding critical friends.) We invite you to tailor both practices to what works best for you. Below is an overview of how to engage in these practices.

archaeology of self The "deep excavation and exploration of beliefs, biases, and ideas that shape how we engage in the work [of equity]" (Sealey-Ruiz, 2022, p. 22).

CULTIVATING JOURNALING AND DIALOGUE PRACTICES TOWARD EQUITABLE CS ED

PREPARING FOR YOUR REFLECTION

Before diving into a prompt, take a moment to settle into a calm space. Remember that these practices are a safe space for honest introspection and open discussion. Let curiosity guide your approach. Be willing to challenge your existing perspectives and embrace the opportunity to learn from diverse viewpoints.

PENNING YOUR REFLECTIONS

Dedicate some quiet time to capturing your reflections. Delve into your chosen prompt. Let your pen flow freely, capturing your thoughts, feelings, and questions without a filter. Feel free to draw, write, code, or use any other way of recording your reflections. Take as long as you need. Be unafraid to explore personal experiences and assumptions, connecting your reflections to the broader context of (in)equity and CS Ed.

SHARING YOUR INSIGHTS

Join forces with a critical friend, an accountability buddy, or a small team. In this space, share your written musings, engage in respectful dialogue, and learn from each other's perspectives. Listen actively, ask clarifying questions, and offer open-minded support. Remember that the goal is not to reach a specific conclusion. Instead, work to enrich your understanding through shared exploration.

COLLECTIVELY DIALOGUING

Come together in a larger group to debrief your individual and partnered reflections. Share key takeaways, insights, and lingering questions. This collective dialogue acts as a catalyst for further learning. It also nurtures a supportive community to explore equity issues in CS.

CONTINUING THE JOURNEY

Periodically return to your journal. Reflect on your learning journey thus far. How has your understanding of equity issues evolved? How can you apply these insights to your future work, in classrooms, communities, or beyond? Let your journal serve as a roadmap for action, encouraging you to contribute to a more inclusive and equitable CS field.

Remember that journaling and dialogue are merely steppingstones on your path to embracing equitable change in CS. Let curiosity be your compass, dialogue your fuel, and action your ultimate destination.

This chapter provides prompts to reflect on the following topics:

1. Unpacking identity
2. Talking about race, identity, and power
3. Examining school experiences
4. Understanding your relationship to computing and CS
5. Considering your motivations
6. Relating your motivations to your students

Each topic begins with some background context and a rationale, followed by some questions to invite reflection. Feel free to focus on a specific question instead of all of them, follow the topics in any order, or return to a topic more than once. These topics are meant as a guide for your own personal journey, so you should use them in ways that are most helpful to you.

REFLECTION TOPIC 1: UNPACKING IDENTITY

Psychologist Beverly Daniel Tatum (2003) writes about "the complexity of identity." She notes that identity is not just about how you self-define but also about who the world tells you that you are, and how you and others like you are represented in the world. Are people like you missing from the story? Highlighted or privileged in the story?

Many aspects of identity combine with social contexts to help us integrate the past, the present, and the future into a cohesive sense of self. Tatum (2003) argues that there are seven core components of identity that most shape people's experiences in the United States: age, class, disability, gender, racialization/race, religion, and sexual orientation. Other salient identity markers in U.S. culture include our language practices, our nationality/ethnicity, our immigration status, our political party, and our geographic locations.

Identities are socially negotiated between the way we perceive ourselves and the way others and society position us. For example, in his book *Dreams from My Father* (1995), former President Barack Obama described how his own identity as a Black man developed in relation to the different places he lived. Because conceptualizations of race differ across cultures, Obama's experiences around race were not the same in Indonesia, Hawaii, and the continental United States. Although he was a Black man living in each of these places, the way he understood this identity and the way others interacted with him differed greatly across contexts.

The distinction between how society assigns us identities and how we choose to identify ourselves is sometimes complicated. An individual may identify as belonging to a particular racial group, but when filling out a government survey, that option might not appear. An individual might self-identify as a member of a socially marginalized racial group but may have physical features that lead others to assume that the individual is racialized as white, affording them certain social privileges (known as "passing"). How we and others self-identify and how identities are assigned to us based on social norms are important distinctions to be aware of.[2]

While individuals may experience marginalization or oppression for different reasons in different contexts, in the United States, certain identity groups have been systematically afforded privileges while other groups have been systematically afforded disadvantages. This inequity is due to long-standing historical and present-day processes that shape individual action and institutional practices. (See Chapter 5 for more on this.) For example, people racialized as Black Americans have been systematically afforded less power in U.S. society. Those racialized as white Americans have been afforded more power through processes like slavery, Jim Crow laws, and many other ways that racism has been reproduced in society over time. Groups have fought to change this reality over time, but racism remains a persistent fact of U.S. life. Because identity-based inequity shapes U.S. society, CS, and CS Ed, reflecting on our own identities is key to developing self-awareness.

How someone identifies with regard to one aspect of their identity (e.g., race or gender) doesn't necessarily imply a certain life experience. The labels applied to a person's identity may influence, but do not fully determine, their experiences. How people are socially identified in categories is a dynamic process. The theory of **intersectionality**, explored in Chapter 5, can shed light on how marginalization is experienced uniquely by groups at the intersections of multiple identity categories (Crenshaw, 1991).

As teachers, our identities can afford us privileges and/or disadvantages in our professional lives. For example, Kohli (2018) describes the racist microaggressions and race evasive discourse that racially minoritized teachers reported having to navigate. These oppressions took a toll on their ability to stay in the teaching workforce.

intersectionality A theory that asserts that different aspects of people's identity (e.g., disability, gender, race) overlap and intersect in ways that result in oppression that cannot be understood or addressed by focusing on each identity separately (Crenshaw, 1991; Collins, 2019).

---
2. Efforts to articulate this distinction have led to expressions like "racialized as" that imply that racial identity labels are socially constructed, and individuals may or may not self-identify with those labels.

The questions below will help you begin to unpack how power dynamics are connected to your identity and how they shape how you experience and perceive your teaching context and how others perceive you in that space. As you consider your many interrelated identities, we also invite you to think about how you can become what scholar activist Bettina Love calls "coconspirators."[3] Coconspirators is a positive term that describes those who move beyond allyship to take action and conspire against inequitable systems. They draw on the power and privilege afforded to them by society to work toward equitable change in educational spaces (Love, 2019).

> ### REFLECTION TOPIC 1 JOURNAL PROMPTS
>
> What are your many identities? Ask yourself . . .
>
> - What are your identities and many selves?
>
> - Are some of these identities more salient to you in some contexts than others? Why?
>
> - Which identities come readily to mind when you think about yourself? Which identities are not as salient for you (your dead angles)? Why?
>
> - Which identities are sources of pride for you? Why?
>
> - Which identities do you have a more complicated relationship with? Why?
>
> - How do institutions in society privilege and/or disadvantage people with identities like yours?
>
> - Have you ever had to suppress or repress particular identities in particular settings or institutions?
>
> - Have you ever had to suppress or repress particular identities in school? Do you have identities that were celebrated or cultivated in school?
>
> - Have you ever had empowering interactions with others related to one or more of your identities? Disempowering interactions?

---

3. Love spells this word without a hyphen.

> *Explore Further!* Try this social identity wheel activity from the Facing Histories and Ourselves project.⁴
>
> ---
> 4. The social identity wheel activity can be found at https://www.facinghistory.org/resource-library/social-identity-wheel

REFLECTION TOPIC 2: TALKING ABOUT RACE, IDENTITY, AND POWER

We all have different identities. We also have different comfort levels and experiences with talking about power and identity. Given our cultural backgrounds, some topics may be considered "taboo" or unacceptable to talk about in a given community. Some of us may hesitate to have conversations on topics like race, gender and sexual orientation, and power out of fear that such conversations could get us in trouble. Because these topics are hotly contested in the United States, some avoid conversations about power and identity entirely. In some states and districts, discussing such topics in classrooms might even be grounds for disciplinary action, a lawsuit, or harsh community backlash. This reality has been manifest in recent years through book bans and legislation limiting how teachers can discuss topics like race and gender.⁵

Some educators may feel more comfortable bringing up these topics and questioning social hierarchies. They may have had firsthand experience coping with oppressive conditions. They may have been in environments where curiosity about these issues was encouraged. They may be coming from a place of privilege, so they risk less by bringing up issues related to power. Or, they may have not experienced negative impacts from talking about these issues.

It is important to recognize that those who may feel comfortable talking about some issues of identity and power may feel less comfortable or prepared to talk about others. For example, one chapter author, a white Jewish woman, grew up talking about the effects of **antisemitism** with friends, family, and members of her community. Yet she also internalized a climate that put taboos around discussions about disability and race.

Part of building an equity toolkit is becoming more comfortable discussing issues of power and identity. Becoming a CS equity teacher leader

antisemitism A system of prejudice, discrimination, and hostility toward Jewish people.

---
5. You can track legislation related to different equity-related topics at https://www.edweek.org/policy-politics/map-where-critical-race-theory-is-under-attack/2021/06 and https://www.hrc.org/resources/state-maps

means engaging in these topics proactively with students and colleagues. You can create a solid foundation for engaging in dialogue on these topics by considering your own socialization into these topics, triggers that are difficult for you, and dead angles related to these concepts.

REFLECTION TOPIC 2 JOURNAL PROMPTS

How have you been socialized to discuss or avoid conversations about issues of identity and power? Ask yourself . . .

- How old were you when you first learned about issues related to:
  - **Ableism** and disability?
  - Class, wealth, and **classism**?
  - Diversity in sexual orientations and **homophobia**?
  - Gender, **sexism**, and **transphobia/transmisia**?
  - Homelessness and housing insecurity?
  - Immigration, ethnicity, and national identity?
  - Language diversity and language injustice?
  - Race and **racism**?
  - Religious diversity?
- What were those different experiences like? How did they make you feel?
- How, if at all, did your family members, caregivers, and teachers discuss race, culture, and other human differences? What was your personal experience with these conversations?
- Was your curiosity about these issues actively encouraged? Actively silenced?
- What are your triggers that signal an encounter with an equity issue that you are unfamiliar or uncomfortable with?
- What coping strategies do you use to navigate an encounter with an equity issue that you are unfamiliar or uncomfortable with?

---

ableism Implicit or explicit social preference for nondisabled bodies and minds that creates prejudice and oppression of disability and disabled people (Shew, 2020).

classism A system of prejudice and discrimination in favor of people with higher socioeconomic status (e.g., upper middle-class) and against people with lower socioeconomic status (e.g., lower class).

homophobia A system of prejudice and discrimination against or fear or discomfort with people who identify as LGBTQIA2S+.

sexism A system of prejudice and discrimination based on gender and gender identity that privileges men and oppresses women, non-binary, and gender-fluid individuals.

transphobia/transmisia Both terms describe a system of prejudice and discrimination against people who are transgender or non-binary and a fear or discomfort with people who are transgender or non-binary. "Transmisia" emphasizes how prejudice and discrimination are linked to hatred, revulsion, and disgust, rather than fear (KosmicKult, 2020). It is an alternative to ableist language connected with the word "phobia" (Planned Parenthood, n.d.).

racism A system of prejudice and discrimination based on race that privileges individuals racialized as white and oppresses racially minoritized individuals.

REFLECTION TOPIC 3: EXAMINING SCHOOL EXPERIENCES

Like most aspects of our lives, people's experiences with schooling are shaped by social and political influences related to identity. School systems may have biases embedded toward or against students with particular identities. For example, you may have been offered many opportunities to sign up for extracurricular programs to enrich your learning outside of school, or you may have had no such opportunities.

Your interpersonal interactions with classmates and educators also likely influenced how you experienced schooling. For example, if you are a member of a group that is afforded less power in society, you may have been exposed to oppressive conditions, prejudice, or microaggressions related to that identity that have added up over time. If you are a member of a group that is typically afforded more social power, you may have received positive messages about your potential. Or perhaps your experiences resist these patterns for particular reasons.

Your experiences affect your impressions of school growing up, which can inform how you currently teach. It's important to understand these schooling experiences so that you can understand why you may react in certain ways to things in your current school environment. Reflecting on your schooling experiences can also help you avoid recreating harms you may have experienced and help you pass on opportunities that were afforded to you.

It is equally important to recognize how your experiences may not be shared by students in your school, even when they share similar identities. These differences may be due to students' personal lives, how schools function, or how society has changed over time.

REFLECTION TOPIC 3 JOURNAL PROMPTS

What has been your relationship with schooling? Ask yourself . . .

- What do you remember about your different schooling experiences?

- What were some of your experiences with systems of oppression and advantage at school?

- Did you have teachers who made things relevant to your personal experiences, your interests, identities, and background?

> - Why did you become an educator? How, if at all, did that choice relate to aspects of your identity? How, if at all, did that choice relate to your experiences in school?

REFLECTION TOPIC 4: UNDERSTANDING YOUR RELATIONSHIP TO COMPUTING AND CS

How we relate to CS is shaped by our exposure to it. And our exposure to computing is often shaped by broader systems of oppression and advantage (see Chapter 5). Like any school subject, there are ways in which we have been encouraged or discouraged to engage with CS. Some of us may have been provided with access to new tools and technology at home from a young age. Others may have had to rely on low-resourced schools to expose them to technology. Some of us may have been encouraged to tinker with code or have been praised for our creativity for trying to "hack" or "mod" our favorite games. Others may have been outright discouraged from or denied access to CS or been informed that CS exploration was a waste of time.

In formal school settings, you may have been told that you were smart enough to take a CS class, or you may have been told that you would never make it in that environment. You may have associated technology with a nerdy subculture, which might have attracted you to computing or repelled you away. All of these factors affect your relationship to CS and influence how you talk to students and colleagues about their CS abilities. Understanding our own relationship to CS can help us break unhealthy cycles of exclusion and create more inclusive CS experiences for others.

> ### REFLECTION TOPIC 4 JOURNAL PROMPTS
>
> What has been your relationship with computing and CS? Ask yourself . . .
>
> - What does it mean to be a computer scientist?
> - Do you identify as a "computer scientist" or as a "techie person"?
> - Where do you find joy and/or meaning in CS or in computing?
> - What were some of your experiences with systems of oppression and disadvantage in CS?

> - How might your experiences navigating the world with your different identities shape your beliefs about who is thought to be capable of engaging in CS?
> - How might your experiences shape your beliefs about what computing is for?

REFLECTION TOPIC 5: CONSIDERING YOUR MOTIVATIONS

Educators come to teaching for many reasons, and CS educators come to CS teaching for many reasons. To promote equitable practices, it's important to understand your "why," or your motivation(s) for what you do. Are you looking to prepare the next generation for economic opportunities? Do you hope to support young people in expressing themselves creatively about issues they care about? Are you looking to promote skills like problem solving, collaborating, and persistence? Is coding with young people fun and fulfilling for you?

Our whys are unique and may be connected to our own histories. For example, some educators may feel a responsibility to provide opportunities for children because they did not get those same opportunities when they were students themselves. Conversely, they may wish to provide those opportunities because they did experience them as students and found them powerful and motivating.

Our whys propel us to act and keep us motivated on tough days. At the same time, not all rationales promote equitable classroom practices. For instance, we may make assumptions about who can thrive in CS based on our own experiences with **gatekeeping** in the field. Similarly, we should interrogate or challenge motivations for CS Ed that are rooted in savior complexes seeking to "save" or "rescue" marginalized groups through technology. These motivations can reproduce deficit narratives about students and disempower them. The following prompts will help you consider your own motivations for teaching CS.

gatekeeping Institutional policies and structures that control who gets to participate in opportunities and who has access to resources in ways that limit the participation of marginalized groups.

> ### REFLECTION TOPIC 5 JOURNAL PROMPTS
>
> Why are you motivated to teach CS? Ask yourself . . .
>
> - Which (if any) parts of your history and identity (e.g., disability, gender, language practices, race) have influenced your connection to CS?

> - How does CS intersect with your everyday life, your goals, and your identity?
> - How might your personal experiences with CS and technology relate to why you teach CS?
> - Is there a formative experience that you've had that helped you develop a sense of why CS is significant or consequential in your own or in others' lives?
> - Are there communities that you are a part of that use CS for purposes that are close to your heart?
> - What is the role of CS in the world?
> - How do you feel that CS plays a role in social justice?
>
> Explore Further! This CS Visions Toolkit from Computer Science for All is an additional resource that can help you determine your why and your vision for CS education.[6]
>
> ---
> 6. Access the Visions Toolkit at https://web.archive.org/web/20250121043919/https://csforall.org/visions/

REFLECTION TOPIC 6: RELATING YOUR MOTIVATIONS TO YOUR STUDENTS

Your whys and your experiences should inform and motivate your classroom work. At the same time, it is important to recognize that your students' whys will likely be different from yours because of their differing identities and experiences. Focusing on a narrow set of purposes for CS Ed in your classroom, like getting a high-paying job as a software engineer, might leave out students who don't resonate with that rationale. CS educator Christina built on this idea:

> Oftentimes, educators have their vision of what "needs" to be done, but students' ideas can give more depth to the discussion or topic. By including a broader scope of ideas and having students push for what they think is important or interesting, we might better be able to address equity in the classroom.

Listening to students' interests and motivations can help you shape your curriculum or standards in ways that meet your students' interests and goals.

To explore this topic, it's important to think about who your students are and how you get to know about their backgrounds, experiences, interests, and talents. As you narrow in on your motivations, consider how *who* your students are might shape the motivations they have. Consider as well how their experiences with CS and CS Ed might be shaped by their different identities and how those identities have been positioned in society. Reflections like these can help you understand how historical and current power dynamics shape your experiences with your students.

REFLECTION TOPIC 6 JOURNAL PROMPTS

Putting your experiences and your whys into perspective. Ask yourself . . .

- Who are your students? What do you know about their experiences and cultural and language practices?

- How can you learn more about your students' experiences, beliefs, and motivations?

- How might the roles of CS be similar in your life and your students' lives? How might they be different?

- How might your reason(s) for caring about CS intersect with your students' experiences and concerns about CS?

- How might your experiences with systems of advantage and oppression in schooling and in CS (see Chapter 5) be similar to and different from those of your students?

REVISITING AMANDA AND YEIDY'S STORIES

Amanda and Yeidy are not the only ones who have found journaling, dialogue, and reflection beneficial. Many of the teachers we have worked with shared how these practices helped them develop self-awareness and gave examples of how their learning led to changes in their practice. Journaling, dialogue, and reflection are key to building an equity toolkit and the foundation for an equity-oriented praxis.

Amanda concluded her thoughts with the following reflection on journaling as a practice:

> Journaling has made me a deeply reflective person and a more understanding, empathetic, and equitable teacher. Discussing with others has also allowed me to connect more with people of different

backgrounds and engage in meaningful conversations with like-minded individuals who will challenge boundaries and encourage us to think critically.

I would like to share that it is okay to go deep. There is no shame in writing and thinking critically about our implicit biases and our own identities. Let your words flow freely and be fearless; it will make you a better teacher.

REFLECTION QUESTIONS

1. What do you think about the journaling and dialogue practices described in this chapter? How can you see them being beneficial? What challenges might arise trying to engage in these practices?

2. The topics covered in this chapter are not comprehensive. What other topics might you benefit from reflecting on as you engage in equity work in your setting?

TAKEAWAYS FOR PRACTICE

- Choose one topic and journal about it. Reflect on the experience and consider how you might adapt the journaling practices described in this chapter to fit your personal preferences and circumstances.

- Engage in dialogue with a critical friend about a topic in this chapter. Reflect on the new insights that you came away with as a result of your conversation.

GLOSSARY

Term	Definition
ableism	Implicit or explicit social preference for nondisabled bodies and minds that creates prejudice and oppression of disability and disabled people (Shew, 2020).
affinity group	A group of people with shared identities who come together to connect around a common goal.
antisemitism	A system of prejudice, discrimination, and hostility toward Jewish people.
archaeology of self	The "deep excavation and exploration of beliefs, biases, and ideas that shape how we engage in the work [of equity]" (Sealey-Ruiz, 2022, p. 22).

classism	A system of prejudice and discrimination in favor of people with higher socioeconomic status (e.g., upper middle-class) and against people with lower socioeconomic status (e.g., lower class).
critical friend	A supportive person with whom there is a relationship of trust who can provide constructive feedback and ask difficult questions related to equity.
dead angle	An issue or topic related to equity that a person lacks awareness of or experience with or holds negative biases in ways that prevent equitable change. It also avoids ableism implicit in terms like "blind spot."
gatekeeping	Institutional policies and structures that control who gets to participate in opportunities and who has access to resources in ways that limit the participation of marginalized groups.
homophobia	A system of prejudice and discrimination against or fear or discomfort with people who identify as LGBTQIA2S+.
intersectionality	A theory that asserts that different aspects of people's identity (e.g., disability, gender, race) overlap and intersect in ways that result in oppression that cannot be understood or addressed by focusing on each identity separately (Crenshaw, 1991; Collins, 2019).
praxis	The combination of teaching practices and theory. This guide supports praxis by providing theories about equity that help teachers develop mindsets to take transformative action toward equitable CS education.
racism	A system of prejudice and discrimination based on race that privileges individuals racialized as white and oppresses racially minoritized individuals.
self-efficacy	A belief in one's ability to accomplish a task or achieve a goal.
sexism	A system of prejudice and discrimination based on gender and gender identity that privileges men and oppresses women, non-binary, and gender-fluid individuals.
transmisia/ transphobia	Both terms describe a system of prejudice and discrimination against people who are transgender or non-binary and a fear or discomfort with people who are transgender or non-binary. "Transmisia" emphasizes how prejudice and discrimination are

	linked to hatred, revulsion, and disgust, rather than fear (KosmicKult, 2020). It is an alternative to ableist language connected with the word "phobia" (Planned Parenthood, n.d.)
trigger	A topic or conversation that surfaces strong emotions or memories; triggers can motivate equitable action or reproduce inequitable patterns.

REFERENCES

Collins, P. H. (2019). *Intersectionality as critical social theory*. Duke University Press. https://doi.org/10.1215/9781478007098

Copur-Gencturk, Y., Cimpian, J. R., Lubienski, S. T., & Thacker, I. (2020). Teachers' bias against the mathematical ability of female, Black, and Hispanic students. *Educational Researcher, 49*(1), 30–43. https://doi.org/10.3102/0013189X19890577

Crenshaw, K. (1991). Mapping the margins: Intersectionality, identity politics, and violence against women of color. *Stanford Law Review*, *43*(6), 1241–1299. https://doi.org/10.2307/1229039

Kohli, R. (2018). Behind school doors: The impact of hostile racial climates on urban teachers of color. *Urban Education, 53*(3), 307–333. https://doi.org/10.1177/0042085916636653

KosmicKult. (2020, July 19). Hate is NOT fear: Reframing homophobia, biphobia, and transphobia. *Medium*. https://medium.com/@kosmickult/hate-is-not-fear-reframing-homophobia-biphobia-and-transphobia-beabec366dc6

Love, B. L. (2019). *We want to do more than survive: Abolitionist teaching and the pursuit of educational freedom*. Beacon Press.

Obama, B. (1995). *Dreams from my father*. Three Rivers Press.

Planned Parenthood. (n.d.). *What's transphobia, also called transmisia?* Planned Parenthood. https://www.plannedparenthood.org/learn/gender-identity/transgender/whats-transphobia

Price-Dennis, D., & Sealey-Ruiz, Y. (2021). *Advancing racial literacies in teacher education: Activism for equity in digital spaces*. Teachers College Press.

Rodgers, C. R., & Scott, K.H. (2008). The development of the personal self and professional identity in learning to teach. In Cochran-Smith, M. Feiman-Nemser, McIntyre, D. J., & Demers, K. E. (Eds.), *Handbook of Research on Teacher Education* (3rd ed., pp. 732–755). Routledge & Association of Teacher Educators. https://doi.org/10.4324/9780203938690

Sealey-Ruiz, Y. (2022). An archaeology of self for our times: Another talk to teachers. *English Journal, 111*(5), 21–26. https://doi.org/10.58680/ej202231819

Shew, A. (2020). Ableism, technoableism, and future AI. *IEEE Xplore, 39*(1), 40–85. https://doi.org/10.1109/MTS.2020.2967492

Stevenson, H. C. (2014). *Promoting racial literacy in schools: Differences that make a difference*. Teachers College Press.

Tatum, B. D. (2003). *Why are all the Black kids sitting together in the cafeteria: And other conversations about race*. Basic Books.

RESOURCE 1: JOURNAL PROMPTS REFERENCE

This resource provides all of the journal prompts from the chapter consolidated into a single reference.

REFLECTION TOPIC 1: UNPACKING IDENTITY

What are your many identities? Ask yourself . . .

- What are your identities and many selves?
- Are some of these identities more salient to you in some contexts than others? Why?
- Which identities come readily to mind when you think about yourself? Which identities are not as salient for you (your dead angles)? Why?
- Which identities are sources of pride for you? Why?
- Which identities do you have a more complicated relationship with? Why?
- How do institutions in society privilege and/or disadvantage people with identities like yours?
- Have you ever had to suppress or repress particular identities in particular settings or institutions?
- Have you ever had to suppress or repress particular identities in school? Do you have identities that were celebrated or cultivated in school?
- Have you ever had empowering interactions with others related to one or more of your identities? Disempowering interactions?

REFLECTION TOPIC 2: TALKING ABOUT RACE, IDENTITY, AND POWER

How have you been socialized to discuss or avoid conversations about issues of identity and power? Ask yourself . . .

- How old were you when you first learned about issues related to:
  - Ableism and disability?
  - Class, wealth, and classism?

- Diversity in sexual orientations and homophobia?
- Gender, sexism, and transphobia/transmisia?
- Homelessness and housing insecurity?
- Immigration, ethnicity, and national identity?
- Language diversity and language injustice?
- Race and racism?
- Religious diversity?

- What were those different experiences like? How did they make you feel?
- How, if at all, did your family members, caregivers, and teachers discuss race, culture, and other human differences? What was your personal experience with these conversations?
- Was your curiosity about these issues actively encouraged? Actively silenced?
- What are your triggers that signal an encounter with an equity issue that you are unfamiliar or uncomfortable with?
- What coping strategies do you use to navigate an encounter with an equity issue that you are unfamiliar or uncomfortable with?

REFLECTION TOPIC 3: EXAMINING SCHOOL EXPERIENCES

What has been your relationship with schooling? Ask yourself . . .

- What do you remember about your different schooling experiences?
- What were some of your experiences with systems of oppression and advantage at school?
- Did you have teachers who made things relevant to your personal experiences, your interests, identities, and background?
- Why did you become an educator? How, if at all, did that choice relate to aspects of your identity? How, if at all, did that choice relate to your experiences in school?

REFLECTION TOPIC 4: UNDERSTANDING YOUR RELATIONSHIP TO COMPUTING AND CS

What has been your relationship with computing and CS? Ask yourself . . .

- What does it mean to be a computer scientist?
- Do you identify as a "computer scientist" or as a "techie person"?
- Where do you find joy and/or meaning in CS or in computing?
- What were some of your experiences with systems of oppression and disadvantage in CS?
- How might your experiences navigating the world with your different identities shape your beliefs about who is thought to be capable of engaging in CS?
- How might your experiences shape your beliefs about what computing is for?

REFLECTION TOPIC 5: CONSIDERING YOUR MOTIVATIONS

Why are you motivated to teach CS? Ask yourself . . .

- Which (if any) parts of your history and identity (e.g., disability, gender, language practices, race) have influenced your connection to CS?
- How does CS intersect with your everyday life, your goals, and your identity?
- How might your personal experiences with CS and technology relate to why you teach CS?
- Is there a formative experience that you've had that helped you develop a sense of why CS is significant or consequential in your own or in others' lives?
- Are there communities that you are a part of that use CS for purposes that are close to your heart?
- What is the role of CS in the world?
- How do you feel that CS plays a role in social justice?

REFLECTION TOPIC 6: RELATING YOUR MOTIVATIONS TO YOUR STUDENTS

Putting your experiences and your whys into perspective. Ask yourself . . .

- Who are your students? What do you know about their experiences and cultural and language practices?
- How can you learn more about your students' experiences, beliefs, and motivations?
- How might the roles of CS be similar in your life and your students' lives? How might they be different?
- How might your reason(s) for caring about CS intersect with your students' experiences and concerns about CS?
- How might your experiences with systems of advantage and oppression in schooling and in CS (see Chapter 5) be similar to and different from those of your students?

RESOURCE 2: THERAPEUTIC TECHNIQUES TO SUPPORT REFLECTION

Engaging in journaling, dialogue, and reflection on topics like those explored in this chapter can surface strong emotions and memories. We offer some techniques below that can help you navigate triggers that may arise as you engage in these practices.

Practice	Description
Active Listening	Active listening involves paying close attention to what someone is saying, asking questions to clarify understanding, and repeating the speaker's statements to ensure comprehension. Developing a practice of active listening scaffolds empathy development, patience, and the management of emotionally charged responses.
Creative Expression	Creative expression refers to conveying knowledge, emotions, and ideas through mediums such as art, coding, dance, music, and writing. Creative expression can allow you to freely explore your emotions and experiences.
Controlled Breathing	Controlled breathing involves intentionally focusing on your breath, often counting, deepening, or lengthening the breath as a way to help regulate the nervous system and increase oxygen in the body. Practicing controlled breathing exercises can help regulate emotions and manage stress.

Practice	Description
Debate	Debate involves creating space for individuals to express and articulate differing perspectives on challenging topics. Participating in debate in an emotionally supportive environment can enhance argumentation and advocacy skills and promote comfort in assertiveness and public engagement.
Journaling	Journaling involves recording personal thoughts, feelings, and experience in some way. Journaling supports mindful and constructive self-reflection and allows for a non-judgmental space to examine one's awareness of and feelings about issues of inequity.
Mindful Relaxation	Practicing mindfulness and relaxation techniques such as meditation, yoga, or progressive muscle relaxation can promote emotional well-being and reduce stress and anxiety.
Peer Co-Counseling	Sharing strategies for coping with and addressing bias and inequity helps expand one's emotional vocabulary while providing space for collective thought and collaborative action.
Role Play and Drama	Role-playing and drama exercises create opportunities to explore different perspectives and experiences related to bias and inequity while developing communication and empathy skills.
Self-Care	Self-care involves taking action to care for oneself holistically, in all aspects of one's personal well-being and happiness, particularly in times of stress. What self-care looks like is different for each individual, and it might encompass emotional, mental, physical, social, and spiritual facets of life.
Storytelling	Storytelling can promote self-expression and help individuals understand their own experiences with more clarity. Listening to the stories of others can promote intercultural competence and awareness of others' experiences.

critical friend A supportive person with whom there is a relationship of trust who can provide constructive feedback and ask difficult questions related to equity.

RESOURCE 3: FINDING CRITICAL FRIENDS

A **critical friend** can provide you with support on your journey of personal development toward equity. Having a group of critical friends is a central part of building your equity toolkit. Here are some thoughts on finding critical friends.

WHAT IS A CRITICAL FRIEND?

A critical friend is a supportive person with whom you share a relationship of trust. They are someone who can ask difficult questions related to equity, someone who you can dialogue with about equity issues, and someone who can provide you with constructive and critical feedback.

Critical friends should help each other:

- create a safe space that maintains trust;
- encourage open, honest dialogue that includes different perspectives;
- listen actively; and
- challenge assumptions and dead angles.

WHO CAN BE A CRITICAL FRIEND?

- In some cases, it may help to find critical friends who might have had similar experiences (e.g., affinity groups).
- It's also important to have critical friends who contribute perspectives that are different from your own.
- When looking for critical friends, look widely. Don't assume people should be critical friends only because of their identities. It is especially important for individuals who are afforded privilege to not put additional work or undue burden on marginalized individuals as those with privilege seek to better understand oppression and inequity.

7

Setting Your Computer Science Equity Commitments

Lloyd Talley, Sara Vogel, Sarane James, Spence J. Ray, Christy Crawford, Lauren Vogelstein, Christopher Hoadley, Wendy Barrales, Stephanie T. Jones, and the Computer Science Educational Justice Collective

Acknowledgements: Melissa Parker

CHAPTER OVERVIEW

This chapter builds on previous chapters, inviting readers to set commitments and lead out in equity-centered computer science education (CS Ed). The chapter considers making commitments in four areas: (1) self-awareness and personal learning; (2) ways of seeing and being with others; (3) advancing CS pedagogy; and (4) advocating for equitable change in CS Ed. The chapter also offers tools to create a plan for setting commitments and identifying goals that work toward change.

CHAPTER OBJECTIVES

After reading this chapter, I can:

- Explain how commitments are part of an equity-oriented journey.
- Set commitments as a CS educator that are specific to myself, my students, and my CS Ed context.

- Identify action steps I can take to work toward equity in my CS Ed context.

KEY TERMS

advocacy; commitment; critical consciousness; deficit framings; host leadership; praxis; savior complex

CHRISTINA'S STORY

Chapter 6 focused on journaling, dialogue, and reflection as key practices in developing self-awareness and the ability to discuss inequity. An important next step is setting **commitments**, or pledging to a course of action, that will work toward equity in CS Ed. This chapter will explore four areas where you can commit to engage in a journey of equity-oriented **praxis**.

To get started, let's hear from Christina, a CS teacher who has made multiple commitments as part of her equity journey that have led to changes in her classroom and her work as an educator.

commitment A statement that involves aligning personally with a set of values and pledging to a course of action based on those values.

praxis The combination of teaching practices and theory. This guide supports praxis by providing theories about equity that help teachers develop mindsets to take transformative action toward equitable CS Ed.

> When I first started my own equity journey, I felt surprised by how much I didn't know or understand. I thought that I was familiar with equity, but there is more to equity in the classroom than your own experiences. By participating in different professional developments, I was able to broaden my understanding and pedagogy. I was able to put words to things that I felt or knew. It's been an amazing journey that continues.
>
> I made many commitments as an equity-centered CS teacher. I have learned a lot of valuable information and skills to apply what I've learned in my classroom.
>
> I have committed to my own personal development. Constantly taking professional development [PD] and doing readings make me think about equity in CS.
>
> I have committed to becoming an advocate for CS and equity in my school community. I "fight" for CS for all students.
>
> I am committed to giving students a voice in the CS classroom. This is hard for students because they are not accustomed to being in charge of their learning. I hope this develops as they get more comfortable.

Christina's story illustrates how making commitments leads to taking action. Christina's commitment to personal development led her to take PDs and read. Her commitment to advocacy led her to "fight" for CS opportunities for all students. However, her story also shows how commitments are part of the ongoing process of working toward equity in CS Ed. For example, her commitment to giving students a voice in the classroom is not something that is always comfortable for students because it is new. This commitment is something that Christina and her students are still working on. In this chapter, you'll consider which commitments can best help you take action in your CS Ed settings.

COMMITTING YOURSELF TO A JOURNEY

As an educator in CS, you stand at the threshold of a discipline and an industry that continues to reshape our world. Computing is social and political—computing fields and tools can improve lives but also cause harm and perpetuate injustice. This tension is often not made explicit in classrooms where students are learning CS. Teachers who explicitly acknowledge power dynamics in CS fields and education in their classrooms can promote more relevant, inclusive, and empowering CS Ed for everyone.

As Christina's story shows, this work is a journey. The nature of this journey requires committing yourself to ongoing efforts that promote and center equity. While you make personal commitments focused on your own sphere of influence, this work is not meant to be done alone. Equity work is most successful when you are supported in your commitments by colleagues, school and district leadership, and broader institutions and policies. Your role requires working to develop personal self-awareness, working for change in your classroom and beyond, and engaging in shared leadership in community.

This chapter considers four areas in which you can make commitments and plan to take action for yourself, your students, and your teaching to serve as an advocate and leader.

These areas include:

1. self-awareness and personal learning;

2. ways of seeing and being with others;

3. advancing CS pedagogy; and

4. advocacy for equitable change in CS Ed.

We provide examples of commitments in each area to help you get started. But we also invite you to draw on your reflections from previous chapters,

Setting Your Computer Science Equity Commitments 149

especially Chapter 6, to create commitments that represent yourself, your identities, your work, and the communities that you are a part of.

AREA #1: SELF-AWARENESS AND PERSONAL LEARNING

The first area involves committing to taking action to understand yourself and your own identity, to strengthen your ability to engage in dialogue about equity issues, and to continue your personal learning. We invite you to commit to developing your knowledge about social dynamics that shape educational contexts broadly and within CS and CS Ed specifically. This includes things like expanding your understanding about issues related to topics like class, disability, gender and sexual orientation, language, and race and ethnicity. An important related skill is learning to take stock of your in-the-moment emotional reactions to issues of identity and power. Developing this self-awareness is essential to adequately respond to equity-related challenges in the classroom. We begin with critical self-reflection and then become students of historical and contemporary social inequities in computing, computing education, and the wider society. We can then examine the veracity of our own assumptions and beliefs and take steps toward interrupting harmful myths. We can also give ourselves grace, space, and time to do this work. There is no way to develop perfect self-awareness. Everyone will make mistakes, learn, and move forward. The key is to continue in the process. Changing our own ideas over time is necessary to change how we show up for our students.

AS AN EQUITY-CENTERED CS TEACHER, I COMMIT TO . . .

1. **Critical and continuous learning** about systems of oppression and advantage, historical events, and racial frameworks that shape CS and CS Ed power dynamics and my own relationships to tools and technology.

2. **Self-awareness and examination of internal attitudes and beliefs** about issues related to social identity and social justice in the CS classroom and the larger world.

CS teacher Amanda shared an example of how her classroom practices changed as a result of her commitment to continual learning and an awareness of her own racial identity in relation to her students and her CS curriculum.

> Every February, my fifth graders and I watch the film *Hidden Figures*. We have been doing this for the past three years. Each year, we get a little deeper into the unjust treatment of people of color. I stop the movie at various parts, and we talk about the segregation, how the women highlighted in the movie had to work harder to meet higher standards than everyone else and were likely not compensated fairly. We have also had conversations about allyship and how a few men helped lift women up while others brought the women down.
>
> During my first year showing this film, I did not get too deep into the issues of race. I felt uncomfortable as a white woman and did not want to offend or say the wrong thing. However, I have learned that these conversations need to be had. Students are thinking critically about the injustices that were happening at the time, and I was challenged to facilitate a meaningful conversation about race, identity, and the harsh history of our country's past. I believe having these conversations around the movie and around current events helps my students understand me, and I think it meant something that a white female teacher was criticizing the behavior of other white people in power.

Amanda's commitment to critical learning about issues related to race and gender led to rich discussions about social justice topics with her students. Her awareness of her own internal hesitancy to engage in conversations about race and her commitment to continued learning allowed her to take action and deepen her conversations with her students in ways that addressed broader issues of identity and power.

AREA #2: WAYS OF SEEING AND BEING WITH OTHERS

deficit framings Broadly held beliefs, including stereotypes, that identify groups of people as lacking or deficient in some way (Louie et al., 2021; Steele, 2011).

The second area to consider is how you perceive and share spaces with others, including students and their families, your colleagues, and the communities to which you belong.

Because our own perspectives shape the work we do in classrooms, we must critically examine and expand the lenses through which we view those around us. Some teachers perceive students through **deficit framings** and focus on what students lack or cannot do. This may lead to **savior complexes**, or a sense of needing to "save" or "rescue" marginalized groups. By contrast, students know when a teacher values who they are as a full person and respects their dignity as a learner by "recogniz[ing] and cultivat[ing] one's mind, humanity, and potential" (Espinoza et al., 2020, p. 326). We can counter deficit narratives about learners by learning about our students and respecting their humanity, their full identities, their insights and contributions, and their potential. When we see and interact with students in these ways, students are more likely to feel a greater sense of belonging and succeed.

Respecting the dignity of our students and cultivating their humanity and potential can be done in many ways. One key way is supporting our students to enact changes that they think are important in the world. We can use our classrooms, curriculum, and pedagogical practices as tools that promote our students' **critical consciousness**, or a social and political awareness of how social inequities are created and reproduced. Critical consciousness is a powerful tool for students who are afforded power based on their identities and those who may be marginalized because of their identities. As students come to recognize their own power, even as youth, they can use computing to become change agents in their communities and beyond.

savior complex Attitudes and actions where a person believes that they are responsible for "saving" or "rescuing" others by fixing their problems. The person acting as a "savior" often has a sense of superiority and takes action without the consent of those they are "helping," denying their agency.

critical consciousness A social and political awareness that allows for a critique of how cultural norms, values, and institutions reproduce social inequities (Ladson-Billings, 1995).

AS AN EQUITY-CENTERED CS TEACHER, I COMMIT TO . . .

3. **Seeing and valuing all students (all people)**, their cultures, histories, and ways of being in the world and to empowering students to explore these experiences in CS Ed.

4. **Empowering and preparing students to enact change** through the critical examination of CS and by lifting up students' own goals and purposes for computing.

Amanda, the CS teacher from the previous section, shared one of her commitments related to seeing and being with students:

> I decorate my classroom with posters of diverse innovators and design lessons where students learn about amazing computer scientists. I am committed to holding my students to high standards. I want to challenge them with fun projects that will allow my students to think critically.
>
> A colleague runs a European Explorer project every year. Students research an explorer, print pictures, and create a board. This

year, I plan to challenge that teacher and ask her to collaborate on a more meaningful project. I would like to plan a project where students critically examine everything the explorers did. Instead of placing these men, who initiated the beginning of colonization, on pedestals, I want the students to create a Scratch project that tells the whole story of European Exploration!

Amanda's commitment has already shaped her practice—from how she decorates her classroom to her curriculum to the expectations she has for her students. Even more significantly, Amanda's commitments are guiding her current and future work. Her plans to take action by inviting her colleague to revise an existing project will engage students in critically examining the role of colonization and create a more equity-oriented learning opportunity.

AREA #3: ADVANCING CS PEDAGOGY

Another place to commit to take action is with regard to CS pedagogy. It has been well documented that CS is often taught in ways that can exclude some groups. Given the history of inequitable practices in CS Ed, we invite you to consider commitments related to advancing pedagogy in ways that support all learners to take part in deep, rigorous CS learning (Hammond, as cited in Rebora, 2021).

Accomplishing this goal involves building on the diversity of learners and their backgrounds. As Black feminist scholar, educator, and activist bell hooks noted in her book *Teaching to Transgress*, "pedagogy must insist that everyone's presence is acknowledged. That insistence cannot be simply stated. It has to be demonstrated through pedagogical practices." (hooks, 1994, p. 8). Culturally and linguistically responsive pedagogies acknowledge everyone's presence and affirm, value, and extend the diverse abilities, experiences, language practices, and identities of marginalized communities. They involve teaching responsively by developing new strategies to learn about our students and to transform the way we teach based on what we learn. Such approaches push back on the notion that the cultures that dominate CS and CS Ed now are the only or best cultures for CS. These kinds of pedagogies deepen and transform learning for all students, including those from dominant groups, and they can especially benefit marginalized students (Eglash et al., 2013; Lachney et al., 2021; Mirakhur et al., 2021; Vogel et al., 2020). The remainder of this guide (Chapters 8–17) focuses on specific techniques, rooted in critical pedagogy and research in equity-centered CS Ed, that can help you accomplish goals related to these commitments.

> **AS AN EQUITY-CENTERED CS TEACHER, I COMMIT TO ...**
>
> 5. **Continually tailoring programming and pedagogy** to best nurture and empower the social development of individual students in all of their uniqueness, intersectional identities, and individual needs.
>
> 6. **Advocating for the individual educational needs of students** in CS Ed to administrators, colleagues, and other stakeholders.

CS teacher Brandie shared an example of an activity that she incorporated into her CS instruction that was tailored to students' interests and also worked to develop their critical consciousness.

Brandie explained her approach:

> Last year, I started *What's News in Tech?* lessons. I was inspired by wanting to incorporate current events into the curriculum so that students were knowledgeable about current developments in tech, but I also wanted students to be critical of the tech—considering benefits and harms.
>
> I was inspired by the Teaching Black History All Year Institute presented by Sonja Cherry-Paul and Colleen Cruz who shared a note-taking structure that included four key components. I created my own structure for analyzing tech and guided the kids in using this graphic organizer. (See Figure 1.)

Figure 1. Graphic Organizer to Evaluate Technology Tools

Problem it solves:	**How it works:**
• What problem is it trying to solve? • Who does this technology help?	• How are computers used in this technology? • Why do you think it was designed like this?
Pros & Cons	**Reactions & Questions**
• Is it good at solving the problem? • Does everyone get to use this technology? Why or why not? • Could it be harmful?	• What feelings and ideas are you having? • What do you want to know more about to really understand it?

(center: TECHNOLOGY)

> I was intentional about including the second and third question in the Pros and Cons section because I thought it was a good way to include equity as a lens through which to analyze text. Having the questions present as an expectation for the kids to think about was a powerful framework for teaching kids to be critical about accessibility, effectiveness, and the impact of technology on everyone.

Brandie's commitment to equity-centered pedagogy led her to tailor an existing tool and adapt it to her CS context. This move empowered her students to develop skills to critically analyze technological tools and their impact on society through an equity lens.

AREA #4: ADVOCACY FOR EQUITABLE CHANGE IN CS ED

advocacy Publicly supporting and championing policies and changes that support equity-oriented CS Ed. Advocacy involves taking action to disrupt the status quo.

An equity-oriented praxis also includes shared leadership and **advocacy** for broader equitable changes in CS educational policies and structures. No individual person can wave a magic wand and make CS, education, or anything else equitable. And yet, as professionals and teachers, CS educators can make a tremendous difference in how just or unjust the lives of our students will be. The ways we show up, the choices we make, the relationships we form in classrooms, and how we use our own voices to amplify students' voices have profound impacts on society and on students. It can be tempting to imagine solving problems of oppression in CS by focusing solely on our own classrooms. Yet these problems, by their nature, require engaging the larger world, and as education professionals, we have an ethical responsibility to do so.

The National Equity Project describes this advocacy as leading as a "host" rather than as a "hero" (National Equity Project, n.d.). Hero leadership is described by the National Equity Project as "planning the work and working the plan." Because a hero approach is often done in isolation or is disconnected from the communities impacted by an inequitable status quo, hero leadership may fall short of lasting change and can lead to savior complexes. By contrast, **host leadership** requires building coalitions across communities that involve listening, multiple perspectives, and working collectively for change. Liberatory design mindsets can help build these coalitions (Anaissie et al., 2021). Liberatory design mindsets include building relational trust, practicing self-awareness, recognizing oppression, embracing complexity, focusing on human values, seeking

host leadership Building coalitions across communities that draw on multiple perspectives to work collectively for equity-oriented change.

liberatory collaboration, working with fear and discomfort, attending to healing, working to transform power, exercising creative courage, taking action to learn, and sharing instead of selling ideas. Enacting these orientations in community with others can allow groups to navigate the complexity of equity work and develop creative and lasting solutions. Change may begin in our own classrooms, but by necessity it must be larger, encompassing not only our own hearts and minds but the hearts and minds of those around us.

AS AN EQUITY-CENTERED CS TEACHER, I COMMIT TO . . .

7. **Recognizing my own role** in the systems of oppression and **working to disrupt** systems of oppression and injustice

   - in my own mind;
   - in ways of working in the world;
   - in standards set for students;
   - in CS curricula;
   - in the CS profession; and
   - in systems of schooling.

8. **Empowering and educating colleagues** on tech literacy, CS integration, and CS innovations through an equity lens.

9. **Being a host, not a hero**, in CS equity work and professional learning communities.

PLANNING FOR CHANGE

Committing to equity work in CS Ed is a multi-layered process. Figure 2 illustrates this idea through three nested circles that cover the four areas explored in this chapter. While equity work starts within, it quickly expands outward to encompass leading for transformative change.

Figure 2. Committing to Equity Work

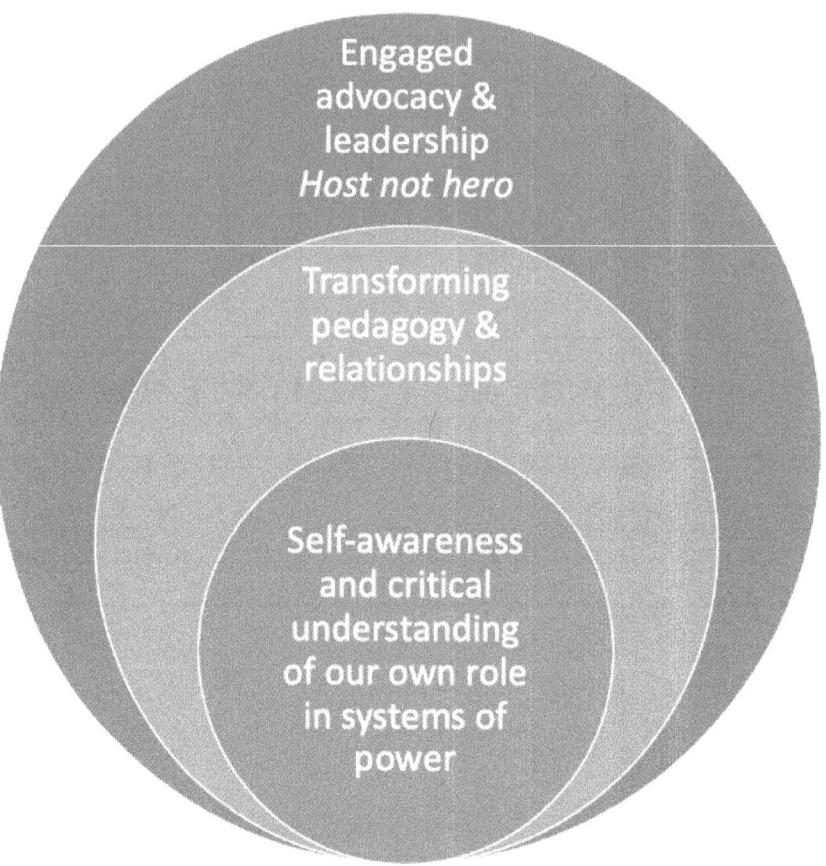

Committing to equity work across these different areas might feel overwhelming. But it is important to remember that this work is not something to be accomplished all at once. Small, consistent efforts can make a big difference, a concept that scholar Ruha Benjamin referred to as "viral justice" (Benjamin, 2022). Commitments help provide a sense of purpose and direction on our journey, offering an orientation that can guide our everyday actions. It may help to translate your commitments into small, concrete action steps. You might break down a broader commitment into actions that span different amounts of time. (e.g., Today, I will . . . ; This week, I will . . . ; This month, I will . . . ; This quarter or semester, I will . . .). The size of your commitments and actions is not important. What matters most is that you find ways that work for you and are consistent in your efforts on this journey.

We invite you to try setting a commitment below. Consider the thoughts, ideas, and experiences that have come to your mind as you have read this chapter. Resource 1 is a similar worksheet that can help you identify and set your CS equity commitments.

> **SETTING CS EQUITY COMMITMENTS**
>
> 1. As an equity-centered CS teacher, I commit to . . .
> 2. Transforming this commitment into action,
>   - Today, I will . . .
>   - This week, I will . . .
>   - This month, I will . . .
>   - This quarter or semester, I will . . .

REVISITING CHRISTINA'S STORY

Christina's practice of setting commitments and taking action as part of her own equity journey has continued, and she has identified ways to hold herself accountable and to monitor her growth. Christina shared:

> I have conversations with my students to find out if I have achieved my goals for the lesson or the unit. I encourage the students to be honest about my teaching, and I ask for suggestions. I explain that like them, I am a work in progress. I also tell them that they are helping the next group of students. I self-evaluate my work against a rubric, and I try to see if I hit the goals that I want. I see my commitments making a difference in students' engagement. Not just with me, but with the content and with their peers. Students feel confident in what they know, and they share and correct each other during discussions or while working on a project. I also know we are making progress because students are finding new ways that I haven't discussed or taught and are teaching me. I love that!

Christina also highlighted how her efforts have been amplified as she has joined in communities beyond her classroom and moved toward advocacy:

> One thing that has been helpful for me has been being a part of an affinity group. Sitting with like-minded educators and discussing topics that affect us and our communities makes a tremendous difference in my understanding and comfort level. Through discussions, I have been able to develop ways to become a changemaker in my community.

Like Christina, in this chapter we have invited you to begin a journey of transformation. This journey will make your own CS teaching more inclusive and equitable and help you advocate for equitable changes in CS Ed and CS fields. To change how our classrooms function, we have to focus on our own roles in systems of oppression or liberation and better understand how power affects both the historical and current world of CS. As we raise our own self-awareness of how those systems have affected our experiences with society, with schooling, and with technology, we can commit ourselves to being a part of more systemic change. That will, of course, impact how we teach or what we might do in our own classrooms, but it can also put us on a path to act as advocates, leaders, and movement builders in our communities. As we become "hosts not heroes," we turn personal goals for equity into shared work toward equitable change.

REFLECTION QUESTIONS

1. Which suggested commitments from this chapter resonate with you? What ideas come to mind for how those commitments apply to your own CS Ed context?

2. What stands out to you about making commitments and taking action from the teacher examples in this chapter? How can you remind yourself that this work is an ongoing process and journey?

TAKEAWAYS FOR PRACTICE

- If you haven't already, set some commitments based on this chapter. The chapter resources can help with this.

- Identify 2–3 individuals with whom you can share your commitments. Create an action plan to periodically check in with them and discuss your progress, challenges that have arisen, and successes that you've experienced.

GLOSSARY

Term	Definition
advocacy	Publicly supporting and championing policies and changes that support equity-oriented CS Ed. Advocacy involves taking action to disrupt the status quo.

commitment	A statement that involves aligning personally with a set of values and pledging to a course of action based on those values.
critical consciousness	A social and political awareness that allows for a critique of how cultural norms, values, and institutions reproduce social inequities (Ladson-Billings, 1995).
deficit framings	Broadly held beliefs, including stereotypes, that identify groups of people as lacking or deficient in some way (Louie et al., 2021; Steele, 2011).
host leadership	Building coalitions across communities that draw on multiple perspectives to work collectively for equity-oriented change.
praxis	The combination of teaching practices and theory. This guide supports praxis by providing theories about equity that help teachers develop mindsets to take transformative action toward equitable CS Ed.
savior complex	Attitudes and actions where a person believes that they are responsible for "saving" or "rescuing" others by fixing their problems. The person acting as a "savior" often has a sense of superiority and takes action without the consent of those they are "helping," denying their agency.

REFERENCES

Anaissie, T., Cary, V., Clifford, D., Malarkey, T., & Wise, S. (2021). *Liberatory design: Mindsets and modes to design for equity.* Liberatory Design. https://static1.squarespace.com/static/60380011d63f16013f7cc4c2/t/60b698f388fe142f91f6b345/1622579446226/Liberatory+Design+Deck_June_2021.pdf

Benjamin, R. (2022). *Viral justice: How we grow the world we want.* Princeton University Press. https://doi.org/10.1515/9780691222899

Eglash, R., Gilbert, J. E., Taylor, V., & Geier, S. R. (2013). Culturally responsive computing in urban, after-school contexts: Two approaches. *Urban Education, 48*(5), 629–656. https://doi.org/10.1177/0042085913499211

Espinoza, M. L., Vossoughi, S., Rose, M., & Poza, L. E. (2020). Matters of participation: Notes on the study of dignity and learning. *Mind, Culture, and Activity, 27*(4), 325–347. https://doi.org/10.1080/10749039.2020.1779304

hooks, b. (1994). *Teaching to transgress.* Routledge. https://doi.org/10.3366/para.1994.17.3.270

Lachney, M., Bennett, A. G., Eglash, R., Yadav, A., & Moudgalya, S. (2021). Teaching in an open village: A case study on culturally responsive computing in compulsory education. *Computer Science Education, 31*(4), 462–488. https://doi.org/10.1080/08993408.2021.1874228

Ladson-Billings, G. (1995). But that's just good teaching! The case for culturally relevant pedagogy. *Theory Into Practice, 34*(3), 159–165. https://doi.org/10.1080/00405849509543675

Louie, N., Adiredja, A. P., & Jessup, N. (2021). Teacher noticing from a sociopolitical perspective: The FAIR framework for anti-deficit noticing. *ZDM-Mathematics Education, 53*, 95–107. https://doi.org/10.1007/s11858-021-01229-2

Mirakhur, Z., Fancsali, C., & Hill, K. (2021). The potential of CR-SE for K-12 computer science education: Perspectives from two leaders. *Voices in Urban Education, 50*(1). https://doi.org/10.33682/3en3-cbgn

National Equity Project. (n.d.). *Networks and communities of practice.* https://web.archive.org/web/20240808060608/https://www.nationalequityproject.org/networks

Rebora, A. (2021). Zaretta Hammond on equity and student engagement. *Educational Leadership, 79*(4), 14–18. https://www.ascd.org/el/articles/zaretta-hammond-on-equity-and-student-engagement

Steele, C. M. (2011). *Whistling Vivaldi: How stereotypes affect us and what we can do.* W. W. Norton & Company.

Vogel, S., Hoadley, C., Castillo, A. R., & Ascenzi-Moreno, L. (2020). Languages, literacies and literate programming: Can we use the latest theories on how bilingual people learn to help us teach computer literacies? *Computer Science Education, 30*(4), 420–443. https://doi.org/10.1080/08993408.2020.1751525

RESOURCE 1: MY COMMITMENTS TO EQUITABLE CS ED

Use this resource as a guide to set your own personal commitments to equitable CS Ed in your setting. Feel free to draw on the suggested commitments in this chapter (see Resource 2) and make them your own.

Area #1: Self-Awareness and Personal Learning	
As an equity-centered CS teacher, I commit to . . .	
Transforming this commitment into action,	
Today, I will . . .	
This week, I will . . .	
This month, I will . . .	
This quarter or semester, I will . . .	
Area #2: Ways of Seeing and Being with Others	
As an equity-centered CS teacher, I commit to . . .	

Transforming this commitment into action,	
Today, I will . . .	
This week, I will . . .	
This month, I will . . .	
This quarter or semester, I will . . .	
Area #3: Advancing CS Pedagogy	
As an equity-centered CS teacher, I commit to . . .	
Transforming this commitment into action,	
Today, I will . . .	
This week, I will . . .	
This month, I will . . .	
This quarter or semester, I will . . .	

Area #4: Advocacy for Equitable Change in CS Ed	
As an equity-centered CS teacher, I commit to . . .	
Transforming this commitment into action,	
Today, I will . . .	
This week, I will . . .	
This month, I will . . .	
This quarter or semester, I will . . .	

I will hold myself accountable by . . .	
I can find support from . . .	

Commitment check-ins				
Date	Progress	Successes	Challenges	Next Steps

RESOURCE 2: SUGGESTED COMMITMENTS TO EQUITABLE CS ED

This resource provides an overview of all of the suggested commitments from this chapter.

AS AN EQUITY-CENTERED CS TEACHER, I COMMIT TO . . .

1. **Critical and continuous learning** about systems of oppression and advantage, historical events, and racial frameworks that shape CS and CS Ed power dynamics and my own relationships to tools and technology.

2. **Self-awareness and examination of internal attitudes and beliefs** to issues related to social identity and social justice in the CS classroom and the larger world.

3. **Seeing and valuing all students (all people)** as well as their cultures, histories, and ways of being in the world and to empower students to explore these experiences in CS Ed.

4. **Empowering and preparing students to enact change** through the critical examination of CS and by lifting up students' own goals and purposes for computing.

5. **Continually tailoring programming and pedagogy** to best nurture and empower the social development of individual students in all of their uniqueness, intersectional identities, and individual needs.

6. **Advocating for the individual educational needs of students** in CS Ed to administrators, colleagues, and other stakeholders.

7. **Recognizing my own role** in the systems of oppression and **working to disrupt** systems of oppression and injustice

    - in my own mind;
    - in ways of working in the world;
    - in standards set for students;
    - in CS curricula;
    - in the CS profession; and
    - in systems of schooling.

8. **Empowering and educating colleagues** on tech literacy, CS integration, and CS innovations through an equity lens.

9. **Being a host, not a hero**, in CS equity work and professional learning communities.

8

Getting Started with Digital Racial Literacy in Computer Science Education

Lloyd Talley and the Computer Science Educational Justice Collective

CHAPTER OVERVIEW

This chapter introduces the concept of digital racial literacy as an application of frameworks that examine racial literacy in the context of technology. Digital racial literacy involves developing students' awareness of the relationships between race and technology, preparing students to manage emotions connected to racism in computer science (CS), and empowering students to critique and use technology to disrupt inequities. The chapter begins by exploring how racism and racial-ethnic bias shape computing. It then considers how to promote digital racial literacy in CS education (CS Ed) through internal reflection and self-examination and through an examination of racial socialization processes. The chapter concludes with strategies to develop digital racial literacy in CS classrooms. This chapter is intentionally written for self-reflective practice in community with others. It is highly recommended that this chapter is read and discussed individually and with colleagues or critical friends to pause, reflect, and identify steps to take action.

CHAPTER OBJECTIVES

After reading this chapter, I can:

- Identify ways that racial bias has impacted technology.

- Define digital racial literacy and explain its connection to CS and CS Ed.

- Reflect on my racial identities and experiences in preparation for developing my students' digital racial literacy.

- Define racial socialization and identify ways that students are socialized about race in my CS Ed context.

KEY TERMS

critical race theory; digital racial literacy; Four I's of Oppression and Advantage; racial-ethnic; racial-ethnic socialization; racial literacy; racism; RECAST framework

BRANDIE'S STORY

Brandie is an elementary CS teacher committed to an equity-oriented CS practice. One of her commitments involves helping students become aware of inequities that exist in technology fields. Brandie described a lesson she created for her students:

> I created a lesson for my fifth grade students to introduce them to the book *Power On!* by Jane Margolis and Jean Ryoo. I wanted students to come to the conclusion that homogeneity in CS is dangerous and can lead to a range of unintended consequences. I showed a video of the seemingly harmless technology of an automatic soap dispenser that would not dispense soap for a Black user. I watched as the students tried to make sense of how it worked perfectly every time for the white person, or even when a white paper towel was placed in front of the sensor, but not the Black hand.

Through her lesson Brandie sought to develop her students' **digital racial literacy** about technology—their awareness of bias in technology, their ability to navigate emotions that surface when exploring racial and ethnic issues in tech, and their ability to take action to disrupt inequity in tech. In this chapter, we'll consider the relationships between race and ethnicity, technology, and CS Ed as part of understanding the important need to develop digital racial literacy in CS Ed.

digital racial literacy
Fostering digital racial literacy in CS Ed involves:

1) Developing students' awareness of the role of human bias in shaping algorithmic bias and the ways in which racially marginalized communities are represented in and threatened by current and existing technologies.

2) Preparing students and colleagues to manage the emotions they will face as they interact with CS products and possible workplace experiences that embed racism.

3) Empowering students to critique the impact of technologies on their communities and in their daily lives and to use technology to disrupt systems of oppression and galvanize their communities.

THE RACIALIZED LANDSCAPE OF COMPUTING AND CS ED

> Tech is racist and sexist and ableist because the world is so. Computers just reflect the existing reality and suggest that things will stay the same—they predict the status quo. By adopting a more critical view of technology, and by being choosier about the tech we allow into our lives and our society, we can employ technology to stop reproducing the world as it is, and get us closer to a world that is truly more just.
>
> —Broussard (2023)

racism A system of prejudice and discrimination based on race that privileges individuals racialized as white and oppresses racially minoritized individuals.

In her powerful text, *More than a Glitch*, professor and journalist Meredith Broussard shares the above quote that serves as a stark reminder of the pervasive social biases that are deeply entrenched in our society. One of the most pervasive of these systems is **racism**. By racism, we mean the individual prejudice, systemic oppression, and inequitable access to power and resources that result from perceived differences between one socially constructed racial category and another (Harris, 1993; Kendi, 2019).[1] CS educators face immense challenges, as they are at the front lines of teaching in a world that is inherently racist and where technology, rather than serving as a neutral tool, instead serves to embed, amplify, and perpetuate racism.

Educators bear a profound responsibility to support children and young people to navigate this complex landscape and to work together to achieve a more just and inclusive understanding of technology. The enormity of this task is underscored by the need to teach the technical aspects of computing as well as address deeply ingrained biases to dismantle the discriminatory structures embedded within the field.

Despite ongoing efforts to reduce harm and bias in tech, these efforts have often fallen short. In part, this is due to a lack of attention to developing the digital racial literacy of those who work in tech-related industries. By digital racial literacy, we mean an awareness of bias in technology, an ability to navigate emotions that surface when exploring racial and ethnic issues in tech, and an ability to take action to disrupt inequity in tech (Talley, 2022). Digital racial literacy brings together existing frameworks (Daniels et al., 2019; Price-Dennis & Sealey-Ruiz, 2021; Stevenson, 2014) to offer a concrete application of these ideas in CS Ed.

---

1. We recognize that racism also encompasses inequitable access to power and resources based on socially constructed ethnic categories. In this chapter, when we refer to race, we also include ethnicity in that discussion. The term "racial-ethnic" is used to emphasize this relationship.

This chapter will help educators get started on their journey to develop digital racial literacy. It begins with an overview of the realities of computing and computing education in a racialized world to build factual awareness. The remainder of the chapter explores what we mean by digital racial literacy in CS and how we promote it in our CS classrooms. Journaling and reflection prompts are embedded throughout the chapter to help readers develop emotional preparedness. (See Chapter 6 for further guidance on journaling and dialogue practices.)

COMPUTING IN A RACIALIZED WORLD

A complex web of racial biases affects every facet of society, perpetuating disparities that span all **Four I's of Oppression** (ideological, institutional, interpersonal, and internalized; see Chapter 5). Computing technologies and their deployment in marginalized communities amplify negative racial biases in our society and unjustly impact these communities. As was introduced in Chapters 2 and 3, racial biases shape algorithms that impact everything from search engine results to job hiring processes to criminal sentencing procedures. Below are some specific examples of how racial bias in technology pervades tech industries.

> **Four I's of Oppression and Advantage** A theory that illustrates how systems of oppression and advantage (like ableism, classism, or racism) are produced across multiple layers of society. The four I's are ideological, institutional, interpersonal, and internalized. (See Bell, 2013; Chan & Coney, 2020; Chinook Fund, n.d.; Kuttner, 2016.)

RACIAL BIAS IN THE TECHNOLOGY INDUSTRY

FACIAL RECOGNITION TECHNOLOGY

Facial recognition technology has been found to have significant accuracy differences based on race. A study by the National Institute of Standards and Technology found that facial recognition algorithms were more likely to misidentify Asian and African American faces, leading to higher rates of false-positive identifications and greater potential for false arrests. This bias in facial recognition technology disproportionately impacts racially marginalized communities who are more likely to be wrongfully arrested and face other negative consequences (Grother et al., 2019).

HEALTHCARE ALGORITHMS

Healthcare algorithms have been found to perpetuate racial bias by providing less accurate medical diagnoses for individuals from certain racial groups. For example, one study found that Black patients were less likely to be referred for specialized care when using an algorithm for managing chronic diseases. This type of bias leads to inadequate treatment for individuals from racially marginalized communities and worsens existing health disparities (Obermeyer et al., 2019).

JOB ADVERTISEMENTS

Job advertisements and recruiting practices in the tech industry have been found to perpetuate racial bias. Research has found that job postings for tech positions use language that is more likely to appeal to white candidates and discourage applications from underrepresented groups. Additionally, recruiters have been found to rely heavily on personal networks for candidate referrals, which can further entrench existing racial and ethnic disparities (Cesario et al., 2020).

EDUCATIONAL TECHNOLOGY

Education technology has been found to perpetuate racial bias by providing fewer educational opportunities for students from certain racial groups. One study found that online education resources tended to feature characters that were mostly white, while Black and Hispanic characters were underrepresented. This lack of diversity in educational materials contributes to existing educational disparities and impacts future career opportunities for students from racially marginalized communities (Laskowski & Kumar, 2018).

RIDE-SHARING ALGORITHMS

Ride-sharing algorithms have been found to perpetuate racial bias by providing less reliable service to passengers from certain racial and ethnic groups. A study found that ride-sharing services were more likely to cancel rides requested by passengers with African American sounding names. This type of bias contributes to existing transportation disparities and negatively impacts individuals from racially marginalized communities who rely on ride-sharing services (Ge & Knittel, 2019).

Racial biases embedded in technology play a significant role in perpetuating injustice across many areas of social life. At the same time, some have mobilized computing tools and technologies to promote social activism and to advocate for racial justice. Activist groups have organized in digital spaces, including social media. One notable example is the #BlackLivesMatter social media strategy, led by Tamia Mallory. See Table 3 in Chapter 4 for additional examples.

COMPUTING EDUCATION IN A RACIALIZED WORLD

Statistical realities cast a somber light on the impact of racial biases on the state of computing education. Black, Latine, and Indigenous youth in the United States are excluded from CS Ed at alarming rates.[2] Furthermore, these groups often encounter barriers that impede their access to quality CS Ed, contributing to a troubling lack of diversity in the field. Asian youth across many ethnic groups also face stereotyping and harassment in CS Ed.

The tech workforce, access to CS Ed, and new technology development are all inherently political and subject to the racialization processes embedded in U.S. society. This reality raises the stakes for CS educators who want to advance equitable CS Ed. Acknowledging the severity of these issues in the real world can be scary. However, we must not avoid empowering our students to be informed consumers of technology and their social world. When confronted with a field that has been shown to both exclude and perpetuate harm toward racially marginalized communities, CS educators might feel helpless and overwhelmed. The task can seem even more difficult when we are asked to promote the **racial-ethnic** diversification of the CS industry and to prepare students to be wise consumers of technology as central goals of many CS Ed efforts in schools today.

Despite broad-scale efforts to increase equitable practice in CS, translating these aims into tangible classroom practices remains challenging. Much rich work is being done examining race in relation to CS and CS Ed using a variety of different constructs (see, for example, Jones & melo, 2021; Lachney et al., 2019; Lachney et al., 2023; Tanksley, 2023; Tanksley, 2024). The concept of digital racial literacy aids in translating equity aims into classroom practice. Central to these efforts is promoting students' awareness of and ability to manage topics related to race-ethnicity in their daily lives and tech spaces, particularly for students

racial-ethnic This term recognizes race and ethnicity as social constructions. Both race and ethnicity—and the conflicts that emerge related to them—are relevant to issues of inquiry in CS and CS Ed. This term captures how both constructs need to be considered as part of developing digital racial literacy.

---

2. See the On Terminology section of this guide for an explanation on our use of different identity-related terms.

who are underrepresented in tech, such as African American students, Latine students, and students from Indigenous nations.

WHAT DO WE MEAN BY DIGITAL RACIAL LITERACY IN CS?

CS educator Dawn shared an example of how she worked to promote students' awareness of topics related to race and ethnicity in their lives:

> I have shared with my CS students facial recognition biases in the industry and how women or people of color have struggled to get to the management level in the field. Many of my students were surprised to learn that. For some students, it was their first CS class, and they had no context for what the technology industry was like. A lot of them were honest that they wanted to enter the field because they would make a high salary. For some of my Asian students, they believed that they just have to do coding, and there is no need to socialize. In my AI [artificial intelligence] class, I tried very hard to clear these misconceptions and make sure my students worked in partner groups or teams to collaborate and include each other.

As Dawn's example shows, many of the issues that impact equity in CS and CS Ed are undergirded by a fundamental lack of digital racial literacy. CS Ed often falls short of preparing students to gain an awareness of bias in technology, an ability to navigate emotions that surface when exploring racial and ethnic issues in tech, and an ability to take action to disrupt inequity in tech (Talley, 2022).

While scholarly frameworks like **critical race theory** are helpful to understand macro level racial inequities, they fail to instruct us in the day-to-day practices that will shape a more equitable CS field (Bell, 2023; Delgado & Stefancic, 2023; Ledesma & Calderón, 2015). By contrast, digital racial literacy can help educators assess their own readiness for discussing and confronting topics related to racial bias with students in their classrooms. It can also help teachers prepare students to be knowledgeable consumers of tech and prepare those who aspire to tech careers for the racialized encounters they will experience in the workforce.

Digital racial literacy can be especially empowering for minoritized students who have experienced marginalization around race and ethnicity. Yet ultimately, this kind of learning helps *all* students become more conscientious makers and consumers of technology. Incorporating digital

critical race theory
A scholarly theory that frames race as a socially constructed reality embedded into society. Critical race theory recognizes racism as complex and intersectional with other social identities. It seeks to center racially marginalized voices through a commitment to challenge the status quo and work toward social justice (Bell, 2023; Delgado & Stefancic, 2023; Ledesma & Calderón, 2015).

racial literacy practices into computing education helps students develop an appreciation of how racial-ethnic minoritized people have shaped CS and recognize how our actions can shape the future diversity of the tech workforce and the experiences of their fellow citizens.

Race and racial conflicts impact educational spaces broadly. Seeking to address this reality, Stevenson (2014) developed frameworks to explore notion of **racial literacy**. Racial literacy involves a historical and factual awareness of racial issues in the classroom and the emotional preparedness needed to discuss and engage with these issues. Stevenson proposed the **Racial Encounter Coping Appraisal Socialization Theory (RECAST) framework** as a practical way to address racial stress and trauma. It has three components: READ, RECAST, and RESOLVE. READ focuses on developing a historical and factual awareness of race and racial politics and of your own racial identity. RECAST offers strategies to manage and cope with racial stress and trauma, including developing emotional preparedness. RESOLVE focuses on addressing and taking action against the root causes of racial tension and trauma. The RECAST framework is explored in greater detail in Chapter 9.

As discussed above, race intersects with the digital world in important and unique ways. Given the need to make technologies and the industries that produce them more racially equitable and diverse, practitioners and scholars have defined what it means to practice racial literacy specifically within the realm of technology. Building on Stevenson's (2014) work, Daniels and colleagues (2019) developed a foundational definition for racial literacy in technology.

RACIAL LITERACY IN TECHNOLOGY
(Daniels et al., 2019)

Racial literacy in technology involves:

- an intellectual understanding of how structural racism operates in algorithms, social media platforms, and technologies not yet developed;

- an emotional intelligence concerning how to resolve racially stressful situations within organizations; and

- a commitment to take action to reduce harms to racially marginalized communities.

---

racial literacy The historical and factual awareness of racial issues in the classroom and the emotional preparedness needed to discuss and engage with these issues (Stevenson, 2014).

RECAST framework The Racial Encounter Coping Appraisal Socialization Theory or RECAST framework offers support to address racial stress and trauma and discuss racial topics in the classroom. The RECAST framework has three parts:
1. READ or becoming aware of racial stress and trauma
2. RECAST or managing and coping with racial stress
3. RESOLVE or taking action against the root causes of racial tension (Stevenson, 2014).

These tenets provide a set of broad goals for CS educators to aspire to as they orient themselves to teaching youth about racial-ethnic contributions and bias in CS.

Scholars Price-Dennis and Sealey-Ruiz (2021) have considered specifically how to support teachers to develop racial literacy in the digital age. They offer strategies such as archaeology of the self as a process that allows teachers to come to terms with how racism, stereotypes, and bias shape them individually. These strategies are practical ways that support developing racial literacy in tech.

HOW CAN WE PROMOTE DIGITAL RACIAL LITERACY IN CS CLASSROOMS?

Digital racial literacy pairs Daniels and colleagues' (2019) racial literacy in tech framework with Price-Dennis and Sealey-Ruiz's (2021) focus on helping teachers develop racial literacy and applies them through Stevenson's (2014) RECAST theory of racial literacy. Digital racial literacy offers a novel way for teachers and students to concretely engage with racial inequity in technology. Within the computer classroom, digital racial literacy can be translated into the following three efforts.

DIGITAL RACIAL LITERACY IN CS ED

Fostering digital racial literacy in CS Ed involves:

1. Developing students' awareness of the role of human bias in shaping algorithmic bias and the ways in which racially marginalized communities are represented in and threatened by current and existing technologies.

2. Preparing students and colleagues to manage the emotions they will face as they interact with CS products and possible workplace experiences that embed racism.

3. Empowering students to critique the impact of technologies on their communities and in their daily lives and empowering students to use technology to disrupt systems of oppression and galvanize their communities.

In terms of classroom practice, this means intentionally incorporating the contributions and experiences of racial-ethnic minoritized people in tech into our classroom practice. It also means exploring with students the harms and challenges that technology presents to racial-ethnic minoritized communities. We must attend to the social-emotional component of this content by embedding appropriate therapeutic and emotional management strategies into our discussions of race-ethnicity to bolster students' abilities to process and face racialized encounters in the tech space. With this intellectual and emotional preparedness, students can then harness CS to promote justice.

There are many avenues to focus on when addressing racial-ethnic inequities in CS. However, there are four that are particularly important in school-based CS Ed. These issues closely follow the CS Ed-to-tech workforce pipeline and are areas that can be directly influenced by CS educators.

AREAS OF DIGITAL RACIAL LITERACY TO INCORPORATE INTO CS ED

TECHNICAL

Students' awareness and knowledge of the technological means by which racial-ethnic bias enters technologies and the means by which communities of color are targeted through these products. (algorithmic bias; data set representation; data sources; programmer-held bias)

REPRESENTATION

Students' appreciation for and recognition of the contributions of racial-ethnic minoritized people in CS and tech.

PIPELINE AND ACCESS

Providing racial-ethnic minoritized students with insight and access to CS coursework and career pathways.

ADVOCACY AND EMPOWERMENT

Enabling students to promote justice in racial-ethnic minoritized communities through technology.

Incorporating these four areas into CS teaching can promote diversity and inclusion in tech and prepare students to promote justice in their local and national communities.

To prepare you as an educator to engage in this work with your students, we invite you to pause and reflect on what you have read so far by completing the following reflection prompts. (See Chapter 6 for additional guidance on journaling and reflection.)

> **REFLECTION 1: DELVING DEEPER**
>
> - How am I intentionally helping students become aware of the impacts of technology and the tech industry on racial-ethnic minoritized communities?
>
> - How am I promoting a better future of racial-ethnic equity through my classroom CS practice?

LOOKING INSIDE: EXPLORING OUR INTERNAL LANDSCAPE

In our journey toward digital racial literacy in CS Ed, it is imperative to begin by turning inward and examining our personal responses to issues of race. Broussard's (2023) quote at the beginning of the chapter serves as a poignant reminder that technology, like any other facet of our society, reflects existing biases and inequalities. To break away from perpetuating the status quo, we must first engage in an introspective process.

Much of this chapter has grown out of a collaboration with the Exploring Equity in Computer Science (EECS) in New York City Public Schools as part of their Computer Science for All initiative (see Preface for more information). When EECS began, there was a measurable need to improve educators' awareness, emotional management, and social justice orientation toward race and ethnicity. In our work with EECS educators, we consistently found that the topic of race-ethnicity is one of the more confusing and viscerally stressful social identity categories that they encounter daily (Crawford et al., 2023). In EECS program sessions, it became evident that many CS educators hold misconceptions about (1) race-ethnicity, (2) how discrimination manifests in tech, and (3) the contributions of marginalized CS innovators. These responses to the stressfulness of racialized experiences are a microcosm of global social dynamics on race, which are especially apparent in CS and tech.

Working with educators across all disciplines, integrating the topics of race and bias into classroom practice consistently elicits similar reactions (Talley, 2021; Talley, 2022). When encountered, these misconceptions are often met with avoidant, fearful, and even angry responses from educators. Similarly, it is difficult for those with a strong passion for racial and ethnic justice to manage their anger, fear, and avoidance when advocating for their views about race and ethnicity in tech. So if you are feeling any of these things right now, know you are not alone.

As we embark on the journey of teaching computing in a racialized world, let us recognize the transformative potential within our hands. The challenges are immense, but the impact of educators in shaping a more equitable future is equally profound. Together, let us navigate the front lines of equitable practice, armed with knowledge, empathy, and a commitment to dismantling the negative biases that pervade our technological landscape. Take a moment to consider your own position with regard to racial-ethnic issues.

REFLECTION 2: DELVING DEEPER

- How do my life experiences, awareness, and coping abilities around racial-ethnic issues impact my classroom practice and convey care and protection to my students?

While Chapter 6 invites you to engage in this process holistically about your identity and past experiences, in this chapter, we invite you to engage in reflection specifically around your racial identities. The prompts below will help get you started (Talley, 2022). Remember you can refer to Chapter 6 for guidance on journaling, as well as supports for navigating emotions that may arise while engaging in this reflection.

ACTIVITY 1: REFLECTING ON YOUR RACIAL IDENTITIES

EXAMINE YOUR PERSONAL RACIAL JOURNEY

Start by embarking on an "archeology of self" (Sealey-Ruiz, 2013; Chapter 6). Reflect on your racial journey, acknowledging your racial identity and the evolving perspectives you hold. Consider how your own experiences and beliefs may shape your approach to teaching CS. It is especially important to reflect on the messages you received from your family and community early in your life.

EXPLORE WHAT TRIGGERS YOU

Delve into the factors that trigger emotional responses in the context of race. Recognize that these responses are a natural reaction to stress rather than an indication of an inability to address the issues at hand. Understanding our triggers allows us to navigate conversations on race with greater empathy and awareness (Stevenson, 2014).

INVESTIGATE YOUR RELATIONSHIP WITH TECH AND DISCRIMINATION IN EVERYDAY LIFE

Consider your relationship with technology and its intersection with issues of discrimination. How do your experiences with technology mirror or challenge societal norms? Investigate the impact of technology on your perceptions and interactions, particularly in the context of racial dynamics.

ARCHAEOLOGY OF SELF

Building on the insights of Price-Dennis and Sealey-Ruiz (2021), acknowledge the importance of an ethical stance and self-work in developing digital racial literacy. Ongoing practice and adopting reflective approaches can enhance your racial self-efficacy, fostering a deeper understanding of your own biases and reactions.

As CS educators, we all possess racial identities and opinions about race in tech. Recognizing that these conversations may be sensitive, we must actively engage in the Archeology of Self to navigate and understand our own emotional responses (Price-Dennis & Sealey-Ruiz, 2021). By doing so, we equip ourselves to create a more inclusive and equitable learning environment, fostering the social-emotional capacities necessary for addressing racial stress and trauma in the CS classroom.

LOOKING AROUND: HOW OUR STUDENTS LEARN ABOUT RACE

CS educators must recognize that race can be a sensitive and challenging topic to discuss in the classroom. However, avoiding these issues leaves a significant gap in CS Ed by continuing patterns of silence and race-evasiveness or avoiding discussions of race and ethnicity, that reproduce existing inequities. To ensure that future technologists understand the human experience and can build technologies that appreciate human diversity, we as CS educators must intentionally support our students' social-emotional capacities and computational abilities.

To explore digital racial literacy in CS, we begin by analyzing the messages about race we deliver in the classroom. By doing so, we can move beyond a limited, unintentional, and haphazard incorporation of race and ethnicity in CS Ed to a more intentional and purposeful practice of digital racial literacy. By examining these messages we can better understand how our own and our students' racial identities have formed.

REFLECTION 3: DELVING DEEPER

- What messages about race-ethnicity and CS am I implicitly and explicitly sending my students? What does this look like in my classroom?

RACE MESSAGES MATTER

Though the practice is centuries old, the concept of racial literacy was formally introduced by sociology scholar France Twine (2004). Twine studied the strategies, messages, and practices that adults, specifically parents and caregivers, use to prepare and buffer their children from the impacts of racial-ethnic bias. Interestingly, her work began with studying the white parents of multi-racial children in the United Kingdom. The parents in this work expressed that at the heart of racial literacy is an acceptance and awareness that racial-ethnic discrimination and bias is unavoidable for racially and ethnically minoritized youth. By accepting this reality, CS educators can recognize the importance of tending to students' racial awareness and preparation as part of their classroom practice. To address this dynamic, we must understand how our students learn about and cope with racial-ethnic bias and stressors in their lives.

racial-ethnic socialization The process by which we as individuals develop racial identities and a sense of racial meaning based on social norms and expectations. Our racial-ethnic socialization shapes our attitudes, beliefs, and behavior, especially related to racial issues (Hughes et al., 2006).

Much of our understanding and management of racialized experiences are derived from socialization messages that inform our racial identity. These ideologies, biases, and reactions to racial encounters are primarily shaped by implicit and explicit messages. This process is known as **racial-ethnic socialization**. Hughes and colleagues (2006) define racial socialization as the "process by which individuals develop racial identities and a sense of racial meaning, which shapes their attitudes, beliefs, and behavior" (p. 7).

The knowledge we receive from family, media, and society compose the majority of these messages. Although a significant portion of children's racial-ethnic learning occurs with caregivers, teachers and peers also play a critical role in the racial socialization of youth. The messages transmitted by caregivers, teachers, and peers are integral in developing students' awareness, understanding, and emotional preparedness to deal with issues of race and ethnicity in all aspects of their lives.

In their research on parental racial socialization in the United States, Hughes and colleagues (2006) identified five common racial socialization messages delivered by parents: (1) egalitarianism; (2) silence about race; (3) preparation for bias; (4) promotion of (mis)distrust; and (5) cultural socialization. Understanding these common racial socialization messages is helpful for educators' self-analysis of their racial socialization trajectories and racial identity development. Table 1 outlines these messages and connects them to classroom practices.

Table 1. Common Racial Socialization Messages and CS Classroom Practices

Racial Socialization Message	CS Classroom Practice
Egalitarianism	
Promoting the idea that all individuals are equal and should be treated fairly regardless of their race or ethnicity. This type of racial socialization message emphasizes the importance of treating everyone with respect and discourages stereotyping and prejudice based on race. Egalitarianism racial socialization messages are intended to promote equality and fairness and to help individuals develop a positive and inclusive view of people from different racial and ethnic backgrounds.	Encourage youth to value individual qualities and cultural knowledge over racial group membership. This message and practice can promote an inclusive and equitable environment for all students regardless of their racial background. *Precaution:* Although this egalitarian message may feel equitable and fair, without balanced acknowledgement of difference, it can become a reinforcement of color-blindness, or a way to ignore the impacts of racism on society and on individuals

Silence About Race	
The absence of direct messages or practices related to racial issues, such as the exclusion of topics related to racial equity and inclusion in educational curricula or the avoidance of discussing incidents of racial bias or discrimination. This lack of discussion can contribute to a culture of racial insensitivity and reinforce systemic racism.	The implicit or explicit avoidance of the topic of race can exclude racially minoritized students from important conversations and contribute to their marginalization. *All* teachers should incorporate conversations about algorithmic racial bias and racial-ethnic leaders in all CS classrooms. Educators should create a safe and inclusive learning environment where students can openly discuss the impact of racial inequality on the tech industry.
Preparation for Bias	
Promoting awareness and preparedness to cope with discrimination can help students of color to navigate potential discrimination they may face.	Teachers can inform their students about incidents of racial bias in tech organizations and marginalized communities to prepare them for possible biases they may encounter in their future careers. Teachers can support students to be co-conspirators and allies, to recognize and disrupt bias when they recognize it, instead of leaving the work only to those experiencing racial bias.
Promotion of (Mis)Distrust	
Practices that emphasize wariness and distrust in interracial interactions can further contribute to racial tensions and discrimination.	Educators should focus on promoting cross-cultural understanding, empathy, and respect to create a more inclusive learning environment for all students.
Cultural Socialization	
Messages and practices that teach children about their racial or ethnic heritage and history; promote cultural customs and traditions; and encourage cultural, racial, or ethnic pride can foster a sense of belonging and pride among students of color.	Teachers can incorporate culturally relevant materials, historical events, and cultural holidays to create a more inclusive and welcoming classroom environment. For instance, teachers might incorporate the tradition of braiding from continental Africa into a lesson regarding computing circuitry to make connections between cultural practices and computing. However, as discussed in Chapter 2, teachers should be sure to incorporate these examples in ways that avoid essentializing students or assuming that such examples are automatically relevant to students from a given background.

Unpacking the implicit and explicit messages about race that educators have received over the course of their life is a necessary reflective step to identify current dispositions and reactions to race-based content. To help with this, review Table 1, and then take a moment to reflect.

> ### REFLECTION 4: DELVING DEEPER
>
> - Which racial socialization messages did I hear as a youth? Which messages do I recognize that are being sent to my students?

It's important to remember that when it comes to digital racial literacy, the work begins with ourselves. As educators, we must be willing to examine our biases and assumptions, our racial identity development, and life course socialization experiences. We can only effectively teach our students digital racial literacy if we actively engage in it ourselves. We must also be willing to listen to our students' experiences and perspectives, recognizing how their identities shape their understanding of and experiences in the world.

Integrating messages about race into CS Ed can enable educators to be intentional and purposeful in their curricula. It can also lay the foundation for how students make sense of and evaluate racialized encounters. By informing our intellectual understanding of common racial socialization messages, we can better appraise racial encounters and assess the stressfulness of race-based events and our coping responses to these events.

REVISITING BRANDIE'S STORY

It may seem daunting to tackle racial issues and develop students' digital racial literacy in CS Ed, but students are able and ready to engage with these ideas. Brandie shared her students' reactions to her *Power On!* lesson:

> It was powerful to see students' shock and upset grow during the lesson as they saw example after example of how a lack of diverse programmers and a diverse data set led to inaccuracies in CS tools that ranged from inconvenient to deadly. At the end of the lesson, as they read how the characters in the story questioned who is creating seemingly racist AI, they learned some statistics about women and people of color having lower access and participation in CS education and careers.

> By fifth grade at my school, students have had a significant number of learning experiences about slavery, racism, and many forms of discrimination, but it was powerful for them to see technology failing in this way as well. I hope it was a powerful lesson for them to see that CS and technology is not neutral and that society's power hierarchies can be replicated through technology too.

Brandie's lesson and her students' reactions illustrate the power that can come from working to develop digital racial literacy in CS Ed. In the next chapters, we'll consider some concrete tools and strategies that you can use to do this work in your own context.

REFLECTION QUESTIONS

1. When have you recognized or experienced racialized bias in technology? After reading this chapter, do other examples come to mind? Why is it important to make students aware of these realities?

2. What stands out to you about the concept of digital racial literacy? What connections do you notice between developing racial literacy in general and developing digital racial literacy within the context of CS Ed?

3. Why do you think it is important to develop our own digital racial literacy in tandem with supporting students to develop their digital racial literacy? What role does racial-ethnic socialization play in the need to develop digital racial literacy?

TAKEAWAYS FOR PRACTICE

- Review the descriptions of the recommended areas of digital racial literacy in CS Ed (Technical; Representation; Pipeline and Access; Advocacy and Empowerment) discussed in the chapter. Consider which of these areas already appear in your current curriculum and where you might make changes to incorporate examples from these areas into your instruction.

- Take some time to reflect on your racial identities by completing Activity 1. Remember that you can journal through writing, drawing, coding, or any other creative medium to convey your thoughts, ideas, and feelings.

GLOSSARY

Term	Definition
critical race theory	A scholarly theory that frames race as a socially constructed reality embedded into society. Critical race theory recognizes racism as complex and intersectional with other social identities. It seeks to center racially marginalized voices through a commitment to challenge the status quo and work toward social justice (Bell, 2023; Delgado & Stefancic, 2023; Ledesma & Calderón, 2015).
digital racial literacy	Fostering digital racial literacy in CS Ed involves: 1) Developing students' awareness of the role of human bias in shaping algorithmic bias and the ways in which racially marginalized communities are represented in and threatened by current and existing technologies. 2) Preparing students and colleagues to manage the emotions they will face as they interact with CS products and possible workplace experiences that embed racism. 3) Empowering students to critique the impact of technologies on their communities and in their daily lives and to use technology to disrupt systems of oppression and galvanize their communities.
Four I's of Oppression and Advantage	A theory that illustrates how systems of oppression and advantage (like ableism, classism, or racism) are produced across multiple layers of society. The four I's are ideological, institutional, interpersonal, and internalized. (See Bell, 2013; Chan & Coney, 2020; Chinook Fund, n.d.; Kuttner, 2016.)
racial-ethnic	This term recognizes race and ethnicity as social constructions. Both race and ethnicity—and the conflicts that emerge related to them—are relevant to issues of inquiry in CS and CS Ed. This term captures how both constructs need to be considered as part of developing digital racial literacy.
racial-ethnic socialization	The process by which we as individuals develop racial identities and a sense of racial meaning based on social norms and expectations. Our racial-ethnic

	socialization shapes our attitudes, beliefs, and behavior, especially related to racial issues (Hughes et al., 2006).
racial literacy	The historical and factual awareness of racial issues in the classroom and the emotional preparedness needed to discuss and engage with these issues (Stevenson, 2014).
racism	A system of prejudice and discrimination based on race that privileges individuals racialized as white and oppresses racially minoritized individuals.
RECAST framework	The Racial Encounter Coping Appraisal Socialization Theory or RECAST framework offers support to address racial stress and trauma and discuss racial topics in the classroom. The RECAST framework has three parts: 1. READ or becoming aware of racial stress and trauma 2. RECAST or managing and coping with racial stress 3. RESOLVE or taking action against the root causes of racial tension (Stevenson, 2014).

REFEENCES

Bell, D. A. (2023). Who's afraid of critical race theory? In E. Taylor, D. Gillborn, & G. Ladson-Billings (Eds.), *Foundations of critical race theory in education* (3rd ed., pp. 30–41). Routledge. https://doi.org/10.4324/b23210-4

Bell, J. (2013). *The four "I's" of oppression*. Begin Within. https://beginwithin.info/articles-2/

Broussard, M. (2023). *More than a glitch: Confronting race, gender, and ability bias in tech*. MIT Press. https://doi.org/10.7551/mitpress/14234.001.0001

Cesario, J., Johnson, D. J., & Eisthen, H. L. (2020). Language in job ads may contribute to underrepresentation in the tech industry. *Proceedings of the National Academy of Sciences, 117*(16), 8981–8984.

Chan, E. L., & Coney, L. (2020). Moving TESOL forward: Increasing educators' critical consciousness through a racial lens. *TESOL Journal, 11*(4), 1–13. https://doi.org/10.1002/tesj.550

Chinook Fund. (n.d.) *4 I's of oppression*. https://chinookfund.org/wp-content/uploads/2015/10/Supplemental-Information-for-Funding-Guidelines.pdf

Crawford, C., Kuyenga, M. A., Talley, L., Mirakhur, Z., & Clark, H. (2023). *Organizing for educational equity in computer science: Lessons from New York*

City's CS4All initiative. New York City Department of Education. https://sites.google.com/schools.nyc.gov/cs4all-equity/about-us/impact-report?authuser=0

Daniels, J., Nkonde, M., & Mir, D. (2019). *Advancing racial literacy in tech: Why ethics, diversity in hiring & implicit bias trainings aren't enough.* Data and Society Fellowships Program. https://datasociety.net/wp-content/uploads/2019/05/Racial_Literacy_Tech_Final_0522.pdf

Delgado, R., & Stefancic, J. (2023). *Critical race theory: An introduction* (4th ed.). NYU Press. https://doi.org/10.18574/nyu/9781479818297.001.0001

Ge, Q., & Knittel, C. R. (2019). Racial and gender discrimination in transportation network companies. *Proceedings of the National Academy of Sciences, 116*(12), 5365–5370.

Grother, P., Ngan, M., & Hanaoka, K. (2019). *Face recognition vendor test (FRVT) part 3: Demographic effects.* National Institute of Standards and Technology. https://doi.org/10.6028/NIST.IR.8280

Harris, C. I. (1993). Whiteness as property. *Harvard Law Review, 106*(8), 1701–1791. https://www.jstor.org/stable/1341787

Hughes, D., Rodriguez, J., Smith, E. P., Johnson, D. J., Stevenson, H. C., & Spicer, P. (2006). Parents' ethnic-racial socialization practices: A review of research and directions for future study. *Developmental Psychology, 42*(5), 747. https://doi.org/10.1037/0012-1649.42.5.747

Jones, S. T. & melo, n. a. (2021). We tell these stories to survive: Towards abolition in computer science education. *Canadian Journal of Science, Mathematics and Technology Education, 21*, 290–308. https://doi.org/10.1007/s42330-021-00158-2

Kendi, I. X. (2019). *How to be an antiracist.* One World.

Kuttner, P. J. (2016). Hip-hop citizens: Arts-based, culturally sustaining civic engagement pedagogy. *Harvard Educational Review, 86*(4), 527–555. https://doi.org/10.17763/1943-5045-86.4.527

Lachney, M., Babbitt, W., Bennett, A., & Eglash, R. (2019). Generative computing: African-American cosmetology as a link between computing education and community wealth. *Interactive Learning Environments, 29*(7), 1115–1135. https://doi.org/10.1080/10494820.2019.1636087

Lachney, M., Allen Kuyenga, M. C., Phelps, J., Yadav, A., & Drazin, M. (2023). "Everybody's searching their roots": Centering Black nature-cultures of belonging in non-compulsory computer science education. *Computer Science Education, 34*(4), 829–863. https://doi.org/10.1080/08993408.2023.2268378

Laskowski, M. P., & Kumar, A. (2018). Representation matters: The effect of avatar race in a virtual world and implications for educational and career opportunities. *Computers & Education, 123*, 147–160.

Ledesma, M. C., & Calderón, D. (2015). Critical race theory in education: A review of past literature and a look to the future. *Qualitative Inquiry, 21*(3), 206–222. https://doi.org/10.1177/1077800414557825

Obermeyer, Z., Powers, B., Vogeli, C., & Mullainathan, S. (2019). Dissecting racial bias in an algorithm used to manage the health of populations. *Science, 366*(6464), 447–453. https://doi.org/10.1126/science.aax2342

Price-Dennis, D., & Sealey-Ruiz, Y. (2021). *Advancing racial literacies in teacher education: Activism for equity in digital spaces*. Teachers College Press.

Sealey-Ruiz, Y. (2013). Building racial literacy in first-year composition. *Teaching English in the Two-Year College, 40*(4), 384–398. https://doi.org/10.58680/tetyc201323603

Stevenson, H. (2014). *Promoting racial literacy in schools: Differences that make a difference*. Teachers College Press.

Tanksley, T. (2023). Employing an abolitionist, critical race pedagogy in CS: Centering the voices, experiences and technological innovations of Black youth. *Journal of Computer Science Integration, 6*(1). https://doi.org/10.26716/jcsi.2023.12.27.49

Tanksley, T. C. (2024). "We're changing the system with this one": Black students using critical race algorithmic literacies to subvert and survive AI-mediated racism in schools. *English Teaching: Practice & Critique, 23*(1). https://doi.org/10.1108/ETPC-08-2023-0102

Talley, L. M. (2021). *Exploring equity in computer science programs* [Professional development program]. New York City Department of Education.

Talley, L. M. (2022). *Exploring equity in computer science pilot series (EECS Pilot): Program plan and curriculum*. New York City Department of Education. https://sites.google.com/schools.nyc.gov/cs4all-equity/eecs/eecs

Twine, F. W. (2004). A white side of black Britain: The concept of racial literacy. *Ethnic and Racial Studies, 27*(6), 878–907. https://doi.org/10.1080/0141987042000268512

9

Applying Digital Racial Literacy in Computer Science Education

Lloyd Talley and the Computer Science Educational Justice Collective

CHAPTER OVERVIEW

This chapter offers two tools to develop digital racial literacy in computer science (CS) and CS education (CS Ed). First, the chapter introduces and explores Howard Stevenson's (2014) Racial Encounter Coping Appraisal Socialization Theory (RECAST) model by applying the model to a case study of a CS classroom experience. Second, the chapter considers digital racial literacy as a form of social and emotional learning. It offers examples of therapeutic techniques and practices that can be used in CS classrooms to support CS educators and their students in navigating racial stress and trauma. This chapter is intentionally written for self-reflective practice in community with others. It is highly recommended that the chapter is read and discussed individually and with colleagues or critical friends to pause, reflect, and identify steps to take action.

CHAPTER OBJECTIVES

After reading this chapter, I can:

- Explain what the RECAST framework is and identify ways to apply this framework to develop digital racial literacy.
- Explain why digital racial literacy can be understood as social-emotional learning and identify therapeutic practices that can be used to develop digital racial literacy.

KEY TERMS

digital racial literacy; intercultural competence; racial-ethnic; racial self-efficacy; RECAST framework; social-emotional learning; therapeutic practices

KWAME'S STORY

This chapter offers tangible strategies to apply the theories of digital racial literacy introduced in Chapter 8 to the day-to-day work of CS teaching and learning. First, we provide a framework (RECAST) for navigating racial encounters in the classroom (Stevenson, 2014). Second, we consider how developing digital racial literacy is also social-emotional work and explore how teachers can leverage therapeutic techniques to support digital racial literacy development. To get started, let's meet Kwame, an eighth-grade CS teacher.[1]

> In the wake of the George Floyd murder, eighth-grade CS teacher Kwame noticed that his students were distracted.[2] Some expressed feelings of anger and hopelessness during private conferences after his lesson. Disturbed by his students' sadness and also angered by the killing himself, Kwame wanted to do something to address his students the next day.
>
> That evening, he silenced his social media accounts, went for a long-needed jog, made his favorite dinner, and journaled reflectively for thirty minutes about his thoughts on the situation. Then, he drew up a brief lesson plan.
>
> The next day, Kwame began his classes with an emotion cloud and a stress barometer to get a sense of his students' feelings. He also held a moment of silence. Then, pulling from his reflective journal, Kwame discussed his feelings of sadness and distress over the George Floyd murder and connected it to the killings of Emmett Till and Rodney King.[3] Kwame used a write-pair-share activity to have students express their emotions in regard to the strategy. For the writing portion, he encouraged artistic

---

1. This vignette was developed with Kwame's permission.
2. See https://en.wikipedia.org/wiki/George_Floyd and https://en.wikipedia.org/wiki/Murder_of_George_Floyd
3. See https://en.wikipedia.org/wiki/Emmett_Till and https://en.wikipedia.org/wiki/Rodney_King

expression using poems and narrative writing and tools like p5[4] on sites created with html and CSS. Kwame then encouraged students to use their responses to express their feelings and perspectives in an impromptu George Floyd Mattered Town Hall activity. After the Town Hall, Kwame's students wanted to take action to support the memory of George Floyd in their own school and in the community.

The following week, Kwame hosted an in-class Action Brainstorm Bonanza and Unconference to facilitate student thinking on collective action they could take. These activities resulted in students writing emails and letters to their city council and to Congress, advocating for a change to their school's discipline policies and establishing a Black Lives Matter youth group at his school.

You'll return to Kwame's story later to consider the steps that he took to foster his own and his students' digital racial literacy. We turn now to a framework that can help us consider how to develop digital racial literacy in CS classrooms like Kwame did.

THE RECAST FRAMEWORK

As CS continues to grow as a field, educators may wonder, How can we possibly combat systemic racism from our classrooms?[5] The CS students of today are the industry and field leaders of tomorrow. This means they, and we, have great power to re-define and re-make the cultures of the technology industry. Amid the complexities and challenges, there is a resounding call to action for CS educators. Beyond the theoretical discussions, this chapter is a call to engage, to question, and to guide students toward a more informed and conscientious interaction with technology through developing digital racial literacy. As discussed in Chapter 8, **digital racial literacy** involves:

1. Developing students' awareness of the role of human bias in shaping algorithmic bias and the ways in which racially marginalized communities are represented in and threatened by current and existing technologies.

---

digital racial literacy
Fostering digital racial literacy in CS Ed involves:

1) Developing students' awareness of the role of human bias in shaping algorithmic bias and the ways in which racially marginalized communities are represented in and threatened by current and existing technologies.
2) Preparing students and colleagues to manage the emotions they will face as they interact with CS products and possible workplace experiences that embed racism.
3) Empowering students to critique the impact of technologies on their communities and in their daily lives and to use technology to disrupt systems of oppression and galvanize their communities.

---

4. The tool can be found at https://p5js.org
5. We recognize that racism also encompasses ethnic conflict and prejudice based on ethnicity. In this chapter, when we refer to race, we include ethnicity in that discussion. The term "racial-ethnic" is used to emphasize this relationship.

2. Preparing students and colleagues to manage the emotions they will face as they interact with CS products and possible workplace experiences that embed racism.

3. Empowering students to critique the impact of technologies on their communities and in their daily lives and empowering students to use technology to disrupt systems of oppression and galvanize their communities.

There are many tools that can be used to support CS teachers and students to develop digital racial literacy. The **RECAST framework** from Howard Stevenson (2014) is one model that helps explain the relationship among racial encounters, socialization messages (see Table 1 in Chapter 8), and our coping responses to stressful situations. According to Stevenson, overcoming our biases and improving our reactions to racial encounters requires ongoing practice and can't be resolved just through accumulating knowledge.

The RECAST framework offers a practical approach to addressing racial stress and trauma in the CS classroom. The framework has three key components: READ, RECAST, and RESOLVE.

- READ focuses on developing an historical and factual awareness of race and racial politics, and your own racial identity.

- RECAST aims to manage and cope with racial stress and trauma.

- RESOLVE focuses on addressing and taking action against the root causes of racial tension and trauma.

Let's look more closely at how we can apply this framework to the practice of digital racial literacy in CS Ed.

In the READ component, CS teachers can educate themselves about the impacts of issues like algorithmic bias, cyber surveillance, and workplace discrimination in the world. Educators can explore—individually and with their students—the underlying biases that shape the design and implementation of computer systems and software and seek to understand how these biases can marginalize certain groups. Additionally, teachers can work to create a classroom environment that values diversity and inclusivity, where students can feel comfortable expressing their experiences with racial bias in tech.

In the context of RECAST, the increasing use of social media/forums and online communication (e.g., internet, dark web) has created a new source of racial stress for many students. Online racial interactions, such as cyberbullying, trolling, and hate speech can cause significant emotional distress and trauma. Teachers can help students develop coping strategies to manage these stressors, such as mindfulness techniques and therapeutic strategies. They can also encourage students to seek support from counselors or mental health professionals.

Finally, the RESOLVE component of the framework emphasizes the importance of social action and taking steps to address the root causes of racial stress and trauma. In the context of CS, this can involve advocating for greater diversity and inclusivity in the tech industry, challenging the underlying biases in algorithms and computer systems, and promoting social justice.

It is important to note that the growing reliance on virtual communication and technology can also hinder youths' development of in-person social skills and engagement in collective action. Therefore, teachers can also encourage their students to engage in community-based activism and civic activity, helping them build the skills necessary to make a difference in the world. Through these efforts, CS teachers can help students develop the tools and strategies needed to effectively manage and respond to racial stress and trauma in their personal and professional lives.

The socialization that occurs throughout the course of our lives and the coping responses we develop through our experiences shape what Stevenson defines as **racial self-efficacy**, or our belief that we can cope with and manage **racial-ethnic** encounters in everyday life (Stevenson, 2014). As educators develop their digital racial literacy by building ongoing awareness, managing their emotional responses, and committing to promoting social justice through CS, they are better prepared to support their students to do the same. To foster your own and your students' racial self-efficacy, it is essential to focus on developing digital racial literacy as an ongoing practice, including how to address stressful racial-ethnic encounters in the moment.

APPLYING THE RECAST FRAMEWORK IN THE CLASSROOM

CS educator Brandie teaches at a predominantly white school in a district that prioritizes developing students' digital racial literacy.[6] A few years ago, the district started an initiative to develop a curriculum that highlights the racial and cultural challenges of marginalized groups to elevate the voices of those whose stories are not often told. Brandie's fifth-grade students read *Ghost Boys* by Jewell Parker Rhodes. The novel was inspired by Tamir Rice and includes Emmett Till as a character.[7] Brandie

---

racial self-efficacy The belief that one can cope with and manage racial-ethnic encounters in everyday life (Stevenson, 2014).

racial-ethnic This term recognizes race and ethnicity as social constructions. Both race and ethnicity — and the conflicts that emerge related to them — are relevant to issues of inquiry in CS and CS Ed. This term captures how both constructs need to be considered as part of developing digital racial literacy.

---

6. See the On Terminology section of this guide for an explanation on our use of different identity-related terms

7. See https://en.wikipedia.org/wiki/Killing_of_Tamir_Rice and https://en.wikipedia.org/wiki/Emmett_Till

described the novel as "definitely a hard read. The first page starts with the character's internal monologue as he lays on the ground dying after having just been shot." Recognizing the racial stress and trauma that this novel would raise for students, Brandie's fifth-grade team used the RECAST framework to support their students' digital racial literacy as they engaged with the text. In Table 1, Brandie shares what she did as she taught the novel.

Table 1. Applying the RECAST Framework in the Classroom

RECAST Element	Classroom Application
READ	Parents were notified in our monthly newsletter that we were getting ready to read the book so they could familiarize themselves with the story and the themes within the book. We wanted to allow space and time for parents to introduce or discuss topics with their child that felt important to their family before we began reading. We were hopeful that this initial invitation would lead parents to check in and support their child throughout the unit as well.
	I reached out directly to the parent of the one Black girl in my class to make her aware that the book might be particularly challenging for her daughter, considering the discomfort that her daughter had already shown in previous lessons regarding historical racism and discrimination against Black people. Before we began reading the book in class, I sent a copy of the book home for her parents to read themselves, so that they could familiarize themselves with the story and even read the first chapter with their daughter. I hoped this would provide a safe space for her to initially discuss her feelings and consider what she thought might be helpful for her as coping strategies if she were to develop big emotions while in class.
RECAST	At the end of reading the first scene, I knew the students would be disturbed and upset. I used a mood meter to help the students identify and name their feelings. I gave them a moment to sit with their feelings before asking questions that allowed them to share their thoughts, feelings, and questions in open discussion. The mood meter was an important reflection and check-in tool that I used at parts of the story that I thought were emotionally challenging. I asked students to raise their hands to identify which color of the meter they were in. I also asked if they wanted to continue reading or if they needed time to pause and write.
	I bought a special notebook for this unit that students used to write in as they read. The journal was for them, to help them process the story by drawing or writing their feelings, questions, ideas, etc. Additionally, at the end of each day's reading, or at significant parts of the story, I asked students to answer questions. Some of the questions were about their feelings and some were about their thoughts and understanding of the story.
	There were a few times in the unit, such as when the character Emmett Till told the story of his death, that we did a "Chalk Talk." Students sat in groups at tables that had a large piece of chart paper, and they shared their reactions with each other silently by writing on the paper. They read the reactions of others in their group and responded silently by drawing lines to connect and then write their responses. It provided a different way for students to express themselves, process their feelings and the feelings of others, and respond to each other. It's a very powerful outlet for the kids to express their feelings and develop empathy as they learned the feelings of their classmates.

Table 1. Continued

RECAST Element	Classroom Application
RESOLVE	At the end of the unit, students had a choice project in which they could choose the genre and media they wanted to use to respond to the book. Some students wrote poems or did art. Although coding a Scratch project was an option, not many students had strong enough coding skills to efficiently complete a program like that. There was a big showcase and fifth-grade classes from schools across the district got to share their work with each other.

Now that you have read Brandie's experience, reflect on the examples she shared. Where do you notice the different elements of the RECAST framework? How did Brandie develop an awareness of racial stress and trauma for herself? For her students? How did she plan to manage and cope with her own and her students' stress? How did the unit allow students to address and take action against racial tension and trauma?

DIGITAL RACIAL LITERACY AS SOCIAL-EMOTIONAL LEARNING

Because a key component of the RECAST framework involves managing and coping with stress related to racial-ethnic encounters, CS teachers need strategies and approaches to help manage stress. This section considers how to do this in the CS classroom by considering how digital racial literacy can be considered **social-emotional learning** (SEL). SEL refers to learning skills and behaviors to develop healthy identities, manage emotions, and maintain healthy and supportive relationships (Collaborative for Academic, Social, and Emotional Learning [CASEL], n.d.).

social-emotional learning Learning skills and behaviors needed to develop healthy identities, manage emotions, and maintain healthy and supportive relationships (CASEL, n.d.).

> ### REFLECTION 1: DELVING DEEPER
>
> - How can digital racial literacy be understood as a form of social-emotional learning?
> - How do I improve my capacity to address racial issues in technology in caring, sensitive, and healthy ways?

With the technology industry's narrow focus on products and efficiency, issues of emotional and social participation can be overlooked. Similarly, in CS, it is also easy to narrowly focus on students' computational thinking and abilities with little regard to their social-emotional competencies.

However, this narrow focus on computational abilities leaves us with a major challenge. It produces technologists who do not understand the human experience and may not have the ability to build technologies that appreciate human diversity. To address this, CS educators must be proactive and intentional in how they support their students' social-emotional capacities while also developing their computational faculties.

Recognizing feelings related to racial-ethnic encounters as a response to stress rather than as an inability to deal with the issues overall is a key starting place to resolving them. Our CS students today are the CS leaders and workforce of tomorrow and will shape the future of human-technological interaction. With this in mind, developing our students' sociocultural awareness and respect for the contributions and experiences of racial-ethnic minorities in the field is key to a more equitable tech landscape. Even students who may not be inclined to seek a career in CS must be equipped with a basic digital racial literacy to promote racial justice in society.

While SEL programs are typically framed as a broad strategy to promote students' executive functioning and emotional management, digital racial literacy can be leveraged as a specific and targeted form of SEL to address racial-ethnic inequities and disparities in technology fields and in CS Ed. Applying strategies that promote historical accuracy and **intercultural competence**, emotional management, and social/civic empowerment to CS instruction is the cornerstone of an ethical and sensitive practice of digital racial literacy in CS Ed (Talley, 2022). By integrating a digital racial literacy mindset into tech education, we can achieve several learning objectives:

1. Building students' cultural humility and empathy toward multicultural influences in tech.

2. Preparing students for experiences of stress and discrimination that may impact their lives as tech consumers and employees.

3. Providing students with the technical and civic skills to resist and respond to racial-ethnic inequities exacerbated by technologies and producers.

To develop digital racial literacy as a form of social-emotional learning in CS classrooms, educators need strategies to navigate moments of racial stress that will arise when seeking to promote equity-oriented instruction. Because CS and technology are sites where youth develop racial identities and are racially socialized, we must remain aware of and continually attend to how our students interact with technology and its racial implications.

intercultural competence
An awareness of one's own cultural perspectives and identities and an ability to engage effectively with others across cultures.

How will you handle the moments of racial stress that may pervade the classroom?

This question defines your practice of digital racial literacy in the CS classroom. The RECAST theory of digital racial literacy pushes us to recognize our ability to respond to these moments or "encounters" by creating an ongoing and intentional practice of recognizing, processing, and responding to these moments.

Using counseling-based strategies can help educators incorporate digital racial literacy into the CS classroom as a form of social-emotional learning. The use of **therapeutic practices** can create a supportive classroom environment and scaffold students' preparedness to discuss topics of race. Common SEL therapeutic practices include active listening, creative expression, controlled breathing, debate, journaling, mindful relaxation, peer co-counseling, role play and drama, self-care, and storytelling. These techniques and how they can support developing digital racial literacy in CS Ed are described below.

therapeutic practices
Practices that can improve quality of life by addressing and helping manage and resolve discomfort, emotional distress, pain, or stress.

SOCIAL-EMOTIONAL AND THERAPEUTIC PRACTICES TO DEVELOP DIGITAL RACIAL LITERACY IN CS ED

ACTIVE LISTENING

Active listening involves paying close attention to what someone is saying, asking questions to clarify understanding, and repeating the speaker's statements to ensure comprehension. Developing a practice of active listening scaffolds empathy development, patience, and the management of emotionally charged responses. Active listening can help students build stronger relationships with peers, teachers, and other community members and helps promote an inclusive classroom environment.

CREATIVE EXPRESSION

Creative expression refers to conveying knowledge, emotions, and ideas through mediums such as art, coding, dance, music, and writing. Encouraging creative expression can allow students to explore their emotions and experiences related to racial-ethnic bias in a safe and supportive environment.

CONTROLLED BREATHING

Practicing controlled breathing exercises can help students regulate their emotions and manage stress related to racial-ethnic bias. One example of a controlled breathing technique is CLCBE (Calculate, Locate, Communicate, Breathe, and Exhale), developed by Stevenson. This skill is particularly helpful for recasting racial stress and trauma. It involves calculating your stress level on a scale of one to ten, locating where you feel the stress in your body, and communicating what you are saying to yourself during the moment. You then breathe in for four counts and exhale for six counts to allow yourself time to pause, become mindful, and decide how to respond (Ravitch, 2020; Rosati, 2020)

DEBATE

Debate can involve creating space for individuals to express and articulate differing perspectives on challenging topics. Facilitating debate in an emotionally supportive environment allows students to enhance their argumentation and advocacy skills while promoting comfort in assertiveness and public engagement.

JOURNALING

Journaling involves recording personal thoughts, feelings, and experience in some way. Journaling supports mindful and constructive self-reflection and allows for a non-judgmental space for students to examine their awareness of and feelings about issues of inequity in and with technology.

MINDFUL RELAXATION

Practicing mindfulness and relaxation techniques such as meditation, yoga, or progressive muscle relaxation can promote emotional well-being and reduce stress and anxiety related to racial-ethnic bias.

PEER CO-COUNSELING

Peer-to-peer sharing of strategies for coping with and addressing racial-ethnic bias allows students to expand their emotional vocabulary while providing space for collective thought and collaborative action.

ROLE PLAY AND DRAMA

Role-playing and drama exercises allow students to explore different perspectives and experiences related to racial-ethnic bias while developing communication and empathy skills.

SELF-CARE

Self-care involves taking action to care for yourself holistically, in all aspects of your personal well-being and happiness, particularly in times of stress. What self-care looks like is different for each individual, and it might encompass emotional, mental, physical, social, and spiritual facets of life. In the classroom, this might look like extending radical compassion to students and noticing students' body language as a signal of potential needs (Ravitch, 2020).

STORYTELLING

Storytelling can promote students' self-expression and help them understand their own experiences with more clarity. Listening to the stories of others can promote intercultural competence and awareness of other experiences.

Integrating these practices into CS instruction can enable educators to sensitively engage students with race-related CS knowledge. Educators can also use these strategies for themselves as they prepare to engage with these topics with students or colleagues.

APPLYING THERAPEUTIC PRACTICES IN THE CLASSROOM

Brandie drew on therapeutic practices to support her students throughout the *Ghost Boys* unit. She was acutely aware of the racial stress that this unit surfaced and incorporated some of the practices described above into her instruction to support students' digital racial literacy as social-emotional learning. Table 2 illustrates how Brandie integrated these practices into the unit.

Table 2. Applying Therapeutic Practices in the Classroom

Therapeutic Practice(s)	Classroom Application
Controlled breathing and mindful relaxation	During the *Ghost Boys* unit, the students read an article about the Tamir Rice shooting to help them prepare for the introductory scene in the book where the character is on the ground dying from just having been shot. Afterwards, I did a breathing meditation activity with the students in which they closed their eyes, imagined a balloon, filled it with all of their negative feelings, and imagined it floating away out of sight. Many of the students leaned into the experience and appreciated the quiet time. Afterwards, I asked if they thought it helped them calm down and feel more in control of their emotions. The reception was mixed, so I didn't try it again. Instead of doing guided visualizations, I just allowed the students at least a minute of quiet time after difficult scenes because the opportunity to sit silently and think freely in order to process their thoughts and feelings was what they seemed to enjoy most about the visualization experience.
Creative expression	The creative expression aspect of the work came through more in the final project of the unit, so it was more of a resolve activity than a recast activity. Students were given the freedom to choose whatever type of media they wanted and an open opportunity to respond to the text. Although creative expression is presented in the recast section of the framework, for elementary students, giving them some kind of creative project to share their ideas and educate others on the topic they've learned is arguably age-appropriate advocacy/action work as well, which I think can also be considered a resolve activity.
Journaling	Journaling was used throughout the unit when we read *Ghost Boys* as a class. The book was read entirely as a shared read aloud. Students had their own copy of the book, which allowed them to read along as I read aloud. Having their own copy let them refer to text details as they reflected on scenes for journaling and as they participated in class discussions. Reading the text as a read aloud felt important for being able to support the students with the particularly difficult parts of the story. For example, when the main character is experiencing his death in the first chapter, I definitely wanted everyone to stop reading as soon as that scene was over, to help them process, as opposed to just continuing to read at their own pace and not giving that scene the emotional space and processing that it needs. When the journal was introduced, students were told that this was their private place to jot whatever came up for them as we read. Unlike their reader's notebook, which they knew I looked at to assess their comprehension, the journal gave them the freedom and privacy to release and/or explore whatever came up for them. It was clear that most of the students really used their journal as their processing space. As we read, you could see kids' faces reflect their emotions or hear kids react with a gasp or a "what?!" When they were sparked by something, they would immediately open their journal and begin writing or drawing. In the pauses after reading, students recorded quickly in their journal as well because I always gave them a few minutes of quiet time to think and journal before we had any kind of discussion. At the end of the unit, the students took their journals home. I think the journals gave kids a private and unstructured space to express themselves, which is rare because for so much of their class work, we ask them to be so structured.

Take a moment again to reflect on Brandie's experiences. How did Brandie tailor these practices for her students' specific needs? Which practices that she described could apply in your own context? What additional supports might you need?

REVISITING KWAME'S STORY

We close this chapter with an invitation for *you* to revisit Kwame's story and consider how he applied the concepts presented in this chapter. After you reflect, you can find commentary on Kwame's story from the chapter author in Resource 1.

> ### ACTIVITY 1: KWAME'S STORY—
> ### GEORGE FLOYD MATTERED
>
> After learning about the RECAST framework for racial literacy, identify which elements Kwame embodied in his story.
>
> ### KWAME'S STORY: (REPRINTED FROM ABOVE)
>
> In the wake of the George Floyd murder, eighth-grade CS teacher Kwame noticed that his students were distracted. Some expressed feelings of anger and hopelessness during private conferences after his lesson. Disturbed by his students' sadness and also angered by the killing himself, Kwame wanted to do something to address his students the next day.
>
> That evening, he silenced his social media accounts, went for a long-needed jog, made his favorite dinner, and journaled reflectively for thirty minutes about his thoughts on the situation. Then, he drew up a brief lesson plan.
>
> The next day, Kwame began his classes with an emotion cloud and a stress barometer to get a sense of his students' feelings. He also held a moment of silence. Then, pulling from his reflective journal, Kwame discussed his feelings of sadness and distress over the George Floyd murder and connected it to the killings of Emmett Till and Rodney King. Kwame used a write-pair-share activity to have students express their emotions in regard to the strategy. For the writing portion, he encouraged artistic expression using poems and narrative writing and tools like p5 on sites created with html and CSS. Kwame then encouraged students to use their responses. Kwame then encouraged students to use their responses

> to express their feelings and perspectives in an impromptu George Floyd Mattered Town Hall activity. After the Town Hall, Kwame's students wanted to take action to support the memory of George Floyd in their own school and in the community.
>
> The following week, Kwame hosted an in-class Action Brainstorm Bonanza and Unconference to facilitate student thinking on collective action they could take. These activities resulted in students writing emails and letters to their city council and to Congress, advocating for a change to their school's discipline policies and establishing a Black Lives Matter youth group at his school.

RECAST Element	Elements from Kwame's Story
READ: What did Kwame do to be aware of and sense (apprise) the upcoming racial moment in his classroom?	
RECAST: How did Kwame acknowledge the stressfulness of the situation and attend to the social-emotional needs of himself and his students?	
RESOLVE: How did Kwame and/or his students address or take action to reconcile the inequities and injustice in their school or society?	
REASSESS: What affirmation, advice, or support would you offer Kwame moving forward?	
Which therapeutic techniques did Kwame use in his situation? Which additional techniques might be appropriate to use in his situation?	

REFLECTION QUESTIONS

1. After reading this chapter, what stands out to you about the importance of integrating a digital racial literacy mindset into CS Ed?

2. One reality of developing digital racial literacy is that it requires you as an educator to become aware of, manage, and address your own racial stress as a key part of supporting your students to do the same. What resources are available to you in your context to support you in doing this work? What other supports might you need?

TAKEAWAYS FOR PRACTICE

- Select a CS unit, lesson, or activity. Analyze it using the RECAST framework. Consider where you are already incorporating aspects of the framework and where you can make changes to more fully address racial stress and trauma.

- Using the same unit, lesson, or activity from above, identify at least one therapeutic practice that you could incorporate to support students' digital racial literacy as a form of social-emotional learning.

GLOSSARY

Term	Definition
digital racial literacy	Fostering digital racial literacy in CS Ed involves:
	1. Developing students' awareness of the role of human bias in shaping algorithmic bias and the ways in which racially marginalized communities are represented in and threatened by current and existing technologies.
	2. Preparing students and colleagues to manage the emotions they will face as they interact with CS products and possible workplace experiences that embed racism.
	3. Empowering students to critique the impact of technologies on their communities and in their daily lives and empowering students to use technology to disrupt systems of oppression and galvanize their communities.
intercultural competence	An awareness of one's own cultural perspectives and identities and an ability to engage effectively with others across cultures.

racial-ethnic	This term recognizes race and ethnicity as social constructions. Both race and ethnicity—and the conflicts that emerge related to them—are relevant to issues of inquiry in CS and CS Ed. This term captures how both constructs need to be considered as part of developing digital racial literacy.
racial self-efficacy	The belief that one can cope with and manage racial-ethnic encounters in everyday life (Stevenson, 2014).
RECAST framework	The Racial Encounter Coping Appraisal Socialization Theory or RECAST framework offers support to address racial stress and trauma and discuss racial topics in the classroom. The RECAST framework has three parts: 1. READ or becoming aware of racial stress and trauma 2. RECAST or managing and coping with racial stress 3. RESOLVE or taking action against the root causes of racial tension
social-emotional learning	Learning skills and behaviors needed to develop healthy identities, manage emotions, and maintain healthy and supportive relationships (CASEL, n.d.).
therapeutic practices	Practices that can improve quality of life by addressing and helping manage and resolve discomfort, emotional distress, pain, or stress.

REFERENCES

Collaborative for Academic, Social, and Emotional Learning [CASEL]. (n.d.). *What is the CASEL framework?* https://casel.org/fundamentals-of-sel/what-is-the-casel-framework/

Ravitch, S. M. (2020, Aug 11). *Why teaching through crisis requires a radical new mindset.* Harvard Business Publishing Education. https://hbsp.harvard.edu/inspiring-minds/why-teaching-through-crisis-requires-a-radical-new-mindset

Rosati, J. (2020, Oct 22). Recasting the moment: Professor Howard Stevenson on creating change through racial literacy. *The Penn GSE Magazine.* https://www.gse.upenn.edu/news/recasting-moment-professor-howard-stevenson-creating-change-through-racial-literacy

Stevenson, H. (2014). *Promoting racial literacy in schools: Differences that make a difference.* Teachers College Press.

Talley, L. M. (2022). *Exploring equity in computer science pilot series (EECS Pilot): Program plan and curriculum.* New York City Department of Education. https://sites.google.com/schools.nyc.gov/cs4all-equity/eecs/eecs

RESOURCE 1: AUTHOR COMMENTARY ON KWAME'S STORY

The table below provides commentary by the chapter author, offering some possible answers to the questions from the concluding activity in the chapter.

> ### KWAME'S STORY: (REPRINTED FROM ABOVE)
>
> In the wake of the George Floyd murder, eighth-grade CS teacher Kwame noticed that his students were distracted. Some expressed feelings of anger and hopelessness during private conferences after his lesson. Disturbed by his students' sadness and also angered by the killing himself, Kwame wanted to do something to address his students the next day.
>
> That evening, he silenced his social media accounts, went for a long-needed jog, made his favorite dinner, and journaled reflectively for thirty minutes about his thoughts on the situation. Then, he drew up a brief lesson plan.
>
> The next day, Kwame began his classes with an emotion cloud and a stress barometer to get a sense of his students' feelings. He also held a moment of silence. Then, pulling from his reflective journal, Kwame discussed his feelings of sadness and distress over the George Floyd murder and connected it to the killings of Emmett Till and Rodney King. Kwame used a write-pair-share activity to have students express their emotions in regard to the strategy. For the writing portion, he encouraged artistic expression using poems and narrative writing and tools like p5 on sites created with html and CSS. Kwame then encouraged students to use their responses to express their feelings and perspectives in an impromptu George Floyd Mattered Town Hall activity. After the Town Hall, Kwame's students wanted to take action to support the memory of George Floyd in their own school and in the community.
>
> The following week, Kwame hosted an in-class Action Brainstorm Bonanza and Unconference to facilitate student thinking on collective action they could take. These activities resulted in students writing emails and letters to their city council and to Congress, advocating for a change to their school's discipline policies and establishing a Black Lives Matter youth group at his school.

RECAST Element	Elements from Kwame's Story
READ: What did Kwame do to be aware of and sense (apprise) the upcoming racial moment in his classroom?	Kwame demonstrated his awareness of the situation as he . . . • Noticed that his students were distracted and that some expressed feelings of anger and hopelessness. • Connected his reflections about George Floyd to the killings of Emmett Till and Rodney King.
RECAST: How did Kwame acknowledge the stressfulness of the situation and attend to the social-emotional needs of himself and his students?	Kwame managed his own and his students' emotions by . . . • Using his reflective journal to discuss his feelings of sadness and distress over George Floyd's murder. • Silencing his social media accounts, going for a jog, making a favorite meal, and journaling. • Having students write an emotion cloud and a stress barometer. • Holding a moment of silence. • Using a write-pair-share activity to have students express their emotions about the tragedy. • Encouraging artistic expression to express their emotions.
RESOLVE: How did Kwame and/or his students address or take action to reconcile the inequities and injustice in their school or society?	Kwame and his students addressed the issue in their local and broader community by . . . • Encouraging students to host an impromptu George Floyd Mattered Town Hall. • Hosting an Action Brainstorm Bonanza and Unconference. • Having students write emails and letters to the city council and Congress. • Advocating for a change to school discipline policies. • Establishing a Black Lives Matter youth group.

RECAST Element	Elements from Kwame's Story
REASSESS: What affirmation, advice, or support would you offer Kwame moving forward?	Kwame might celebrate the actions that he and his students have already taken and continue to engage in self-care and checking in with his students about their social-emotional needs.

Which therapeutic techniques did Kwame use in his situation?
Which additional techniques might be appropriate to use in his situation?

To manage his own emotions, Kwame engaged in journaling and practiced self-care by silencing his social media, going for a jog, and making a favorite dinner. He supported his students by engaging them in creative expression.
Kwame might also have found it beneficial for himself and for his students to engage in controlled breathing exercises and mindful relaxation. He could also consider inviting students to engage in storytelling about their experiences and emotions and leading the students in his Black Lives Matter youth group through peer co-counseling activities.

10

Auditing Your Digital Racial Literacy Practice

Lloyd Talley and the Computer Science Educational Justice Collective

CHAPTER OVERVIEW

This chapter builds on Chapters 8 and 9 by providing resources for computer science (CS) teachers to examine their CS education (CS Ed) practices through the lens of digital racial literacy. The chapter applies the Racial Encounter Coping Appraisal Socialization Theory (RECAST) framework for racial literacy by offering guidance for educators to complete audits of their CS classroom practice and specific CS lesson plans or activities. This chapter is intentionally written for self-reflective practice in community with others. It is highly recommended that the chapter is read and discussed individually and with colleagues or critical friends to pause, reflect, and identify steps to take action.

CHAPTER OBJECTIVES

After reading this chapter, I can:

- Complete audits of my classroom practice and CS units, lessons, and activities to evaluate how I incorporate digital racial literacy into my CS instruction.

KEY TERMS

audit; digital racial literacy; racial-ethnic; RECAST framework; social-emotional learning; therapeutic practices

YOUR STORY

This chapter builds on Chapters 8 and 9 to give you a chance to apply what you've learned as you audit your CS practices and CS curriculum through the lens of **digital racial literacy**, or the process of developing awareness of the relationships between race and technology, managing emotions connected to racism in tech, and critiquing and using technology to disrupt inequity. Let's begin with a reflection. As we begin, we invite you to apply the different strategies you've been learning about to navigate stressors that might emerge related to developing digital racial literacy (see Table 2 in Chapter 9). Remember that it is important to pause and okay to sit with discomfort. As you practice these strategies yourself, you'll be better prepared to support your students in their own journeys.

> ### REFLECTION 1: DELVING DEEPER
>
> - What tangible shifts can I make to incorporate digital racial literacy into my CS curriculum?
> - Who can I rely on to hold me accountable for improving my practice?

Now that you have been introduced to frameworks and techniques to strengthen your knowledge of digital racial literacy in the CS classroom, this chapter offers two tools to evaluate your current practice: a general digital racial literacy classroom practice audit and an audit to evaluate digital racial literacy within a specific lesson or activity.

CS DIGITAL RACIAL LITERACY CLASSROOM PRACTICE AUDIT

When most people hear the word "audit," fear strikes. However, **auditing**, or systematically reviewing your CS curriculum and instructional practices, can be a valuable way to assess where you are and where you need to grow. Auditing might include analyzing your lesson plans to consider

---

digital racial literacy Fostering digital racial literacy in CS Ed involves:

1. developing students' awareness of the role of human bias in shaping algorithmic bias and the ways in which racially marginalized communities are represented in and threatened by current and existing technologies

2. preparing students and colleagues to manage the emotions they will face as they interact with CS products and possible workplace experiences that embed racism

3. empowering students to critique the impact of technologies on their communities and in their daily lives and empowering students to use technology to disrupt systems of oppression and galvanize their communities.

audit A process of systematically reviewing your curriculum and instructional practices to assess where you are and where you can grow.

how they incorporate social equity issues and your students' identities and lived experiences. It might also involve examining your stress and emotional responses to equity issues that may arise in your classroom and taking steps to manage these emotions healthily.

Technology impacts every aspect of our lives, but the field has been plagued with issues of underrepresentation and bias, particularly against **racial-ethnic** minoritized groups.[1] For this reason, teachers can promote equity and inclusion by developing students' digital racial literacy in CS classrooms by focusing on the areas of:

- technology;
- representation;
- access and workforce development; and
- justice, advocacy, and empowerment.

Chapter 8 unpacks these four areas in greater detail. Audits of how we consider these areas in our CS curricula allow us to address systemic barriers that have prevented racial-ethnic minoritized groups from fully participating in the field of CS. For instance, representation in CS has historically been limited to a small group of people, leading to a lack of diversity in mainstream technology development (see Chapters 2 and 3). Access and workforce development determine who has the opportunity to enter into and succeed in the field. Promoting justice, advocacy, and empowerment helps address the power dynamics often at play in technology development and usage. Exploring and engaging in discussions about these topics with students can promote more equitable CS learning.

The Classroom Practice Audit tool below (Tables 1a-c; Talley, 2022) can be used to assess your efforts in promoting equity and inclusion in your CS spaces. Drawing on the **RECAST framework** introduced in Chapter 9 (Stevenson, 2014), the tool is divided into the three parts of the framework: READ, RECAST, and RESOLVE. The audit builds on Stevenson's framework by applying it specifically to developing digital racial literacy. The READ section focuses on awareness and knowledge of issues related to racial-ethnic minoritized people in CS. The RECAST section addresses emotional management and therapeutic practices for students related to racism in tech, and the RESOLVE section focuses on social action and understanding to disrupt racial inequity in tech. Teachers can

---

1. We recognize that racial issues also encompass ethnicity. In this chapter, we include ethnicity in discussions of race. The term "racial-ethnic" is used to emphasize this relationship.

racial-ethnic This term recognizes race and ethnicity as social constructions. Both race and ethnicity—and the conflicts that emerge related to them—are relevant to issues of inquiry in CS and CS Ed. This term captures how both constructs need to be considered as part of developing digital racial literacy.

RECAST framework The Racial Encounter Coping Appraisal Socialization Theory or RECAST framework offers support to address racial stress and trauma and discuss racial topics in the classroom. The RECAST framework has three parts:

1. READ or becoming aware of racial stress and trauma

2. RECAST or managing and coping with racial stress

3. RESOLVE or taking action against the root causes of racial

use the questions provided in each category to reflect on their efforts in promoting equity and inclusion in CS and identify areas for improvement.

Digital Racial Literacy Classroom Practice Audit Tool

Table 1a. READ (Awareness): Knowledge of Racial Issues in CS

Focal Area	Audit Questions
Technology	Do I make my students aware of systemic algorithm bias and its impact on marginalized communities?
Representation	Do I inform my students of CS and STEM trailblazers from racial-ethnic minoritized groups? Do my CS examples and projects offer representations of these trailblazers?
Access and Workforce Development	How do I increase my students' awareness of opportunities and racial disparities in the tech workforce?
Justice, Advocacy, and Empowerment	Do my CS projects reflect the implications of implementing this technology for racial-ethnic minoritized people?

Table 1b. RECAST (Emotional Management): Social-Emotional Learning and Therapeutic Practices

Focal Area	Audit Questions
Technology	Are my students guided to express their emotions and beliefs about algorithmic bias and racial injustice mediated by CS?
Representation	How can I allow my students to process their emotions related to the disparities in representation in tech and CS?
Access and Workforce Development	Have I attended to students' emotions and hope about entering the tech workforce? Have I prepared my students for possible racial bias in tech roles? Have I checked with my racial-ethnic minoritized students about their feelings of belongingness?
Justice, Advocacy, and Empowerment	Have I facilitated opportunities for sharing and emotional development?

Table 1c. RESOLVE (Action): Social Action and Understanding

Focal Area	Audit Questions
Technology	Do my students have an understanding of the processes by which racial bias enters CS products?
Representation	Have I created space to allow my students to engage in meaningful discussions and take action against racial bias in technology?
Access and Workforce Development	What pathways have I created for students to pursue opportunities in tech, considering and addressing racial disparities?
Justice, Advocacy, and Empowerment	How have I helped my students leverage CS to create positive social change? Have I created opportunities for my students to organize and mobilize on their own?

By applying the READ-RECAST-RESOLVE framework to CS pedagogy, classroom management, and ethics, CS teachers can work toward creating more equitable and inclusive learning environments for all students. This requires a commitment to ongoing self-reflection, learning, and action, as well as a willingness to engage in difficult conversations and challenge systemic inequalities inside and outside the classroom.

ACTIVITY 1: PERFORM A CLASSROOM PRACTICE AUDIT

Now it's your turn to complete a classroom practice audit.

1. Reflect on your classroom practices and how they promote equity and inclusion in CS.

2. Utilize the Classroom Practice Audit tool (Tables 1a-c) to address the areas of technology; representation; access and workforce development; and justice, advocacy, and empowerment.

3. Respond to the questions within each category to evaluate your efforts and identify areas for improvement.

CS DIGITAL RACIAL LITERACY UNIT PLAN, LESSON PLAN, OR ACTIVITY AUDIT

Similar to the above Classroom Audit, the CS Digital Racial Literacy Unit Plan, Lesson Plan, or Activity Audit (Table 2; Talley, 2022) is a reflective journey that empowers you to critically assess and enhance the social impact of your CS lessons. Again applying the RECAST framework (Stevenson, 2014) to digital racial literacy development, this activity invites you to revisit one of your favorite lesson plans focusing on the domains of READ, RECAST, and RESOLVE.

In the READ section, examine how your lesson plan incorporates a relevant social issue to contextualize your CS lesson within social equity in the real world. Consider whether you have invited your students to be critical thinkers by analyzing how the CS concept at hand can shape possibilities and contribute to inequities. Take a moment to reflect on how your students' lived experiences and identities might influence their interpretation of the technology or CS assignment.

In the RECAST section, assess whether you have integrated relevant social, emotional, and coping skills into your lesson to model stress management and promote digital racial literacy among your students. Explore how you have examined your own stress about social equity issues that may surface during the CS lesson, recognizing the importance of creating a supportive learning environment.

Finally, in the RESOLVE section, consider whether you have asked your students to develop a social action response or plan to address the real-world implications of the technology and social inequity discussed in your lesson. Evaluate whether you have equipped your students with concrete sociopolitical knowledge or skills, like as digital organizing or Freedom of Information Act requests, to operationalize and address their social equity concerns through a CS project.

Throughout your audit, consider how you might scaffold students' abilities to engage with these topics by incorporating elements of **social-emotional learning** (SEL), including the **therapeutic practices** introduced in Chapter 9.

This audit is an opportunity for growth and refinement, aiming to elevate the social impact of your CS lessons. Embrace the chance to make your lessons more inclusive, relevant, and empowering for your students. Let's embark on this journey of self-reflection and improvement together.

---

social-emotional learning Learning skills and behaviors needed to develop healthy identities, manage emotions, and maintain healthy and supportive relationships (Collaborative for Academic, Social, and Emotional Learning, n.d.).

therapeutic practices Practices that can improve quality of life by addressing and helping to manage and resolve discomfort, emotional distress, pain, or stress.

Table 2. Racial Literacy Unit Plan, Lesson Plan, or Activity Audit

Domain	Prompt	SEL or Therapeutic Lesson Element to Support Students
READ	☐ I have incorporated a relevant social issue to contextualize my CS lesson and connect it to equity in the real world.	
	☐ I have exposed my students to or have invited them to be critical of how this CS concept can shape possibility and inequity.	
	☐ I have considered how my students' lived experiences and identities shape their interpretation of this technology/CS assignment.	
RECAST	☐ I have incorporated relevant social, emotional, and coping skills to model stress management and digital racial literacy with my students.	
	☐ I examined my stress about the social equity issues that may surface during my CS lesson.	
RESOLVE	☐ I have asked my students to develop a social action response/plan to address or further explore the real-world implications of this technology and social inequity.	
	☐ I gave my students concrete socio-political knowledge or skills to address their social equity concerns through a CS project.	

> **ACTIVITY 2: PERFORM A UNIT, LESSON, OR ACTIVITY AUDIT**
>
> Now it's your turn to complete a unit plan, lesson plan, or activity audit:
>
> 1. Take a moment to revisit one of your favorite units, lesson plans, or CS activities.
>
> 2. Use the prompts provided in Table 2 to assess your lesson in the domains of READ, RECAST, and RESOLVE. Provide evidence of integration or potential improvement for each prompt.

CONSIDERATIONS FOR AUDITING YOUR PRACTICE

Many CS educators have audited their practice in their efforts to increase opportunities to develop digital racial literacy in their CS instruction. Here we share some considerations based on their experiences.

First, when completing the audit process, it is important to give yourself enough time and space to complete the task. This includes taking care of yourself and managing your own racial stress that may arise as part of the process. The therapeutic techniques in Chapter 9 can support you in this. CS educator Jami recommended:

> I think the most important thing is to give yourself time to truly reflect instead of trying to squeeze your current practices to meet the requirements. I've seen teachers try to make their current practices "fit" into the audit criteria to "accomplish the task" instead of truly assessing where they can improve.

Remember that making equity-oriented change is an ongoing process. It is okay to make small changes as part of a consistent effort to improve. CS educator Brandie acknowledged some of the challenges that might arise in planning changes based on the results of your audit:

> Since discussing race and equity is not usually a thing that can be quickly mentioned or discussed, making sure that it's done well without taking a lot of time away from the main objectives of the lesson can be challenging.

It can be important to find a balance between developing digital racial literacy well and still ensuring that standards and objectives are met. Similarly, Brandie noted that "talking about issues of race and equity are and can be heavy." Jami added that it's important to balance engaging students with these important issues but also "center joy and the accomplishments of marginalized communities."

Second, while completing your audit, it is important to remember your students and consider their identities, needs, and backgrounds. Brandie and Jami shared that their students experienced lessons focused on digital racial literacy in different ways. Brandie teaches at a predominately white school:

> Lessons and activities focused on discrimination can be particularly difficult for students who are of the cultural group of focus. They are often the only one in the class, and there is a particular discomfort with that to be aware of before discussing certain topics with the class.

Jami faces a different but related challenge. Her school is predominantly Latine.[2] She noted:

> This can make discussions about race challenging because most of the content we cover is about the Black American experience, so many Latine students feel that it is a topic that isn't relevant to them. I highlight ways in which Black activists supported Latin American independence movements and show examples of groups working together to help students understand that injustice hurts all of us.

As you consider changes to make based on your audits, consider what supports different students in your class might need and how you can make your instruction relevant to students with different experiences and backgrounds. While Brandie and Jami acknowledged that this process was challenging, they both emphasized the importance of preparing to engage students about these topics.

Finally, it may seem daunting to seek to develop digital racial literacy due to concerns about how students will respond. Some educators, especially those who teach elementary grades, may feel that students are too young to engage with these topics. While *how* you engage students

---

2. See the On Terminology section of this guide for an explanation on our use of different identity-related terms.

and the supports you provide may differ based on students' ages, it is possible. Brandie described her fifth-grade students' reactions to lessons that developed digital racial literacy:

> The students were shocked and appalled by the examples of bias that they learned. Throughout the lesson there were many open-mouthed shocked faces, audible gasps, questions, and other reactions. Kids were upset that tech could fail so severely in ways that were so hurtful to humans and that the failures were around race. Their sense of injustice and their desire to correct it is pretty developed, so seeing bias surface so strongly in the realm of technology was eye-opening and impactful for the students.

Ethan, a middle school CS teacher, shared similar responses from his older students:

> Students have enjoyed discussing their feelings and creating projects to help mitigate bias. Many of my middle school students felt passionate about fairness and enjoyed creating projects to support social justice. Students often felt empowered when they were working toward solving a real-world problem.

Students come to the classroom with a familiarity with technology, an awareness of inequity, and many feelings and questions. Providing students with support to develop digital racial literacy in connection with technology and opportunities to take action is an essential part of becoming an equity-oriented CS educator.

REVISITING YOUR STORY

Now that you've completed the audits, take a moment to reflect on the insights you gained from the process and the changes and enhancements you envision for your teaching.

REFLECTION 2: DELVING DEEPER

- What key takeaways did you gain from completing the audits?
- How can you further integrate digital racial literacy principles into your CS instruction?
- Are there specific strategies or actions you plan to implement based on what you found in your audit?

As a CS educator, you are at the front lines of CS Ed and workforce development. Your knowledge of the sociocultural landscape of CS is integral to your students' development. Digital racial literacy frameworks are critical because they offer practical guidance on identifying and addressing social equity issues in real-world contexts. Without digital racial literacy, we risk perpetuating and exacerbating social inequities in CS Ed and the tech workforce.

The consequences of not engaging in digital racial literacy in CS classrooms are vast and dire. Ignoring the intersection of race and technology may inadvertently perpetuate harmful stereotypes or allow implicit bias to go unchecked. However, with a concerted effort to recognize and challenge structural inequalities in CS, you can avoid excluding and marginalizing students in your classroom.

We must be intentional in our approaches to teaching CS. This means incorporating relevant social issues and critical discussions of real-world racial bias in tech into our curriculum. It also includes ensuring that our examples and projects reflect the implications of implementing technology for racial-ethnic minoritized communities. We can prioritize offering our students concrete civic and sociopolitical knowledge and skills that they can use to operationalize and address their social equity concerns through CS projects.

As educators, we must be willing to examine our own biases and assumptions, as well as our racial identity development and life course racial socialization messages. We can only effectively teach our students digital racial literacy if we actively engage in it ourselves. We must also be willing to listen to our students' experiences and perspectives, recognizing how their identities shape their understanding of and experiences in the world.

Ultimately, engaging in digital racial literacy in your CS classroom is crucial for advancing equity and inclusion in tech and preparing your students to be informed and responsible citizens in an increasingly diverse and complex world. By prioritizing digital racial literacy in your practice, you help create a more just and equitable society that recognizes and values the unique contributions of all individuals of various racial and ethnic backgrounds. Ultimately, advancing equity in CS requires ongoing learning, growth, and action. We can create a more inclusive and equitable future for all by continuing to develop our digital racial literacy practice.

REFLECTION QUESTIONS

1. Have you ever completed an audit before? If so, what were the benefits? If not, how do you think auditing your practice can help you become a more equity-oriented CS educator?

2. How might you be able to connect what you've noticed about your practice and what you've learned from this chapter to the equity commitments you set in Chapter 6?

TAKEAWAYS FOR PRACTICE

- Use the tools in this chapter to complete an audit of digital racial literacy in your CS education context. Consider how you might create a plan to set goals to improve, check in on your progress, and re-audit your practices periodically.

GLOSSARY

Term	Definition
audit	A process of systematically reviewing your curriculum and instructional practices to assess where you are and where you can grow.
digital racial literacy	Fostering digital racial literacy in CS Ed involves: 1. developing students' awareness of the role of human bias in shaping algorithmic bias and the ways in which racially marginalized communities are represented in and threatened by current and existing technologies 2. preparing students and colleagues to manage the emotions they will face as they interact with CS products and possible workplace experiences that embed racism 3. empowering students to critique the impact of technologies on their communities and in their daily lives and empowering students to use technology to

	disrupt systems of oppression and galvanize their communities.
racial-ethnic	This term recognizes race and ethnicity as social constructions. Both race and ethnicity—and the conflicts that emerge related to them—are relevant to issues of inquiry in CS and CS Ed. This term captures how both constructs need to be considered as part of developing digital racial literacy.
RECAST framework	The Racial Encounter Coping Appraisal Socialization Theory or RECAST framework offers support to address racial stress and trauma and discuss racial topics in the classroom. The RECAST framework has three parts: 1. READ or becoming aware of racial stress and trauma 2. RECAST or managing and coping with racial stress 3. RESOLVE or taking action against the root causes of racial tension.
social-emotional learning	Learning skills and behaviors needed to develop healthy identities, manage emotions, and maintain healthy and supportive relationships (Collaborative for Academic, Social, and Emotional Learning, n.d.).
therapeutic practices	Practices that can improve quality of life by addressing and helping to manage and resolve discomfort, emotional distress, pain, or stress.

REFERENCES

Collaborative for Academic, Social, and Emotional Learning (n.d.). *What is the CASEL Framework?* https://casel.org/fundamentals-of-sel/what-is-the-casel-framework/

Stevenson, H. (2014). *Promoting racial literacy in schools: Differences that make a difference.* Teachers College Press.

Talley, L. M. (2022). *Exploring equity in computer science pilot series (EECS Pilot): Program plan and curriculum*. New York City Department of Education. https://sites.google.com/schools.nyc.gov/cs4all-equity/eecs/eecs

11
Language Injustice in Computer Science Education

Sara Vogel, Christopher Hoadley, Lauren Vogelstein, Wendy Barrales, Sarane James, Laura Ascenzi-Moreno, Jasmine Y. Ma, Joyce Wu, Felix Wu, Jenia Marquez, Stephanie T. Jones, and the Computer Science Educational Justice Collective

CHAPTER OVERVIEW

This chapter examines how inequities related to language manifest in computer science (CS) and CS education (CS Ed). It explores examples of how language injustice operates at ideological, institutional, interpersonal, and internalized levels in CS and CS Ed contexts. The chapter concludes by considering how CS educators can work toward language justice in their CS Ed settings.

CHAPTER OBJECTIVES

After reading this chapter, I can:

- Identify inequities related to language in CS and CS Ed.
- Explain how language injustice is manifested in CS Ed at the ideological, institutional, interpersonal, and internalized levels.
- Define language justice and give examples of language justice in CS Ed.

KEY TERMS

bi/multilingual learners; Four I's of Oppression and Advantage; gatekeeping; intersectional identities; language ideologies; language injustice; language justice; raciolinguistic ideologies; standard English

JOHN'S STORY

Linguistic diversity is ever increasing in contemporary K-12 U.S. classrooms, including CS classrooms. Teachers may find themselves wondering how to reach all learners, regardless of how they communicate. This question is complex and multilayered and involves deeply understanding the students we are trying to support and the policies and beliefs about language that shape our educational spaces. To begin exploring these issues, let's meet John, a sixth-grade CS student.

As you read the introduction to John's story below, consider these questions: What do you notice and wonder about John? How is he described here?

MEET JOHN

During our work at one New York City public school, the PiLa-CS [Participating in Literacies and Computer Science] team met John.[1] John was a sixth-grade student who had immigrated to New York City from East Africa during fifth grade. He used four languages in his daily life: Amharic, Arabic, English, and Tigrinya. When he enrolled in school, he was labeled an English Language Learner, or ELL. Because of this label, John had English as a New Language (ENL) class incorporated into his schedule several times per week. He would typically leave his general education classes during certain literacy or social studies periods to attend his ENL classes.

In his ENL pull-out class, his teacher asked John and his classmates to use Scratch to tell a family story.[2] John decided to animate an important moment in his family's history: when he and his family walked from Eritrea to Ethiopia for three days at the beginning of their journey as refugees.

---

1. PiLa-CS is a research-practice partnership focused on supporting bi/multilingual learners in CS Ed. For more information, see the Preface.
2. Scratch is a programming environment that allows users to design and code their own digital stories, games, and animations at https://scratch.mit.edu.

LANGUAGE AND EQUITY IN CS ED

Have you ever been judged for how you speak or write? Many people share the experience of feeling excluded when their way of communicating doesn't align with how others are communicating. Sometimes this is because they misunderstood an "inside joke," or felt out of place for not using the right "techie jargon," or because they pronounced words differently than someone else. Others have had experiences of being mocked or stigmatized for their accent or for using languages or varieties deemed "inappropriate" to a particular situation.

While people may feel judged for their language in interpersonal interactions, inclusion and exclusion based on language are also structural features of our society. Language-based inequities occur systematically across many institutions, fields, and contexts, including education and CS Ed. **Bi/multilingual learners**, or students who use more than one language and who may be learning English, often experience significant marginalization in school.[3] Bi/multilingual students may be separated from their peers in remedial-style English classes that have lowered expectations for academic learning and limited ways for bi/multilingual students to show what they do know. Standardized tests measure what students know and can do in English but fail to consider what students can express using other languages and modalities. Furthermore, bi/multilingual students may not have opportunities to learn CS at all. In 2022, for example, about 11.2% of students were designated English learners but only about 5.6% of them were enrolled in CS (100Kin10.org, 2022). In CS classrooms that do serve bi/multilingual learners, resources may not be provided in languages that students and their families can understand.

Bi/multilingual learners aren't the only ones who experience marginalization due to their language and communication practices. CS programs may not have the resources or expertise to support learners with speech disabilities or other language-related disabilities. Educators may (even unwittingly) lower expectations for learners who have accents or speech patterns they perceive as "ethnic" or "uneducated" or for students who appear to not know specific technical or disciplinary vocabulary.

School systems and educational policies use many terms to label learners who are bi/multilingual and who are learning English at school. John, for example, was labeled as an English Language Learner (ELL)

> **bi/multilingual learners**
> We use this term to emphasize students' varied and dynamic linguistic resources. We use multilingual to highlight how we may not be able to assume that a learner only uses two languages and may have a broader linguistic repertoire (Holdway & Hitchcock, 2018).

---

3. In this chapter we use the term "bi/multilingual learners" to emphasize these students' linguistic resources. We also opt to use this term because it is strengths-based. We use it synonymously with emergent bilinguals. These terms stand in contrast to terms such as "English Language Learner" or "Limited English Proficient." See the On Terminology section of this guide for an explanation on our use of identity-related terms.

at his school. Each label used in education is attached to associations and assumptions about learners and educational expectations for them (García & Kleifigen, 2018). The terms have important consequences for students' experiences in school.

Historically, the U.S. federal government has labeled bi/multilingual students with terms that take a deficit-based perspective on their abilities (e.g., limited English proficient, language-minority). This approach embeds those deficit views into U.S. schooling structures. Other labels center white, middle class, **"standard" English** language and culture as the desirable norm (e.g., ELL; culturally and linguistically diverse children; language minority students). In recent years, many school systems, states, and educators have worked to shift those perspectives by using terms that highlight both the assets of these students and the historical and ideological systems that marginalize them (e.g., emergent bi/multilingual; racialized bi/multilingual). A more comprehensive list of these labels and their associations appear in Table 1.

Throughout these chapters, you'll notice that we use several of the terms in the table. We use "bi/multilingual learner" and "emergent bi/multilingual learner" to foreground students' rich and fluid language practices. When we use "language-minoritized" or "racialized," we seek to highlight how systems marginalize those who are perceived to have language practices that don't conform to a dominant standard. In some cases, we may also refer to bi/multilingual learners who are receiving services for English learning at school as "bi/multilingual English Learners."

standard English A socially constructed, idealized form of English that is not used by people in everyday life (Chang-Bacon, 2020; Flores & Rosa, 2015).

Table 1. Language Labels in U.S. Educational Settings

Label	Assumptions and Associations
Limited English Proficient	This label was used in federal policy until 2015. It "focuses on the students' limitations rather than their potential" (García et al., 2008, p. 7).
Culturally and Linguistically Diverse Children	This label mistakenly equates diversity with individuals who culturally and/or linguistically deviate from white, middle class, standard English norms.
English as a Second Language Students	This label refers to a subject and not to people. It neglects that students may be multilingual, not just bilingual (García et al., 2008).

Label	Assumptions and Associations
Language Minority Students	This label can "offer a legal basis for [students'] rights and accommodations" but neglects the idea that bi/multilingualism is the norm around the world (García & Kleifgen, 2018, p. 3).
English Language Learner/ English Learner (ELL/EL)	This label is used in U.S. federal policy and by most U.S. states and localities. It foregrounds that these students are and should be learning English rather than leveraging the language assets they already possess (García & Kleifgen, 2018).
Multilingual Learner	This term is used in some states' (e.g., New York) policy documents. It foregrounds students' flexible and bi/multilingual assets and language use.
Emergent bi/multilingual	This term foregrounds students' flexible and bi/multilingual assets and language use. Additionally, it "recognizes the fact that our linguistic performances are always emerging, depending on the task that we are asked to perform" (García & Kleifgen, 2018, p. 5).
Language-minoritized	This term acknowledges how systems perceive the language resources of some students as a problem for institutions to "fix" (Flores, 2020) rather than as an asset or resource (Ruíz, 1984).
Racialized bi/multilingual	This term acknowledges that systems multiply the marginalization of bi/multilingual students who are racialized in society as African, Black, Latine, Middle Eastern, and so on, and/or who are low-income, recent immigrants.

Using different terms to refer to students is not just a semantic exercise or a case of "political correctness." The terms that are used link the experiences of individual learners to the larger systems that are at the root of those experiences (Brooks, 2020; García, 2009b). CS educator Aaron shared what this looks like in his context:

> The ELL label still holds negative stigma in our school with the assumption that ELL students don't behave as well as "honors" or "gen-ed" [general education] students. The label has had a

negative impact on students' behavior because the expectations are set low and students fall in line with this environment of judgment even before a real interaction happens.

I use the term bi/multilingual learners as often as I can, and this is often met with inquiries to clarify what I mean. I think identifying a problem with the language commonly used in schools is a great first step, but it reveals the larger issue of professional development not acknowledging updates in equitable language.

While Aaron's experience highlights the assumptions embedded in these terms, they also have real, material consequences for how students are taught. John's ELL label meant that he was entitled to English learning support and services. In his school's ENL program, a specialized teacher with training in Teaching English to Speakers of Other Languages (TESOL) was tasked with "pushing in" to content classes (e.g., math, science) to provide supports to students with ELL labels. The TESOL teacher also "pulled out" students, especially those just beginning to learn English, to a smaller classroom for differentiated activities a few times each week. John received both supports at different times throughout the week.

Local and state policies to support students with the ELL label vary and can have drawbacks that create gaps for students and their different needs. While being in a smaller pull-out ENL class might help students like John adapt to a new cultural and educational setting in a new country, being in those classes also means students miss out on opportunities, like computing, that are happening simultaneously in the general education classroom. In New York State, where John lives, one option to fulfill policy mandates for students with the ELL label is through bilingual education models. In this setting, students receive content instruction in both their home language and English and are not typically "pulled out" of content classes. There is a Spanish-English bilingual program at John's school but not one that includes languages that John uses, which are less common in his neighborhood. Bilingual education is only required in New York City when more than fifteen students in two consecutive grades speak the same language. This approach creates gaps and differential learning opportunities for students who use a variety of languages but who may not live near others who share those languages.

John, like all students with the ELL label, is expected to make progress toward passing his state's standardized English proficiency test each year. His school is evaluated based on his and his peers' growth. This pressure could lead educators and administrators to focus solely on English learning at the expense of other content areas (Menken & Solorza, 2014). John's school could run the risk of making English learning the most salient aspect of his identity, obscuring how he uses other languages in his daily life (Amharic, some Arabic, Tigrinya). Without care, school policies could end up segregating students like John from the general education population in an effort to push for standardized test performance, stigmatizing John throughout his schooling experiences. The realities described in this chapter give insight into the complex ways that language is entangled with issues of equity in CS Ed.

LANGUAGE INJUSTICE

The stigmas that can follow students in connection with language-related labels are symptomatic of a larger issue that shapes their experiences in schools, in CS Ed, and in CS fields: **language injustice**.

Language injustice is the systematic denial of people's rights to use the language practices of their families,cultures, and communities, or the systematic privileging of certain groups' language practices over others'.

The details of John's story illustrate some of the ways that language injustice plays out in school settings.

language injustice The systematic denial of people's rights to use the language practices of their families, cultures, and communities or the systematic privileging of certain groups' language practices over others'.

JOHN'S LANGUAGE BACKGROUND

John had experiences in many different places, from his hometown in Eritrea, to refugee camps in Ethiopia, to his home, community, and school in New York City. Across all of these contexts, he regularly had to make decisions about how to use language. These were not always easy decisions.

John shared that being multilingual helped him because he could speak to people in their preferred language. He also discussed his decision to use Amharic as a refugee in Ethiopia, sharing that because of the ongoing conflicts between groups in those two countries, he feared he would be physically harmed if he spoke his home language, Tigrinya. John understood that language is linked to power and that aggressors could use language to identify a person's tribe, sect, religion, or region, potentially putting that person in danger.

While John was proud of Tigrinya, calling it "his language," he predominantly used English at school in New York. For example, for his family history Scratch project, he used the English version of Scratch—even though there were versions available in his other languages—because nobody else spoke the other languages he knew. John shared that it was important to him to use the language that others around him would understand to best connect with them, and he prioritized others' comfort and needs in a caring manner.

While he chose to use English for his project, the use of English at school was a complicated issue that he grappled with. During one focus group with John, he spontaneously posed a question to the group:

"I have a question about the thing—Is it a good thing to only speak English? Or uh, like, or another country like language? Because like if you speak English like, people know, like, what kind of language you speak. But if you speak like my language, people—people doesn't know like my language more popular. Is that a good thing only to learn English? That way people could speak to you, like, and they don't-. They know that English is, like, all people know that. English is like American—uh like they speak American people? And pe- uh like, is it only—is it good thing to just learn American?" (Focus Group, May 31, 2019)

John's story highlights that bi/multilingual learners are often navigating far more than their own communication goals when they decide which language to use in different situations. These students are grappling with schools, tools, and communities shaped by language injustice because society marks students' language practices. Sometimes these practices are marked in ways that privilege students, but more often, language practices are marked in ways that marginalize students. Language injustices have been enacted against many learners whose language practices do not conform to the dominant group. This may include students who are Asian, Black, Latine, recent immigrants, children of immigrants, low income, language disabled, from rural areas, or some combination. For example, students who use creolized or vernacular-based varieties of English often don't receive labels like those that appear in Table 1.[4] However, because their language practices differ from the white, middle-class, "standard"

---

4. Examples of vernaculars include African American Vernacular English, Southern American English, or Cockney English. Vernaculars have distinct grammar and vocabulary patterns that are often considered "nonstandard." Examples of creoles include Gullah, Jamaican Patois, and Trinidadian Creole. These are languages in their own right, based in English as a result of colonization and/or enslavement.

English norm, they face language injustice and marginalization in school settings.

Language injustice manifests at the four levels of the **Four I's of Oppression and Advantage** framework we introduced in Chapter 5. It permeates society's dominant *ideologies*, or systems of ideas about how society works. It also gets embedded in our *institutions*, shapes our *interpersonal* interactions, and gets *internalized* by individual people (Chinook Fund, n.d.). It is present in technology and computing fields, which use language to **gatekeep** and produce tools with embedded biases that fail to meet the needs of linguistically diverse societies. It is present in schooling and in CS Ed, where students who use—or who are perceived to use—language differently from the dominant "standard" English norm are marginalized. In the next sections, we examine language injustice at each of these four levels.

IDEOLOGICAL LANGUAGE INJUSTICE

One way that language injustice is perpetuated is through damaging **language ideologies**. Language ideologies are ideas, values, and assumptions about languages, language speakers, and language use that link language to broader social and political systems in different contexts (Irvine & Gal, 2000).

Teachers and students may notice how language ideologies influence the contexts around them. For example, John picked up on how English is centered in the United States, and how the language practices of white, upper- and middle-class "standard" English speakers are privileged over all other means of communication. The idea that using this kind of "standard" language indicates intelligence and capability is a language ideology, not an objective reality. Similar language ideologies exist in global contexts. For example, in Spanish-speaking communities, some Colombian or Argentinian varieties of Spanish are thought to be more prestigious than varieties from the Caribbean.

Deficit-based language ideologies are pervasive in the U.S. school system, and school is framed as a place to "fix" students and families who speak languages other than "standard" English. This is particularly pertinent to African American Vernacular English (AAVE). School cultures often misappropriate various AAVE terms as "slang," which positions all usage of AAVE as "nonstandard" and "inappropriate" for academic settings or writing. This ideology not only limits students' AAVE linguistic expression in the classroom but also broadly undervalues AAVE as a language. AAVE is framed as "a collection of slang terms" or as a "less-than-complete language," instead of the full, robust language that linguists have identified it as (e.g., Smokoski, 2016). The effects of this

---

Four I's of Oppression and Advantage A theory that illustrates how systems of oppression and advantage (like ableism, classism, or racism) are produced across multiple layers of society. The four I's are ideological, institutional, interpersonal, and internalized. (See Bell, 2013; Chan & Coney, 2020; Chinook Fund, n.d.; Kuttner, 2016). See also Chapter 5.

gatekeeping Institutional policies and structures that control who gets to participate in opportunities and who has access to resources in ways that limit the participation of marginalized groups.

language ideologies Ideas, values, and assumptions about languages, language speakers, and language use that link language to broader social and political systems in different contexts (Irvine & Gal, 2000).

raciolinguistic ideologies
Sets of ideas that draw on racism to shape dominant ideas about language (Flores & Rosa, 2015).

intersectional identities
A theory that recognizes how people's different identities (e.g., disability, gender, race) overlap and intersect, creating access to privilege or resulting in oppression in ways that cannot be understood or addressed by considering each identity separately (Crenshaw, 1991; Collins, 2019).

language ideology have material impacts that marginalize and limit students' authentic language use.

Language ideologies also intersect with other kinds of oppressive ideologies in our society, including ideologies about race. Language scholars Flores and Rosa (2015) introduced the concept of **raciolinguistic ideologies** to describe the politicized nature of how racialized bi/multilingual people are perceived by "white listening subjects." These subjects are not so much individual people as they are the social norms that condition us to accept white, middle-class language practices as "standard." Given students' **intersectional identities**, students may be both racially marginalized and considered a language-minority, experiencing multiple and unique forms of marginalization.

INSTITUTIONALIZED LANGUAGE INJUSTICE

Oppressive language ideologies are also taken up by the policies and practices of institutions, becoming embedded in the tools those industries create. In the technology industry, the interfaces of many tech platforms are only available in English and a handful of other global languages. This limitation disadvantages many users and creators. For instance, Facebook suspended the accounts of many Native American users because Facebook systems did not interpret their names as "real names" (Holpuch, 2015). Voice recognition software is less effective at processing the language of people with "non-standard" accents (Paul, 2017). Software support for non-Roman scripts—or even for letters of the Roman alphabet that include accent marks and other symbols—is often absent, buggy, or prohibited (e.g., Fox, 2018). Artificial intelligence models have been shown to perpetuate extreme raciolinguistic stereotypes against speakers of AAVE. These dialect prejudices are more severe than any experimentally recorded human ones, as the artificial intelligence models are more likely to suggest that speakers of AAVE "be assigned less prestigious jobs, be convicted of crimes, and be sentenced to death" (Hoffman et al., 2024, n.p.). These patterns demonstrate the impact of institutionalized language injustice.

CS educators Alexis and Jennifer described how their bi/multilingual learners have been impacted by embedded linguistic biases in technology. Alexis described how "my Bengali and Chinese-speaking students face more challenges in the classroom than my Spanish-speaking students do.[5] Videos and subtitles are often not available in their native languages."

---

5. We preserve Alexis' original terms here and wish to note that what we commonly refer to as "Chinese" in English is not a single language but represents a family of languages and dialects, including Cantonese and Mandarin. The political and ideological nature of these named language boundaries is discussed further in Chapter 12.

Jennifer added, "It's definitely easier to translate with some languages than others. The keyboards for Russian and other Asian languages are different, and it makes translating harder." These examples illustrate how English language-centric designs limit using technology to effectively support bi/multilingual students in CS classrooms.

Harmful language ideologies are also taken up by educational institutions, marginalizing some students and maintaining the linguistic supremacy of students who use language in "standard" ways. Historically across North America, Indigenous and Native American children were forcibly sent to boarding schools to "civilize" and assimilate them. These efforts included violently imposing English and punishing children for using languages other than English (Smithsonian, 2020; Suina, 1985). Violent means were also used to punish immigrant children for using home languages at school (García, 2009a). Some states continue to have laws on the books that make it illegal to educate students bilingually in public schools (Gómez, 2022), and other states have only repealed similar laws as recently as 2015 (Freedberg, 2016).

A common institutional practice is to educate students labeled as ELLs in "English-only" contexts. This approach perpetuates language ideologies that position bi/multilingual learners at a deficit. However, bi/multilingual learners are already fluent in varied and complex language practices. John, for example, spoke four different languages. Yet the ELL label emphasizes only students' "standard" English language status, tying their intelligence to their scores on English proficiency exams and what they can demonstrate about their academic achievement using English. In some schools, schedules are designed to prioritize English learning over all other kinds of learning. As mentioned earlier, ENL teachers are often asked to pull bi/multilingual students out of class during CS time because CS is considered "enrichment," but English learning is considered mandatory. Luckily for John and his classmates, their ENL teacher, Ms. Kors, took care to integrate CS into her class.

Even when students are able to access computing education, institutionalized marginalization can occur through assessments that depend on using the language of the dominant group. In one study, researchers found that middle schoolers designated as ELLs according to the state did worse than other students on text-heavy CS story problems but actually performed better on interviews related to open-ended, authentic final projects (Grover et al., 2016). These findings highlight how students who use language differently may be more successful than traditional metrics show. Bias may be embedded into these metrics in ways that do not enable students to demonstrate their actual abilities (Ascenzi-Moreno & Seltzer, 2021). The ways that language injustice manifests within institutions like the technology industry and computing education puts language minoritized users and learners at a disadvantage.

INTERPERSONAL AND INTERNALIZED LANGUAGE INJUSTICE

Language injustice also manifests interpersonally in interactions between people. In education, this might look like students teasing each other for their accents or for being in the ENL class. It could also appear when teachers tell Black students they are "articulate" when they don't use AAVE. In CS industries, interpersonal injustice might include people who might be excluded for not using the right tech jargon, not knowing the right nerdy cultural references, or not using certain programming languages. It might look like a tech firm hiring manager not hiring an engineer because their accent seems non-standard. For instance, April Christina Curley, a Black employee at Google, described how her manager told her that what they perceived as a prominent Baltimore accent was a "disability" that should be disclosed and that it "intimidated" others in the company (Duffy, 2020; Kirby, 2021). These technical contexts feed into broader methods of marginalization against those who don't use language in the way traditionally dominant or powerful groups do. Language injustice also gets internalized by people, as speakers come to feel pride or shame in how they speak based on their experiences navigating systems and interactions.

STRIVING FOR LANGUAGE JUSTICE IN CS ED AND BEYOND

Bi/multilinguals and other language-minoritized learners come to school with experiences of language marginalization and with thoughts and opinions about it. Educators looking to promote equitable practices in their computing courses must grapple with language injustice. This might include discussing language injustice with students and becoming aware of how language injustice is part of the hidden curriculum in schooling. Educators can work to lower barriers for CS learners who are marginalized around language and to support all learners to notice and push back against oppressive language ideologies in tech tools and cultures. Disrupting inequities around language in CS Ed also involves striving for language justice.

Scholar April Baker-Bell (2020) writes specifically about **language justice** (or as she calls it, **linguistic justice**) in the context of supporting and sustaining the cultural and linguistic practices of Black students:

> [Linguistic justice is] a call to action: a call to radically imagine and create a world free of anti-blackness. A call to create an education system where Black students, their language, their

language (linguistic) justice Challenging white supremacy and dismantling linguistic racism to ensure that all people have the right to use the language practices of their families, cultures, and communities, eliminating the systematic privileging of certain groups' language practices over others' (Baker-Bell, 2020).

literacies, their culture, their creativity, their joy, their imagination, their brilliance, their freedom, their resistance MATTERS. (p. 2)

It is important to note that these linguistic practices are not limited to regional dialects of AAVE, as Black students, like all students, do not exist as a linguistic monolith. For Baker-Bell, linguistic justice is rooted in challenging white supremacy rather than uplifting any specific language practice. By working to dismantle anti-Black linguistic racism, she argues that educators can support Black students and, indeed, any speakers whose language practices deviate from white, middle-class, standard American English norms.

CS teachers can also promote language justice in their classrooms and spheres of influence. How might they do this? Teachers can learn to notice how language-minoritized students resist linguistic injustice daily, especially in the context of computing and technology activities. For example, at John's middle school, students were asked to use a "personalized" automated learning software called iReady. iReady was only available in English, and students were expected to engage with it quietly and independently for test prep. Many students covertly conferred with each other, speaking in home languages and attempting to use translation software to support their use of the tool. One student, Andy, exercised critical consciousness, remarking that *"programadores debieron pensarse como dos veces"* ("programmers should think twice") before releasing iReady as an English-only product. Andy's classmate Mariposa added: "I think it's racist because it doesn't have two languages, it only have one. So it's much difficult for kids that doesn't know English." Furthermore, the school didn't have another technology class available. Andy remarked that if their classmates didn't learn CS and coding, the students might think that computing was limited to iReady rather than encompassing more expansive and creative media (for more, see Vogel, 2020). These students' actions resisted the language injustices they recognized at their school and in educational technology.

Instead of ignoring these moments or treating them as "off-task" tangents, teachers can build on students' language practices and attitudes about language. Teachers who value language justice welcome the kinds of conversations that Andy, Mariposa, and John had around language, power, and technology. They support students to refine their critical consciousness around the potential biases of technology in relationship to language. Teachers can help students navigate choices related to language and technology in the CS classroom and beyond. They can provide opportunities to prototype or design new kinds of tools or digital artifacts to help students and their communities better learn, share, inquire, and express themselves.

Educators who care about language injustice can also become advocates outside of the classroom. There's a long history of parents, educators, and communities fighting for linguistic justice, including the right to educate children using home languages.[6] CS teachers can become involved at a systemic level by developing culturally and linguistically relevant CS curricula, ensuring that English learning services do not conflict with computing coursework, and considering the experiences of bi/multilingual learners and their families when making school policy decisions.

REVISITING JOHN'S STORY

John's story in this chapter shows some of the ways that language injustice can operate in CS Ed. Even as a relative newcomer to U.S. schooling, John was already aware of how language ideologies embedded in institutional policies and structures influenced his interactions with those around him and shaped the language choices he made. At the same time, John's varied and rich linguistic repertoire is a powerful resource for learning. In the next chapter, we'll consider how John's teacher, Ms. Kors, created opportunities for John to draw on his linguistic and cultural expertise as he worked on his Scratch family history project. Learning to recognize and center students' language practices is a key part of moving toward more linguistically just ways of teaching and computing.

REFLECTION QUESTIONS

1. What are some of your own language practices? Are there words, expressions, or language varieties that you use in some contexts or with some people but not others? How do you determine which language(s) or varieties to use and when?

2. Which languages or language varieties are welcome in your classroom or school? How do you communicate to students what ways of communication are (or are not) acceptable in different contexts?

---

6. For example, Chinese American families sued the San Francisco United School District in 1974 to protest the school district's lack of meaningful education for Chinese speaking students in the district. As a result of this ruling, it was decided that schools had to provide students new to English with support to access the curriculum. Puerto Rican activists, also in 1974, sued the New York City Board of Education, and the settlement, the Aspira Consent Decree, declared the right to transitional bilingual education and ESL for New York City students. While both pieces of legislation established bilingual education programs, language injustice persists within and outside of these bilingual programs for racialized bi/multilingual students.

3. What are some of the language ideologies that influence your CS context(s)? Where do you notice these ideologies appearing in institutional policies or interpersonal interactions? In the technology and computing tools you use?

TAKEAWAYS FOR PRACTICE

- Examine your school or district's policies for language learners. Consider which terms are used as labels for students and what embedded assumptions and associations are connected to those labels. How do local policies and practices in your context reinforce or resist those assumptions?

- Consider the story about Andy, Mariposa, and John in the section "Striving for Language Justice in CS Ed and Beyond." Choose a CS tool that is commonly used in your context. Analyze how linguistically accessible it is. What supports or modifications could you provide students—or have students develop—to make the tool more linguistically just?

GLOSSARY

Term	Definition
bi/multilingual learners	We use this term to emphasize students' varied and dynamic linguistic resources. We use multilingual to highlight how we may not be able to assume that a learner only uses two languages and may have a broader linguistic repertoire (Holdway & Hitchcock, 2018).
Four I's of Oppression and Advantage	A theory that illustrates how systems of oppression and advantage (like ableism, classism, or racism) are produced across multiple layers of society. The four I's are ideological, institutional, interpersonal, and internalized. (See Bell, 2013; Chan & Coney, 2020; Chinook Fund, n.d.; Kuttner, 2016). See also Chapter 5.
gatekeeping	Institutional policies and structures that control who gets to participate in opportunities and who has access to resources in ways that limit the participation of marginalized groups.
intersectional identities	A theory that recognizes how people's different identities (e.g., disability, gender, race) overlap and

	intersect, creating access to privilege or resulting in oppression in ways that cannot be understood or addressed by considering each identity separately (Crenshaw, 1991; Collins, 2019).
language ideologies	Ideas, values, and assumptions about languages, language speakers, and language use that link language to broader social and political systems in different contexts (Irvine & Gal, 2000).
language injustice	The systematic denial of people's rights to use the language practices of their families, cultures, and communities or the systematic privileging of certain groups' language practices over others'.
language (linguistic) justice	Challenging white supremacy and dismantling linguistic racism to ensure that all people have the right to use the language practices of their families, cultures, and communities, eliminating the systematic privileging of certain groups' language practices over others' (Baker-Bell, 2020).
raciolinguistic ideologies	Sets of ideas that draw on racism to shape dominant ideas about language (Flores & Rosa, 2015).
standard English	A socially constructed, idealized form of English that is not used by people in everyday life (Chang-Bacon, 2020; Flores & Rosa, 2015).

REFERENCES

100Kin10. (2022). *Belonging: What we know about belonging and how to cultivate it in STEM classrooms*. https://docs.google.com/presentation/d/1GIVR_ELq8bQu8vLa7ACRUAxOqG0la2X39poMLs6SrS0/edit#slide=id.p3

Ascenzi-Moreno, L., & Seltzer, K. (2021). Always at the bottom: Ideologies in assessment of emergent bilinguals. *Journal of Literacy Research, 53*(4), 468–490. https://doi.org/10.1177/1086296X211052255

Baker-Bell, A. (2020). *Linguistic justice: Black language, literacy, identity, and pedagogy*. Routledge. https://doi.org/10.4324/9781315147383

Bell, J. (2013). *The four "I's" of oppression*. Begin Within. https://beginwithin.info/articles-2/

Brooks, M. D. (2020). *Transforming literacy education for long-term English learners: Recognizing brilliance in the undervalued*. Routledge. https://doi.org/10.4324/9781315151236

Chan, E. L., & Coney, L. (2020). Moving TESOL forward: Increasing educators' critical consciousness through a racial lens. *TESOL Journal, 11*(4), 1–13. https://doi.org/10.1002/tesj.550

Chang-Bacon, C. K. (2020). Monolingual language ideologies and the idealized speaker: The "new bilingualism" meets the "old" educational inequities. *Teachers College Record, 123*(1), 1–19. https://doi.org/10.1177/016146812112300106

Chinook Fund. (n.d.) *4 I's of oppression*. https://chinookfund.org/wp-content/uploads/2015/10/Supplemental-Information-for-Funding-Guidelines.pdf

Collins, P. H. (2019). *Intersectionality as critical social theory*. Duke University Press.

Crenshaw, K. (1991). Mapping the margins: Intersectionality, identity politics, and violence against women of color. *Stanford Law Review, 43*(6), 1241–1299.

Duffy, K. (2020, Dec 22). A Black ex-Googler claimed she was told by a manager that her Baltimore-accented speech as a "disability" and later fired. *Business Insider*. https://www.businessinsider.com/google-fired-employee-diversity-recruiter-baltimore-accent-was-disability-2020-12?op=1%5C

Flores, N. (2020). From academic language to language architecture: Challenging raciolinguistic ideologies in research and practice. *Theory into Practice, 59*(1), 22–31. https://doi.org/10.1080/00405841.2019.1665411

Flores, N., & Rosa, J. (2015). Undoing appropriateness: Raciolinguistic ideologies and language diversity in education. *Harvard Educational Review, 85*(2), 149–171. https://doi.org/10.17763/0017-8055.85.2.149

Fox, A. (2018, Feb 28). *Why a Telugu character is bricking Apple devices*. Make Tech Easier. https://www.maketecheasier.com/why-telugu-character-bricking-apple-devices/

Freedberg, L. (2016, Nov 14). *Bilingual education vote in California another shift from bitter 1990s conflicts*. EdSource. https://edsource.org/2016/bilingual-education-vote-in-california-another-shift-from-bitter-1990s-conflicts/572692

García, O. (2009a). Education, multilingualism and translanguaging in the 21st century. In T. Skutnabb-Kangas, R. Phillipson, A. K. Mohanty, & M. Panda (Eds.), *Social justice through multilingual education* (pp. 140–158). Multilingual Matters. https://doi.org/10.21832/9781847691910-011

García, O. (2009b). Emergent bilinguals and TESOL: What's in a name? *TESOL Quarterly, 43*(2), 322–326. https://doi.org/10.1002/j.1545-7249.2009.tb00172.x

García, O., & Kleifgen, J. A. (2018). *Educating emergent bilinguals: Policies, programs, and practices for English learners*. Teachers College Press.

García, O., Kleifgen, J. A., & Falchi, L. (2008). From English language learners to emergent bilinguals. *Equity Matters: Research Review No. 1*. Campaign for Educational Equity, Teachers College, Columbia University.

Gómez, L. (2022, Jan 28). *Push to repeal English-only education appears abandoned in 2022*. AZ Mirror. https://azmirror.com/briefs/push-to-repeal-english-only-education-appears-abandoned-in-2022/

Grover, S., Pea, R., & Cooper, S. (2016, Feb). Factors influencing computer science learning in middle school. In *Proceedings of the 47th ACM Technical Symposium on computing science education* (pp. 552–557). Association for Computing Machinery. https://doi.org/10.1145/2839509.2844564

Hoffman, V., Kalluri, P. R., Jurafsky, D., & King, S. (2024). *Dialect prejudice predicts AI decisions about people's character, employability, and criminality*. Cornell University. https://arxiv.org/abs/2403.00742

Holpuch, A. (2015, Feb 16). Facebook still suspending Native Americans over "real name" policy. *The Guardian.* https://www.theguardian.com/technology/2015/feb/16/facebook-real-name-policy-suspends-native-americans

Holdway, J., & Hitchcock, C. H. (2018). Exploring ideological becoming in professional development for teachers of multilingual learners: Perspectives on translanguaging in the classroom. *Teaching and Teacher Education, 75,* 60–70. https://doi.org/10.1016/j.tate.2018.05.015

Irvine, J. T., & Gal, S. (2000). Language ideologies and linguistic differentiation. In P. Kroskrity (Ed.), *Regimes of language: Ideologies, polities, and identities* (pp. 35–83). School of American Research Press.

Kirby, D. (2021, Jan 22). *April Christina Curley spoke out against racism at Google. Her story points to the struggles Black women face in tech.* Technical.ly. https://technical.ly/company-culture/april-christina-curley-google/

Kuttner, P. J. (2016). Hip-hop citizens: Arts-based, culturally sustaining civic engagement pedagogy. *Harvard Educational Review, 86*(4), 527–555. https://doi.org/10.17763/1943-5045-86.4.527

Menken, K., & Solorza, C. (2014). No child left bilingual: Accountability and the elimination of bilingual education programs in New York City schools. *Educational Policy, 28*(1), 96–125. https://doi.org/10.1177/0895904812468228

Paul, S. (2017, Mar 20). Voice is the next big platform, unless you have an accent. *Wired.* https://www.wired.com/2017/03/voice-is-the-next-big-platform-unless-you-have-an-accent/

Ruíz, R. (1984). Orientations in language planning. *NABE Journal, 8*(2), 15–34. https://doi.org/10.1080/08855072.1984.10668464

Smithsonian. (2020). Boarding schools: Struggling with cultural repression. In *Native words, native warriors.* https://americanindian.si.edu/nk360/code-talkers/boarding-schools/

Smokoski, H. L. (2016). *Voicing the other: Mock AAVE on social media.* [Unpublished master's thesis, City University of New York.]

Suina, J. H. (1985). *"And then I went to school": Memories of a Pueblo childhood.* Rethinking Schools. https://rethinkingschools.org/articles/and-then-i-went-to-school/

Vogel, S. (2020). *Translanguaging about, with, and through code and computing: Emergent bi/multilingual middle schoolers forging computational literacies.* [Doctoral Dissertation], City University of New York. https://academicworks.cuny.edu/cgi/viewcontent.cgi?article=5015&context=gc_etds

12
Translanguaging in Computer Science Education

Sara Vogel, Christopher Hoadley, Lauren Vogelstein, Wendy Barrales, Sarane James, Laura Ascenzi-Moreno, Jasmine Y. Ma, Joyce Wu, Felix Wu, Jenia Marquez, Stephanie T. Jones, and the Computer Science Educational Justice Collective

CHAPTER OVERVIEW

This chapter unpacks the term "translanguaging" and offers it as a theory to promote language justice for bi/multilingual learners in computer science education (CS Ed). It explores how translanguaging as an everyday practice is perceived in deficit ways because of power and social inequity. It also provides examples of how to interpret students' language practices through asset-based lenses. The chapter then considers how taking up translanguaging in CS classrooms makes space for students to draw on their full language repertoires as resources for learning. It concludes by examining the three components of translanguaging pedagogy: stance, design, and shifts.

CHAPTER OBJECTIVES

After reading this chapter, I can:

- Define translanguaging as a theory.
- Explain how translanguaging promotes language justice for students.

- Identify stances, designs, and shifts that can be implemented to leverage translanguaging in CS pedagogy.

KEY TERMS

academic language; bi/multilingual learners; critical consciousness; language repertoire; language resources; languaging; raciolinguistic ideologies; standard English; theory; translanguaging design; translanguaging pedagogy; translanguaging shifts; translanguaging stance; translanguaging theory

JOHN'S STORY

One of the first steps toward promoting language justice in CS Ed is to examine and interrogate how we as educators interpret how people, and especially our students, use language. Do we perceive students as competent communicators and meaning makers? Or do we instead focus on deficits and what students lack? While most teachers want to do the former, we may find ourselves doing the latter when students express meaning in ways that we are not accustomed to or find difficult to parse, or when we don't have enough time to stop and think about what our students are really trying to do.

In this chapter, we revisit John, a sixth-grade student in a New York City public middle school who had immigrated to New York City from Eritrea in East Africa during fifth grade. From John, we can learn how to more sensitively interpret what students say and do in ways that promote equity.

As we learned in Chapter 11, John used four languages in his daily life: Amharic, Arabic, English, and Tigrinya. Labeled as an English Language Learner (ELL) by the district when he enrolled in school, John was placed in an English as a New Language (ENL) class. His ENL teacher, Ms. Kors, worked to integrate CS into their class. She asked her students to use Scratch to tell a family story. John decided to animate an important moment in his family's history: when he and his family walked from Eritrea to Ethiopia for three days at the beginning of their journey as refugees.

In the classroom moment below, John interacts with a Participating in Literacies and Computer Science (PiLa-CS) researcher.[1] As you read this example, we invite you to consider the perspectives you bring: How would you interpret what John is meaning here?

---

1. PiLa-CS is a research-practice partnership focused on supporting bi/multilingual learners in CS Ed. For more information, see the Preface.

INTERPRETING LANGUAGE PRACTICES

In order to create his family history Scratch project, John had to become acquainted with many computational ideas and make choices to express his ideas in code. During this process, John wanted to program his sprites (or characters) to speak one at a time, which required him to carefully sequence "wait () secs" code blocks between the blocks for the characters' dialogue.

John was asked by a PiLa-CS researcher to explain how this code functioned. In his explanation, John drew two different stick figures representing Scratch sprites and then shared how he wanted them to greet each other using spoken language and gestures. The following captures part of John's explanation:

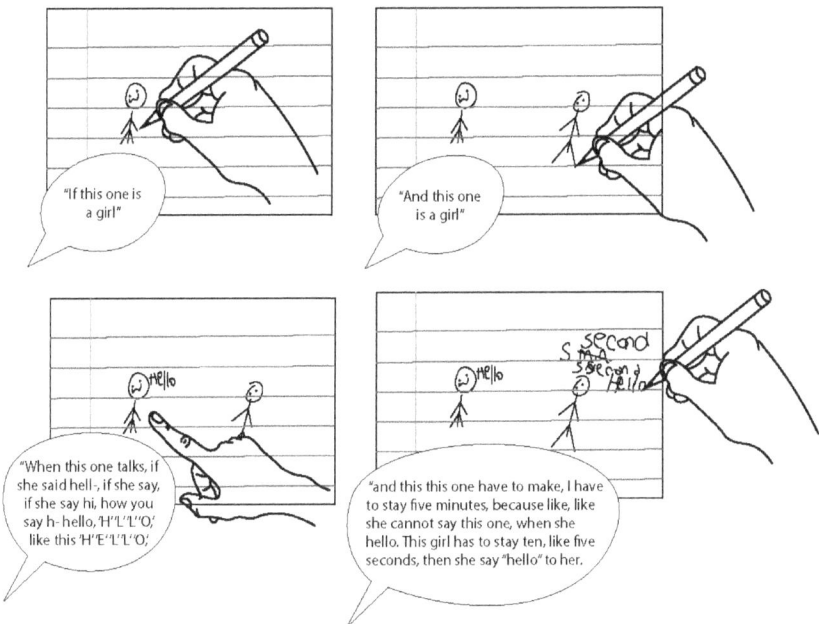

How do you interpret what John is meaning here? (Excerpted from Vogel [2020].)

INTERPRETING STUDENTS' LANGUAGE PRACTICES

There are many ways that teachers might interpret what John is doing here. When students communicate with us, we try to make sense of and interpret their communication through different **theories**, or sets of ideas

theory A set of ideas based on scholarship and practice that are used to explain and interpret how society works.

used to explain how society works.[2] In John's case, we draw on theories we have about how people learn language and use language to learn. Based on our theories, we make judgments about what language counts as "articulate," "academic," or "appropriate" in CS classrooms.

The theories that educators use to interpret language shape what they do in classrooms. For example, using a theory that connects how well a student can use "academic language" to intelligence might lead an educator to identify "problems" with how John shared his ideas. They might label what John was doing with spoken language as "stuttering," with him "struggling" to get his words out. Using this theory, they might conclude that he didn't understand how to code in Scratch. These kinds of deficit-based framings of students can lead educators to provide remedial education around vocabulary and conclude that some students need simplified curricula.

Other theories, however, might lead educators to interpret what John was trying to communicate in a different way. These theories help educators recognize and parse all of the resources—language and communication tools—that John orchestrated in his explanation. John coordinated his words with drawings and gestures and even went on to expand his explanation by asking the researcher to act out the conversation idea together, embodying what it meant for talk to overlap. If our theories help us attend to these many resources, we can recognize that John had an in-depth understanding of the idea that in an animated dialogue, wait time must be programmed in, even if humans take it for granted in a conversation. He also demonstrated his understanding of how code in the language of Scratch is spatially organized.

Attending to all of John's communicative resources would help an educator develop asset-based perspectives on his learning, creating more opportunities for John and other students to fully express themselves. Below, we introduce a theory from linguistics, sociolinguistics, and bilingual education called translanguaging that can help us view students through asset-based perspectives.

translanguaging theory
A theory of language that argues that people have one system of language features and practices that they draw on to make meaning, learn, and express themselves. These features and practices defy the named languages (like English, Spanish, etc.) that society has used to categorize language.

WHAT IS TRANSLANGUAGING?

Translanguaging theory offers a way to center the dynamic and fluid ways that people use language. It helps educators pay attention to the full range of ways that students communicate, without evaluating them against a perceived "standard" way of speaking.

---

2. See Chapter 5 for some theories about equity and inequity that shape this guide.

Translanguaging theory calls attention to how there are two ways of thinking about what language is. When used colloquially, "language" might be used as a noun to refer to a collection or system of sounds, syntaxes, signs, and symbols, which have been politically labeled with a name: Arabic, English, Hindi, Mandarin, Spanish, and so on. But "language" can also refer to the act of communicating itself, a verb. This definition highlights that language is a general competence. Bilingual education scholar Ofelia García uses the verb **languaging** to reflect that language is something people *do* in social contexts. Languaging and communication are universal capacities, even if using particular language systems like English, Mandarin, and Spanish are not. Translanguaging theory captures this idea.

languaging A verb used to indicate how language is something that people *do* in social contexts rather than emphasizing language as a noun referring to a static linguistic system.

TRANSLANGUAGING THEORY

Translanguaging theory posits that:

1. People have only *one* system of language features and practices—one general language repertoire—that they draw on to make meaning, learn, and express themselves.

2. These features and practices defy the named languages (English, Spanish, etc.) that society has used to categorize language (García & Wei, 2014).

To unpack this theory, let's start with the first part: people have one language repertoire.

Just like John, all of us have a collection of resources we use to communicate, make sense, and learn. That collection includes words, sounds, syntaxes, gestures, signs, symbols, objects (like things in our environment, clothes, media, and tools), and social knowledge about how, when, and where to use those forms in different contexts. We call that collection our communicative repertoire (Rymes, 2014) or our **language repertoire**. The features of that repertoire are our **language resources**.

Translanguaging recognizes that people have one, unified repertoire of language features and practices that they draw on when they communicate and make meaning. In recognizing this, translanguaging attempts to rectify past theories that argued that different languages (like Arabic, English, and Spanish) lived separately in the mind. According to those theories, when people communicate, they access each mental system separately, with bilinguals only being able to use one of their different systems at any time. This kind of argument led to misconceptions that there was

language repertoire A collection of resources used to communicate, make sense of the world around us, and learn.

language resources A collection of words, sounds, and syntaxes, gestures, signs, symbols, objects, and social knowledge about how, when, and where to use those forms in different contexts that make up our language repertoire.

only so much "space" in the brain for different languages. Operating with those traditional language theories, educators would probably insist John use his home languages less to reduce confusion, problematically neglecting the assets of his language repertoire, and being complicit in assimilationist forms of education.

Translanguaging theorist Dr. Ofelia García argued that these older theories didn't capture the dynamic ways that most people, and especially bi/multilingual people, actually do language (García, 2009).[3] For example:

- In talking with bilingual friends, bilinguals often use words from different languages in the same sentence to capture concepts and ideas that don't translate.

- A bilingual physics student from Latin America who studied abroad in the United States might be nervous about giving a research talk in what would be considered her "native" language, Spanish, because she learned concepts and ideas about physics in English.

- Many young bilinguals in the United States are encouraged to practice English and not to speak a home language at home. They may be more comfortable listening to and understanding a home language than English but more comfortable speaking and writing in English than their home language.

Traditional theories would suggest that individuals in the circumstances above were less "balanced bilinguals" or were more "dominant" in one language over another. But that idea locates deficiencies and differences in those bilingual people relative to a monolingual standard. Bilinguals are not two monolinguals in one (Grosjean, 2012). As García and others have pointed out, people don't use or acquire languages as they appear in the dictionary. We acquire and use different language resources depending on the context around us and our purposes for communicating.

Another major limitation of traditional language theories is that they posit that named languages are a reality in our brains. But named languages (French, Hebrew, Hindi, etc.) are social and political designations (Otheguy et al., 2015). This reality is clear when we consider the experiences of someone growing up in Scotland and someone growing up in

---

3. In this chapter we use the term "bi/multilingual learners" to emphasize these students' linguistic resources. We also opt to use this term because it is strengths based. We use it synonymously with "emergent bilinguals." These terms stand in contrast to terms such as "English Language Learner" or "Limited English Proficient." See the On Terminology section of this guide for an explanation on our use of identity-related terms.

Louisiana. While they may both be recognized as speakers of "English," they might still find communication with each other difficult. So why are both of those people recognized as speakers of English? Moreover, why are certain minority languages, such as Occitan and Patwah, referred to as "dialects" rather than languages?[4]

One answer to this question can be traced back to colonialism, imperialism, and nation-state building. Scholar Max Weinreich captured this idea during a lecture in the 1940s:

אַ שפּראַך איז אַ דיאַלעקט מיט אַן אַרמיי און פֿלאָט
a shprakh iz a dialekt mit an armey un flot
"A language is a dialect with an army and navy" (Max Weinreich)

This quote captures that traditional power dynamics dictate the ability to decide what counts as a "language," and what is merely a "dialect." People speak how they speak, but politics often shape, police, or value/devalue language practices based on our conceptions of named languages.[5]

This leads to the second part of translanguaging: people's language repertoires do not conform to the named languages (like English, Spanish, etc.) that society has used to categorize language. Translanguaging's "trans-" prefix captures this reality. When we communicate, the ideas we have and the purposes we have for expressing those ideas determine the language we use for our thinking, not the boundaries of the named language. People draw on words, sounds, syntaxes, ideas, gestures, signs, symbols, rhythms, and cadences that they pick up from all of their life experiences.

Translanguaging can help educators attend to the many ways that our students communicate meaning, rather than solely evaluating their speech.[6] Instead of assessing John's language against an arbitrary "standard," we might consider all of the ways that John communicated meaning as he explained his Scratch code. This way, we get a better sense of what he understood about the computational concept of "sequencing."

---

4. Occitan is spoken in southern France, northern Spain, and parts of Italy. Patwah is spoken in Jamaica.

5. As one historical example, several hundred years ago, the northern part of the Indian subcontinent was said to speak a single language termed "Hindustani." However, differences in language use shaped by religion, ethnicity, and the partition of India and Pakistan became codified as two named languages, Hindi and Urdu, written in different scripts. Social pressure has increased to use Persian-derived words in Pakistan and Sanskrit-derived words in India. Although many linguists still consider these registers of a single language, the difference holds power in social and political identities.

6. To learn more about translanguaging, check out the video *Episode 2: Translanguaging 101* at https://www.pila-cs.org/videos

INTERPRETING JOHN'S TRANSLANGUAGING

Even though John only spoke in words that are recognized as English, he translanguaged, drawing on multiple communicative resources to express himself:

- John drew a quick sketch of two stick figures on either side of the page to represent two sprites (*programmable objects such as characters*) in Scratch (*symbols*).

- He wrote text next to each character, carefully sequencing their dialogue in a way that matched how a programmer would code (*words*).

- He gestured to one sprite and then another as he wrote, indicating who was speaking at what time (*gestures*).

- As he wrote the response from the second sprite, he explained and wrote a time amount on top of the sprite on the left because "this girl has to stay ten, like five seconds, then she say 'hello' to her," sharing his awareness of the function of Scratch's "wait" blocks in the context of his dialogue project (*words, sounds, symbols*).

Looking at how John translanguaged—how he coordinated his use of words, drawings, writing, and gestures to communicate his understanding—can help us get a better sense for what he knows and has learned.[7]

Something important to note here is that John tailored his speech to his English-speaking audience, which meant he didn't use all of his language resources including the Amharic, Arabic, and Tigrinya he knows. Can you imagine what he could have expressed about his understanding if he had been able to use his full language repertoire?

CS teachers may allow students to use their full language repertoire without recognizing it. One teacher, Jennifer, explained, "I realize I do a ton of [translanguaging] and never gave it a name." Jennifer described how her students use "diagrams, planning, acting, facial and hand expressions, a mix of languages [and] peer translations" to communicate and convey what they understand. Using translanguaging theory to interpret students' communication has important implications for challenging systems of power and oppression, which we unpack in the next section.

---

7. See Chapters 16 and 17 for more information on the Universal Design for Learning framework, another resource that helps teachers design instruction and assessment that more effectively supports students to demonstrate their learning.

TRANSLANGUAGING, POWER, AND RACISM

As we learned above, the language practices of people are dynamic and defy the language categories that societies have constructed. Translanguaging happens all of the time. For example, think about . . .

- An academic whose manuscript is filled with words specific to their field, Latinisms like "in situ" or "a priori," or equations, charts, and graphs.

- Teens who use the latest memes to share in-jokes with each other.

- A programmer who uses code and comments to ensure others can follow progress they've made on an open-source project.

- The last time you sent a text message to a friend that included gifs or emojis.

- Times you used context to guess words in a science textbook that you didn't understand.

- Times you've used language that would have been considered "inappropriate" or "swearing" in a situation to help you make a point.

- When deaf individuals use signs from standard sign languages as well as signs specific to their communities or families in conjunction with vocalizing and text messaging to communicate (Swanwick, 2016).

- When families with young children use made up words or imitations of their child's pronunciation to share their affection for each other.

Some of the boundary-crossing and defying nature of the language practices described above might seem mundane to you and go unremarked upon day to day. Other examples might stick out more. This is because while translanguaging describes how everyone communicates, some translanguaging practices are more socially marked than others. Some translanguaging moves might mark someone as part of a particular community or help someone identify a certain way. For instance, using techie words and l33t speak (using characters other than letters to modify the spelling of words) might mark someone as a "geek" or "techie" person.[8] But some

---

8. To learn more about l33t speak, visit https://en.wikipedia.org/wiki/Leet

forms of translanguaging are marked because they are associated with groups that are assigned less or more power in society because of -isms like ableism, classism, homophobia, racism, sexism, transphobia, and xenophobia. Depending on context, when people use language associated with groups racialized as Asian, Black, Indigenous, or Latine, or language associated with immigrants, working classes, LGBTQ+ communities, and other marginalized groups, they might be perceived as inferior, uneducated, or transgressive.[9] When people use language currently associated with power and status (including the practices of people of white, heterosexual, cis, male, middle/upper class, college-educated backgrounds), they might be perceived as intelligent, dexterous, or creative.

Elizabeth Acevedo (2015) performs her spoken-word poem, "Afro-Latina" as a compelling example of how language gets marked differently depending on the person using it.[10] In her poem, Acevedo translanguages by leveraging a host of language resources: words that would be recognized as "English," "Spanish," or "Spanglish;" gestures; rhythmic phrasing; singing; and a reference to "*la negra tiene tumbao*" (a line from a song by Afro-Latina artist Celia Cruz). She relays her pride around her identity and unique language practices. She also shares her experiences navigating a society that does not value her and her families' ways of being and communicating. She calls out the ways that society labeled her mother's language "broken English" and how she internalized that stigma for a time.

Acevedo's mother's language was deemed "broken." But plenty of people may use language the same way as her mother and not be stigmatized for it. For example, white American tourists who try to make themselves understood through gesture or machine translation software when they have trouble communicating with spoken language abroad are not, in general, systematically stigmatized for those practices because they are afforded more political power. Similarly, language practices used by marginalized groups might be appropriated by groups who hold more social and political power and, in the process, might be perceived as "cool" without actually affording additional power to marginalized groups.

Everyone translanguages, because everyone's language practices cross and go beyond named language boundaries. But society does not perceive the translanguaging of all people equally.

Over the years, educators have responded to the social marking of language in a variety of ways. Historically, the approach was to help students who

---

9. See On Terminology for more on our use of identity-related terms.
10. View Acevedo's video at https://www.youtube.com/watch?v=tPx8cSGW4k8

used language outside of a dominant norm assimilate by suppressing home languages and working to diminish their accents. As the Civil Rights movement brought attention and power to language-minoritized groups, many educators took up "additive" approaches rooted in teaching kids to "code-switch," or recognize when it would be "appropriate" to use home languages and when to use the dominant language. This code-switching approach was intended to empower students in an unjust society (for a summary of these movements, see Flores & Rosa, 2015).

But recently, some educators have critiqued that additive approach. They have called attention to the **raciolinguistic ideologies** present in societies, or the ways that racism shapes dominant ideas about language. Scholars Nelson Flores and Jonathan Rosa argue that institutions and individuals become "white listening subjects" when they perceive the linguistic performance of racialized people as deviant or at a deficit, no matter how technically their speech conforms to the "standard" (Flores & Rosa, 2015). There are many examples of raciolinguistic ideologies playing out in our society and schools:

- Higher ed professors and K-12 teachers often perceived grammar errors in the speech and essays of Black and Latine students, even though the speech and writing technically complied with standard grammar rules (Alim, 2007; Flores & Rosa, 2015).

- Princess Charlotte, the young daughter of British Royals, has been praised in the popular press for growing up bilingual, while mainstream press accounts of racialized immigrant young people's budding bilingualism is often portrayed in mainstream outlets as a problem to solve (Rosa & Flores, 2017)

- In popular culture, the Spanish practices of many Latine politicians and celebrities are often judged more harshly than those of their white counterparts (Flores, 2016).

raciolinguistic ideologies
Sets of ideas that draw on racism to shape dominant ideas about language (Flores & Rosa, 2015).

These points highlight a key tension: even if a racialized person is code-switching and using language in ways that conform to a dominant standard, it does not mean they can overcome the effects of racism. Dr. April Baker-Bell underscores this point in her book, *Linguistic Justice: Black Language, Literacy, Identity, and Pedagogy* (2020).

> If y'all actually believe that using "standard English" will dismantle white supremacy, then you not paying attention! If we, as teachers, truly believe that code-switching will dismantle

white supremacy, we have a problem. If we honestly believe that code-switching will save Black people's lives, then we really ain't paying attention to what's happening in the world. Eric Garner was choked to death by a police officer while saying "I cannot breathe." Wouldn't you consider "I cannot breathe" "standard English" syntax? (p. 2)

Most, if not all, educators would accept that schools should not impose a language forcibly on students or demand that they "subtract" their home languages. Yet there are still many who argue for an approach that promotes teaching students how to speak "appropriately" or to code-switch in school. Emphasizing that students should speak **standard English** at school or in "professional" environments suppresses their identities as emergent bi/multilinguals or speakers of marginalized varieties of language. It conveys to students that their methods of communication, and even they themselves, are inferior. The language practices our students already use are powerful, valid, and as important as "standard" English. Furthermore, these practices can support them to do CS.

standard English A socially constructed, idealized form of English that is not used by people in everyday life (Chang-Bacon, 2020; Flores & Rosa, 2015).

WHY MIGHT EDUCATORS TAKE UP TRANSLANGUAGING?

In schools, we often restrict students from using their full language repertoires to communicate, in part because schooling expects students to learn to use standard English in "academic" ways. Translanguaging can help educators question the nature and politics of categories like "standard English" and "**academic language**." For example, translanguaging theory helps us ask:

academic language Specialized language used in academic settings.

- Why do named languages exist in the first place? Who decides what the "standard" is?

- Why are certain kinds of language (e.g., words, phrases, and styles used in Black, Latine, and working-class communities) perceived as more/less "proper" or "academic"?

- Why are block-based programming languages like Scratch perceived as less "real" than text-based programming languages like Python?

- How can we elevate speakers who use language in ways that are typically devalued in schools and CS?

- How can we notice and learn more about *all* of the ways students communicate, from home language practices to memes, emojis, and other digital literacies students engage in?

Translanguaging refocuses our attention on the rich and dynamic language practices that students like John already leverage in a given moment (Otheguy et al., 2015). Translanguaging helps us center students' assets. It helps us acknowledge that all people's language repertoires, including those of our students who may be labeled as "English language learners," are already full and always dynamic.

By advocating for teachers to take up translanguaging perspectives, we are not saying you shouldn't teach your students the language necessary to pass a test or ace a job interview. But your students are more than a passed test or job interview. Students should feel free to use any method of communication that will help them learn and to strategically choose the method of communication that will get them the best results in any given situation. Their diverse language practices are an asset, not a hindrance.

As we strive toward equitable practices in CS Ed, especially for students who have been marginalized for the ways they or their families use or are perceived to use language, translanguaging theory can help teachers look beyond whether their students' language practices conform to notions like "perfect English" or "perfect Spanish" and instead pay attention to and value the rich ways students and their communities already express themselves.

When we take up a translanguaging orientation as educators, we put less stock in evaluating how students communicate against a "standard" and instead commit ourselves to help learners:

- Value their identities as bi/multilinguals or users of particular varieties used in their communities.

- Engage with complex content using their full language repertoires.

- Leverage students' existing and complex understandings of language politics.

- Extend their language repertoires to include new practices for different contexts, audiences, and purposes.

- Navigate and push back against a world where language ideologies are imposed by society.

- Build community across language difference.

It is especially important to teach with your bi/multilingual students' translanguaging in mind because their vast language resources are repressed in classrooms more often than many other students' resources. Even when students have the opportunity to use more of their language repertoire than they normally do in school, they often choose not to, perhaps to better connect with their classmates. For instance, although John could have used Scratch in Amharic, he felt a need to restrict his language use to English and even raised the question if using "American" or "English" is better than his translanguaging. Resisting deficit-based language ideologies in the classroom takes time and necessitates creating trusting relationships with students. CS teacher Aaron reflected on how he might use translanguaging to build classroom relationships:

> I have always looked at language as one-dimensional, not paying much mind to cultural, dialectical, and regional differences within a language. . . . I feel like this is a great opportunity to [use] various movies and do a "make your own captions" activity. Essentially, the student hears what the actor/actress is saying in their own words, then must translate it to how the student would say the same thing, but in their own way. This practice reflects listening and absorbing language to show its connection to how we speak for ourselves.

Aaron recognized his own limited definition of language and worked to expand it by recognizing all language varieties as valuable. His activity allows students to use their language repertoires to intentionally move between the context of the movie and their own language practices. This approach would likely build community within Aaron's classroom.

As Aaron's example shows, translanguaging underscores that people use different language and other expressive resources to communicate with different audiences, in different contexts, for different purposes (e.g., to express, to inform, to learn, to persuade, to push back) over their life course. Teachers can help students develop those abilities to deploy their language resources strategically and to reason explicitly about their choices.

As CS teachers who care about equitable practice, we can also support students to develop **critical consciousness**. Language plays a key role in that process. Students might choose to push back on dominant language ideologies. For example, educator and scholar Dr. Jamila Lyiscott (2014) shares in her spoken-word essay how she uses her different language practices in different situations and for different purposes, including to critique society.[11]

critical consciousness
A social and political awareness that allows for a critique of how cultural norms, values, and institutions reproduce social inequities (Ladson-Billings, 1995).

---

11. Watch Lyiscott's talk at https://www.ted.com/talks/jamila_lyiscott_3_ways_to_speak_english

We believe that using a translanguaging lens in teaching can promote equitable practices in your classroom because it starts from the assumption that learners' full language capacities—what they are already good at—is helpful for their learning, instead of focusing on measuring students against external named languages to demonstrate deficiencies.

LEVERAGING TRANSLANGUAGING IN YOUR TEACHING

Students already translanguage all of the time in classrooms. Your job as a teacher is to design learning experiences and supports that help students use their dynamic and rich language resources to learn. This approach is called **translanguaging pedagogy**.

Translanguaging pedagogy is a way of teaching that builds on students' diverse language backgrounds. It isn't just accepting students' diverse language repertoires. It involves explicitly supporting students to leverage the resources in their existing repertoires and to develop new ones.

Translanguaging pedagogy includes three parts: your stance as an educator, your designs for learning, and the shifts in practice you make to respond to students in the moment.

TRANSLANGUAGING STANCE

When we use the word "stance" in this context, we mean it as a belief system that shapes how you approach your students. A **translanguaging stance** is an orientation that frames language diversity across and within individuals as a resource, not a deficit. CS educators who practice translanguaging pedagogy take up a stance that is curious and open about students' language practices. They learn about how students express themselves and make meaning. They also learn about students' experiences with reading, writing, and technology in and outside of school, within the United States, and for some students, abroad.

Ms. Kors' translanguaging stance was embodied in the family history Scratch project she designed for John's ENL class. Ms. Kors asked students to share more about themselves and their family history, inviting them to use language practices that would be authentic to their story in the final product. John took up this invitation and shared a part of his life—his experience as a refugee—with his teacher and peers. The assignment opened up opportunities for John to be acknowledged as the full, complex, and competent community member he already was.

CS teacher Nicole reflected on how understanding translanguaging allowed her to develop a stance to resist deficit perceptions of **bi/multilingual learners** in her context:

---

translanguaging pedagogy A way of teaching that builds on students' diverse language backgrounds, supporting them to leverage existing resources in their language repertoires and to develop new ones.

translanguaging stance An orientation that frames language diversity across and within individuals as a resource, not a deficit.

bi/multilingual learners We use this term to emphasize students' varied and dynamic linguistic resources. We use "multilingual" to highlight how we may not be able to assume that a learner only uses two languages and may have a broader linguistic repertoire (Holdway & Hitchcock, 2018).

In my school, I have heard the terms English as a Second Language (ESL) students, English Language Learners (ELL), English Learners (EL), and multilingual learners. I am now more aware of how using deficit-based framings has made me assess students' language in a negative way. Unfortunately, I am sure I have made assumptions about students' abilities which affected my students in negative ways. [After learning about translanguaging], I can bring different strategies back to my classroom to change my own practices. These efforts will advance my students' communication skills and break some forms of language oppression.

While Nicole shared some of her initial experiences learning about translanguaging, developing a translanguaging stance is an ongoing effort. Educator Tarek Elabsy described his journey:

I've found that the best way to understand my students' language practices is to be truly curious about their experiences. I try to create a classroom where they feel safe to share their thoughts and feelings about language. I also make it a point to listen carefully and really try to understand what they are communicating, even if it's not always clear at first.

One example that comes to mind is when I was teaching a unit on coding. One of my students, Maya, was struggling with some of the programming terms. She kept using a phrase that was a combination of English and Spanish, but it made sense to her. Instead of correcting her, I asked her to explain what she meant, and she did a great job of describing the code in her own words. That moment showed me how important it is to allow students to express their understanding in ways that are authentic to them.

Tarek described how he worked to create a space that resisted assumptions about language and fostered "curiosity" and feelings of safety rather than expectations about one "right" way to use language. He also started from a belief that students were communicating in ways that made sense, even if he didn't understand them initially. As his example with Maya shows, Tarek encouraged his students to communicate using their full language repertoires to show their understanding of concepts beyond the use of specific terminology.

Teachers who take up a translanguaging stance don't try to police students' language. Instead, they work to support students in making decisions about when, how, and why to use particular kinds of language for specific purposes and interactions. They teach with the awareness that language categories (like "standard" and "academic" English) are social constructs that can have real consequences in our students' lives but that we and our students can also be empowered to resist and change (Otheguy et al., 2015).

TRANSLANGUAGING DESIGN

Armed with knowledge about their students, educators who practice translanguaging pedagogy design learning experiences that specifically support students to translanguage. The next chapters will provide approaches for designing with students' language practices and community literacies in mind, but there are many ways to incorporate translanguaging into classroom activities.

Teachers can design lessons that encourage students to use multilingual resources. Many helpful tools are digital and exist online. For example, teachers might model how and when to use machine translation software and programming tutorials in multiple languages. CS teacher Dawn shared how she had one of her students write an essay for a local computing and social justice competition in her student's home language and use Google Translate to generate an English version. While her student won the competition, Dawn reflected how "next time, I would encourage my students to do translanguaging throughout the essay," drawing on all of their linguistic resources to produce their essays.

Of course, not everything is available in languages that reflect how your students communicate, so you might supplement online resources with translanguaging activities like strategically pairing students depending on the activity. Educators might pair students with similar language repertoires for activities that center fluid sense-making or group students with complementary language repertoires to encourage students to learn new language practices in English and in each other's home languages. Other strategies could include posting multilingual word walls, having students make personal bilingual picture dictionaries, and supporting students to consider which language practices they will use to show and tell what they know. Making decisions about how and when to pair students or when to encourage certain language practices will depend on your knowledge of your students and your awareness of power dynamics related to language. The goal in implementing these strategies, however, is to give permission for students to use all of their language in the CS classroom.

Educators can also validate students' language practices during whole class discussions and share-outs. If specialized CS vocabulary or other English learning goals are part of your lessons, you can encourage kids to use all of their language abilities to get there. Or try using activities and language that make sense to students to describe and define such terms. Let students use terms for code and programming they make up or that they use with their families and friends if these help them learn. Ask students to describe, draw, or use their bodies to express their ideas about code and computing. Looking back at how John explained the concept of sequencing, we recognize how he leveraged his multimodal language resources in his understanding and communication. Designing for opportunities like this is key for engaging in translanguaging pedagogy.[12]

Nicole, a CS teacher from New York City, shared how **translanguaging designs** in her after-school CS space let her multilingual learners shine. Nicole organized a 3D printing after-school program for students from all backgrounds. The students had different abilities, spoke different languages, and participated in different school tracks (e.g., gifted programs, general education, special education). Two students were often the first to finish creating using the software and the first to print. Nicole shared that they then helped "other students as they were learning the software. These two students were my multilingual learners. They were able to show students what to do.... They used [the language] they knew to express themselves and [other] students accepted their help to complete the projects. This was an amazing sight to see.... It gave my room a sense of community, computing, and different disciplines at the same time."

TRANSLANGUAGING SHIFTS

The design strategies we mentioned above might come in handy in the moment, as things that students say or do prompt you to make changes to your plan. Being flexible and ready to make **shifts** is the third part of translanguaging pedagogy.

For example, John's teacher Ms. Kors initially wanted to have her students create Scratch projects about Greek mythology to closely align the activity with the sixth-grade curriculum. However, she ultimately chose to have her students tell family stories because she wanted to get to know her students better, given that most of them were newcomers to the United States and her school. What she didn't expect was how students themselves wanted to know more about each other's language and cultural backgrounds. In response to these curiosities, she did things

translanguaging design Pedagogical designs that incorporate translanguaging practices into classroom activities in ways that allow students to use all of their language resources in learning.

translanguaging shifts In-the-moment moves and changes that teachers make to respond to students and allow them to use all of their language resources in learning.

---

12. For more design strategies, check out resources from PiLa-CS at https://nyuscholars.nyu.edu/en/publications/strategies-for-supporting-bimultilingual-learners-in-cs-ed, and our video on the topic, *Episode 3: Translanguaging Pedagogy in CS Ed* at https://www.pila-cs.org/videos. You can also see images and resources from the unit Ms. Kors designed for John's class at https://docs.google.com/presentation/d/1ZZgaVxlRQOy1tq9nuatdvDsoJoAaXZRPMabkQSefeOk/view#slide=id.g8929f6191e_0_286.

like pull up Google maps to geographically locate students' international immigration journeys and created informal opportunities for students to ask each other questions about their language use.

Nicole shared similar small shifts she has used in her classroom to support her students to translanguage:

> Using pictures or gestures definitely helps advance some forms of communication with my students. I also use Google translate and websites that change to different languages. Even changing the language . . . on an iPad has changed the game for me. Using the camera icon on Google translate can help when translating a kid's writing and when I want to write for my students to understand. Using picture cards of vocabulary and having different signs with multiple languages to explain certain things have helped me to assist my students' understanding and communication.

Supporting multilingual learners in your CS teaching doesn't have to mean radically changing your classroom. It means adopting the three parts of translanguaging pedagogy: having a stance of curiosity and acceptance about your students' language use and backgrounds, designing your lessons so that students can leverage all language resources, and adapting or shifting in the moment to build on the language abilities students bring to class. These techniques can also help students with Individualized Education Programs who may use language differently or help monolingual standard English speakers consider deficit language ideologies or biases embedded in their school environments.

REVISITING JOHN'S STORY

John has a rich set of resources that he used to help him complete his family story activity in Ms. Kors' CS class. Drawing on different languages, gestures, drawing, code, and more, John was able to communicate to create and share his story. Ms. Kors' willingness to recognize John's different language resources as assets for learning is at the core of her translanguaging approach. Designing CS learning activities with students' language practices at the center also requires educators to think critically about what they are asking students to learn, and why. In Chapter 13, we examine how considering computing through the lens of language can help us frame CS in more inclusive ways. In Chapter 14, we support teachers to expand learning goals beyond those covered by state standards, considering how students might blend literacies from their own communities, from computing, and from other school disciplines in generative ways.

REFLECTION QUESTIONS

1. How does translanguaging theory fit with or differ from how you think or have thought about language? What can you do to work toward developing a translanguaging stance as an educator?

2. How have you noticed your students use their full language repertoires in different ways to make and express meaning?

3. How do language policies in your settings allow people to or constrain people from using their full language repertoires?

TAKEAWAYS FOR PRACTICE

- Find a language policy relevant to your setting. Analyze it for ways that you notice how raciolinguistic ideologies or other inequities are shaping that policy.

- Analyze an existing CS lesson or activity for how well it allows students to use their full language repertoires. Revise it using translanguaging design.

GLOSSARY

Term	Definition
academic language	Specialized language used in academic settings.
bi/multilingual learners	We use this term to emphasize students' varied and dynamic linguistic resources. We use "multilingual" to highlight how we may not be able to assume that a learner only uses two languages and may have a broader linguistic repertoire (Holdway & Hitchcock, 2018).
critical consciousness	A social and political awareness that allows for a critique of how cultural norms, values, and institutions reproduce social inequities (Ladson-Billings, 1995).
language repertoire	A collection of resources used to communicate, make sense of the world around us, and learn.
language resources	A collection of words, sounds, and syntaxes, gestures, signs, symbols, objects, and social knowledge

	about how, when, and where to use those forms in different contexts that make up our language repertoire.
languaging	A verb used to indicate how language is something that people *do* in social contexts rather than emphasizing language as a noun referring to a static linguistic system.
raciolinguistic ideologies	Sets of ideas that draw on racism to shape dominant ideas about language (Flores & Rosa, 2015).
standard English	A socially constructed, idealized form of English that is not used by people in everyday life (Chang-Bacon, 2020; Flores & Rosa, 2015).
theory	A set of ideas based on scholarship and practice that are used to explain and interpret how society works.
translanguaging design	Pedagogical designs that incorporate translanguaging practices into classroom activities in ways that allow students to use all of their language resources in learning.
translanguaging pedagogy	A way of teaching that builds on students' diverse language backgrounds, supporting them to leverage existing resources in their language repertoires and to develop new ones.
translanguaging shifts	In-the-moment moves and changes that teachers make to respond to students and allow them to use all of their language resources in learning.
translanguaging stance	An orientation that frames language diversity across and within individuals as a resource, not a deficit.
translanguaging theory	A theory of language that argues that people have one system of language features and practices that they draw on to make meaning, learn, and express themselves. These features and practices defy the named languages (like English, Spanish, etc.) that society has used to categorize language.

REFERENCES

Acevedo, E. (2015). *Afro-Latina*. YouTube. https://www.youtube.com/watch?v=tPx8cSGW4k8

Alim, S. H. (2007). Critical hip-hop language pedagogies: Combat, consciousness, and the cultural politics of communication. *Journal of Language, Identity, and Education*, 6(2), 161–176. https://doi.org/10.1080/15348450701341378

Baker-Bell, A. (2020). *Linguistic justice: Black language, literacy, identity, and pedagogy*. Routledge. https://doi.org/10.4324/9781315147383

Chang-Bacon, C. K. (2020). Monolingual language ideologies and the idealized speaker: The "new bilingualism" meets the "old" educational inequities. *Teachers College Record, 123*(1), 1–19. https://doi.org/10.1177/016146812112300106

Flores, N. (2016, July 23). *Tim Kaine speaks Spanish. Does he want a cookie?* The Educational Linguist. https://educationallinguist.wordpress.com/2016/07/23/tim-kaine-speaks-spanish-does-he-want-a-cookie/

Flores, N., & Rosa, J. (2015). Undoing appropriateness: Raciolinguistic ideologies and language diversity in education. *Harvard Educational Review, 85*(2), 149–171. https://doi.org/10.17763/0017-8055.85.2.149

García, O. (2009). Education, multilingualism and translanguaging in the 21st century. In T. Skutnabb-Kangas, R. Phillipson, A. K. Mohanty, & M. Panda (Eds.), *Social justice through multilingual education* (pp. 140–158). Multilingual Matters. https://doi.org/10.21832/9781847691910-011

García, O., & Wei, L. (2014). *Translanguaging: Language, bilingualism and education*. Palgrave Pivot. https://doi.org/10.1057/9781137385765_4

Grosjean, F. (2012). An attempt to isolate, and then differentiate, transfer and interference. *International Journal of Bilingualism, 16*(1), 11–21. https://doi.org/10.1177/1367006911403210

Holdway, J., & Hitchcock, C. H. (2018). Exploring ideological becoming in professional development for teachers of multilingual learners: Perspectives on translanguaging in the classroom. *Teaching and Teacher Education, 75*, 60–70. https://doi.org/10.1016/j.tate.2018.05.015

Ladson-Billings, G. (1995). But that's just good teaching! The case for culturally relevant pedagogy. *Theory Into Practice, 34*(3), 159–165. https://doi.org/10.1080/00405849509543675

Lyiscott, J. (2014). *3 ways to speak English*. TED. https://www.ted.com/talks/jamila_lyiscott_3_ways_to_speak_english?subtitle=en

Otheguy, R., García, O., & Reid, W. (2015). Clarifying translanguaging and deconstructing named languages: A perspective from linguistics. *Applied Linguistics Review, 6*(3), 281–307. https://doi.org/10.1515/applirev-2015-0014

Rosa, J., & Flores, N. (2017). Unsettling race and language: Toward a raciolinguistic perspective. *Language in Society, 46*(5), 621–647. https://doi.org/10.1017/S0047404517000562

Rymes, B. (2014). Communicative repertoire. In C. Leung & B. V. Street (Eds.), *The Routledge companion to English studies* (pp. 287–301). Routledge.

Swanwick, R. (2016). *Languages and languaging in deaf education: A framework for pedagogy*. Oxford University Press.

Vogel, S. (2020). *Translanguaging about, with, and through code and computing: Emergent bi/multilingual middle schoolers forging computational literacies* [Doctoral dissertation], City University of New York. https://academicworks.cuny.edu/cgi/viewcontent.cgi?article=5015&context=gc_etds

13

Literate Programming and Code as a Language Resource

Sara Vogel, Christopher Hoadley, Lauren Vogelstein, Wendy Barrales, Sarane James, Laura Ascenzi-Moreno, Jasmine Y. Ma, Joyce Wu, Felix Wu, Jenia Marquez, Stephanie T. Jones, and the Computer Science Educational Justice Collective

CHAPTER OVERVIEW

This chapter presents the idea of "literate programming," or how code can be used as a form of expression as part of social conversations. It defines literate programming in the context of computer science (CS) and considers how literate programming is relevant to CS education (CS Ed). The chapter illustrates ways to engage students in thinking about code and ways to use code as an expressive medium in and of itself to contribute to conversations.

CHAPTER OBJECTIVES

After reading this chapter, I can:

- Define literate programming and identify ways to support students to communicate with and about code.
- Identify ways that using code can support bi/multilingual students' expression.

KEY TERMS

language repertoire; literate programming; translanguaging

JOHN'S STORY

In Chapters 11 and 12, we met John, a sixth-grade student at a public middle school in New York City. John was in Ms. Kors' English as a New Language (ENL) class. He spoke Amharic, Arabic, English, and Tigrinya and, by **translanguaging** (see Chapter 12), drew on his full **language repertoire** to develop a Scratch-based story about his journey from Eritrea to Ethiopia as a refugee. In this chapter, we consider how Ms. Kors helped John and his classmates think about code in new ways that allowed them to express themselves through their personal narratives.

CODE AS AN EXPRESSIVE RESOURCE

As we aim to support bi/multilingual and language-minoritized students in CS Ed, it is important to consider the power dynamics of computing education that may be excluding those students in the first place.[1] CS is often taught in ways that reinforce narrow notions of what counts as CS, who does CS, and for what purposes. Many CS 101 courses ask students to memorize syntaxes and to create test "toy" projects disembodied from real-life contexts.

But these approaches ignore the fact that code is deeply relevant to the human experience. Code is all around us, shaping how we communicate, entertain, transact, vote, and take civic action—not to mention how we are surveilled, scammed, and persuaded. Instead of treating code as something people use to solve de-contextualized problems, we might frame it as a language resource: a resource that computers can process and that people can mobilize to support communication and expression with other humans. As scholar and educator Tom Lynch writes, "software theorists are quite clear on this: like other languages, software is socially constructed, flawed, fickle, and ideological" (Lynch, 2017, p. 165).

---

translanguaging A theory of language that argues that people have one system of language features and practices that they draw on to make meaning, learn, and express themselves. These features and practices defy the named languages (like English, Spanish, etc.) that society has used to categorize language.

language repertoire A collection of resources (e.g., words, sounds, syntaxes, gestures, signs, symbols, objects, and social knowledge about how, when, and where to use those forms) used to communicate, make sense of the world around us, and learn.

---

1. In this chapter we use the term "bi/multilingual learners" to emphasize these students' linguistic resources. We also opt to use this term because it is strengths based. We use it synonymously with emergent bilinguals. These terms stand in contrast to terms such as "English Language Learner" or "Limited English Proficient." See the On Terminology section of this guide for an explanation on our use of different identity-related terms.

In this chapter, we unpack a philosophy about programming that highlights CS' connections with expression, language, and communication. If we start with the premise that people express and communicate about, with, and through code (Vogel, 2020), then it follows naturally that bi/multilinguals—and all students—already have a lot to contribute and can be more inclusively welcomed into the space.

COMMUNICATING ABOUT AND AROUND CODE: MAKING CODE "LITERATE"

Many people decide that programming and CS is "not for them" because code itself appears like a jumble of inscrutable white text on a black screen. But there are many ways to make code more readable, supporting experts and novices alike. CS teacher Anjeliqe described how the possibility of making code more accessible is one of her favorite parts of her job:

> This is why I like teaching computer science. I am always able to connect different concepts, and it has gotten to the point where many of them are able to make connections themselves. They'll tell me, "Oh, Ms. Martinez, this reminds me of xyz from this class." It just allows them to see how relevant computer science is.

Let's return to John's story to consider how Ms. Kors aimed to make code more readable in her ENL classroom.

COMMUNICATING ABOUT AND AROUND CODE

As students in Ms. Kors' class built their Scratch projects, they:

Storyboarded their stories on paper and used PowerPoint before moving to Scratch.

Role-played what they hoped their code would do using puppets and paper prototypes.

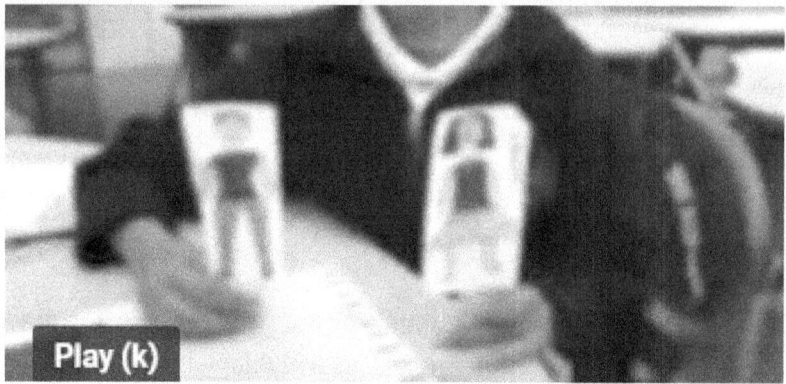

Set the interface of Scratch to display different languages at different times.

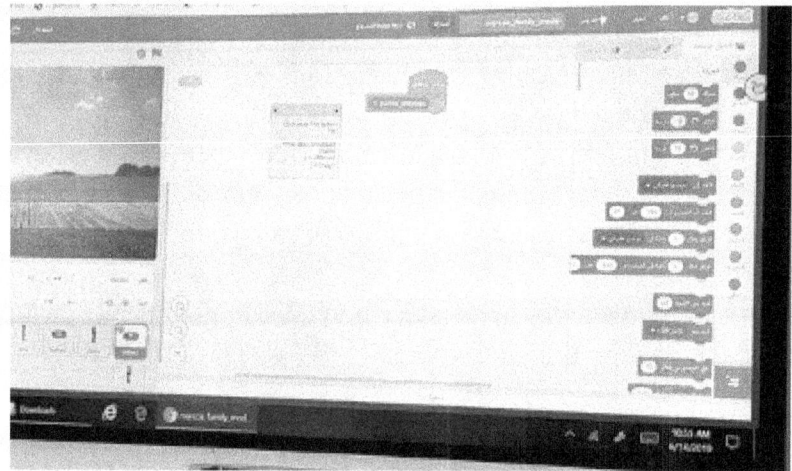

Shared and debugged their code collectively by doing demos at the electronic whiteboard. Students shared their thinking and narrated along using a range of language practices.

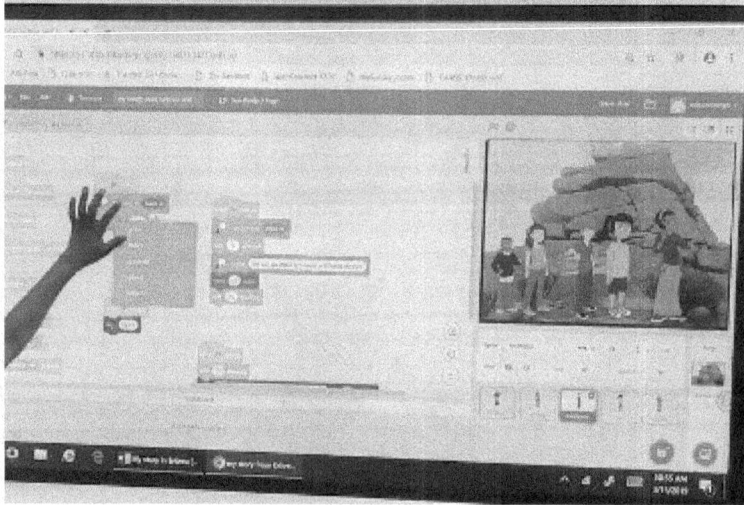

Annotated printed out versions of Scratch code on paper.

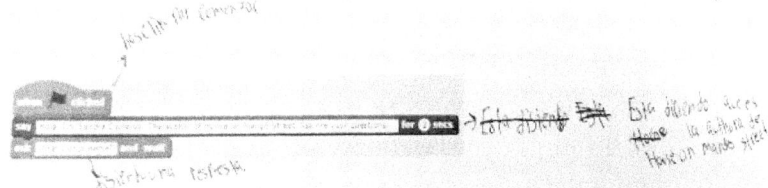

Annotated their code digitally using comments and Scratch's "Notes and Credits" project page section.

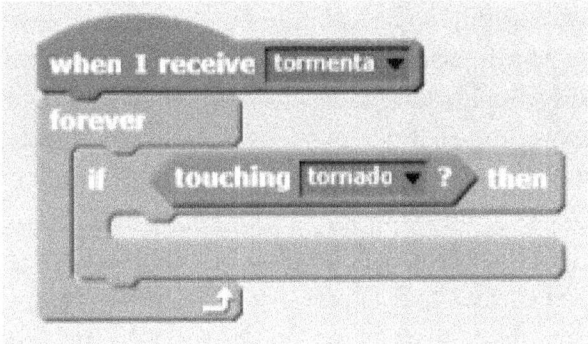

Through all of the teaching moves above, Ms. Kors supported John and his peers to represent code and what they hoped it would do for their projects in a way that was easily understandable for the members of this computing community. Students translanguaged with spoken and written Scratch keywords and human language, diagrams, drawings, and role-play. Other CS teachers, like Jennifer, have taken similar approaches:

> I am a planner by nature and give my students that opportunity.
> I love graphic organizers. Storyboarding with images, text, or a combination is always encouraged. We also act out scenarios before writing code.

These types of "unplugged" activities give students opportunities to, as Jennifer described, "get past the fear of what the code will look like." Students can visualize their thinking in ways that are accessible, motivating, and relevant.

Like John and his classmates, all programmers express themselves about, with, and through code as they engage in broader communities. They use programming languages like Java and C++. They write comments in their code, create flow charts and diagrams, post queries on online forums like stackoverflow.com, share meaningful CS projects with the wider world, critique harmful tech on social media, and so much more (Vogel et al., 2020).

The idea of embracing a broad range of language and communication practices has a long history in the field of CS. Prominent computer scientist Donald Knuth coined the phrase **literate programming** (Knuth, 1984) to emphasize that computer code (programs) are meant to be read and understood by people, not just computers, a stance that we echo here. Knuth advocated that computer scientists should appreciate virtuosic works of programming just like virtuosic works of literature.[2] He argued that treating programs as not only functional but also expressive creations would allow real progress in CS.

> **literate programming**
> An understanding of code as a form of expression that is part of a social conversation because computer code (programs) is meant to be read and understood by people and not just computers (Knuth, 1984).

In addition to advocating that coders should be well read in excellent works of programming, Knuth also advocated that programming itself should involve combining human language and computer programming languages in specific ways. Knuth built systems to support a software development process where programmers first specified and refined with others what their programs should do in human language and then gradually refined these drafts to include a combination of executable code and comments. The result was a clear and expressive "literate" program that could be run on the computer and read (or modified) by other people. Thinking about how to make programs literate for all can help reduce perceptions of programming as the domain of an elite few, what has been metaphorically called a programming "priesthood" (Backus, 1980; Doctorow, 2009; Maz, 2017; Nelson, 1973; Sabelli, 1998).

The idea of literate programming helps us understand that coding is a part of a social conversation, one of many ways that we can express and communicate ideas to and with others. This means that coding is not just about correctness but about how ideas are encoded, expressed, and understood in social contexts. Programmers must consider the other people they are in conversation with.

When we understand that computer programs are for people—not

---

[2]. Visit https://shreevatsa.net/post/programming-pearls/ to explore some of these "Programming Pearls."

just computers—to interact with, we also pay more attention to the ways that language mediates how people learn, solve problems, and collaborate in CS. "Communication about computing" is a core practice identified in the K-12 CS Education Framework (K-12CS.org, 2016). Research has shown that even though students may be able to correctly solve programming problems, if they can't explain how the solutions work, they may not actually understand what they've done (Hoadley et al., 1996). When teachers engage students in talking about computing and pair-programming interactions, they can help develop students' computational thinking (Grover & Pea, 2013; Israel et al., 2017; Werner & Denning, 2009). Tarek Elabsy, a New York City educator, shared how he works to support students' understanding through communicating about code:

> I often encourage my students to explain their code to each other. This helps them develop their communication skills and also makes sure they understand what they've created. I've found that even when students can write code that works, they sometimes have trouble explaining what they did. It's important for them to be able to articulate their thinking.

Social interactions mediated through text comments, code, and tutorials on the Scratch programming platform have been found to support younger students in improving their interactive media projects (Brennan et al., 2011). Similarly, teachers can encourage students to express themselves through multiple modalities such as interviews, drawings, and design journals to show what they know about computing (Brennan & Resnick, 2012), much in the same way that John did in Chapter 12. Attending to students' language use in conversation about and with code is key to supporting robust CS learning.

Inviting students to not just write programs but also read and engage with programs to make them more "literate" can create space for novices to participate in CS. Just like translanguaging pedagogy, the literate programming philosophy helps educators take an asset-based approach where all of a student's linguistic resources can be used to develop new literacies: using human language and pseudocode to leverage into executable code.[3]

---

3. The Participating in Literacies and Computer Science video *Episode 4: What CS Ed Can Offer Bi/Multilinguals* illustrates how a literate programming approach can support multilingual learners' CS and language development. View the video at https://www.pila-cs.org/videos

LEVERAGING CODE FOR EXPRESSION AND CRITICALITY

The literate programming philosophy underscores that computer programs are for people and not just computers—to read and parse. Not only is communicating about and around code integral to sustaining computing communities but people can create through code as its own expressive medium. The assignment John was asked to complete in his ENL class is an example of this.

MS. KORS' CODING ASSIGNMENT

> John's ENL teacher, Ms. Kors, asked her students to use Scratch to code animations of their family history. She chose this assignment because she thought that code would allow students to express themselves in a more expansive way than her traditional written assignments. Students would be able to add more details with the visual features of animations and bring viewers into their stories by leveraging potential interactive elements.
>
> In addition, this assignment allowed students to share parts of themselves that their teachers and peers might now know about them or wouldn't know about them if not for this opportunity to share. John understood this intention behind the assignment. When asked why he thought Ms. Kors wanted students to use Scratch in class, John shared, "because she want us, she she she, she want to know our story" (Focus Group, May 31, 2019).
>
> Through the framing of this project, Ms. Kors challenged notions about what parts of kids' lives are relevant to CS, encouraging students to express personal narratives in code and multimedia. This became apparent when sharing projects meant running students' code as well as taking the class through the code itself. This created new and shared parts of students' language repertoires as they learned how to code together to share their stories.

While many programmers use code for problem-solving (e.g., creating efficient algorithms to sort or search through data), many people who engage in computing, like John, also use code, images, and data for expression and communication. For example:

- The artist Shantell Martin created her own font, Shantell Sans, and shared the story behind how and why she made it on this website.[4]

- The Women of Color archive uses digital technologies to document and preserve the stories of matriarchs of color.[5]

- "Unplugged" CS and knitting projects like Dr. Elisabetta Matsumoto's work with physicists at Georgia Tech and the National Science Foundation funded project Re-Crafting Computer Science (Keune, 2022) bring together code and materials science with ancestral crafting knowledge.[6]

CS teacher Anjeliqe shared her approach to teaching computing in ways that leverage code for expression:

> One of our number one rules when my co-teacher and I teach is for the students to be creative. Both my co-teacher and I did art in addition to CS in college, and we always tell students to demonstrate the artist in them. The more creative the better. Lots of people think coding and CS are boring, but those "boring" parts help you create beauty and interesting things as well.

REVISITING JOHN'S STORY

John's project and the other examples shared in this chapter bring together things that are not traditionally seen as relevant to CS (e.g., refugee journeys, the artistry of handwriting, your abuela's favorite story, knitting, family heritage practices) with computing to represent people's ideas in easy-to-understand, aesthetically beautiful, and compelling ways.

In this chapter, we've explored how leveraging students' translanguaging and code as a "literate" language resource can offer bi/multilingual learners a way to express themselves and participate in conversations that involve CS and coding.

---

4. See https://shantellsans.com/

5. See https://www.wocarchive.com/

6. Learn more about Dr. Matsumoto's work at https://www.nytimes.com/2019/05/17/science/math-physics-knitting-matsumoto.html and more about the Re-Crafting Computer Science project at http://kpeppler.com/#blog

But to truly advance equitable practices in CS, we must also examine the nature of the computing conversations that students take part in: What is being discussed in these conversations? Toward what ends? Who is taking part? Who is left out? These questions are ones we explore in Chapter 14.

REFLECTION QUESTIONS

1. How has code been relevant to your life? How have you used it as a way to express yourself?

2. Which of the strategies from Ms. Kors and her class have you used as part of your coding experiences? Which ones resonate with you as effective to use with students in your context? Why?

TAKEAWAYS FOR PRACTICE

- Find an existing CS lesson or activity. Evaluate how it provides students with opportunities to communicate about and with code. How could you revise the lesson or activity to better leverage code as a medium of expression?

GLOSSARY

Term	Definition
language repertoire	A collection of resources (e.g., words, sounds, syntaxes, gestures, signs, symbols, objects, and social knowledge about how, when, and where to use those forms) used to communicate, make sense of the world around us, and learn.
literate programming	An understanding of code as a form of expression that is part of a social conversation because computer code (programs) is meant to be read and understood by people and not just computers (Knuth, 1984).
translanguaging	A theory of language that argues that people have one system of language features and practices that they draw on to make meaning, learn, and express

themselves. These features and practices defy the named languages (like English, Spanish, etc.) that society has used to categorize language.

REFERENCES

Backus, J. (1980). Programming in America in the 1950s—Some personal impressions. In N. Metropolis (Ed.), *A history of computing in the twentieth century* (pp. 125–135). Academic Press. https://doi.org/10.1016/B978-0-12-491650-0.50017-4

Brennan, K., & Resnick, M. (2012, Apr). New frameworks for studying and assessing the development of computational thinking. In *Proceedings of the 2012 annual meeting of the American Educational Research Association*, Vancouver, Canada (Vol. 1, p. 25).

Brennan, K., Valverde, A., Prempeh, J., Roque, R., & Chung, M. (2011, June). More than code: The significance of social interactions in young people's development as interactive media creators. In *EdMedia+ Innovate Learning* (pp. 2147–2156). Association for the Advancement of Computing in Education.

Doctorow, C. (2009, 12 March). The high priests of IT—And the heretics. *Harvard Business Review*. https://hbr.org/2009/03/the-high-priests-of-it

Grover, S., & Pea, R. (2013). Computational thinking in K–12: A review of the state of the field. *Educational Researcher, 42*(1), 38–43. https://doi.org/10.3102/0013189X12463051

Hoadley, C. M., Linn, M. C., Mann, L. M., & Clancy, M. J. (1996). When, why and how do novice programmers reuse code. In W. Gray & D. Boehm-Davis (Eds.), *Empirical Studies of Programmers: Sixth workshop* (pp. 109–129). Ablex Norwood.

Israel, M., Wherfel, Q. M., Shehab, S., Melvin, O., & Lash, T. (2017). Describing elementary students' interactions in K-5 puzzle-based computer science environments using the Collaborative Computing Observation Instrument (C-COI). *ICER '17: Proceedings of the 2017 ACM Conference on International Computing Education Research* (pp. 110–117). https://doi.org/10.1145/3105726.3106167

K-12CS.org. (2016). *K-12 Computer Science Framework*. https://k12cs.org/

Keune, A. (2022). Material syntonicity: Examining computational performance and its materiality through weaving and sewing crafts. *Journal of the Learning Sciences, 31*(4–5), 477–508. https://doi.org/10.1080/10508406.2022.2100704

Knuth, D. E. (1984). Literate programming. *The Computer Journal, 27*(2), 97–111. https://doi.org/10.1093/comjnl/27.2.97

Lynch, T. L. (2017). How English teachers will save the future: Reimagining computer science as the language art it is. *Journal of English Teaching through Movies and Media, 18*(4), 163–180. https://doi.org/10.16875/stem.2017.18.4.163

Maz, A. (2017, 5 December). A priesthood of programmers. *Jacobite*. https://web.archive.org/web/20171207063309/https://jacobitemag.com/2017/12/05/a-priesthood-of-programmers/

Nelson, T. H. (1973, June 4–8). A conceptual framework for man-machine everything. *Proceedings of the National Computer Conference and Exposition—AFIPS '73*, New York, USA. http://doi.org/10.1145/1499586.1499776

Sabelli, N. H. (1998). We are no longer a priesthood. *Communications of the ACM, 41*(1), 20–21. http://doi.org/10.1145/268092.268100

Vogel, S. (2020). *Translanguaging about, with, and through code and computing: Emergent bi/multilingual middle schoolers forging computational literacies* [Doctoral dissertation, City University of New York]. https://academicworks.cuny.edu/cgi/viewcontent.cgi?article=5015&context=gc_etds

Vogel, S., Hoadley, C., Castillo, A. R., & Ascenzi-Moreno, L. (2020). Languages, literacies and literate programming: Can we use the latest theories on how bilingual people learn to help us teach computational literacies? *Computer Science Education, 30*(4), 420–443. https://doi.org/10.1080/08993408.2020.1751525

Werner, L., & Denning, J. (2009). Pair programming in middle school: What does it look like? *Journal of Research on Technology in Education, 42*(1), 29–49. https://doi.org/10.1080/15391523.2009.10782540

14

What Conversation Is This Code a Part of?

Sara Vogel, Christopher Hoadley, Lauren Vogelstein, Wendy Barrales, Sarane James, Laura Ascenzi-Moreno, Jasmine Y. Ma, Joyce Wu, Felix Wu, Jenia Marquez, Stephanie T. Jones, and the Computer Science Educational Justice Collective

CHAPTER OVERVIEW

This chapter builds on the notion of "literate programming" from Chapter 13 to consider which conversations coding and computing are a part of. The chapter presents a framework called "syncretic computational literacies," or the "three circles," that extends the conversations that coding and computer science education (CS Ed) are a part of. It invites CS educators to consider how code can be connected not only to computational literacies but also to community literacies that center students' interests and backgrounds and disciplinary literacies that connect CS with other school subjects. The chapter concludes with resources for planning CS lessons that make code a part of broader conversations across multiple literacies.

CHAPTER OBJECTIVES

After reading this chapter, I can:

- Explain the concept of syncretic computational literacies and how this approach supports equity-oriented CS education.
- Identify ways to make CS instruction part of larger conversations that connect to students' lives.

KEY TERMS

academic language; community literacies; computational literacies; disciplinary literacies; equity as transformation; hybridity; syncretic; syncretic computational literacies

JOHN'S STORY

A key goal of CS Ed that pushes toward equity as transformation is ensuring that CS learning opportunities center students' values and experiences (Grapin et al., 2023; see Chapter 4 for more on **equity as transformation**). Transformation also involves inviting students to interrogate the status quo of what computing "should" be to include CS and CS Ed in larger conversations. John and Ms. Kors offer an example of one kind of transformative CS learning opportunity. Ms. Kors had asked students to use Scratch to share personal narratives, making their experiences and communities relevant to CS Ed. Let's consider how John took up this invitation in his project.

equity as transformation
A way of thinking about equity that recognizes that because the status quo tends to reproduce inequity, it needs to be transformed. Equity as transformation works to disrupt what is considered "normal" in CS disciplines and industries by valuing and centering marginalized knowledge systems, tools, and people.

JOHN'S FAMILY HISTORY SCRATCH PROJECT

For his family history project, John chose to create a Scratch animation depicting a key moment from his lived experience: when he and his family walked from Eritrea to Ethiopia for three days at the beginning of their journey as refugees.

His project involved coding Scratch sprites that represented the different members of his family and timing the appearance of speech bubbles to depict their conversations as they embarked on their journey. Through his code, John was able to share traits of his family members. He made decisions about which images to use to depict each member of the family, which "text to speech" voices to use for people of different ages and genders, and what dialogue to use to share the ways that they took care of each other.

When asked why he chose to tell this particular family story, John shared that he wanted to tell his class where he came from and to remind them that traveling to a new country means you will miss where you are from:

"I want to tell where I came from and I want to tell people that, like you could travel ano-any country and like you'll miss your fr-place." (John, Focus Group, 5/31/2019).

In choosing to share such an intense and challenging experience, John was able to start conversations in school about his experiences as a refugee that he had not previously shared with teachers. Although this was not Ms. Kors' original intention behind the project, it served as a generative starting point. When asked about the part of his story that he put into Scratch, John shared vivid details from his experience: "I was walk like, I was walking like the, the place like this, it was too sunny. Uh, then, like, we only walk like at the night time. Like, we cannot walk, like at the sun time. [. . .] Only sometimes. Like I bleed [John gestures towards his nose]. My mother cannot let me go at this time. I go in the dark time." (Observation, February 8, 2019).

At the end of the project, during a parent-teacher conference with Ms. Kors, John was able to share his project with his mom. John and his mother shared a tender moment reflecting on this experience while speaking in Tigrinya. John's mother then shared more about their experiences as refugees with John's teacher, elaborating on why this project was so meaningful to her and her family.

Ms. Kors' project was transformational because it centered John's experiences in ways that were powerful for everyone involved and brought CS into a broader conversation about immigration. John's story can help us think deeply about the ideas we are trying to express through code, as well as our motivations, purposes, and intended audiences for computing. To tell his story, John brought in knowledge and practices related to computing (e.g., making decisions in Scratch to depict his family members). John also related the project to the social history of his region of origin and his own family history. And he leveraged practices related to storytelling that are typically taught in language arts.

CODE IN CONVERSATION

In Chapter 13, we considered how code as a "literate" language resource can offer bi/multilingual learners a way to express themselves and participate in conversations that involve CS and coding.[1] But to truly advance equitable practices in CS toward transformation, we also need to examine the nature of the computing conversations that students take part in (Ko et al., 2020). What is being discussed in these conversations? Toward what ends are these conversations moving? Who is taking part? Who is left out?

Even as computing tools, technologies, and cultures have enabled expression and creativity, they have also played a role in advancing inequities, including language injustice as we saw in Chapter 11, and the other forms of inequity explored in this book (see Chapters 2–4, 5, 8, and 15). When we support bi/multilingual learners to participate in CS, we run the risk of uncritically introducing students into fields and industries that have historically marginalized them and their communities and may continue to marginalize them today. These settings might send the message to students that language and learning practices associated with school-based CS and other academic disciplines are more valuable than the language and practices used in students' own communities (Vogel, 2021).

To avoid these pitfalls, educators can attune themselves to the conversations happening around computing that are taking place away from current centers of power, like the tech industry and university CS departments. Educators can help students start new conversations and use practices and language that they learn outside of school to have them. As scholar Yasmin Kafai has argued, "computational participation" is not just about understanding the tools that students inherit but also about changing and remaking a world mediated by computation (Kafai, 2016).

Achieving this equity-as-transformation vision is what we explore in this chapter. As we connect our theories of translanguaging pedagogy (Chapter 12) with the literate programming approach (Chapter 13), we repeatedly pose the question:

What conversation is this code a part of?

There are many conversations that students might have about, with, and through code. As we aim to support equitable participation for bi/multilingual learners in CS Ed, we can consider expanding the types and range of conversations we have with students. We can engage them with computing tools and ideas that go beyond those typically sanctioned by CS courses and industry.

---

1. In this chapter we use the term "bi/multilingual learners" to emphasize these students' linguistic resources. We also opt to use this term because it is strengths-based. We use it synonymously with "emergent bilinguals." These terms stand in contrast to terms such as "English Language Learner" or "Limited English Proficient." See the On Terminology section of this guide for an explanation on our use of different identity-related terms.

SYNCRETIC LEARNING AND LITERACIES

We believe that, similar to how we teach writing across the academic curriculum, computing can and should be connected to domains outside of traditional coding, or what many consider "pure CS." Extending computing might include connecting it to family and community, like John's project did. It could involve integrating computing with other academic disciplines, like language arts and storytelling, also like John's project. In fact, the most important computing conversations touch communities in different ways and go beyond disciplinary boundaries.

Guiding students to connect CS to conversations they are having in other school subjects, in their homes, or in their on- and offline communities enriches learning across the curriculum. Making these connections also supports a more culturally responsive approach to school and learning. There's no best model for this. Ms. Kors' project offers one example, but there are many possible ways to extend computing into larger conversations. Teachers might infuse CS into other subjects like science or social studies through interdisciplinary approaches. Or they might incorporate units that explore the intersections of computing and diverse fields and domains into a stand-alone CS course.

When we bridge school and home knowledge by putting them in conversation with each other, we take up a **syncretic** approach to learning. Syncretic means combining different traditions, perspectives, and practices to create something new. The term helps us highlight that when people bring practices from different spaces (like home and school) together, tensions and sparks result that allow us to create new kinds of literacies. These new literacies transform and improve what and how we learn (Gutiérrez, 2014).

syncretic Combining different cultural, social, or religious beliefs and perspectives to create new practices.

Often, everyday and out-of-school knowledge are brought into classrooms to provide a pathway to accessing forms of school knowledge (sometimes called **hybridity** in research like Gutiérrez et al., 1999). Hybridity as an approach can support equity as access. By contrast, syncretism supports equity as transformation as it highlights how new ideas emerge when home and school knowledge are brought together and both are treated as legitimate. For example, when Elizabeth Acevedo joined language from her various communities in her poetry (see Chapter 12), she not only brought poetry into the conversations in her communities, but she also advanced poetry itself (Acevedo, 2015).[2] When John carefully selected which text-to-speech voices he wanted to code into Scratch sprites to depict his family members, he opened up new conversations with his teachers about programming and the representation of age and gender in digital media.

hybridity Bringing everyday and out-of-school knowledge into the classroom to help students learn academic content (Gutiérrez et al., 1999).

---

2. Watch Acevedo perform her poem at https://www.youtube.com/watch?v=tPx8cSGW4k8

We call the merging together of literacies from different school disciplines, from CS, and from home and community, **syncretic computational literacies**. Teachers can intentionally plan for syncretic computational conversations. One bilingual middle school science teacher did this as she realized that her students were talking about Hurricane María shortly after it devastated Puerto Rico in the fall of 2017. She considered what was "computational" and what was "scientific" within those conversations. Based on her reflections, she developed a unit that guided students to use Scratch to create computational models of the impacts of the storm. The models also leveraged students' own personal experiences and family histories related to hurricanes and storms.[3]

When supporting teachers to think "syncretically," we encourage them to start conversations that enable their students to draw on literacies from three areas: community literacies, disciplinary literacies, and computational literacies. Ms. Kors' assignment and John's project is a good example of what syncretic computational literacies might look like.

COMMUNITY LITERACIES

Community literacies include ways of reading, writing, speaking, creating, and interacting with the world that students learned from friends, family, and other communities. Community literacies encompass all the conversations that are outside of what school traditionally centers. This could include literacies that connect to home languages, as well as cultural practices that aren't part of official, **academic language**. Such practices may come from television shows, dinnertime conversations, or online fan sites. In the case of John's family story, community literacies included conversations about immigration, identity, and belonging.

DISCIPLINARY LITERACIES

Disciplinary literacies include ways of reading, writing, speaking, creating, and interacting with the world in ways that are connected to school subject areas. Disciplinary literacies include scientific discourse in science class, literary discourse in language arts class, historical reasoning in social studies class, and so on. Scientists learn to have discussions around hypotheses and data using certain terms and language practices, mathematicians learn to use a certain kind of argument for a proof, and poets learn to play with and defy the grammatical patterns of prose. Similarly, students learn these specialized ways of talking, writing, and thinking

---

syncretic computational literacies Merging literacies from students' homes and communities, different academic disciplines, and CS to create new types of literacies and conversations.

community literacies Ways of reading, writing, speaking, creating, and interacting with the world that students learned from friends, family, and other communities outside of school.

academic language Specialized language used in academic settings.

disciplinary literacies Ways of reading, writing, speaking, creating, and interacting with the world in ways that are connected to school subject areas and academic disciplines (e.g., history, math, science).

---

3. For more on this unit and others like it, see the *PiLa-CS Educator Resources* page at https://www.pila-cs.org/educator-resources

in their school subjects. These literacies help students communicate with others in and about those disciplines. John's story incorporated disciplinary literacies related to storytelling and narratives from language arts.

COMPUTATIONAL LITERACIES

Computational literacies include real-world conversations where students can use code and computing—not only the way professional programmers might talk to each other but also other CS literacies that underpin computing in a variety of settings. This can include how expert spreadsheet users debug their macros, how digital artists talk about and share their work, how students express their concerns with the ethics of hacking or modding games, and even how CS is used to uphold and bolster racism, sexism, and other societal hierarchies. Some of the computational literacies that John used to tell his story included sequencing and timing speech bubbles to show a conversation and making coding decisions to depict members of his family.

computational literacies Real-world conversations where students use code and computing to create and communicate about CS.

SYNCRETIC COMPUTATIONAL LITERACIES

While community, disciplinary, and computational literacies are each important in their own right, they become more powerful when they are brought into conversation with each other. In this way, they have the potential to become transformative. Figure 1 illustrates our concept of syncretic computational literacies.

Figure 1. Syncretic Computational Literacies

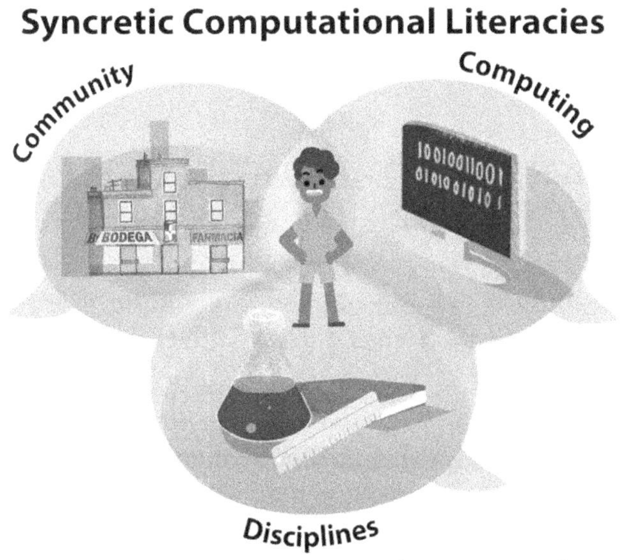

Syncretic Computational Literacies © 2020 by Mulan Fu, Danielle Fuller, and Ezra Posner is licensed under CC BY-SA 4.0

Community, disciplinary, and computational literacies already exist in the world, and students already practice them to varying degrees and in different ways. However, these different literacies are not equally valued, and they are rarely brought together. School curricula often undermine and devalue the knowledge of bi/multilingual learners' communities. And even among academic disciplines, CS is often held apart, framed as an inaccessible way of thinking that only people who have a "techy" bent are able to comprehend.

As CS Ed becomes part of the K-12 schooling core, educators have the opportunity to challenge this siloed reality. Instead of constructing walls and boundaries around the CS field, practitioners can work toward syncretic goals for CS Ed. Such goals value community knowledge as it overlaps with and exists alongside knowledge from computing and other disciplines. If we want to achieve CS for all, we have to dismantle our ideas about computing being a separate and obscure way of thinking and communicating.

One of the best ways to do that is by breaking down the barriers between computing conversations and all of the other conversations our students are having. Because computing is such a new area of conversation for many students, it also provides opportunities for emergent bilinguals to think strategically about language, to anchor computing in diverse cultures, and to bridge home and school conversations. As CS teacher Michelle expressed: "When teachers attempt to marry knowledge that comes from the community with that of academic subjects and computational creativity, students benefit by merging ideas to create a richer understanding of all three." We are bound to create exciting new avenues for CS when it can include the richness of multiple named languages and interweave the significant ways people use the languages of different academic disciplines.

USING SYNCRETIC COMPUTATIONAL LITERACIES (THE THREE CIRCLES) TO DESIGN LEARNING

Looking at CS from a syncretic perspective means drawing inspiration for learning environments from the many conversations about, with, and through code that occur in spaces beyond formal CS classes and professional programming jobs. It means noticing and surfacing the tensions between the different ways of knowing, computing, and using language that come together in these conversations. Having syncretic conversations empowers students to use code to serve their communities, push back against inequitable computing practices, and support their growth and identity development.

"Syncretic computational literacies" is a mouthful. The Participating in Literacies and Computer Science (PiLa-CS) project also frequently calls this idea "the three circles," as visualized in Figure 1 above.[4] Though the idea may appear simplistic, it is clarifying and powerful: you can use the three circles to understand the types of emerging literacies students participate in. You can also use the three circles to brainstorm what kinds of conversations students could have in class and how to design units to support students to have these conversations in your classroom. The three circles can inform how you use the translanguaging pedagogy framework of stance, design, and shifts. For instance, the three circles can be used to think about how to respond in the moment with shifts as students bring in language to the classroom. A teacher might ask: "How can I embrace how students are using language and link it to other literacies?" The three circles can also be used as a tool to think about designing units or activities. Resource 1 is a worksheet that can be used as a tool to bring three circles thinking into unit design.

Tarek Elabsy is a CS educator who has designed activities for his students that bring together community, disciplinary, and computational literacies. As you read his example, try to identify aspects of the three circles and how they came together to create something new:

> I have a student who is a passionate video game player, and he's also learning a lot about different cultures through his family, particularly through their Spanish-speaking traditions. I worked with him to create a video game where he used his coding skills to tell a story about his family's heritage. He incorporated elements of his culture into the game, which made it both engaging and meaningful to him.
>
> This project was a great example of how we can blend different aspects of students' lives to support their learning. It brought together this student's interests in video games, their knowledge of their culture, and their skills in computer science.

Designing and developing syncretic computational conversations in classrooms is one way to promote equitable practices in CS Ed. Doing so breaks down traditional boundaries between school disciplines and communities that have systematically marginalized bi/multilingual learners. It helps us change what counts as academic knowledge in a way that uplifts the brilliance that bi/multilingual learners already bring to the classroom. And it helps us envision what it would be like to have generative computing

---

4. PiLa-CS is a research-practice partnership focused on supporting bi/multilingual learners in CS Ed. For more information, see the Preface.

conversations not only in the offices of tech companies but throughout society and with youth.

REVISITING JOHN'S STORY

Michelle, an art teacher who incorporates CS into her instruction, reflected on what she learned from hearing about Ms. Kors' assignment and what it meant for John and for herself in her own context:

> It is important to expand the norms associated with CS programming to include the interests of less represented participants. John's experience of using Scratch to animate his family's story was such a value to him and the other students in his class. Learning these skills through storytelling and personal history gives kids a creative purpose for the code they use. It also ties family history and community to schooling. Teachers like myself who teach subjects outside of "pure CS" can use programs like Scratch to acquaint our students with CS language within our "other" subject areas. This allows children to gain more resources for communication that they can draw on in the future.

As John's story has shown across these chapters, contrary to myths that computing is "too hard" for bi/multilingual learners, through approaches like translanguaging, coding can become a valuable resource for communication and expression.

REFLECTION QUESTIONS

1. Now that you've read all of John's story, what stands out to you most about his experiences and Ms. Kors' instructional decisions?

2. Reflect on a time when you experienced something **syncretic**, either related to computing or in another part of your life. What were the different pieces that were brought together? What new something was created as a result?

TAKEAWAYS FOR PRACTICE

- Use Resource 1 below to brainstorm a syncretic unit that integrates community, disciplinary, and computational literacies.

GLOSSARY

Term	Definition
academic language	Specialized language used in academic settings.
community literacies	Ways of reading, writing, speaking, creating, and interacting with the world that students learned from friends, family, and other communities outside of school.
computational literacies	Real-world conversations where students use code and computing to create and communicate about CS.
disciplinary literacies	Ways of reading, writing, speaking, creating, and interacting with the world in ways that are connected to school subject areas and academic disciplines (e.g., history, math, science).
equity as transformation	A way of thinking about equity that recognizes that because the status quo tends to reproduce inequity, it needs to be transformed. Equity as transformation works to disrupt what is considered "normal" in CS disciplines and industries by valuing and centering marginalized knowledge systems, tools, and people.
hybridity	Bringing everyday and out-of-school knowledge into the classroom to help students learn academic content (Gutiérrez et al., 1999).
syncretic	Combining different cultural, social, or religious beliefs and perspectives to create new practices.
syncretic computational literacies	Merging literacies from students' homes and communities, different academic disciplines, and CS to create new types of literacies and conversations.

REFERENCES

Acevedo, E. (2015). *Afro-Latina*. YouTube. https://www.youtube.com/watch?v=tPx8cSGW4k8

Grapin, S. E., Pierson, A., González-Howard, M., Ryu, M., Fine, C., & Vogel, S. (2023). Science education with multilingual learners: Equity as access and equity as transformation. *Science Education, 107*, 999–1032. https://doi.org/10.1002/sce.21791

Gutiérrez, K. D. (2014). Integrative research review: Syncretic approaches to literacy learning. Leveraging horizontal knowledge and expertise. In *63rd Literacy Research Association Yearbook*, 48–61. Literacy Research Association.

Gutiérrez, K. D., Baquedano-López, P., & Tejeda, C. (1999). Rethinking diversity: Hybridity and hybrid language practices in the third space. *Mind, Culture, and Activity, 6*(4), 286–303. https://doi.org/10.1080/10749039909524733

Kafai, Y. B. (2016). From computational thinking to computational participation in K-12 education. *Communications of the ACM, 59*(8), 26–27. https://doi.org/10.1145/2955114

Ko, A. J., Oleson, A., Ryan, N., Register, Y., Xie, B., Tari, M., . . . & Loksa, D. (2020). It is time for more critical CS education. *Communications of the ACM, 63*(11), 31–33. https://dl.acm.org/doi/pdf/10.1145/3424000

Vogel, S. (2021). "Los programadores debieron pensarse como dos veces": Exploring the intersections of language, power, and technology with bi/multilingual students. *ACM Transactions on Computing Education (TOCE), 21*(4), 1–25. https://doi.org/10.1145/3447379

RESOURCE 1: THREE CIRCLES WORKSHEET

YOUR TURN TO START A SYNCRETIC COMPUTATIONAL CONVERSATION!

Ready to support your emergent bilingual students in integrated CS activities?

This packet will help you design a unit that brings together computing, your subject area, and your students' communities and language practices.

WHAT TO TEACH? (WHAT CONVERSATION WILL YOU MAKE CODE A PART OF?)

Brainstorm: What are some topics, big ideas, or parts of the curriculum that you want to target in this activity?

How might you integrate literacies from the three circles to support learning those big ideas? How would you draw on students' (bilingual) language repertoires?

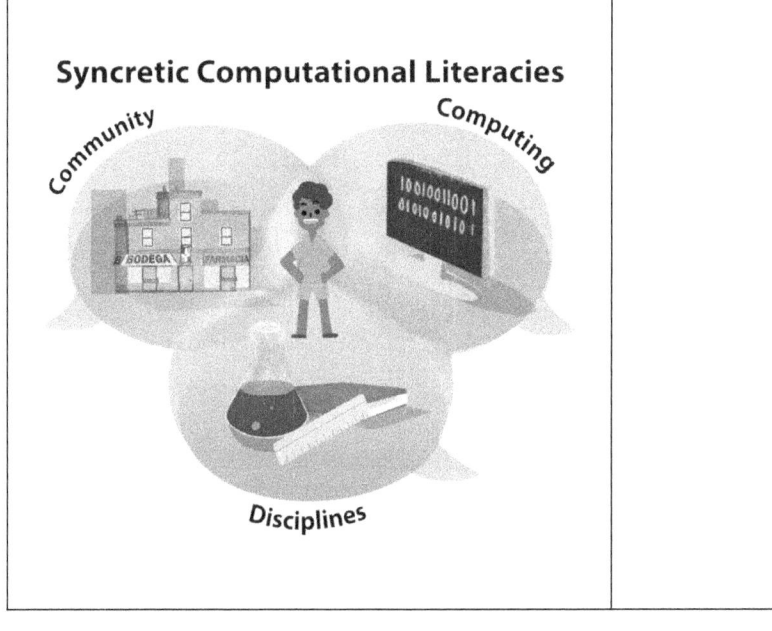

Identify the Specific Objectives you are interested in having students explore.

Literacies and objectives from...	What you want to grow or teach in this activity	What your students already bring to the table
The School Subjects (e.g., ways of talking, listening, writing, creating, reading, critical thinking, and learning in school subjects)		
The Community (e.g., home, friends, family, communities, media)		
Computing (e.g., coding/computing to think about things, solve problems, express themselves in the "real world")		

What would you have your students do/make (e.g., unit/lesson, project)?
What resources do you have?
What resources do you need?
Description of activity

Need more fine-grained strategies for supporting multilingual learners in CSed? Check out the Educator Resources on our website at https://pila-cs.org.

Suggested Resource Citation: Cervantes, F., Vogel, S., Hoadley, C., Aponte, G., Ascenzi-Moreno, L., & Ma, J. (2020, October). Planning for syncretic conversations: Your turn to start a syncretic computational conversation! Participating in Literacies and Computer Science (PiLaCS). https://nyuscholars.nyu.edu/en/publications/planning-for-syncretic-conversations-your-turn-to-start-a-syncret

Planning for Syncretic Conversations: Your Turn to Start a Syncretic Computational Conversation! © 2020 by *Participating in Literacies and Computer Science* is licensed under *CC BY-NC-SA 4.0*

15

Disability, Ableism, and You

Spence J. Ray, Maya Israel, Joanne Barrett, Nykema Lindsey, Carla Strickland, Bethany Daniel, Stephanie T. Jones, and the Computer Science Educational Justice Collective

CHAPTER OVERVIEW

This chapter defines disability and unpacks ableism as a system of oppression that reproduces inequities in computer science (CS) and CS education (CS Ed). Drawing on the theories presented in Chapter 5, the chapter illustrates how ableism intersects with other identities (e.g., linguistic, racial) and creates oppression across four layers of society (ideological, institutional, interpersonal, and internalized). The chapter then examines how disability and ableism shape CS and CS Ed. It concludes with action steps you can take against ableism in your classroom.

CHAPTER OBJECTIVES

After reading this chapter, I can:

- Define disability and explain its role in CS Ed.
- Define ableism and understand how it operates across different layers of oppression.
- Identify ways that disability and ableism shape CS Ed.
- Reflect on personal experiences that have shaped my own perceptions of ableism and disability.

KEY TERMS

ableism; access; accessibility; accommodations; assistive technologies; co-teaching; disability; disabled exceptionalism; dynamic disabilities; dysgraphia; Four I's of Oppression and Advantage; identity-first language; imposter syndrome; Individualized Education Program (IEP); invisible disabilities; medical model of disability; microaggressions; modifications; neurodiversity; paternalism; person-first language; pull out model; push in model; segregated settings; self-contained classroom; social model of disability; technoableism

YOUR STORY

Previous chapters have begun with stories from teachers about their experiences related to the chapter's content. In this chapter, the stories will come from you! The activity below will help you start to connect your prior knowledge and personal experiences to the chapter's content.

> ## ACTIVITY 1: STOP AND JOT OR DOODLE
>
> - Take out a piece of paper or open up a digital notepad or canvas.
> - Spend at least 2–3 minutes thinking about the prompt below.
> - Capture your thinking through writing or drawing.
> - You can use a timer if you'd like.
>
> **Prompt:** Reflect on your own experiences as a student, teacher, and/or parent related to disability in school.
>
> What comes to mind when you think about disability in your school experiences? How was it talked about (or not) in school settings? How was it present (or not) in your relationships with those around you? How might other aspects of your identity (e.g., race, gender, income/socioeconomic status) have played a role in how you experienced and/or learned about disability?

No matter what your experiences are, they are yours, and they inform your perspectives as you read this chapter. Becoming aware of our perspectives helps us know where we're starting from so we can widen our perspectives and deepen our understanding. This reflection serves as a starting point that we'll revisit throughout the chapter. As you read, we hope that you engage in active reflection and challenge assumptions about what we know about students with disabilities in CS Ed.

WHAT IS DISABILITY?

disability Any physical, mental, or emotional variance that impacts, limits, or makes more difficult major life activities in society as it exists today.

Disability is a term that is often used to describe how individual minds and bodies differ from what has been determined by society to be "normal" (Annamma et al., 2013). Traditional notions of disability set expectations for what individuals "should" be able to do to navigate daily life in society and establish a strict binary between ability and disability. We challenge this idea and take a broad understanding of disability. We consider disability as any variance (e.g., cognitive, developmental, neurological, physical, psychological, physical, sensory) that impacts, limits, or makes more difficult major life activities in society as it exists today.

identity-first language A way to talk about disability that centers the disability (e.g., "a disabled person"). For some people with disabilities, identify-first language is an important way to reclaim their disabled identities so that disability is not perceived as negative. It is best to ask individuals whether they prefer identify-first or person-first language.

When it comes to language use about disability, there are two common approaches: **identity-first language** (e.g., a disabled person) and **person-first language** (e.g., a person with a disability). Identity-first language is often used by disabled people who consider their disabilities as an important part of who they are (National Center on Disability and Journalism [NCDJ], 2021). Person-first language is often used to center people rather than their disabilities. Different people have different preferences on which type of language to use and why. Rather than making assumptions, it is best to ask individuals what their preference is, just as you might discuss correct name pronunciation or preferred pronouns. In this chapter, we use identity-first and person-first language to acknowledge both approaches.[1]

person-first language A way to talk about disability that avoids defining people in terms of their disability (e.g., "a person with a disability"). It is best to ask individuals whether they prefer identify-first or person-first language.

We understand disability as a natural part of the human experience. We use the term to describe the spectrum of abilities that we all have, and we recognize that people's abilities change over their life spans (Shew, 2020). While some disabilities are present at birth, others may happen through life experiences. Some disabilities are lifelong; others are temporary. Some disabilities may be developed over time through injustices. For example, research has found that people in lower-income neighborhoods who are regularly exposed to pollution due to environmental injustice are more likely to develop health issues (like asthma) that limit their daily activities (Rauh et al., 2008).

Not all disabilities are treated the same by society. Some disabled people can "pass" or be perceived by others as nondisabled and access related privileges. Some disabilities are marked socially as "more" or

---

1. See the On Terminology section of this guide for a full explanation on our use of different identity-related terms.

"less" normal. For example, wearing contact lenses to correct vision is not generally marked as a disability in U.S. culture. As we'll consider later, the lines between what counts as "normal" vision, low vision, and blindness as a disability are socially designed and constructed (Annamma et al., 2013).

Invisible disabilities (also called non-visible or non-apparent disabilities) are disabilities that are not readily perceived by others. Invisible disabilities might include things like chronic illness or mental illness and other conditions that significantly impact daily living. Some may assume that invisible disabilities don't "count" because they are less apparent. However, these disabilities are very real. People with invisible disabilities may have unique experiences because they are often perceived as nondisabled and are expected to move, think, or behave in normative ways. When these expectations are violated, others may become upset or make incorrect assumptions about the situation.

Similarly, people with **dynamic disabilities** may have fluctuations in their daily functioning. They may be able to walk without assistance one day, need a cane another day, and a wheelchair on another day. The nature of these disabilities can lead other people to interpret those with dynamic disabilities as merely "faking" their problems. This assumption often stems from understanding disability through a binary lens rather than recognizing it as a lived experience that exists along a continuum.

Different experiences with navigating disabilities in society provide us with essential perspectives into our society, and we must be careful not to understand disability as a monolith. We recognize that the lived experiences of people with disabilities vary and are individual. Thus, we hold a dialectical perspective on disability, making room for concepts like **neurodiversity** that people take up as a positive identity that they would not change or instances where non-hearing people consider themselves members of the deaf community but not disabled (Shew, 2020). Yet we also recognize that for other realities, such as chronic pain or terminal illness, some might wish to have their disability cured or treated.

We also adopt an intersectional perspective on disability, acknowledging that the multiple identities of individuals with disabilities influence how they experience both marginalization and privilege (Annamma et al., 2013). Two people with the same disability label may have distinct experiences related to disability depending on other identities based on class, culture, gender, race, sexual orientation, socioeconomic status, and so on. For instance, Kay Ulanday Barrett, a poet and disability activist, discussed their experience at the intersections of race, gender, and disability in a 2016 interview.[2] Barrett described the ways that different spaces confirm

invisible disabilities Disabilities that are not readily perceived by society.

dynamic disabilities Disabilities that have symptoms that fluctuate in severity, and daily functioning varies from day to day.

neurodiversity The recognition that there are a range of differences in how our brains work.

---

2. Access the video at https://www.youtube.com/watch?v=CSHcKFn7zZw

or deny different aspects of their identity. Consider why it is important to take an intersectional perspective on disability.

MODELS OF DISABILITY

There are several ways to think about disability. The most prevalent way in the United States is the **medical model of disability**. The medical model involves a doctor or licensed professional diagnosing a disability and working to "repair" or treat it as fully as possible. Diagnosing disabilities is often highly subjective, requiring individual judgments that can introduce personal biases and reproduce inequity. The medical model frequently leads to an understanding of disability as negative, with disabled people needing to be "fixed" (Shew, 2020) and locates the problem within individuals rather than as a community and systemic challenge that often exists by design (Love et al., 2021).

By contrast, the disability rights community embraces a more comprehensive **social model of disability**. This model does not name differences as good or bad. It simply accepts them as different, acknowledging these differences in minds and bodies as diversity. Rather than understanding disability as an individual problem, the social model emphasizes how society upholds "able-bodied" norms of mind and body. Because of how society is built and organized, it disables some people by design. For example, when society constructed buildings and sidewalks that did not meet the needs of all bodies, we "disabled" some. Without a curb cut or ramp, a person using a wheelchair would be disabled from crossing the street or entering a building. Design features like curb cuts and ramps are less disabling and make a huge difference for access.

The medical and social models of disability can be understood as two ends of a continuum (Figure 1). Many people think about disability in ways that fall somewhere in between, and there are several other models as well.

> **medical model of disability** A model that understands disability as an individual medical problem that should be fixed or cured.

> **social model of disability** A model that understands disability as diversity within minds and bodies, where individuals are disabled because of how society is built and organized.

Figure 1. Models of Disability

The models we choose to use are grounded in histories and ideologies that shape how we understand these issues. For example, the medical model of disability is intertwined with histories of practices (e.g., forced sterilization, institutionalization, incarceration, eugenics, phrenology) that sought to "prove" that people from different racial backgrounds were biologically different and that those racialized as non-white were inferior and even not fully human. These efforts were then used to rationalize violence and oppression against racially minoritized people and people with disabilities (Annamma et al., 2013). Forced sterilization was used to oppress Black and disabled women and was justified through pseudoscience. Genetic testing today has similar parallels in that it may result in "selective abortion of fetuses with markers for autism . . . encourag[ing] the idea that it's better to not exist than to risk being disabled" (as cited in Shew, 2020). Similarly, the social model of disability highlights how, in the United States, disability is profoundly influenced by our post-industrial, capitalist society. Within this model, human value is tied to productivity and the ability to work, resulting in the devaluation of individuals with disabilities because their productivity may not align with capitalist norms, like an eight-hour workday or valuing quantity over quality (Shew, 2020).

> ### REFLECTION 1: DEFINING DISABILITY
>
> - After reading these definitions of disability, consider your response to the activity at the beginning of the chapter. Did reading this section change your thinking? Where does your personal orientation toward disability fall in terms of the models described above?

One goal of this chapter is to make you aware of different ways to think about disability. Considering disability from a variety of perspectives can help us understand it differently. We hope that you will take time to consider different perspectives and be open to broadening your own perspective in ways that are more inclusive of all, regardless of the labels society assigns.

WHAT IS ABLEISM?

Ableism is a loaded term and can describe a range of actions, attitudes, interactions, and statements. Defining it can be tricky. Thomas Hehir, a leading advocate for children with disabilities and a leader in special

ableism Implicit or explicit social preference for nondisabled bodies and minds that creates prejudice and oppression of disability and disabled people (Shew, 2020).

education policy, defines ableism as, "the devaluation of disability [that] results in societal attitudes that uncritically assert that it is better for a child to walk than roll, speak than sign, read print than read Braille, spell independently than use a spell-check, and hang out with nondisabled kids as opposed to other disabled kids" (Hehir, 2002).

Take a moment to reflect on Hehir's definition, using the prompt below.

REFLECTION 2: EXAMINING ABLEISM

- How does society communicate the belief that it is better for children to walk than to roll? To speak than to sign? To read print rather than Braille? To spell independently rather than use a spell-check? Think about how these beliefs are communicated through policies, interactions, designs, and so on.

- What are the implications of valuing "hanging out with non-disabled kids as opposed to other disabled kids"? How does this attitude reflect ableism as a devaluing of disability?

Ableism describes the implicit or explicit social preference for nondisabled bodies and minds that creates prejudice toward disability and disabled people (Shew, 2020). Ableism encompasses beliefs about what "counts" as a "normal" mind and body as determined by society and perpetuates negative narratives about those with disabilities. It includes the explicit discrimination, harm, or oppression that disabled people face in society and the exclusion of disabled people from daily activities by design. Ableism suggests that disability is always negative (Shew, 2020).

paternalism
Treating individuals with disabilities in condescending or patronizing ways that deny them their agency and dignity.

disabled exceptionalism
Narratives that position disabled people as inspirational because they were able to "overcome" their disability and accomplish great things. Disabled exceptionalism objectifies those with disabilities and recenters ableist norms.

However, ableism also manifests in more subtle ways, especially in classrooms and schools. A well-intentioned teacher might talk down to a student with a disability, oversimplifying things and making decisions on behalf of the student. This behavior is referred to as **paternalism** and is one form of ableism (Love et al., 2021). Similarly, school curricula, including CS curricula, often fail to teach disability history. When disability is mentioned, the stories may reinforce ideas of **disabled exceptionalism** where disabled people are centered as an "inspiration" because they were able to "overcome" their disability and accomplish great things (Shew, 2020). But such stories objectify people with disabilities to gratify nondisabled people. Both paternalism and perpetuating disabled exceptionalism dehumanize disabled people by limiting their agency and ability to make decisions and by denying them their dignity as human beings.

Ableism also reproduces privilege available to those who are socially perceived as "able-bodied" or who have the ability to live daily life in ways that are considered "normal" by society. Activity 2 lists some examples of privilege that come from ableism. As you complete the activity, consider which statements you have experienced and/or how a given privilege may not be available to you or those you know because of a disability.

ACTIVITY 2: ABLEISM AND PRIVILEGE

- Read the statements.
- Which statements have you experienced?
- How have these privileges *not* been available to you, either because of a disability or for another reason?

Statements:

1. I can be assured that my entire neighborhood will be accessible to me.
2. In school, I was given learning materials that showed people like me as a role model.
3. I can be assured that assumptions about my mental capabilities will not be made based on my physical appearance.
4. I can do well in challenging situations without being told what an inspiration I must be to other able-bodied people.
5. It is unlikely that my employer will ask me about current or past medical information and feel that they can legitimately do so.
6. I am unlikely to be forcibly subjected to treatment that, though carried out in the name of my health and well-being, might be considered abuse in other contexts.
7. I can be pretty sure of finding people willing to give me career advice that is based around my strengths and ambitions rather than from their assumptions about my sanity or ability level.
8. I can buy posters, postcards, picture books, greeting cards, dolls, toys, magazines, and so on that feature people that look like me and have the same physical status.
9. I can go to a grocery store and know that I can access anything that I need.

> 10. I can enter a clothing store and purchase items without feeling like I am being judged by the personnel who work there.
>
> 11. I am confident that I will be able to find food that I am able to eat when I travel.
>
> 12. I know that if there is a fire or emergency, I will be able to exit the building.

These examples are meant to help you think about some of the invisible privilege that surrounds ableism (McIntosh, 1990). However, it is important to remember that you do not have to be disabled to experience ableism (Lewis, 2021, as cited in Love et al., 2021). Because of intersectional identities, a nondisabled person might say "no" to one or more of these statements for other reasons. For example, a woman wearing a hijab might enter a clothing store and feel judged by the personnel based on her religious practices. Students with racial and gender minoritized identities may not have had learning materials in school that showed people like them as role models. These overlapping experiences can be one way to build solidarity and to recognize how ableism affects everyone.

ABLEISM, PRIVILEGE, AND OPPRESSION

Ableism, like other oppressive systems of power, is often invisibilized for those who align with what society has classified as "normal." CS teacher Kristi shared her perspective on this reality:

> When I had a child in New York City and suddenly had to take a stroller everywhere, I very much saw New York as an ableist city and really hadn't ever seen it that way before. I also remember [learning in professional development] about park bench design and how some cities specifically designed benches for people to not get too comfortable to lay down on as a measure to control [unhoused people]. I remember looking more closely at how benches were designed as well as playgrounds. You start to realize how non-inclusive the world is in so many ways and how most things were designed by and for someone who is not disabled.

As Kristi described, ableism and exclusion are reproduced by design. For example, in cities like New York, not every subway station has an elevator and is accessible. People who use elevators to navigate may have to exit at a different stop from their original destination and find an alternative route. Like any of the "-isms" discussed in Chapter 5, ableism operates at multiple layers of society. Furthermore, ableism doesn't occur in a vacuum; different types of ableist oppression intersect, leading to compounding effects. The sections below give some examples of how ableism manifests across the **Four I's of Oppression and Advantage** we introduced in Chapter 5 (Chinook Fund, n.d.).

ABLEISM AND IDEOLOGICAL OPPRESSION

Ideological layers of ableism are embedded into subconscious ideas and attitudes about disabilities and disabled people within a culture or society. Some common ableist ideologies include assumptions that people with disabilities are less capable or valuable or even less human than people without disabilities. For instance, the media often celebrates people without disabilities who show kindness to a person with disabilities, praising the nondisabled person for doing something "remarkable" instead of something that should be a general courtesy. This news article headline is one example: *Student Commended for Act of Kindness When Matched Against Wrestler with Physical Disability* (ABC News, 2019).

While the intent of stories like this is generally to inspire people to be kind, they send strong implicit ableist messages about what is normal and acceptable in society. Some of these implicit ideas include the following:

- It is a privilege for people with disabilities to receive kindness from others instead of being automatically treated with the same courtesy afforded to nondisabled people.

- People with disabilities need a nondisabled person to "save" them from social rejection or tasks of daily living.

- It's okay to use the image and/or story of a person with a disability without their consent.

- People with disabilities are less valued than the nondisabled person who was kind to them.

Similar news stories sometimes appear related to other marginalized identities, such as examples of kids being nice to a trans student or a recent immigrant at school. While kindness and courtesy are important traits, these stories reproduce ideological assumptions about marginalized groups. Intersectionality also plays a role in these situations, as a trans student or immigrant student with disabilities might have amplified consequences (e.g., safety and legal implications) to having their images made public because of their multiple identities.

> **Four I's of Oppression and Advantage** A theory that illustrates how systems of oppression and advantage (like ableism, classism, or racism) are produced across multiple layers of society. The four I's are ideological, institutional, interpersonal, and internalized. (See Bell, 2013; Chan & Coney, 2020; Chinook Fund, n.d.; Kuttner, 2016). See also Chapter 5.

Kristi, the CS teacher we met earlier, shared an example of how she recognized ableism operating at the ideological level in her own life:

> The historical ways we've read about disabilities as young people (at least for me) has been mostly . . . negative and [that] we're "supposed to feel bad" for those individuals, . . . [like] the generic character in the wheelchair or with other disabilities would always be "weaker" than the others and less valuable to the friend group. . . . Also in mainstream TV, the main characters are rarely those with disabilities, undervaluing them as either actors in general and/or as characters in shows.

Kristi pointed to many of the ableist ideologies described above, such as a need to pity people with disabilities as weaker and less valuable. Kristi also named how these ideologies are reproduced in our culture through how we are taught about disability in school and how disability is represented in entertainment. Kristi offered a counterexample as she described a book she read with her child where "one of the main (and coolest) superheroes was in a wheelchair and I remember thinking how cool they wrote the story to be inclusive like this." Efforts that counter dominant beliefs about disability can work to disrupt the ableist ideologies embedded in our society.

ABLEISM AND INSTITUTIONAL OPPRESSION

Institutional ableism includes the ways that negative biases about people with disabilities are built into the law, social structures and policies, school systems, digital technologies, and so forth (Annamma et al., 2013). While a common narrative is that laws protect people, sometimes they also uphold negative biases and structures that allow ableism to continue. Beratan (2006) described institutional ableism as "discriminatory structures and practices . . . [and] uninterrogated beliefs about disability [that are] deeply ingrained within educational systems (n.p.)." Beratan named how institutional ableism involves structures and practices but also draws in ideological layers of oppression through the "uninterrogated beliefs about disability" that are embedded in education. He argued that because of institutional and ideological ableism, "even the most well-intentioned policies [maintain] the . . . oppression of existing hierarchies" (n.p.).

technoableism The belief that technology is a "solution" for disability and that disabled people can be "fixed" by technology (Shew, 2020).

One way that institutional ableism manifests is through **technoableism**, or the belief that technology is a "solution" for disability and that disabled people can be "fixed" by technology (Shew, 2020). On the contrary, ableist biases embedded in technology disproportionately impact people with disabilities. For instance, automated virtual proctoring systems are tools used to monitor educational test taking and are intended to prevent cheating. These systems surveil test takers through cameras and microphones and monitor the user's screen, keyboard, and mouse. Disabled test takers "are more likely to be flagged as potentially suspicious . . . simply because of the ways disabled people already exist and because of disability-specific access needs when test-taking" (Center for Democracy and Technology [CDT], 2022, p. 8). Needs like extended breaks or the use of screen readers are "more likely to be flagged or prohibited" by these systems, impacting test takers' performance (CDT, 2022, p. 8).

In CS Ed contexts, institutional ableism can appear in many ways. For example, the tools and curricula developed for and adopted by schools and districts are not always accessible or easily usable for those with disabilities. As CS educator Karime noted, "Just because something is on a computer doesn't intrinsically make it accessible." Schools and districts often do not consider **accessibility** when making adoption and purchasing decisions, leading to technology tools that exclude many students with disabilities. Similarly, school structures and policies may keep students with disabilities out of CS Ed classes. Kristi shared an example from the high school where she works. Depending on where a student lives or the school district they attend, they may be separated into self-contained classes or schools, or they may be integrated with their peers. Kristi described her experience:

> Because CS is an "enrichment" class, it isn't prioritized at all for students [with Individuals Education Programs (IEPs)], as the school wants to ensure those students "get all the core subjects" like Biology to graduate.

accessibility The process of making activities, environments, information, and interactions available to people with different needs.

Kristi's example highlights the layers that can exist within institutional ableism. Because biology is valued as a "core" subject for high school, it's considered valuable to offer an inclusion option. However, students with disabilities are not provided the same opportunities to access CS educational opportunities; there is no CS inclusion option and CS courses are not offered in their special education setting.

ABLEISM AND INTERPERSONAL OPPRESSION

Interpersonal ableism happens in social interactions between people. These interactions encompass language and actions. Any time that nondisabled people deny or discount the lived experiences of disabled people, this is a form of interpersonal oppression (Bennett & Rosner, 2019; Shaw, 2020).

Authors Sari Solden and Michelle Frank (2019) offer examples of three types of messages that can be considered interpersonal ableism (Table 1). These messages often perpetuate ableist language and paternalistic attitudes and can be understood as forms of ableist **microaggressions**.

> **microaggressions**
> Common, everyday slights (verbal or behavioral) toward socially marginalized groups or individuals; microaggressions may be intentional or unintentional, but they still significantly impact those receiving them.

Often, interpersonal ableism appears in educational contexts as deficit language about disabled students and/or reduced expectations for those students that limit what they are capable of. Kristi described a situation that she experienced at her school while talking with a special education colleague: "The colleague kept remarking about how 'my kids just can't do that' or identifying a specific student as 'lazy' or 'difficult' rather than acknowledging the needs that student may have that aren't being met." Similarly, Rebecca described how a teacher in her school refused to support a student identified as needing special education services in a CS activity "because he was struggling with logging into his computer. She said he couldn't even log in, so she didn't see how he could follow

Table 1. Interpersonal Ableism (Adapted from Solden & Frank, 2019)

Type	Explanation	Examples
You message	Messages stated directly to the disabled person that result from "misunderstanding, misinterpreting, or conflating" individuals' character and their disability (Solden & Frank, p. 32)	"You're so smart. You don't need accommodations."
They message	Indirect messages that people make about others with similar disabilities. These messages are not directed to a person with a disability. In fact, the speaker may not know that their comment was heard by someone with a disability. The hearer's disability may stay "hidden." However, the messages implicitly convey to the disabled person what is and is not socially acceptable.	Sam, an undiagnosed student with ADHD overhears a teacher remark, "Ugh. Jordan is so ADHD [attention deficit hyperactivity disorder]. They need to be on medication" Sam wonders, "Do they think that about me? What would they think about me if they knew I had ADHD?"
Duh! message	Messages or "suggestions" offered as "solutions" to a disability. These messages trivialize the realities of disabilities and often assume that people with disabilities aren't capable of finding solutions on their own or merely haven't tried these seemingly "obvious" answers to a "simple" problem. These suggestions are likely all things that individuals have tried and/or use consistently, but they are inadequate to address the complexities of people's lived realities.	"Have you thought about making a list?" "What about putting it in your calendar?" "Just use a timer." "Try making the font larger." "Have you tried getting more sleep?"

the CS activity." These examples reflect interpersonal ableism because they reproduce the idea that students with disabilities are less capable of learning than their nondisabled peers.

ABLEISM AND INTERNALIZED OPPRESSION

Internalized ableism describes how disabled people absorb negative beliefs about disability that shape how they perceive themselves. These negative beliefs are often heard from multiple sources, including interpersonal experiences with others, laws, and messaging about disability in culture and society. Solden and Frank (2019) identify "absorbed messages" as one type of internalized ableism. These messages were likely internalized unconsciously but shape ideas about what is expected, valued, and not valued by society and how people with disabilities can(not) meet those expectations. Absorbed messages may sound like, "Other people do this. Why can't I?" "Why can't I be normal?" "Why is this so hard for me?" "What is wrong with me?"

People without disabilities can also have internalized ableism, manifested as ableist biases that disabilities are "bad" and that people with disabilities need to be "fixed." Most, if not all of us, will experience some type of disability over the course of our lives. Ableist biases can be transformed inward to become internalized ableism. Similarly, people with disabilities can also hold ableist biases. Because disabilities are so varied, a person with one type of disability might accept their disability but think of another disability as something to be ashamed of.

In CS Ed, internalized ableism can limit what a student attempts or believes is possible for them to accomplish. Internalized ableism might appear as disabled individuals feeling shame about their disability and inferior to their nondisabled peers, not asking for **accommodations**, feeling like they don't deserve accommodations, or placing unrealistic expectations on themselves. Internalized ableism can influence whether a student enrolls in a CS course, persists when presented with a coding challenge, or attempts to participate in a robotics competition. **Imposter syndrome** leads students to discount abilities that they have, and the internalized messages that get replayed (either consciously or unconsciously) can make students feel bad about themselves when they do not need to.

Kristi shared an example of internalized ableism that she recognized in her classes:

> I have announced my CS class as a course option some of my sophomores could take with me the following year. I've heard several students with IEPs say that "it's too hard for me" or "I'll never be able to do that." [This] just solidifies the idea that

accommodations Changes to a learning environment or to the presentation of curricular content that are offered to help students access content and complete learning tasks that are a regular part of the curriculum. Examples include using a microphone, arranging seating to facilitate movement, or using assistive technologies.

imposter syndrome Feelings and beliefs of intellectual and professional inferiority or incompetence; "a perceived self-doubt in one's abilities and accomplishments compared with others, despite evidence to the contrary" (Walker & Saklofske, 2023, n.p.).

society, relationships, and experiences around them have shaped this belief inside of them about what they can and cannot achieve, especially when it comes to CS.

Internalized ableism can be resisted. Intrapersonal awareness, or an awareness of one's internal dialogues and beliefs, and support to challenge negative internalized beliefs can empower a student to take risks. In contrast to what Kristi shared, many other CS teachers have shared examples of how CS has been a powerful way for students with disabilities to create and express themselves in new ways that have strengthened their self-efficacy and confidence.

DISABILITY AND ABLEISM IN PUBLIC EDUCATION

Disability and ableism in U.S. education are intertwined with the special education system in public schools. Special education is built on a legal model of disability that is guided by the Individuals with Disabilities Education Act (IDEA) and other laws and regulations (U.S. Department of Education, 2004). There are currently approximately 7.2 million students, or about 15% of all students, who are identified as having a disability according to IDEA and who receive special services as part of their public education (National Center for Education Statistics [NCES], 2024). Section 1400 of IDEA frames disability in this way:

> Disability is a natural part of the human experience and in no way diminishes the right of individuals to participate in or contribute to society. Improving educational results for children with disabilities is an essential element of our national policy of ensuring equality of opportunity, full participation, independent living, and economic self-sufficiency for individuals with disabilities. (U.S. Department of Education, 2004)

dysgraphia A learning disability that may affect a person's physical ability to write and/or impact their ability to express their thoughts through writing.

Drawing on medical models of disability, IDEA identifies thirteen categories of disabilities that are used to identify and provide services for students. Some of these categories include autism, intellectual disabilities, specific learning disabilities (e.g., **dysgraphia**, dyslexia), and speech, hearing, and visual impairments. While these categories are useful to support many students, they are also limiting. For example, according to IDEA, traumatic brain injury is identified as a disability category, but severe emotional trauma that may be transient is not. Neither is ADHD, despite being well established as a neurodevelopmental disorder within the medical model of disability. However, students with these disabilities may need services and resources to support their full participation in school. Additionally, research shows that a significant proportion of students, especially students of color and multilingual learners, with disabilities are likely not identified and do not receive any support services (Lai et al., 2024; Learning Disabilities Association of America, 2020). This reality means that we need to think broadly about our students and their needs, beyond the legal and medical models that shape disability policies in schools.

In working toward the goals of equal educational opportunity and full participation stated in IDEA, most students with disabilities are taught alongside their peers in general education classrooms. This effort is referred to as inclusion. Inclusion of students with disabilities in general education classrooms has been shown to be at worst neutral—and more often beneficial—to both disabled and nondisabled students, academically and socially (Ruijs & Peetsma, 2009). While all students benefit from inclusion approaches, it is important to point out that including students with disabilities in general education settings is primarily for their own benefit and not the benefit of their nondisabled peers.

Students with disabilities may have an **Individualized Education Program** (IEP), a legal document that outlines services and support that the student will receive. Teachers in general education classrooms must provide support and accommodations that meet the requirements in the IEP. Services may also include **co-teaching** models, where a general education teacher and a special education teacher both teach in the same classroom, having a special education teacher **push in** and support students with disabilities in their general education classrooms or having students with disabilities be **pulled out** of general education classes to receive support from a special education teacher in smaller classes. Depending on students' needs, students with disabilities may also be educated in **self-contained classrooms** separate from their general education peers.

Ideally, classrooms are designed in ways that ensure that all students, including those with disabilities, have **access** to learning opportunities that are accessible to them. Access refers to making sure that all students have the opportunity to participate in CS learning experiences. The U.S. Department of Education's Office for Civil Rights (OCR) has defined accessibility as ensuring that "a person with a disability is afforded the opportunity to acquire the same information, engage in the same interactions, and enjoy the same services as a person without a disability in an equally effective and equally integrated manner, with substantially equivalent ease of use" (OCR, 2013).

Individualized Education Program (IEP) A legal document mandated by federal law (IDEA) that outlines services and support that a student with disabilities will receive as part of their public education (U.S. Department of Education, 2004).

co-teaching An instructional model where a general education teacher and a special education teacher teach together in the same classroom.

push in model An instructional model where a special education teacher pushes into, or enters a general education classroom, to support students with disabilities for a given amount of time.

pull out model An instructional model where students with disabilities are pulled out of, or leave their general education classrooms, to receive specialized support from a special education teacher for a given amount of time.

self-contained classroom An instructional model where students with disabilities are educated in a special education classroom rather than a general education classroom.

access Giving all students the opportunities and support they need to participate in CS.

modifications Changes to what a student is expected to learn or produce. Examples include shortening an assignment or adjusting a grading scale so that spelling doesn't count toward a grade.

assistive technologies Technology that helps people with disabilities perform tasks more easily or safely so that they can live, move, participate, and contribute in society more fully. Assistive technologies may include devices (e.g., walkers, prosthetics), materials (e.g., curricular aids), services (e.g., technical assistance), or software (e.g., screen readers).

Ensuring access through accessibility may take place through accommodations or **modifications** to the classroom environment or to curricular materials. Accommodations are changes that allow students to participate in a learning activity without changing the activity itself. Modifications are changes to what students are expected to learn. Accommodations might include things like the teacher using a microphone to support a student who is hard of hearing, arranging seating to facilitate movement, using fonts and color schemes that are easy to read for people with dyslexia or colorblindness, or providing resources like screen readers and other **assistive technologies**. Modifications might include things like shortening assignments, adjusting the grading scale (e.g., spelling and grammar don't "count" toward the grade), or having students answer fewer multiple-choice questions on a test instead of producing an open-ended response. In U.S. public education, legal requirements for providing access through accommodations and modifications are part of the IEP process. Teachers should also consider needs that students might have that are not mandated by special education requirements.

Accessibility doesn't automatically result in equity. Many use the analogy of accessibility as helping people with disabilities get onto any playing field, even an unequal one (see Annamma et al., 2013). Like the baseball analogy used in Chapter 4, accessibility doesn't ensure that the playing field is even, nor does it ensure that everyone is able to enjoy full participation in the ways they want to participate. While access is an important first step, it often falls short of full, inclusive, and equitable participation.

In part, this is because the intersections of ableism with racism, classism, language injustice, and other forms of societal oppression manifest uniquely in special education. Black, Indigenous, and Latine students, as well as bi/multilingual learners, are overall underrepresented in special education and cannot access needed services. These same students are also overrepresented in some regions of the country and in certain disability categories. They are more likely to be placed in more restrictive or separate educational settings like self-contained classrooms (Webb, 2020). Racially and linguistically minoritized students face this double bind because of their intersectional identities (Cioè-Peña, 2020; Wilt et al., 2022). For example, a minoritized student who has trouble listening in class may be punished for their behavior instead of an educator thinking to check the child's ability to hear. The simultaneous under- and overrepresentation of marginalized students is influenced by a myriad of factors, including test bias, poverty, insufficient or ineffective instruction, a lack of resources, and a lack of qualified professionals with the skills and knowledge to work with students of diverse backgrounds (Blanchette, 2009; Sullivan & Artiles, 2011).

In particular, racially and linguistically marginalized students tend to be overrepresented in disability categories that are highly stigmatized or highly interpretive, where identifying a disability involves subjective judgments by educators (Finch, 2012; Annamma et al., 2013). Overrepresentation in certain categories (e.g., emotional and behavioral disorders, specific learning disabilities, intellectual disabilities) involves personal biases introduced in the evaluation process in addition to institutional and systemic issues like those above that contribute to reproducing this inequity.

These realities are tied to the relationship between racism and ableism. Special education legislation requires students with disabilities to be placed in the least restrictive environment that meets their needs, beginning with the general education classroom setting. However, scholars have identified how racially marginalized students are overrepresented in self-contained special education classrooms, which can be understood as an informal way to continue racial segregation processes in schools after the Brown v. Board ruling (Harry & Klingner, 2022). Recognizing this reality, disability scholars often refer to self-contained classrooms as **segregated settings** to emphasize the intersections between race and disability.

segregated settings A term used by disability scholars to describe how self-contained classrooms often reproduce racial segregation because of the overrepresentation of racially marginalized students in these settings.

DISABILITY AND ABLEISM IN CS ED

While CS Ed has been focused on increasing access to and participation in K-12 CS learning opportunities, learners with disabilities have not always been a part of those efforts. We know that if learners with disabilities have effective instruction and accessible tools and materials, they succeed in CS Ed (Israel et al., 2015). However, many disabled students enter CS classrooms that are inaccessible and are taught by teachers who may not believe in their ability and their right to learn CS alongside their peers.

The problem of providing access to CS Ed for all students is compounded because students with disabilities in self-contained classrooms are more likely to be excluded from CS courses. When students are provided with opportunities to engage in CS learning, their CS time is prioritized as less important than other subject areas. Kristi's example earlier highlighted this reality, where biology courses as a "core subject" were available to all students, but CS courses were not. Similarly, students who require special services are often pulled out of their general education classes during CS time. In co-teaching settings, the special education teacher is often not present for the CS class. In CS classes when paraeducators are present, they may not feel comfortable with the CS content and may be less able to support students in CS classes. As a result, students are left with a curriculum that is either below their abilities, or they are not provided with adequate scaffolding to access the general curriculum. These realities specifically shaped CS educator Karime's plans: "This is the reason why I entered a dual program in CS and special education. Most CS classes are taught in settings without a special education co-teacher, and I felt ill-equipped to support the special education students in my classes."

The lack of inclusion of students with disabilities in CS Ed is a social justice issue. Inclusion of *all* students in general education CS classrooms benefits students and society as a whole. Students with disabilities bring unique perspectives to CS. Their experiences with technology can impact future directions and advances in computing and design that support technology users with a range of different disabilities (Shew, 2020). All students, regardless of social or medical labels, should be given the opportunity to learn CS. What some students learn may be modified or different, but they can all participate in meaningful ways. Perhaps computing helps them develop skills like self-regulation or allows them to create artifacts that bring joy or perhaps they will go on to create world-changing technologies or enact social policies that shape the way we interact with emerging technologies. An inclusive mindset does not discriminate and provides learning opportunities for all students.

Because of how disability is framed in society broadly and in schools and CS Ed specifically, teachers play an important role in actively working to change how disability is perceived. One teacher, Molly, told her experience as she studied about disability and listened to the stories disabled people shared. Molly recalled that learning more about disability and ableism changed her perspectives:

> [M]y preconceived notions began to unravel. I recalled my own classroom, where I had sometimes underestimated the potential of my students with disabilities. A wave of realization washed over me. I had been limiting my students' narratives, viewing them through a lens of what they could not do rather than celebrating what they could achieve.

What can you do to resist ableism and support students with disabilities in your CS classroom? One important consideration is to find ways to include and incorporate voices of disabled people into your curriculum. In addition, Spence Ray and Maya Israel (n.d.), disability scholars who work in CS Ed, have provided a helpful overview of things you can do in their guide, *Combatting Ableism in Education*.[3] These suggestions can help

---

3. Access the guide at https://drive.google.com/file/d/1w6gP0yisJ1TpCgEP ae8kni1Z9mnzmNID/view

you think about how to recognize and combat ableism in your teaching broadly. In the next chapters, we'll consider some specific approaches that can help you better meet all students' needs.

REVISITING YOUR STORY

Now that you have learned more about disability and ableism, let's dig deeper into your story from the beginning of the chapter. Complete the reflection below to capture your deeper understandings of disability and ableism.

> ### REFLECTION 3: YOUR EXPERIENCE WITH DISABILITY AND ABLEISM
>
> - Take 10–15 minutes or longer thinking about the prompt below. You can use a timer if you'd like.
>
> - Choose Option 1 (collage) or Option 2 (timeline) to capture and express your thinking.
>
> - Once you have created your collage or timeline, consider sharing aspects of your work with a partner or group, and listen as other people share theirs.
>
> *PROMPT:*
>
> What defining experiences have shaped or continue to shape your perception of disability and ableism throughout your life? Experiences might include books or media that made a strong impression on you as a child, important relationships in your life, teaching experiences, or perhaps the personal development of your identity as a person with a disability.
>
> *OPTION 1:*
>
> Create a digital or mixed-media collage. Consider including images, words, headlines, emojis, audio clips, and anything else you can think of to creatively express your defining experiences

with disability and ableism. Below is a sample collage. It depicts some feelings and experiences of an individual through their schooling and with their relationships with family and friends.

OPTION 2:

Create a digital or paper timeline of your experiences. The timeline can be a linear listing of experiences or include multimedia artifacts. Color code each timeline entry to indicate the emotional or affective aspects of the experience. For example, you may use red for an unpleasant experience that made you angry, yellow for a positive experience, or several bright colors for intense and mixed emotions around a profoundly life-changing event. It's up to you how you want to create this code. Below is a sample timeline created by the authors of this chapter.

MY PERSONAL EXPERIENCE WITH DISABILITIES
A brief history from my earliest memories

ELEMENTARY SCHOOL	START OF MIDDLE SCHOOL	END OF MIDDLE SCHOOL	HIGH SCHOOL	COLLEGE	GRAD SCHOOL	YOUNG ADULT
I would see the "special ed" classroom across from the office. They were kept separate from the other students and classes.	Made a new friend. She couldn't get together much because she had to babysit all the time for her brother Peter with Down syndrome.	Got to know Peter well and looked forward to playing with him when I visited her house.	Grandmother had strokes and was paralyzed and could not speak. We took turns as a family nursing her for 3 years.	Dad had heart attacks and strokes and became disabled.	Peter died from cancer at age 23.	Became a teacher and without any training, had students placed in my class. I would do the best I could without guidance.

REFLECTION QUESTIONS

1. This chapter focused primarily on your personal experiences with disability and ableism. What kinds of training and preparation have you received (or not) around disability and ableism in your role as an educator?

2. How is ableism present in your work contexts? What ideas do you have now to challenge ableism in these spaces?

TAKEAWAYS FOR PRACTICE

- Create a list of your top 5 takeaways from this chapter that you can apply in your classroom or with your students right away. This might include your personal framings of how you think about your students or concrete action steps. Share your list with a colleague.

GLOSSARY

Term	Definition
ableism	Implicit or explicit social preference for nondisabled bodies and minds that creates prejudice and oppression of disability and disabled people (Shew, 2020).
access	Giving all students the opportunities and support they need to participate in CS.
accessibility	The process of making activities, environments, information, and interactions available to people with different needs.
accommodations	Changes to a learning environment or to the presentation of curricular content that are offered to help students access content and complete learning tasks that are a regular part of the curriculum. Examples include using a microphone, arranging seating to facilitate movement, or using assistive technologies.
assistive technologies	Technology that helps people with disabilities perform tasks more easily or safely so that they can live, move, participate, and contribute in society more fully. Assistive technologies may include

	devices (e.g., walkers, prosthetics), materials (e.g., curricular aids), services (e.g., technical assistance), or software (e.g., screen readers).
co-teaching	An instructional model where a general education teacher and a special education teacher teach together in the same classroom.
disability	Any physical, mental, or emotional variance that impacts, limits, or makes more difficult major life activities in society as it exists today.
disabled exceptionalism	Narratives that position disabled people as inspirational because they were able to "overcome" their disability and accomplish great things. Disabled exceptionalism objectifies those with disabilities and recenters ableist norms.
dynamic disabilities	Disabilities that have symptoms that fluctuate in severity, and daily functioning varies from day to day.
dysgraphia	A learning disability that may affect a person's physical ability to write and/or impact their ability to express their thoughts through writing.
Four I's of Oppression and Advantage	A theory that illustrates how systems of oppression and advantage (like ableism, classism, or racism) are produced across multiple layers of society. The four I's are ideological, institutional, interpersonal, and internalized. (See Bell, 2013; Chan & Coney, 2020; Chinook Fund, n.d.; Kuttner, 2016). See also Chapter 5.
identity-first language	A way to talk about disability that centers the disability (e.g., "a disabled person"). For some people with disabilities, identify-first language is an important way to reclaim their disabled identities so that disability is not perceived as negative. It is best to ask individuals whether they prefer identify-first or person-first language.
imposter syndrome	Feelings and beliefs of intellectual and professional inferiority or incompetence; "a perceived self-doubt in one's abilities and accomplishments compared with others, despite evidence to the contrary" (Walker & Saklofske, 2023, n.p.).

Individualized Education Program (IEP)	A legal document mandated by federal law (IDEA) that outlines services and support that a student with disabilities will receive as part of their public education (U.S. Department of Education, 2004).
invisible disabilities	Disabilities that are not readily perceived by society.
medical model of disability	A model that understands disability as an individual medical problem that should be fixed or cured.
microaggressions	Common, everyday slights (verbal or behavioral) toward socially marginalized groups or individuals; microaggressions may be intentional or unintentional, but they still significantly impact those receiving them.
modifications	Changes to what a student is expected to learn or produce. Examples include shortening an assignment or adjusting a grading scale so that spelling doesn't count toward a grade.
neurodiversity	The recognition that there are a range of differences in how our brains work.
paternalism	Treating individuals with disabilities in condescending or patronizing ways that deny them their agency and dignity.
person-first language	A way to talk about disability that avoids defining people in terms of their disability (e.g., "a person with a disability"). It is best to ask individuals whether they prefer identify-first or person-first language.
pull out model	An instructional model where students with disabilities are pulled out of, or leave their general education classrooms, to receive specialized support from a special education teacher for a given amount of time.
push in model	An instructional model where a special education teacher pushes into, or enters a general education classroom, to support students with disabilities for a given amount of time.
segregated settings	A term used by disability scholars to describe how self-contained classrooms often reproduce racial segregation because of the overrepresentation of racially marginalized students in these settings.

self-contained classroom	An instructional model where students with disabilities are educated in a special education classroom rather than a general education classroom.
social model of disability	A model that understands disability as diversity within minds and bodies, where individuals are disabled because of how society is built and organized.
technoableism	The belief that technology is a "solution" for disability and that disabled people can be "fixed" by technology (Shew, 2020).

REFERENCES

ABC News. (2019, Jan 6). *Student commended for act of kindness when matched against wrestler with physical disability.* ABC News. https://www.goodmorningamerica.com/news/video/student-commended-act-kindness-matched-wrestler-physical-disability-60195112

Annamma, S. A., Connor, D., & Ferri, B. (2013). Dis/ability critical race studies (DisCrit): Theorizing at the intersections of race and dis/ability. *Race Ethnicity and Education, 16*(1), 1–31. https://doi.org/10.1080/13613324.2012.730511

Bell, J. (2013). *The four "I's" of oppression.* Begin Within. https://beginwithin.info/articles-2/

Barrett, K. U. (2016, May 5). *#RaceAnd: Kay Ulanday Barrett* [Video]. YouTube. https://www.youtube.com/watch?v=CSHcKFn7zZw

Bennett, C. L., & Rosner, D. K. (2019, May 4–9). The promise of empathy: Design, disability, and knowing the "other." *CHI Conference on Human Factors in Computing Systems Proceedings.* Association for Computing Machinery, 1–13. https://doi.org/10.1145/3290605.3300528

Beratan, G. D. (2006). Institutionalizing inequity: Ableism, racism and IDEA 2004. *Disability Studies Quarterly, 26*(2). https://doi.org/10.18061/dsq.v26i2.682

Blanchett, W. J. (2009). A retrospective examination of urban education: From Brown to the resegregation of African Americans in special education—It is time to "go for broke." *Urban Education, 44*(4), 370–388. https://doi.org/10.1177/0042085909338688

Center for Democracy and Technology [CDT]. (2022). *Ableism and disability discrimination in new surveillance technologies: How new surveillance technologies in education, policing, health care, and the workplace disproportionately harm disabled people.* https://cdt.org/wp-content/uploads/2022/05/2022-05-23-CDT-Ableism-and-Disability-Discrimination-in-New-Surveillance-Technologies-report-final-redu.pdf

Chan, E. L., & Coney, L. (2020). Moving TESOL forward: Increasing educators' critical consciousness through a racial lens. *TESOL Journal, 11*(4), 1–13. https://doi.org/10.1002/tesj.550

Chinook Fund. (n.d.) *4 I's of oppression*. https://chinookfund.org/wp-content/uploads/2015/10/Supplemental-Information-for-Funding-Guidelines.pdf

Cioè-Peña, M. (2020). Raciolinguistics and the education of emergent bilinguals labeled as disabled. *Urban Review, 53*, 443–469. https://doi.org/10.1007/s11256-020-00581-z

Eisenmenger, A. (2019, Dec 12). *Ableism 101*. Access living. https://www.accessliving.org/newsroom/blog/ableism-101/#:~:text=Lack%20of%20compliance%20with%20disability,children%20with%20disabilities%20in%20institutions

Elainey, A. (2016, Apr 5). *Casual ableist language*. [Video]. YouTube. https://www.youtube.com/watch?v=a1rrSXkFqGE

Finch, M. E. H. (2012). Special considerations with response to intervention and instruction for students with diverse backgrounds. *Psychology in the Schools, 49*(3), 285–296. https://doi.org/10.1002/pits.21597

Harry, B., & Klingner, J. (2022). *Why are so many students of color in special education? Understanding race and disability in schools* (3rd ed.). Teachers College Press.

Hehir, T. (2002). Eliminating ableism in education. *Harvard Educational Review, 72*(1), 1–33. https://doi.org/10.17763/haer.72.1.03866528702g2105

Israel, M., Wherfel, Q. M., Pearson, J., Shehab, S., & Tapia, T. (2015). Empowering K–12 students with disabilities to learn computational thinking and computer programming. *TEACHING Exceptional Children, 48*(1), 45–53. https://doi.org/10.1177/0040059915594790

Kuttner, P. J. (2016). Hip-hop citizens: Arts-based, culturally sustaining civic engagement pedagogy. *Harvard Educational Review, 86*(4), 527–555. https://doi.org/10.17763/1943-5045-86.4.527

Lai, I., Lipscomb, S., & Johnson, A. (2024). *Appropriate identification of children with disabilities for IDEA services: A report from Recent National Estimates*. U.S. Department of Education, Institute of Education Science, National Center for Educational Evaluation and Regional Assistance. https://files.eric.ed.gov/fulltext/ED652735.pdf

Learning Disabilities Association of America. (2020). *Core principles: Disproportionality in identification for special education*. https://ldaamerica.org/core-principle-disproportionality-in-identification-for-special-education/\#:\~:text=A%20number%20of%20researchers%20(Elder,et%20al.%2C%202008)

Love, H. R., Nyegenye, S. N., Wilt, C. L., & Annamma, S. A. (2021). Black families' resistance to deficit positioning: Addressing the paradox of black parent involvement. *Race Ethnicity and Education, 24*(5), 637–653. https://doi.org/10.1080/13613324.2021.1918403

McIntosh, P. (1990). White privilege: Unpacking the invisible knapsack. *The Legislative Library of the Northwest Territories*. https://www.jstor.org/stable/community.30714426

National Center on Disability and Journalism. (2021). *Disability language style guide*. https://ncdj.org/style-guide/

National Center for Education Statistics. (2024). *Students with disabilities.* https://nces.ed.gov/programs/coe/indicator/cgg/students-with-disabilities

Office of Civil Rights, United States Department of Education. (2013). *Resolution Agreement South Carolina Technical College System.* https://www.ed.gov/sites/ed/files/about/offices/list/ocr/docs/investigations/11116002-b.pdf

Rauh, V. A., Landrigan, P. J., & Claudio, L. (2008). Housing and health: Intersection of poverty and environmental exposures. *Annals of the New York Academy of Sciences, 1136*(1), 276–288. https://doi.org/10.1196/annals.1425.032

Ray, M., & Israel, M. (n.d.). *Combatting ableism in education.* Project Tactic. https://drive.google.com/file/d/1w6gP0yisJ1TpCgEPae8kni1Z9mnzmNID/view

Ruijs, N. M., & Peetsma, T. T. D. (2009). Effects of inclusion on students with and without special educational needs reviewed. *Educational Research Review, 4*(2), 67–79. https://doi.org/10.1016/j.edurev.2009.02.002

Shew, A. (2020). Ableism, technoableism, and future AI. *IEEE Xplore, 39*(1), 40–85. https://doi.org/10.1109/MTS.2020.2967492

Solden, S., & Frank, M. (2019). *A radical guide for women with ADHD: Embrace neurodiversity, live boldly, and break through barriers.* New Harbinger Publications.

Sullivan, A. L., & Artiles, A. J. (2011). Theorizing racial inequity in special education: Applying structural inequity theory to disproportionality. *Urban Education, 46*(6), 1526–1552. https://doi.org/10.1177/0042085911416014

U.S. Department of Education. (2004). Individuals with disabilities education act. Public Law 108–446. Individuals with Disabilities Education Act, 20 U.S.C. § 1400. https://sites.ed.gov/idea/

Walker, D. L., & Saklofske, D. H. (2023). Development, factor structure, and psychometric validation of the impostor phenomenon assessment: A novel assessment of imposter phenomenon. *Assessment, 30*(7), 2162–2183. https://doi.org/10.1177/10731911221141870

Webb, P. E. (2020). *Disproportionality in special education: The factors of over-representation, lack of inclusion and its impact on student success* [Master's thesis, Bethel University]. Spark Repository. https://spark.bethel.edu/etd/649

Wilt, C. L., Annamma, S. A., Wilmot, J. M., Nyegenye, S. N., Miller, A. L., & Jackson, E. E. (2022). Performing color-evasiveness: A DisCrit analysis of educators' discourse in the U.S. *Teaching and Teacher Education, 117*, 1–12. https://doi.org/10.1016/j.tate.2022.103761

RESOURCE 1: CHALLENGING ABLEIST LANGUAGE

One way that ableism gets reproduced in everyday actions is through language. There are many phrases we use that have a history connected to ableism and disability. The activity below provides a chance to reflect on some of these expressions.

ACTIVITY

1. **Read** each expression in column 1.

2. **Describe** how the expression is ableist in column 2.

3. **Identify** a different, non-ableist phrase you could use instead in column 3.

Column 1 Ableist phrase	Column 2 Why is this expression ableist?	Column 3 Alternative phrase
Example: I'm not **crazy** about how this shirt looks on me.	Crazy originally described (pejoratively) people who struggled with mental illness. Using it to state a preference minimizes the realities of those who live with mental illness.	I don't love how this shirt looks on me.
1. Pay attention! You're so **ADD**.		
2. It was freezing this morning and now it's so hot! The weather is so **bi-polar** today.		
3. She just **turned a blind eye** to that behavior.		
4. Neither of us knew what we were doing. It was like **the blind leading the blind**.		
5. He totally didn't get what I was saying. My ideas **fell on deaf ears**.		
6. That's so **lame**.		
7. You're such a **nut job**.		
8. I'm so **OCD** about my clothes.		
9. She's acting like a **psycho**.		
10. That's **retarded**.		
11. How can you be so **stupid**?		
12. That is the **dumbest** thing I've ever heard.		

REFLECTION

Now that you've completed the activity, take a moment to reflect on what you have learned.

1. What did you notice about how or when these expressions are used? Were there patterns to what made the expressions ableist?

2. Are there any expressions listed above that you use regularly? Did other expressions come to mind that you would add to the list? How can you choose alternatives in your own communication to make your language less ableist?

Examples adapted from Eisenmenger (2019) and Elainey (2016).

16

Unpacking the Universal Design for Learning Framework

Joanne Barrett, Maya Israel, Spence J. Ray, Nykema Lindsey, Carla Strickland, Stephanie T. Jones, & the Computer Science Educational Justice Collective

CHAPTER OVERVIEW

This chapter introduces an instructional planning approach known as the Universal Design for Learning (UDL) framework. The UDL framework is an approach to instruction that can be applied to computer science education (CS Ed) to benefit all students and meet their different needs. The chapter explores mindsets that support using UDL to design instruction, provides an explanation of the UDL framework, and considers how CS teachers might use the framework in their planning.

CHAPTER OBJECTIVES

After reading this chapter, I can:

- Identify mindsets that support designing instruction with the UDL.
- Describe components of the UDL framework and explain how those components inform instructional design.

KEY TERMS

accessibility; accommodations; advocacy; deficit narratives; Individualized Education Program (IEP); neuro-variability; othering; Universal Design for Learning (UDL)

HANA'S STORY

Hana[1] is a technology teacher who teaches elementary CS. At her school, CS is an elective, so Hana sees most of the students on a weekly basis. Because she teaches so many different students, Hana has become very aware of the diverse backgrounds and needs of her learners, including those who have **Individualized Education Programs (IEPs)** and need additional learning supports. She wants to learn more about how to design and plan inclusive lessons that meet the needs of all her students. She has heard about one approach that might help—the UDL framework. Hana plans to talk more with colleagues who use this approach and explore how it can help her create a CS learning environment that is more welcoming to her students' diverse needs.

MEETING ALL STUDENTS' NEEDS

Hana's situation is not unique. Many educators feel ill-prepared to meet students' different learning needs. In this chapter, we'll examine a framework called the **Universal Design for Learning (UDL)**. UDL can help us develop and create instruction that better meets the needs of all of our diverse learners. To get started, use the prompt below to reflect on what a classroom that meets all students' needs might be like.

REFLECTION 1: CS FOR ALL

- Take out a piece of paper or open up a digital notepad or canvas.
- Spend at least 2–3 minutes thinking about the prompt below.
- Capture your thinking through writing or drawing.
- You can use a timer if you'd like.

Prompt: What does an inclusive, accessible classroom mean to you? What does it look like? What does it sound like? What are students doing? How are they engaging with those around them?

Sidebar definitions:

Individualized Education Plan (IEP) A legal document mandated by federal law (IDEA; U.S. Department of Education, 2004) that outlines services and support that a student with disabilities will receive as part of their public education.

Universal Design for Learning (UDL) An instructional planning and teaching approach that seeks to meet the needs of all learners by reducing barriers to learning. The three principles of UDL include providing learners with (1) multiple means of engagement; (2) multiple means of representation; and (3) multiple means of action and engagement (CAST, 2024).

---

1. Hana is a composite character based on the experiences of several New York City–based CS teachers (Kristi Jones, Jennifer Romeo, and Rebecca Young).

Supporting all learners in CS Ed requires three things: (1) inclusive mind-sets and beliefs that all learners can learn CS and deserve to be included in CS Ed; (2) equity-focused pedagogical practices that actively incorporate supports, strategies, and accessible tools that meet the needs of students with disabilities but also help all learners; and (3) advocacy to ensure that all learners can enjoy full participation in CS Ed. Let's look at how the UDL framework provides us with the resources listed above that we need to support all learners in CS Ed.

WHAT IS UNIVERSAL DESIGN FOR LEARNING?

Before we explore the details of UDL, let's begin by reflecting on your own teaching.

> ### REFLECTION 2: UDL "QUIZ"
>
> Think about your own teaching. Have you ever done any of these things?
>
> - Provided choice in activities to your learners.
> - Made learning goals explicit to your students.
> - Allowed learners to use speech-to-text or text-to-speech to complete assignments.
> - Scaffolded learning by starting with an activity with fewer components, working toward more complex activities.
> - Helped students manage their emotions when they were working on something difficult or frustrating.

If you answered yes to any of the instructional practices above, you have implemented aspects of UDL! While some parts of UDL may be new—like the framework itself or its applications to CS Ed—when teachers learn about the UDL framework for the first time, they often indicate that they already use some, if not many, of the practices. However, they have not yet had the opportunity to think about those practices in terms of the overall UDL framework. As you learn about UDL, you'll notice the practices that you already implement and identify new practices to incorporate into your teaching that will increase **accessibility** and full participation in your classroom.

accessibility The process of making activities, environments, information, and interactions available to people with different needs.

So what is UDL? UDL is an instructional planning approach that focuses on how to include the broadest range of learners by reducing barriers to learning, considering accessibility, and increasing the flexibility of instruction (Center for Applied Special Technology [CAST], 2018). Essentially, UDL helps us answer a fundamental teaching question: How can we plan and teach in ways that include all learners? UDL draws on our increasing understanding of neuroscience and how the brain works to think about learning through a commitment to the full participation of all learners.

MINDSETS FOR USING UDL

Before designing instruction using UDL, it's important to understand the foundational mindsets that support a UDL approach. As an entry point into exploring these mindsets, take a moment to reflect on your students.

> ### REFLECTION 3: YOUR STUDENTS
>
> Think about the students in your classroom or educational setting.
>
> - What things motivate your learners?
> - What challenges do they face?
> - What background experiences do they have?
> - What language do they use?

UDL MINDSET 1: THERE IS NO SUCH THING AS THE "AVERAGE LEARNER."

As your reflection probably showed, your learners are very diverse. In fact, while society perpetuates the myth of an "average learner" who *should* be able to do certain things in a classroom, neuroscience has shown that an average learner does not exist! In his book *The End of Average*, scientist Todd Rose explains that there is so much variation among humans that there is no such thing as the average learner (Rose, 2016). We each have a unique learning profile that reflects our preferences, strengths, and areas of challenge. The differences between our learning profiles are more diverse than our fingerprints! So to take up a UDL mindset, we first need to debunk the myth of the average learner.

Instead of learning patterns that follow a non-existent "average" student, we each have an individual, jagged learning profile. Our jagged learning profiles reflect how we are each inclined toward some tasks while we struggle with others. Similarly, we have deeper background experiences (including power dynamics we may have encountered) in some areas than in others and that can affect us in positive or negative ways. Our learning profiles also change based on whether we are tired, hungry, energized, happy, and many other factors.

Rose (2016) shared a story of what can happen when we try to design for "average." During World War II, the U.S. Air Force tried to design a "perfect" seat in their fighter planes that would fit all pilots. To try to meet everyone's needs, they built a seat that fit the average of measurements from many pilots. Instead, the seat didn't work for any of the pilots because none of them had measurements that fit the average. Learning from this experience, they instead designed a seat that was adjustable to each pilot's unique measurements.

UDL tries to do the same. Rather than teaching to the "average" student, UDL seeks to widen what "counts" as average. UDL intentionally designs for student variation and builds in options so that each student can adjust the learning experience to fit their specific needs.

UDL MINDSET 2: ALL STUDENTS DESERVE ACCESS TO CS EDUCATION.

We use the term "CS for all" a lot in CS Ed. But what does this mean? We've explored some definitions elsewhere in this guide (see Chapters 1 and 4). From a UDL perspective, CS for all means recognizing the following:

- All students can learn CS, but not all students will learn CS in the same way.

- All students can participate in CS in a meaningful way, even if what they learn is modified to meet their needs. Expectations and outcomes for learners may be different. However, to ensure justice, we must keep expectations true to a learner's abilities and be careful not to impose limitations based on our own biases or preconceived ideas of what learners are or "should" be capable of doing.

- As teachers, what we do matters! Even small changes to our mindsets and actions can result in big differences that shape how students feel included, valued, and part of the classroom community.

UDL MINDSET 3: WE ARE NOT TRYING TO "FIX" OUR LEARNERS. INSTEAD, WE ARE TRYING TO REMOVE BARRIERS IN THE LEARNING ENVIRONMENT.

After reading the above statement for mindset 3, take a moment to reflect on your own settings. What are some barriers that you have noticed during CS instruction or in CS Ed settings?

When we plan our CS instruction, we try to anticipate the barriers that would prevent all of our students from being able to fully participate. Sometimes, considering barriers leads us to identify challenges that the students are facing, and we frame the barrier as something that the students need to change or fix. For example, a teacher might notice, "My students can't read the directions in this CS assignment." The teacher might "blame" students for failing to succeed at the CS assignment because of their reading levels or other "problems" located within the student. Framing barriers in this way often perpetuates **deficit narratives** about students' (lack of) abilities.

deficit narratives Broadly held beliefs, including stereotypes, that identify groups of people as lacking or deficient in some way (Louie et al., 2021; Steele, 2011).

Thinking about barriers from a UDL perspective allows us to flip the narrative. Instead of naming the problem in terms of the student, we can consider how students' struggles indicate a challenge in the accessibility of the learning materials. Taking a UDL mindset would lead us to frame the teacher's noticing instead as, "The text complexity and formatting of the directions are barriers to understanding this CS assignment." A teacher facing this challenge from a UDL perspective might simplify the language in the directions, break down the directions into smaller steps, and use fonts and formatting that make the directions easier to read and follow for students with different needs. This shift moves us away from pathologizing and **othering** our students. It also provides us with clear directions toward solutions. See Resource 1 for an activity to practice flipping deficit narratives about students to framings that take up UDL perspectives.

othering The process of treating a group of people (often those with minoritized or marginalized identities) as intrinsically different from the dominant social norm.

UNPACKING UDL

Now that we've thought about the mindsets that teachers should have to adopt UDL approaches, let's examine the framework itself more closely. UDL is an instructional planning and teaching approach based on research about how people learn (CAST, 2018). It helps us think about our learning environments, our curriculum, and our instructional approaches to proactively meet the needs of all learners by reducing barriers to learning. Because UDL is intended to be universal, it seeks to meet all students' needs, regardless of background, language, abilities, and physical limitations. UDL offers a strong foundation for teachers to provide accommodations and modifications required for students with IEPs.

The UDL approach and framework was developed by the CAST based on neuroscience research. Our brains are made up of billions of neurons that receive information from the world around us and process it. Those neurons are wired together in unique ways for each individual person. This explains why there is no such thing as an average learner. CAST uses the term **neuro-variability** to describe how no two human brains are alike (CAST, 2018). Just as no two fingerprints are the same, there are infinite possibilities in the variation of human brains. Neuro-variability provides evidence that learners do not have a single learning style, despite popular beliefs to the contrary. Instead, learners rely on many parts of the brain working together, which changes in different contexts and in response to different conditions (CAST, 2018).

neuro-variability A term developed by CAST to describe how no two human brains are alike and that, consequently, there is no one "right" way to learn.

UDL seeks to capture how we are each unique in why we want to learn, what information we take in and how we process it, and how we demonstrate our understanding of what we have learned. To accomplish this, UDL is based on three networks within our brain: recognition networks that impact "what" we learn, strategic networks that impact "how" we learn, and affective networks that impact "why" we learn. The video UDL at a Glance provides an overview of the different components of UDL that are built based on our understanding of the three networks above.[2]

Universal Design for Learning draws on (1) an understanding of the brain's affective networks to design for *multiple means of engagement*, (2) an understanding of the brain's recognition networks to design for *multiple means of representation*, and (3) an understanding of the brain's strategic networks to design for *multiple means of action and expression*. These three principles are the foundation of UDL (CAST, 2024). *Engagement* allows us to attend to the "why" of learning, *representation* allows us to think about the "what" of learning, and *action and expression* allows us to consider the "how" of learning.

Within each of the three overarching principles, UDL provides guidelines to think about how to enact each principle. In turn, each guideline has considerations that teachers can incorporate into their instructional design. All the guidelines for a principle work together to provide students with access, support, and executive functioning through the learning process (CAST, 2024). Let's explore each of the principles in more detail.

---

2. View the video at https://www.youtube.com/watch?v=bDvKnY0g6e4

ENGAGEMENT: THE "WHY" OF LEARNING

Thinking about engagement allows us to consider what is important to our students and what motivates them. Learners come into CS Ed with different motivations, interests, challenges, and experiences. Providing students with multiple ways to engage allows them to connect to computing in ways that are relevant to them and that meet their different needs.

The three guidelines for the principle of designing for multiple means of engagement are:

- Welcoming interests and identities
- Sustaining effort and persistence
- Emotional capacity

Some considerations that teachers might think about as they design for multiple means of engagement include things like designing in ways that optimize choice and autonomy; nurture joy and play; optimize challenge and support; foster belonging and community; and promote individual and collective reflection. See all of the considerations for the principle of engagement in CAST's full guidelines.[3]

REPRESENTATION: THE "WHAT" OF LEARNING

Thinking about engagement allows us to consider how our students prefer to take in information. It also invites us to reflect on how those preferences might change based on the content area, students' prior experiences with information, and even their mood. Providing students with multiple representations of information allows them to access content in relevant ways that meet their needs.

The three guidelines for the principle of designing for multiple means of representation are:

- Perception
- Language and symbols
- Building knowledge

Some considerations that teachers might think about as they design for multiple means of representation include things like supporting multiple

---

3. To learn more, visit https://udlguidelines.cast.org/engagement/

ways to perceive information; clarifying vocabulary, symbols, and language structures; illustrating content through multiple media; connecting prior knowledge to new learning; and cultivating multiple ways of knowing and making meaning. See all of the considerations for the principle of representation in CAST's full guidelines.[4]

ACTION AND EXPRESSION: THE "HOW" OF LEARNING

Thinking about action and expression allows teachers to consider students' preferences for how they learn and strengths they bring to learning. Action and expression includes physical action and different types of communication. Designing for multiple means of action and expression enables students to learn in ways that work best for them and to show what they know in ways that are responsive to their different needs.

The three guidelines for the principle of designing for multiple means of action and expression are:

- Interaction
- Expression and communication
- Strategy development

Some considerations that teachers might think about as they design for multiple means of representation include varying and honoring different methods for response, navigation, and movement; using multiple media and tools for communication, construction, composition, and creativity; and helping students set meaningful goals and learn to anticipate and plan for challenges. See all of the considerations for the principle of representation in CAST's full guidelines.[5]

WHY USE UDL?

UDL pushes back on traditional understandings of curriculum as a static whole, with lessons building on previous lessons in a single, established, linear way. In this traditional approach, each lesson needs to be differentiated with **accommodations** to learners' needs. One of the advantages of designing for learning with the UDL framework is that you build the curriculum to be more accessible for all students from the beginning by removing barriers before they become a part of the learning environment.

accommodations Changes to a learning environment or to the presentation of curricular content that are offered to help students access content and complete learning tasks that are a regular part of the curriculum. Examples include using a microphone, arranging seating to facilitate movement, or using assistive technologies.

---
4. To learn more, visit https://udlguidelines.cast.org/representation/
5. To learn more, visit https://udlguidelines.cast.org/action-expression/

For example, if a lesson requires students to listen to an audio file, designing with UDL would ensure that students had access to a closed-captioned file, subtitles in multiple languages, or a file with someone signing the content. These different options could help all students, including those with different learning needs and preferences. The teacher may need to provide additional accommodations such as listening in a quiet setting to someone with a hearing impairment or sensory processing disorder. But designing curricula with UDL focuses on learners from the beginning to create an initial design that benefits all learners.

While a teacher reviewing the entire guidelines document might feel overwhelmed at first, it is important to not think of the guidelines as a giant checklist. Instead, it is a framework that with thought and consideration can help teachers create learning experiences that will be beneficial to all students. There is also a lot of overlap between the UDL principles and what teachers already do. The UDL framework provides a new way of thinking about learning as a whole, centering the goal of guiding students to become expert learners who are purposeful and motivated, resourceful and knowledgeable, and strategic and self-directed. UDL can be seen as a new lens to look through. Instead of traditional approaches that want to change the learner to fit the shoe, UDL empowers learners to find their own shoes and take meaningful steps toward limitless learning.

This kind of limitless CS learning is a journey, and an important part of that journey is advocating for all students to be included in CS opportunities. **Advocacy** involves publicly supporting a cause, idea, or policy and garnering support from colleagues and administrators. It requires listening to and learning from students and using our privilege to raise up the goals and interests of less-privileged groups (see Love, 2019). Advocacy also fosters and amplifies self-advocacy. It is an act of critical teacher-leadership (Bradley-Levine, 2018). UDL can be a key resource in our advocacy efforts.

advocacy Publicly supporting and championing policies and changes that support equity-oriented CS education. Advocacy involves taking action to disrupt the status quo.

At the same time, it is critical to remember that advocacy itself is a journey. You are not expected to fix a broken system single-handedly. Such expectations are neither fair nor healthy nor possible. Instead, focus on growth by taking steps to advocate where you are at, within your circle of influence. Wherever you are along the journey, you can make a difference. UDL allows you to make that difference in all instructional contexts and with all learner populations, working toward full participation in CS Ed.

Because you are likely already implementing many UDL practices even if you haven't named them as such, we offer the following reflection activity as a way for you to think about how you are already applying the three UDL principles in your instruction.

> # REFLECTION 4: UDL AND ME
>
> Consider the following questions.
>
> ## UDL PRINCIPLE 1: MULTIPLE MEANS OF ENGAGEMENT (THE "WHY" OF LEARNING)
>
> - How are you engaging learners?
> - How do you recruit their interest?
> - How do you help them sustain effort?
> - Do you help students reflect on their learning?
> - How do you foster their sense of belonging and community?
>
> ## UDL PRINCIPLE 2: MULTIPLE MEANS OF REPRESENTATION (THE "WHAT" OF LEARNING)
>
> - How is information presented to the learners?
> - Do you use multiple formats (e.g., text, video, demonstrations)?
> - How do you activate background knowledge?
> - How can you be sure your content is free of biases?
> - How do you promote understanding across different uses of language?
>
> ## UDL PRINCIPLE 3: MULTIPLE MEANS OF ACTION AND EXPRESSION (THE "HOW" OF LEARNING)
>
> - How are students demonstrating their learning?
> - Do you give a choice in products?
> - Do you provide opportunities for physical action?
> - Have you challenged exclusionary practices?
> - How do you help students set and achieve goals?

The different answers you provided are evidence that you are already implementing aspects of UDL! As you continue to reflect, you may also identify ways that you are already taking up UDL mindsets and engaging in advocacy for all of your students. In the next chapter, we'll explore how to integrate UDL into CS instruction specifically.

REVISITING HANA'S STORY

As Hana talked with and learned from colleagues, she recognized several things she already did in her classroom that aligned with the UDL principles. For example, Hana prioritized representing information in multiple ways (through providing students with physical objects that they could manipulate, pictures, videos, written text and through reading text aloud). Thinking about her teaching from a UDL perspective helped Hana realize how these practices were supporting all her students, including her multilingual learners and students with disabilities, in ways that she hadn't acknowledged before.[6]

Hana decided to add a few more UDL options into her instructional design. As she developed her next CS unit, Hana focused on the principle of action and expression and empowered her students to work through their project with a variety of approaches, including videos, guided handouts, and paired work partners. Hana was excited to notice how these changes allowed all of her students to be more successful and deepened their engagement, including for some of her students with disabilities who had struggled in the past. Hana realized that they had likely struggled not because of their abilities but because of barriers that had been present in the learning environment. Now that Hana had removed those barriers, her students were finding new ways to succeed and enjoy CS.

At the same time, most of the changes that Hana made were ones that she felt applied to learning and classrooms generally. Hana wondered if there were specific things she could do to improve her students' ability to learn and engage in computing. Chapter 17 explores Hana's wondering further.

REFLECTION QUESTIONS

1. Now that you have read the chapter, how would you describe an inclusive, accessible classroom? (See Reflection 1.)

2. How might you explain UDL and its associated mindsets to a

---

6. See the On Terminology section of this guide for an explanation on our use of different identity-related terms.

colleague who believes very strongly in an average learner? Who doesn't necessarily recognize the importance of giving CS learning opportunities to all learners? Who tends to describe students through deficit narratives?

TAKEAWAYS FOR PRACTICE

- Consider the classroom and educational spaces. How are the physical designs, technology, resources, curricula, interactions, and so on accessible (or not)? Identify one change that you can enact to make your space more accessible.

- Chapters 15 and 16 were written to incorporate UDL principles into their designs. Look back through the chapters, especially the embedded activities. Make a list of things you notice about how the chapters incorporate UDL.

GLOSSARY

Term	Definition
accessibility	The process of making activities, environments, information, and interactions available to people with different needs.
accommodations	Changes to a learning environment or to the presentation of curricular content that are offered to help students access content and complete learning tasks that are a regular part of the curriculum. Examples include using a microphone, arranging seating to facilitate movement, or using assistive technologies.
advocacy	Publicly supporting and championing policies and changes that support equity-oriented CS education. Advocacy involves taking action to disrupt the status quo.
deficit narratives	Broadly held beliefs, including stereotypes, that identify groups of people as lacking or deficient in some way (Louie et al., 2021; Steele, 2011).
Individualized Education Program (IEP)	A legal document mandated by federal law (IDEA; U.S. Department of Education, 2004) that outlines services and support that a student with disabilities will receive as part of their public education.

neuro-variability	A term developed by CAST to describe how no two human brains are alike and that, consequently, there is no one "right" way to learn.
othering	The process of treating a group of people (often those with minoritized or marginalized identities) as intrinsically different from the dominant social norm.
Universal Design for Learning (UDL)	An instructional planning and teaching approach that seeks to meet the needs of all learners by reducing barriers to learning. The three principles of UDL include providing learners with (1) multiple means of engagement; (2) multiple means of representation; and (3) multiple means of action and engagement (CAST, 2024).

REFERENCES

Bradley-Levine, J. (2018). Advocacy as a practice of critical teacher leadership. *International Journal of Teacher Leadership, 9*(1), 47–62. https://eric.ed.gov/?id=EJ1182705

Center for Applied Special Technology. (2018). *UDL and the learning brain.* https://www.cast.org/wp-content/uploads/2024/12/cast-udlandthebrain-20220228-a11y.pdf

Center for Applied Special Technology. (2024). *The UDL guidelines.* https://udl-guidelines.cast.org/

Louie, N., Adiredja, A. P., & Jessup, N. (2021). Teacher noticing from a sociopolitical perspective: The FAIR framework for anti-deficit noticing. *ZDM-Mathematics Education, 53,* (95–107). https://doi.org/10.1007/s11858-021-01229-2

Love, B. L. (2019). *We want to do more than survive: Abolitionist teaching and the pursuit of educational freedom.* Beacon Press.

Rose, T. (2016). *The end of average: How we succeed in a world that values sameness.* HarperOne.

Steele, C. M. (2011). *Whistling Vivaldi: How stereotypes affect us and what we can do.* W. W. Norton & Company.

U.S. Department of Education. (2004). Individuals with disabilities education act. Public Law 108–446. Individuals with Disabilities Education Act, 20 U.S.C. § 1400 https://sites.ed.gov/idea/

RESOURCE 1: DEVELOPING UDL MINDSETS: FLIPPING THE NARRATIVE TO IDENTIFY BARRIERS TO ACCESS

As discussed earlier in the chapter, a key mindset to implementing UDL is to shift from blaming students for learning challenges to identifying how barriers in the learning environment are preventing students from accessing learning experiences. The activity below provides a chance to practice flipping these narratives.

ACTIVITY

1. **Read** each situation.

2. **Think about** the assumptions (ableist, racist, classist, etc.) embedded in each statement.

3. **List** some of these assumptions in row 2.

4. **Think about** how these assumptions show up as barriers in the learning environment.

5. **Write** a flipped narrative that removes the barriers for the student.

Situation (Example)	Eliana doesn't have strong enough English skills to do well on today's CS activity.
Embedded Assumptions	English is the only language that students can use to do the activity. Eliana doesn't have any other resources or background knowledge that can help her complete the activity.
Flipped Narrative	I need to include a translanguaging option for today's activity. This will allow Eliana to use all of her meaning-making resources to understand and complete the coding challenge.

Situation 1	If Maria could decode informational texts better, she would thrive in science class.
Embedded Assumptions	
Flipped Narrative	

Situation 2	Eleanor can't pay attention in class when directions are given.
Embedded Assumptions	
Flipped Narrative	

Situation 3	Alex's home life is terrible, so he is often angry and upset when he arrives at school.
Embedded Assumptions	
Flipped Narrative	

Situation 4	David is our worst discipline issue. He is always out of his seat and never stops talking to his neighbors or interrupting whole group instruction.
Embedded Assumptions	
Flipped Narrative	

REFLECTION

Now that you've completed the activity, take a moment to reflect on what you've learned.

1. Because UDL is an instructional approach that can help disrupt ableism, consider what you learned about ableism

in Chapter 15. How are ableist beliefs embedded in the statements above?

2. How were you able to remove ableist assumptions as you flipped the narratives?

3. What did you notice about how beliefs changed from the original scenario to the flipped narrative?

4. How did the language used change from the original scenario to the flipped narrative?

5. What habits and practices appeared in your flipped narratives that promote and sustain a UDL mindset?

6. How did flipping the narrative through a UDL mindset change how you interpreted the scenarios?

7. How is what we pay attention to different in the flipped narratives through a UDL mindset?

17

Universal Design for Learning in Computer Science Education

Maya Israel, Spence J. Ray, Joanne Barrett, Nykema Lindsey, Carla Strickland, Stephanie T. Jones, & the Computer Science Educational Justice Collective

CHAPTER OVERVIEW

This chapter applies the Universal Design for Learning (UDL) framework introduced in Chapter 16 specifically to computer science education (CS Ed) contexts. It provides examples of how the different components of the UDL framework can inform CS lessons. It also offers resources to plan CS lessons that leverage the UDL framework.

CHAPTER OBJECTIVES

After reading this chapter, I can:

- Explain how the UDL framework applies to K-12 CS Ed.
- Apply the three instructional approaches aligned with the three UDL principles (multiple means of engagement, representation, and action/expression) to K-12 CS Ed.

KEY TERMS

assistive technologies; culturally sustaining pedagogies; Frayer model; literate programming; Universal Design for Learning (UDL)

HANA'S STORY

In Chapter 16, we met Hana,[1] an elementary teacher who teaches CS as an elective. In seeking to learn more about implementing the UDL in her CS classroom, Hana spoke with a colleague, Jessica, who had made some successful changes. Jessica shared some of the things she did in her CS classroom to incorporate UDL principles for her students:

> I found ways to scaffold learning experiences and to provide students with multiple entry points. I plan lessons with centers and choice built in. When introducing an activity, I frontload all success criteria. I explain directions, provide a copy of the slides in Google Classroom, and sometimes use Flip or Loom [video making tools] to create videos that model the activities for students. I also include pictures and examples of previous projects for some assessments. I have Scratch cards and books that are always available and a quiet station for those who just feel that they can't work in a larger group setting that day. I also always keep a Lego station and typing station so there is always an out for the day if needed. Overall, I try to provide choice and clear expectations so students can pick activities that reinforce key concepts, skills, and strategies but also allow space for self-selection and creativity.

Hana was inspired by seeing Jessica's examples. She decided to go back to the UDL framework and map Jessica's strategies onto the framework then build on her earlier changes to intentionally develop lesson plans that made space for multiple means of engagement, representation, and action and expression.

REVISITING THE UDL FRAMEWORK

Chapter 16 introduced the **Universal Design for Learning**, or UDL, framework (Center for Applied Science Technology [CAST], 2024). UDL is an instructional planning and teaching approach based on research about how people learn (CAST, 2018). It seeks to meet all students' needs by removing barriers from learning environments, curricula, and instructional approaches. Recall that the UDL guidelines emphasize three principles:

Universal Design for Learning (UDL): An instructional planning and teaching approach that seeks to meet the needs of all learners by reducing barriers to learning. The three principles of UDL include providing learners with (1) multiple means of engagement, (2) multiple means of representation, and (3) multiple means of action and engagement (CAST, 2024).

---

1. Hana is a composite character based on the experiences of several New York City–based CS teachers (Kristi Jones, Jennifer Romeo, and Rebecca Young).

designing for learning through (1) multiple means of engagement; (2) multiple means of representation; and (3) multiple means of action and expression.[2]

This chapter considers how UDL can be applied directly to CS Ed in ways that eliminate barriers for learning. For some learners, barriers to CS include a lack of accessible tools or materials or a lack of pedagogical approaches that specifically address their strengths or areas of challenge. For instance, some students may struggle with programming assignments that are not scaffolded and start with a "blank coding canvas." This kind of assignment design can leave learners without contexts or clues to begin an activity. Learners might benefit from learning coding through multimodal approaches that include scaffolding to complete multistep problems.

Providing multiple entry points is one way to anticipate barriers to participation that draw on UDL principles (Barrett & Israel, 2023). Offering different options to engage with an activity allows students to choose how they participate. It also offers them different ways of expressing their understanding. Activity 1 gives you an opportunity to experience what this looks like. In this guided exploration activity, you can choose between various versions of a Scratch program that teaches about weather.[3] All of the versions of the program have the same aim, but there are different entry points for you to examine and modify the code. Take 5–10 minutes to explore the options.

ACTIVITY 1: MULTIPLE ENTRY POINTS EXPLORATION

1. Choose one of the activities.

2. Spend about 5 minutes exploring the project. Set a timer if you'd like.

3. Explore at least one other activity option.

Option 1: Use and modify existing code

In this version of the project, you can play and remix code that has already been constructed.

---

[2]. View the UDL Guidelines at https://udlguidelines.cast.org/

[3]. We provide examples of Scratch as a tool that is readily available for use in K-12 classrooms.

Objective: The cloud will produce rain drops or snowflakes depending on the temperature. Click on the tree to input a change of temperature.

Link: https://scratch.mit.edu/projects/755700720

Option 2: Debug a "buggy" program

In this version of the project, you need to find and fix a bug in the program to make it work as intended.

Objective: The cloud will produce rain drops or snowflakes depending on the temperature. In this version, if the temperature is 32°F, the snowflakes do not appear. Click on the tree to input a change of temperature.

Link: https://scratch.mit.edu/projects/755740047

Option 3: Construct from "exploded" code

In this version of the project, you will reconstruct a code that has been deconstructed. All of the Scratch blocks that you need are in the workspace, but they are not connected.

Objective: The cloud will produce rain drops or snowflakes depending on the temperature. Click on the tree to input a change of temperature.

Link: https://scratch.mit.edu/projects/755767176

Option 4: Extension Activity

If you have completed at least one version of this activity, you can add on to this activity by considering other aspects of the code to change.

Reflection: Which method(s) did you try? How could you use a similar approach in your classroom? What benefits and challenges can you anticipate in using this approach?

The three approaches presented in Activity 1 illustrate how to give students multiple entry points into CS through explicit code-remixing, fixing buggy code, and a Parsons Problem or exploded code (Barrett & Israel, 2023). There are also other entry points and ways to engage students with both the content (weather and precipitation) and the code. These are illustrated in Figure 1.

Figure 1. Scratch Weather (Precipitation) Simulation with Multiple Entry Points

Entry Point	Scratch sample code
Full worked example https://scratch.mit.edu/projects/755743929	
Adding a clone https://scratch.mit.edu/projects/755733329	
Intro demo is not complete (i.e., 32° degrees is incorrect) https://scratch.mit.edu/projects/755700720	

Entry Point	Scratch sample code
Corrected "or" logic version https://scratch.mit.edu/projects/755740047	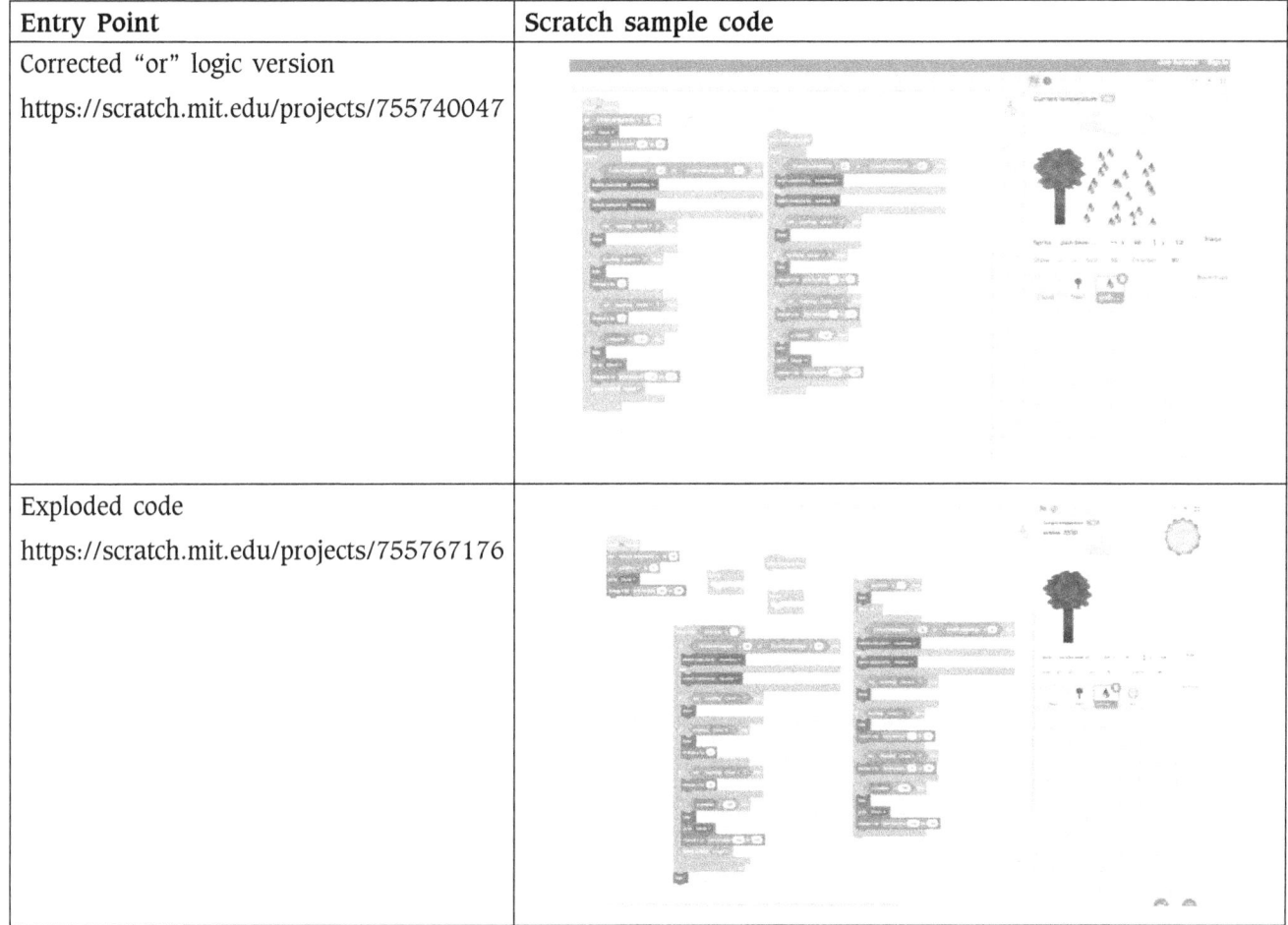
Exploded code https://scratch.mit.edu/projects/755767176	

Using or combining these approaches creates opportunities for discussions with students. CS teachers might ask students questions like:

- How can you improve the existing code?
- What enhancements can you make to the project?

These questions provide ample opportunities to engage with content and computing. Some enhancements may require a few steps, while others may be more complex. For instance, in the above Scratch projects, it is always precipitating. Another version includes a new feature to stop the precipitation: pressing the "s" key will bring out the sun.[4] Other possible enhancements include adding movement for the cloud, collecting accumulated snow at the bottom of the stage, or even adding a rainbow for a few seconds after the arrival of the sun. Each change allows students to think deeply about the science concepts related to precipitation and

---

4. View the version at https://scratch.mit.edu/projects/755743929

the code needed to create the enhancement. Finding different entry and exploration points that speak to the needs and skills of learners is one important way to meet multiple UDL guidelines at once.

Throughout the remainder of the chapter, we'll explore in greater detail how each of the three principles of UDL applies to CS Ed (Israel et al., 2017). While we consider each one separately, in reality, they often overlap. And, as was mentioned in Chapter 16, you may find that you are already implementing strategies in your classroom that align with the principles we examine here.

DESIGNING FOR MULTIPLE MEANS OF ENGAGEMENT

The principle of designing for multiple means of engagement involves considering how to remove barriers to participation. One of these barriers might include getting started with an activity, as Activity 1 illustrated. Other barriers can include seeing the activity as irrelevant or uninteresting, losing motivation to complete the activity, or getting frustrated and giving up on completing the activity. We can remove these and other barriers by designing learning experiences and environments that welcome students' interests and identities, help them manage emotions, and support them to persist and give sustained effort to a learning task.

In this section, we'll consider how designing for multiple means of engagement in the CS classroom can include (1) welcoming interests and identities; (2) helping students sustain effort and persistence; and (3) developing students' emotional capacity.

WELCOMING INTERESTS AND IDENTITIES

A key part of engaging students in CS learning is capturing their interest in learning opportunities. One important way to accomplish this is by giving students choice. A major tenet of UDL is to build learner agency so that learners become purposeful, strategic, and action-oriented (CAST, 2024). If you look back at Activity 1, you'll see that you were provided with choices. You decided how you wanted to approach the activity by looking at the options and choosing the version you wanted to explore. The same holds true for our students. We can make choices clear and explicit for learners, especially at the start of a new project. Offering students choice increases engagement because it provides students with agency, empowering them to take action and direct their own learning.

Another important way to capture students' interest is to let them tailor their CS learning to be relevant to their lives. For example, when students are learning about fractional parts along a number line, they can be given a choice in how to demonstrate their understanding of the concept. One option would be to animate a math story problem in Scratch. In the figure below, for example, the student animated a story where a monkey moved across a number line on a magic carpet. Students could select sprites that were interesting to them to make CS fun and personally relevant.

Other chapters in this book (e.g., chapters 2, 4, and 12–14) also consider how to make CS relevant to students' lives and backgrounds as part of **culturally sustaining pedagogies**. These approaches go beyond capturing students' daily hobbies and preferences, taking up students' cultures and backgrounds as resources for learning. Ms. Kors' assignment in chapters 12 through 14 is one example. Students' identities can also be incorporated into CS in a variety of other ways. For instance, a CS project might ask students to create a story about a family holiday tradition. One student might share about Easter, another about Kwanzaa, and a third about Ramadan, with each student sharing cultural practices that are meaningful to them and their families and communities. When students have autonomy to add personal relevance to their work, they are more likely to want to engage with that work.

culturally sustaining pedagogies Ways and approaches to teaching that value and center students' cultural identities, practices, and ways of knowing as resources for learning rather than excluding or eradicating students' cultures from the classroom (see Ladson-Billings, 2021; Paris & Alim, 2017).

Figure 2. A Student's Personal Scratch Project

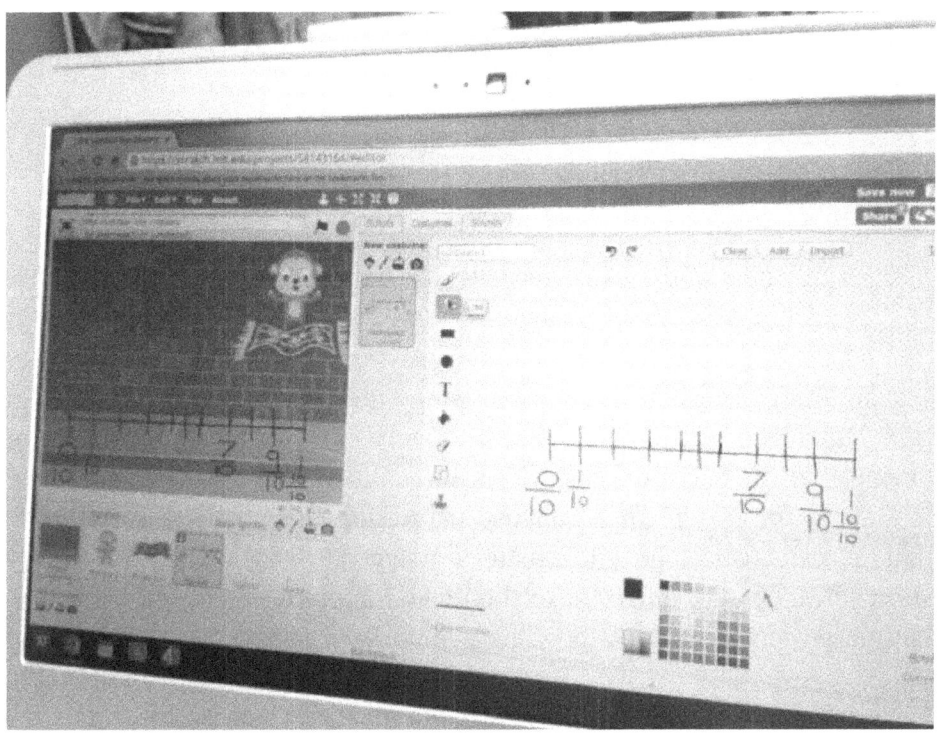

Other strategies to recruit students' interest include providing scaffolds that minimize common "pitfalls" related to both the content and computing skills students need. Teachers can structure activities that allow for students to work on projects at different paces and for different amounts of time and provide students with options to increase or decrease sensory stimulation (e.g., listening to music or using noise cancelling headphones). These strategies engage students in CS learning through tools that support them toward success and allow them to tailor their learning to meet their individual needs and interests.

SUSTAINING EFFORT AND PERSISTENCE

Students are often motivated to participate in CS because it is fun! Yet once students begin to code, they will inevitably create something that does not work as they expected. When code doesn't work according to plan, it can make CS learning difficult and frustrating. Engaging students in CS requires them to maintain their interest and persist in learning activities, even when it is difficult.

One way to help sustain students' effort and persistence is by providing them with positive learning objectives that make students aware of what they have already accomplished. These learning objectives or goals are restated as "I can" statements that make goals concrete and explicit for learners (Israel & Lash, 2020). The goals can address both content and computing aspects of a task. Examples from the Action Fractions Polygon Partners lesson include the following (Learning Trajectories for Everyday Computing [LTEC], n.d.):[5]

- I can identify attributes of polygons.

- I can use math language to write instructions (pseudocode) that a friend can follow to create a polygon.

- I can give and receive feedback to improve directions to animate a polygon in Scratch.

Teachers can encourage students to gauge their own understanding of "I can" statements and provide us with feedback in a variety of ways. For example, at the beginning of the lesson, students can evaluate how they feel about the statement: I can use math language to write pseudocode that a friend can follow to create a polygon. Students can physically show a thumbs up, down, or to the middle; press a green, red, or yellow button; or point to a corresponding symbol (see Figure 3). At the end of

---

5. View this resource at http://everydaycomputing.org/lessons/action-fractions/grade-3/polygon-partners

Figure 3. Student Self-Evaluation for "I Can" Statements

the lesson, teachers can check in again. Students' responses may change to indicate growth in understanding.

Other strategies to sustain students' effort and persistence in CS include explicitly discussing the role of perseverance and problem solving in CS and celebrating students' efforts to persevere and problem solve in the classroom. Teachers can provide additional supports and extension activities to maintain students' engagement. Activity 1 at the beginning of the chapter provides an example of an extension activity as Option 4. Collaboration is also a key way to sustain effort and persistence. Teachers can design activities that use pair programming and group work, giving students clearly defined roles as part of the task. Teaching students how to give and receive feedback on each other's work and building in opportunities to share ideas with peers sustains engagement through collective learning.

EMOTIONAL CAPACITY

Supporting student engagement also requires supporting self-regulation throughout learning activities. Coding inherently involves things not working according to plan. Helping students learn how to deal with frustration and debug their code is crucial to keeping them engaged.

One approach for teaching debugging as a skill is to use strategies like the Debugging Detective (Universal Design for Learning for Computer Science [UDL4CS], 2021; Figure 4).[6] This activity includes questions like, "What did I want my code to do?" and "What happened when I ran my code?" followed by a series of yes/no questions that cue students to think about their code. As they do, they can analyze what went wrong and find potential new avenues to try to fix it.

Teachers can also help students with self-regulation by facilitating personal coping skills and strategies. Acknowledging difficulty and frustration as a reality is important. Strategies for dealing with frustration can be taught as part of social-emotional learning (see Chapter 9). Other supports that teachers can design into their learning experiences to support self-regulation include setting clear expectations for the learning

---

6. View this resource at https://udl4cs.education.ufl.edu/debugging-detective/.

Figure 4. Debugging Detective

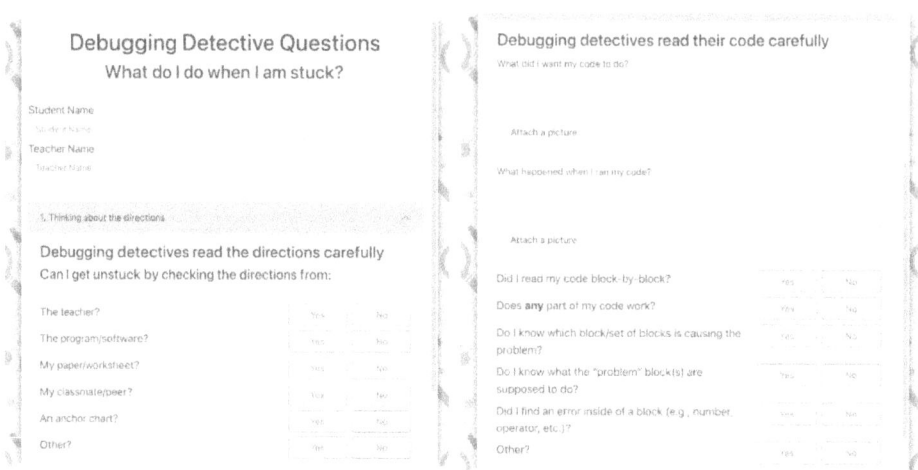

task, having students collaborate with others, teaching students to ask for help, and using assessment rubrics that evaluate both content and process. Breaking up coding with opportunities to reflect on the process through activities like turn-and-talks, written questions, and self- or peer assessment can also sustain engagement.

DESIGNING FOR MULTIPLE MEANS OF REPRESENTATION

The principle of designing for multiple means of representation involves removing barriers for students in terms of how information is presented and how students take it in. There is no single way that information can or should be represented that is optimal for all students. We can remove barriers to representation by providing information in multiple ways (e.g., visual, auditory, physical models), giving students control to adjust how they receive information, and scaffolding students' understanding of information.

In this section, we'll consider how designing for multiple means of representation in the CS classroom can include providing students with options for (1) perception, (2) language and symbols, and (3) building knowledge.

PERCEPTION

Giving students options to perceive information is a key part of providing them with multiple means of representation. Supporting perception involves offering students information in multiple modalities, offering them information in formats that they can adjust, and offering them information that incorporates a variety of perspectives (CAST, 2024).

Given that students process information in multiple modalities, we can go beyond using only auditory or visual information. Instead, we can include alternatives and multiple ways to access content. This might include offering students written instructions and videos of how to complete a CS activity and allowing them to model code through unplugged physical representations and manipulatives before coding on a device. Offering students choices around how they perceive information might also mean using tools that allow students to adjust formatting to more easily perceive the information, such as changing the text size on instructions, adjusting volume on videos, adding closed-captions, and reading alternative text for any images. These moves can help enable all learners access information.

We can also provide students with worked examples of code (Skudder & Luxton-Reilley, 2014; Muldner et al., 2022). By worked examples, we mean scripts that use relevant and instructive variable names and include comments or documentation that might scaffold or explain what particular segments of code are meant to do. Showing students worked examples of code can model good **literate programming** practice (Knuth, 1984; see Chapter 13) and be an important way to support students' perception. Worked examples illustrate not just the outcome of a code, but the *process* of creating the code by showing how programs decompose larger problems into smaller ones. Students can then use those code chunks to solve new problems that are similar to those they are attempting (Margulieux et al., 2013). This approach provides a multimodal way of presenting information. Many CS curricula and tools include worked examples. When worked examples are not available, we can create our own or have students create tutorials for each other (Figure 5; Israel & Ray, 2024).

literate programming
An understanding of code as a form of expression that is part of a social conversation because computer code (programs) is meant to be read and understood by people and not just computers (Knuth, 1984).

Figure 5. Sample Worked Examples for a Scratch Project

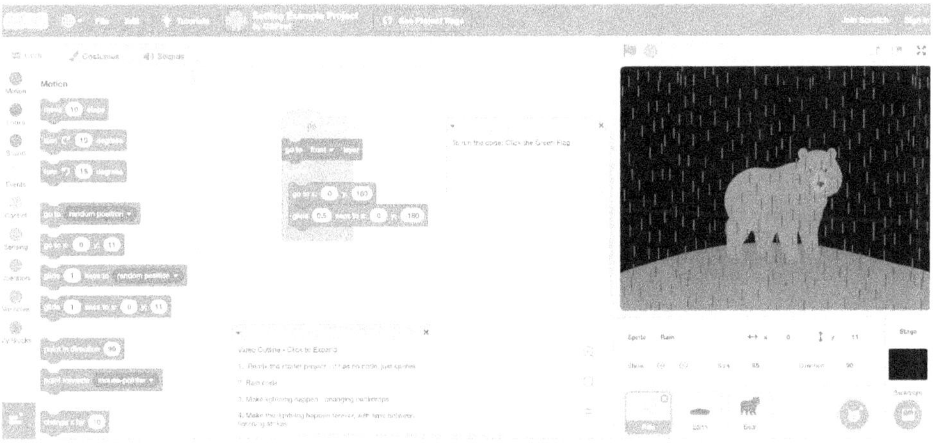

The strategies above support students' sensory perception, but it is also important for learners to recognize and perceive themselves and others in CS. A final consideration for incorporating perception involves providing students with information that authentically represents diverse perspectives and identities (CAST, 2024). Incorporating examples of computer scientists who represent a range of backgrounds is one way to do this. (See Chapters 1 and 2 for some examples.)

LANGUAGE AND SYMBOLS

CS includes many new concepts, some of which are abstract and could become barriers for learners. As with many disciplines, expertise means becoming familiar not only with the concepts but also with how to use professional ways of representing those concepts (Kozma et al., 2009). Providing students with multiple means of representation includes supporting them to learn and use the language and symbols related to CS and coding. Teachers can explicitly teach and review computing vocabulary including concepts like code, animations, algorithms, loops, and so on (see Figure 6; Israel & Ray, 2024). Teachers should also teach and review content-specific vocabulary. For instance, in the Scratch example at the beginning of the chapter, a teacher might focus on vocabulary terms like "precipitation," "atmosphere," and "temperature." Teachers can support students to use content and computing terms by representing language and symbols in a variety of ways. This might include anchor charts or reference sheets with images of code blocks or common syntax posted in the classroom (see Figure 7, photo credit: Todd Lash).

Figure 6. Representations of Computing Vocabulary

Figure 7. Representations of Computing Symbols

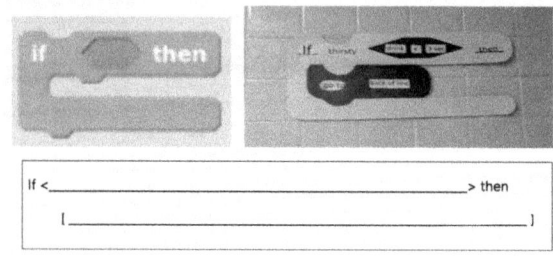

One unique challenge in CS is that students may already have an understanding of a term in one context that takes on a different meaning in CS. For example, the term "variable" is one that students may be familiar with from their math courses. However, a variable in CS and the process of assigning its values in relation to an equal symbol might feel very different from students' experiences with variables in math (Schanzer, 2017). Rewiring a new neural pathway for something already familiar can be challenging. It is important to consider how to introduce or remap concepts for learners.

In considering how to teach concepts like this, teachers might consider questions like:

- What existing knowledge do students already have about the concept?
- Is that knowledge accurate for the CS context?
- Can I build on their existing knowledge?
- Do I need to modify or expand it for the CS context?

A **Frayer model** is one way to introduce new concepts or familiar concepts in a new context. This model places the concept at the center of the map then explores the concept across four quadrants—a definition, facts and/or characteristics, examples, and non-examples. Figure 8 shows a Frayer model about precipitation. This content-related model could be used to frame a lesson for students who are learning to code by using Scratch to build out the weather concept presented in the examples in Activity 1.

Frayer model A graphic organizer that helps students learn new vocabulary words and understand their meanings. The model places the vocabulary word/concept at the center of the map then explores the term across four quadrants: a definition, facts and/or characteristics, examples, and non-examples to clarify what the concept is not.

Figure 8. Precipitation Frayer Model

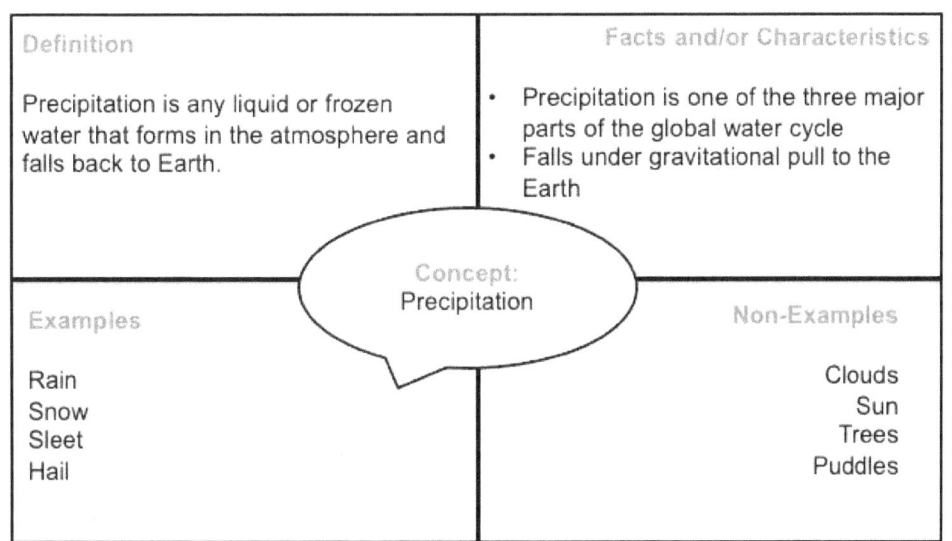

Frayer models can also be used for CS concepts. In Activity 1, loops are required to keep precipitation falling, so Figure 9 shows a model for the CS concept of loops used in relation to the science concept of precipitation.

Figure 9. Loops Frayer Model

Definition	Facts and/or Characteristics
Loops – a sequence of instructions that will repeat until a condition is reached or changed	• Loops reduce the amount of code needed because they are reused • Loops cause codes to repeat • Need a stopping condition
Examples	Non-Examples
Rain drop continue to move down the stage until it reaches the lowest limit and then gets sent back to the cloud location. It repeats this behavior until the sun is clicked to stop the behavior.	Clicking on the sun stops the precipitation sprite from falling. A clone is created (additional raindrops or snowflakes) as part of the behavior within the loop but they are not the loop itself.

Concept: Loops

Offering students multiple ways to build their understanding of language and symbols and relate the language to CS concepts supports accessibility, comprehensibility, and clarity and is key to ensuring shared understanding for all learners (CAST, 2024).

BUILDING KNOWLEDGE

It is not enough to simply present information in multiple ways. We must also build students' knowledge about that information. One important way to do this is by drawing on students' background knowledge, or what they already know about the topic in terms of content and relevant computing concepts. To uncover students' background knowledge, teachers can ask guiding questions. For Activity 1, questions might include:

- What are the conditions for snow?
- How do we simulate a snowflake falling from the sky in our program?
- What do we need to do with the snowflake to make it fall over and over again?

Teachers can also ask questions and invite students to ask questions throughout learning activities. These comprehension checkpoints show what students are understanding and what barriers might still exist to comprehension. They can also guide teachers to scaffold the next steps to expand students' learning. Additional concepts that could be explored based on Activity 1 might include:

- Accumulation of rain vs. accumulation of snow
- Conditions for a rainbow
- Representing hail or sleet by dividing the stage into zones of varying temperatures
- Introducing the water cycle

Other ways to build students' knowledge include providing graphic organizers to help students "translate" programs into pseudocode and using relevant analogies between coding concepts and other content areas. CS teacher Melissa had one of her students do this themselves when they connected CS terms to literacy examples (see Chapter 1). The student compared a sprite in Scratch to a character in a story and the Scratch stage to the story's setting. These parallels made CS concepts more accessible and concrete, supporting all learners' comprehension.

DESIGNING FOR MULTIPLE MEANS OF ACTION AND EXPRESSION

The principle of designing for multiple means of action and expression focuses on how students learn. It involves removing barriers related to how students will interact with each other and with the content, how they will plan to learn, and how they will show what they've learned. We can think of this principle as representing the choice and voice that students get in how to express their learning.

In this section, we'll consider how designing for multiple means of action and expression in the CS classroom can include providing students with options for (1) interaction, (2) expression and communication, and (3) strategy development.

INTERACTION

Interaction describes how students engage with both learning materials and the learning space. CS teachers need to consider barriers that students might face when moving around the classroom (e.g., seating arrangements, narrow aisles), engaging with unplugged learning materials (e.g., whiteboards, physical manipulatives), and engaging with technology (e.g., keyboards, track pads, screens, software, online programs). Removing these barriers ensures that all students can engage in CS learning experiences.

Some ways to facilitate interaction as a way of providing access to how students learn CS include selecting coding apps and websites that offer keyboard shortcuts in addition to dragging and dropping with a mouse and providing students with **assistive technology** like larger or smaller mice or touch-screen devices. Teachers can also offer their own code as templates for students or lead unplugged CS activities that help students engage with coding ideas by physically representing relationships between abstract computing concepts.

Teachers can involve students in designing and programming projects that provide multiple means of action and expression through interaction and access. For example, the Scratch weather example from the beginning of the chapter intentionally lacked user instruction. Students could make recommendations about how to communicate to users how best to engage with the project. Some alternatives to make the project more user-friendly might include having students:

- Create an audio file that plays to tell users where to click at the start of the game.
- Create a message to be displayed at the start of the simulation.
- Create a message to be displayed after a certain length of time.
- Halt all action and focus the user input as the center of attention.

Another way to facilitate interaction is by teaching CS in ways that support collaboration (Lash et al., n.d.). Teachers may need to explicitly teach and model collaboration as a learning goal in and of itself. This process might involve arranging the classroom to facilitate collaboration through seating arrangements and anchor charts with sentence stems and prompts that help students unpack a problem with their peers. Resources like the Collaborative Discussion Framework (Lash & Park, 2015) may be useful. Teachers might also experiment with different models of collaborations (e.g., partners, small groups, using a timer, offering more or less structured collaboration models) to find what best meets the needs of all students.

---

assistive technologies
Technology that helps people with disabilities perform tasks more easily or safely so that they can live, move, participate, and contribute in society more fully. Assistive technologies may include devices (e.g., walkers, prosthetics), materials (e.g., curricular aids), services (e.g., technical assistance), or software (e.g., screen readers).

EXPRESSION AND COMMUNICATION

Expression and communication focus on how students are able to share what they know, have learned, and are learning. Offering choices for how students communicate, scaffolding the process of creating products that represent learning, and honoring the many different ways that students communicate are important considerations for this guideline.

CS teachers can provide students with options for expression and communication by letting students show what they know through unplugged activities and different kinds of computing software and materials. Some of these possibilities might include supporting students to express themselves through pseudocode, physical manipulatives, flowcharts, and comments in code or to use block-based programming interfaces like Alice, code.org, and Scratch.[7] Supporting expression through code can include providing students with options that include starter code they can remix and/or having students create physical manipulatives of commands, blocks, or lines of code. Teachers can also support expression and communication throughout the learning process by offering sentence starters or checklists to help students collaborate, give feedback, and explain their work. Giving students opportunities to practice computing skills and content through projects that build on prior lessons also supports them in showing what they know.

One key way to design for multiple means of action and expression is to give students choice in how they express and communicate what they know. This might look like giving students options for how they show evidence of completing an assignment. For example, instead of creating a model in Scratch, students might create a storyboard or an illustration of a model. Even when students use Scratch, they could have choice in how they represent aspects of their model. They might use existing sprites, search for sprites online, or draw or paint their sprites by hand. These options allow students to express their learning and communicate it to others.

STRATEGY DEVELOPMENT

Strategy development involves helping students "develop the capacity to act skillfully and purposefully" (CAST, 2024, n.p.). This includes teaching students to manage short-term responses to learning and to set, plan, and monitor progress toward long-term goals.

---

7. Visit these sites at https://www.alice.org/, https://code.org/ and https://scratch.mit.edu/

There are many strategies that teachers can offer to support strategy development as part of learning to code. Some of these include guiding students to set goals for long-term projects, which can be supported by providing students with graphic organizers that facilitate planning, goal-setting, and debugging. Figure 10 is an example of a checklist that students could use to ensure that their project has all required components and aligns with the assessment rubric (Jeong et al., 2017). Teachers might also use planned checkpoints during lessons that verify students' understanding of computing skills and academic content and their progress toward learning goals. Teachers can provide students with examples of completed products and embed prompts throughout a project or lesson that invite students to stop and plan, test, or debug. Providing explicit instruction on skills like asking for help, providing feedback, and problem solving can help students express themselves throughout the coding process. Teachers can also demonstrate debugging strategies for students using think-alouds. Finally, having students record their progress over time can allow them to recognize their learning and growth.

Figure 10. Project Completion Checklist excerpted from Jeong et al., 2017[8]

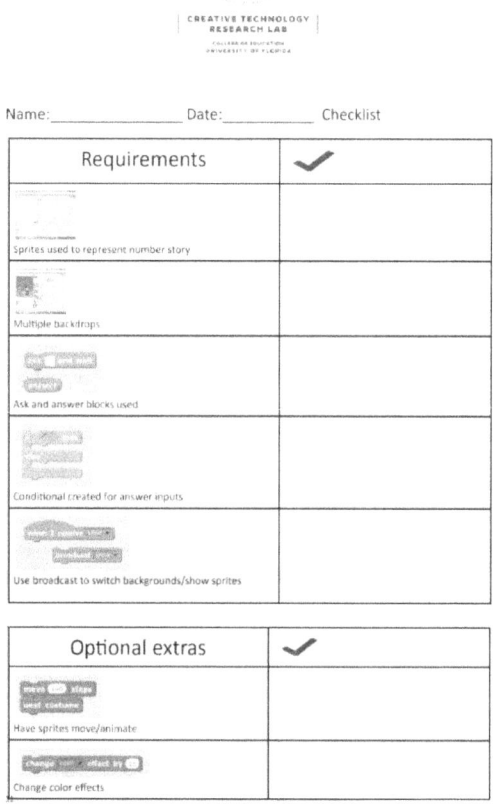

---

8. View the worksheet and other resources at https://docs.google.com/document/d/1_FVQOiam6tlfLQkTyunw7pvBlCX8LodhX3t2Trhg1Dw/edit?tab=t.0

As has been mentioned, debugging is an especially important skill for students to develop as they learn CS. Debugging requires self-regulation related to emotional capacity and developing strategies and executive functioning. The metacognitive strategies that are required to debug and are developed through debugging reinforce the importance of strategy development.

One explicit debugging strategy is referred to as the "reuse strategy" by Ko and colleagues (2019). This strategy involves helping students identify the behavior they want to implement in their program and then find and use code created elsewhere to help them achieve their goals. The reuse strategy provides feedback to students about their goals, what they are trying to code, and what pieces of code they may already have seen that could help them achieve their goal. For example, in the multiple iterations of the weather simulation from Activity 1, the working models of code support the downward movement of sprites, disappearing and reappearing, user interaction through clicking on a sprite, creating clones to create multiple sprites, or using a sprite (i.e., the sun) to act as a trigger to stop all movement. Students could reuse these working models to create new actions in their own programs. Supporting students to develop strategies to manage challenges, solve problems, and identify solutions are key aspects of CS learning.

USING THE UDL FRAMEWORK AS A RESOURCE IN CS ED

As mentioned earlier, the goal of the UDL framework is to anticipate barriers to learning and design learning experiences that reduce or eliminate as many barriers as possible. While it will not be possible to fully eliminate all barriers for every student, anticipating and removing barriers helps your learners have the best learning experience possible and should always be a part of our goals as CS educators.

The UDL framework can guide your efforts to identify and brainstorm possibilities. Remember to begin by designing measurable goals and outcomes for computing and content. Plan ahead of time how you will assess your learners' progress and achievements. Consider creating an assessment plan that addresses barriers that students may encounter, such as providing multiple entry points to a project or choices that allow learners to take ownership of their learning. Allow students to express their learning in meaningful ways. Finally, spend time reflecting. Honest, supportive reflection helps teachers grow and enables us to create the best possible environments for our students to succeed.

Now that you have read this chapter, consider the strategies that Jessica shared with Hana at the beginning. Where do you see different aspects of UDL informing Jessica's instructional approach?

ACTIVITY 2: APPLYING UDL IN CS ED

1. Read Jessica's comments.

2. Identify the different strategies Jessica describes.

3. Make connections between Jessica's strategies and the UDL framework. You can highlight or underline connections, make a list or mindmap, or just think about what you notice.

I found ways to scaffold learning experiences and to provide students with multiple entry points. I plan lessons with centers and choice built in. When introducing an activity, I frontload all success criteria. I explain directions, provide a copy of the slides in Google Classroom, and sometimes use Flip or Loom [video making tools] to create videos that model the activities for students. I also include pictures and examples of previous projects for some assessments. I have Scratch cards and books that are always available and a quiet station for those who just feel that they can't work in a larger group setting that day. I also always keep a Lego station and typing station so there is always an out for the day if needed. Overall, I try to provide choice and clear expectations so students can pick activities that reinforce key concepts, skills, and strategies but also allow space for self-selection and creativity.

REVISITING HANA'S STORY

Hana was excited to make connections between UDL and her CS curriculum. Hana began implementing these changes to strengthen her instruction. Every day, she started and ended her lessons with "I can" statements to help students monitor their own learning. She hung anchor charts around her room with reminders of key CS terms for students to reference. She also gave students options for how they shared their final projects, letting them represent their work through a combination of code, drawing, diagrams, math problems, and writing.

Over time, Hana noticed that all of her students felt more successful in CS, including her students with IEPs. Other teachers had claimed that CS would be too hard for those students, but Hana watched as they excelled in her class and gained confidence. Hana recognized how the UDL framework guided her to design CS learning experiences that eliminated barriers to learning and benefited all of her students.

REFLECTION QUESTIONS

1. Which strategies and designs described in this chapter have you either seen done or used yourself? Which most resonated with you as ones you would like to try?

2. The UDL framework is used across all content areas. Based on what you read in this chapter, how does UDL specifically support learners within the unique context of CS Ed?

TAKEAWAYS FOR PRACTICE

- Choose a CS activity that you have used or would like to use with students. Redesign it to offer students multiple entry points to get started with the activity and/or multiple options to show what they have learned and demonstrate completion of the activity.

- Reflect on your CS Ed context and identify 2–3 barriers in the learning environment that students face. Which design principles in this chapter can help you address those barriers and remove them for learners?

GLOSSARY

Term	Definition
assistive technologies	Technology that helps people with disabilities perform tasks more easily or safely so that they can live, move, participate, and contribute in society more fully. Assistive technologies may include devices (e.g., walkers, prosthetics), materials (e.g., curricular aids), services (e.g., technical assistance), or software (e.g., screen readers).
culturally sustaining pedagogies	Ways and approaches to teaching that value and center students' cultural identities, practices, and ways of knowing as resources for learning rather than excluding or eradicating students' cultures

	from the classroom (see Ladson-Billings, 2021; Paris & Alim, 2017).
Frayer model	A graphic organizer that helps students learn new vocabulary words and understand their meanings. The model places the vocabulary word/concept at the center of the map then explores the term across four quadrants: a definition, facts and/or characteristics, examples, and non-examples to clarify what the concept is not.
literate programming	An understanding of code as a form of expression that is part of a social conversation because computer code (programs) is meant to be read and understood by people and not just computers (Knuth, 1984).
Universal Design for Learning (UDL)	An instructional planning and teaching approach that seeks to meet the needs of all learners by reducing barriers to learning. The three principles of UDL include providing learners with (1) multiple means of engagement, (2) multiple means of representation, and (3) multiple means of action and engagement (CAST, 2024).

REFERENCES

Barrett, J., & Israel, M. (2023). Scaffolding block coding through multiple entry points. *WiPSCE '23: Proceedings of the 18th WiPSCE Conference on Primary and Secondary Computing Education Research* (pp. 1–2). *https://doi.org/10.1145/3605468.3609756*

Center for Applied Special Technology. (2018). *UDL and the learning brain.* https://www.cast.org/binaries/content/assets/common/publications/articles/cast-udlandthebrain-20220228-a11y.pdf

Center for Applied Special Technology. (2024). *The UDL guidelines.* https://udl-guidelines.cast.org/

Israel, M., & Lash, T. (2020). From classroom lessons to exploratory learning progressions: Mathematics + computational thinking. *Interactive Learning Environments, 28*(3), 362–382. https://doi.org/10.1080/10494820.2019.1674879

Israel, M., Lash, T., & Ray, M. (2017). *Universal Design for Learning within computer science education.* Creative Technology Research Lab, University of Florida.

Israel, M., & Ray, S. (2024, Apr 6). *UDL in CS education.* [Professional development session]. Exploring Equity in Computer Science, New York City Public Schools, New York City, NY, USA.

Jeong, G., Lash, T., & Israel, M. (2017). *Helpful strategies for project planning during K-12 computer science instruction.* Project TACTIC: Teaching All Computational Thinking Through Inclusion and Collaboration. Creative Technology Research Lab, University of Illinois. https://ctrl.education.illinois.edu/TACTICal/project-planning.html

Knuth, D. E. (1984). Literate programming. *The Computer Journal, 27*(2), 97–111.

Ko, A. J., LaToza, T. D., Hull, S., Ko, E. A., Kwok, W., Quichocho, J., Akkaraju, H., & Pandit, R. (2019). Teaching explicit programming strategies to adolescents. *SIGCSE '19: Proceedings of the 50th ACM Technical Symposium on Computer Science Education* (pp. 469–475). https://doi.org/10.1145/3287324.3287371

Kozma, R., Chin, E., Russell, J., & Marx, N. (2009). The roles of representations and tools in the chemistry laboratory and their implications for chemistry learning. *Journal of the Learning Sciences, 9*(2), 105–143. https://doi.org/10.1207/s15327809jls0902_1

Ladson-Billings, G. (2021). *Culturally relevant pedagogy: Asking a different question.* Teachers College Press.

Lash, T., Jeong, G., Wherfel, Q., & Israel, M. (n.d.) *Helpful strategies for peer collaboration during K-12 computer science instruction.* Project TACTIC: Teaching All Computational Thinking Through Inclusion and Collaboration. Creative Technology Research Lab, University of Florida. https://ctrl.education.ufl.edu/wp-content/uploads/sites/5/2020/06/CTRL-*TACTIC-PeerCollaboration.pdf*

Lash, T., & Park, M. (2015). *The collaborative discussion framework.* Campaign Unit 4 School District. https://ctrl.education.ufl.edu/wp-content/uploads/sites/5/2020/06/CTRL-CollabFramework.pdf

Learning Trajectories for Everyday Computing. (n.d.). *3rd grade lesson: Polygon partners.* http://everydaycomputing.org/lessons/action-fractions/grade-3/polygon-partners

Margulieux, L. E., Catrambone, R., & Guzdial, M. (2013). Subgoal labeled worked examples improve K-12 teacher performance in computer programming training. *Proceedings of the Annual Meeting of the Cognitive Science Society, 35*, 978–983. https://escholarship.org/uc/item/170185bh

Muldner, K., Jennings, J., & Chiarelli, V. (2022). A review of worked examples in programming activities. *ACM Transactions on Computing Education, 23*(1), 1–35. https://doi.org/10.1145/3560266

Paris, D., & Alim, H. S. (2017). *Culturally sustaining pedagogies: Teaching and learning for justice in a changing world.* Teachers College Press.

Schanzer, E. (2017, Jan 9). *Integrating computer science in math: The potential is great but so are the risks.* AMS Blogs. https://blogs.ams.org/matheducation/2017/01/09/integrating-computer-science-in-math-the-potential-is-great-but-so-are-the-risks/

Skudder, B., & Luxton-Reilly, A. (2014). Worked examples in computer science. *Proceedings of the Sixteenth Australasian Computing Education Conference* (pp. 59–64). https://crpit.scem.westernsydney.edu.au/confpapers/CRPITV-148Skudder.pdf

Universal Design for Learning for Computer Science (UDL4CS). (2021). *Debugging detective.* https://udl4cs.education.ufl.edu/resources/debugging-detective/

GLOSSARY

Ableism: Implicit or explicit social preference for nondisabled bodies and minds that creates prejudice and oppression of disability and disabled people (Shew, 2020).

Academic language: Specialized language used in academic settings.

Access: Giving all students the opportunities and support they need to participate in computer science (CS).

Accessibility: The process of making activities, environments, information, and interactions available to people with different needs.

Accommodations: Changes to a learning environment or to the presentation of curricular content that are offered to help students access content and complete learning tasks that are a regular part of the curriculum. Examples include using a microphone, arranging seating to facilitate movement, or using assistive technologies.

Advocacy: Publicly supporting and championing policies and changes that support equity-oriented CS education. Advocacy involves taking action to disrupt the status quo.

Affinity group: A group of people with shared identities who come together to connect around a common goal.

Antisemitism: A system of prejudice, discrimination, and hostility toward Jewish people.

Archaeology of self: The "deep excavation and exploration of beliefs, biases, and ideas that shape how we engage in the work [of equity]" (Sealey-Ruiz, 2022, p. 22).

Assimilation: Processes through which minoritized and marginalized groups are encouraged or forced to adopt dominant norms and practices.

Assistive technologies: Technology that helps people with disabilities perform tasks more easily or safely so that they can live, move, participate, and contribute in society more fully. Assistive technologies may include devices (e.g., walkers, prosthetics), materials (e.g., curricular aids), services (e.g., technical assistance), or software (e.g., screen readers).

Audit: A process of systematically reviewing your curriculum and instructional practices to assess where you are and where you can grow.

Biases: Attitudes, beliefs, or actions for or against an idea or group when compared with another; may be conscious or unconscious.

Bi/multilingual learners: We use this term to emphasize students' varied and dynamic linguistic resources. We use "multilingual" to highlight how we may not be able to assume that a learner only uses two languages and may have a broader linguistic repertoire (Holdway & Hitchcock, 2018).

Broadening participation: A way of thinking about equity, similar to access, that seeks to increase the participation of members of underrepresented and/or marginalized groups in CS and CS Education (CS Ed). These groups have historically been excluded from computing fields.

Classism: A system of prejudice and discrimination in favor of people with higher socioeconomic status (e.g., upper middle-class) and against people with lower socioeconomic status (e.g., lower class).

Commitment: A statement that involves aligning personally with a set of values and pledging to a course of action based on those values.

Community literacies: Ways of reading, writing, speaking, creating, and interacting with the world that students learned from friends, family, and other communities outside of school.

Computational literacies: Real-world conversations where students use code and computing to create and communicate about CS.

Co-teaching: An instructional model where a general education teacher and a special education teacher teach together in the same classroom.

Critical consciousness: A social and political awareness that allows for a critique of how cultural norms, values, and institutions reproduce social inequities (Ladson-Billings, 1995).

Critical friend: A supportive person with whom there is a relationship of trust who can provide constructive feedback and ask difficult questions related to equity.

Critical race theory: A scholarly theory that frames race as a socially constructed reality embedded into society. Critical race theory recognizes racism as complex and intersectional with other social identities. It seeks to center racially marginalized voices through a commitment to challenge the status quo and work toward social justice (Bell, 2023; Delgado & Stefancic, 2023; Ledesma & Calderon, 2015).

Culturally sustaining pedagogies: Ways and approaches to teaching that value and center students' cultural identities, practices, and ways of knowing as resources for learning rather than excluding or eradicating students' cultures from the classroom (see Ladson-Billings, 2021; Paris & Alim, 2017).

Dead angle: An issue or topic related to equity that a person lacks awareness of or experience with or holds negative biases in ways that prevent equitable change. It also avoids ableism implicit in terms like "blind spot."

Deficit narratives: Broadly held beliefs, including stereotypes, that identify groups of people as lacking or deficient in some way (Louie et al., 2021; Steele, 2011).

Digital racial literacy: Fostering digital racial literacy in CS Ed involves (1) developing students' awareness of the role of human bias in shaping algorithmic bias and the ways in which racially marginalized communities are represented in and threatened by current and existing technologies; (2) preparing students and colleagues to manage the emotions they will face as they interact with CS products and possible workplace experiences that embed racism; and (3) empowering students to critique the impact of technologies on their communities and in their daily lives and empowering students to use technology to disrupt systems of oppression and galvanize their communities.

Disability: Any physical, mental, or emotional variance that impacts, limits, or makes more difficult major life activities in society as it exists today.

Disabled exceptionalism: Narratives that position disabled people as inspirational because they were able to "overcome" their disability and accomplish great things. Disabled exceptionalism objectifies those with disabilities and recenters ableist norms.

Disciplinary literacies: Ways of reading, writing, creating, and interacting with the world in ways that are connected to school subject areas and academic disciplines (e.g., history, math, science).

Diversity: Collectives of individuals with different identities, perspectives, experiences, and backgrounds. Diversity is often described in terms of social categories like age, disability, gender identity and sexual orientation, educational background, language, national origin, race and ethnicity, religion, and socioeconomic status.

Dynamic disabilities: Disabilities that have symptoms that fluctuate in severity, and daily functioning varies from day to day.

Dysgraphia: A learning disability that may affect a person's physical ability to write and/or impact their ability to express their thoughts through writing.

Equality: An approach to addressing inequity that focuses on giving everyone the same resources and opportunities.

Equity as access: Giving all students the opportunities and support they need to participate in CS. Equity as access emphasizes giving everyone what they need to participate in mainstream CS. This approach recognizes that members of marginalized groups may not have the same opportunities to participate in CS, leading to a focus on broadening participation in CS and CS Ed.

Equity as transformation: A way of thinking about equity that recognizes that because the status quo tends to reproduce inequity, it needs to be transformed. Equity as transformation works to disrupt what is considered "normal" in CS disciplines and industries by valuing and centering marginalized knowledge systems, tools, and people.

Erasure: Processes and efforts that render invisible the presence and labor of marginalized and oppressed groups.

Essentialization: Reducing the complexity inherent in people or groups and portraying them in stereotypical ways.

Ethnocomputing: The study of computational practices that are entwined in marginalized/minoritized communities' cultural practices (Eglash et al., 2006).

Exclusion: Processes and efforts that limit the presence and participation of marginalized and oppressed groups in a space.

Four I's of Oppression and Advantage: A theory that illustrates how systems of oppression and advantage (like ableism, classism, or racism) are produced across multiple layers of society. The four I's are ideological, institutional, interpersonal, and internalized. (See Bell, 2013; Chan & Coney, 2020; Chinook Fund, n.d.; Kuttner, 2016.)

Frayer model: A graphic organizer that helps students learn new vocabulary words and understand their meanings. The model places the vocabulary word/concept at the center of the map then explores the term across four quadrants: a definition, facts and/or characteristics, examples, and non-examples to clarify what the concept is not.

Funds of knowledge: Funds of knowledge describe the bodies of knowledge, cultural practices, and ways of interacting that students bring into classrooms with them from their home communities and cultures. Funds of knowledge may include students' academic and personal background knowledge, lived experiences, skills to navigate everyday social contexts, and world views based on broader historical and cultural influences (González et al., 2005; Washington Office of Superintendent of Public Instruction, 2023).

Gatekeeping: Institutional policies and structures that control who gets to participate in opportunities and who has access to resources in ways that limit the participation of marginalized groups.

Generative computing: Computing approaches that connect computational thinking and computing practices to local community practices in culturally responsive ways (Lachney et al., 2019).

Homophobia: A system of prejudice and discrimination against or fear or discomfort with people who identify as LGBTQIA2S+.

Host leadership: Building coalitions across communities that draw on multiple perspectives to work collectively for equity-oriented change.

Hybridity: Bringing everyday and out-of-school knowledge into the classroom to help students learn academic content (Gutiérrez et al., 1999).

Identity-first language: A way to talk about disability that centers the disability (e.g., "a disabled person"). For some people with disabilities, identify-first language is an important way to reclaim their disabled identities so that disability is not perceived as negative. It is best to ask individuals whether they prefer identify-first or person-first language.

Ideological oppression: Dominant sets of beliefs and values that justify and maintain systems of oppression; often disguised as "common sense."

Ideologies: Systems of ideas that circulate in society. Dominant ideologies perpetuate ideas that reinforce the supremacy of certain groups over others.

Imposter syndrome: Feelings and beliefs of intellectual and professional inferiority or incompetence; "a perceived self-doubt in one's abilities and accomplishments compared with others, despite evidence to the contrary" (Walker & Saklofske, 2023, n.p.).

Individualized Education Program (IEP): A legal document mandated by federal law (IDEA, 2004) that outlines services and support that a student with disabilities will receive as part of their public education.

Inequity: Injustice or unfairness that is created and reproduced by social forces. It is important to remember that "fairness" does not mean "sameness," so working to right unfairness and inequity does not mean just giving everyone the same thing.

Institutional oppression: Structures and policies within institutions that disadvantage certain groups and benefit others.

Intercultural competence: An awareness of one's own cultural perspectives and identities and an ability to engage effectively with others across cultures.

Internalized oppression: Acceptance of negative stereotypes about one's own group, leading to self-doubt and discouragement.

Interpersonal oppression: Prejudice and discrimination experienced by individuals or small groups in interpersonal interactions.

Intersectionality: A theory that recognizes how people's different identities (e.g., disability, gender, race) overlap and intersect, creating access to privilege or resulting in oppression in ways that cannot be understood or addressed by considering each identity separately (Crenshaw, 1991; Collins, 2019).

Invisible disabilities: Disabilities that are not readily perceived by society.

Language agnostic: Computing approaches that focus on core computing skills that can be applied across different programming languages.

Language ideologies: Ideas, values, and assumptions about languages, language speakers, and language use that link language to broader social and political systems in different contexts (Irvine & Gal, 2000).

Language injustice: The systematic denial of people's rights to use the language practices of their families, cultures, and communities or the systematic privileging of certain groups' language practices over others'.

Language (linguistic) justice: Challenging white supremacy and dismantling linguistic racism to ensure that all people have the right to use the language practices of their families, cultures, and communities, eliminating the systematic privileging of certain groups' language practices over others' (Baker-Bell, 2020).

Language repertoire: A collection of resources used to communicate, make sense of the world around us, and learn.

Language resources: A collection of words, sounds, and syntaxes, gestures, signs, symbols, objects, and social knowledge about how, when, and where to use those forms in different contexts that make up our language repertoire.

Languaging: A verb used to indicate how language is something that people *do* in social contexts rather than emphasizing language as a noun referring to a static linguistic system.

Literate programming: An understanding of code as a form of expression that is part of a social conversation because computer code (programs) is meant to be read and understood by people and not just computers (Knuth, 1984).

Marginalization: The social process of excluding or oppressing individuals who hold identities that are devalued or differ from society's "ideal" norm.

Marginalized/minoritized identities: Identity categories that are devalued by society, often because they are different from what society has established as the "ideal" norm. Those with marginalized/minoritized identities often face oppression and exclusion from mainstream society. We use marginalized and minoritized as adjectives to emphasize how social processes actively construct inequity (Black et al., 2023). The term "minoritized" emphasizes historical systematic oppression and may be used regardless of whether an identity group actually represents a numerical minority in a context (see Black et al., 2023; Flores & Rosa, 2015).

Matrix of domination: Intersecting systems of power that produce distinct and interlocking forms of oppression (Combahee River Collective, 1977; Collins, 2019).

Medical model of disability: A model that understands disability as an individual medical problem that should be fixed or cured.

Microaggression: Common, everyday slights (verbal or behavioral) toward socially marginalized groups or individuals; microaggressions may be intentional or unintentional, but they still significantly impact those receiving them.

Modifications: Changes to what a student is expected to learn or produce. Examples include shortening an assignment or adjusting a grading scale so that spelling doesn't count toward a grade.

Neurodiversity: The recognition that there are a range of differences in how our brains work.

Neuro-variability: A term developed by the Center for Applied Special Technology (CAST) to describe how no two human brains are alike and that, consequently, there is no one "right" way to learn.

Opportunity hoarding: Processes through which privileged groups control and prevent access to resources for marginalized groups.

Othering: The process of treating a group of people (often those with minoritized or marginalized identities) as intrinsically different from the dominant social norm.

Paternalism: Treating individuals with disabilities in condescending or patronizing ways that deny them their agency and dignity.

Person-first language: A way to talk about disability that avoids defining people in terms of their disability (e.g., "a person with a disability"). It is best to ask individuals whether they prefer identify-first or person-first language.

Praxis: The combination of teaching practices and theory. This guide supports praxis by providing theories about equity that help teachers develop mindsets to take transformative action toward equitable CS Ed.

Pull out model: An instructional model where students with disabilities are pulled out of, or leave, their general education classrooms to receive specialized support from a special education teacher for a given amount of time.

Push in model: An instructional model where a special education teacher pushes into, or enters, a general education classroom to support students with disabilities for a given amount of time.

Racial-ethnic: This term recognizes race and ethnicity as social constructions. Both race and ethnicity—and the conflicts that emerge related to them—are relevant to issues of inquiry in CS and CS Ed. This term captures how both constructs need to be considered as part of developing digital racial literacy.

Racial-ethnic socialization: The process by which we as individuals develop racial identities and a sense of racial meaning based on social norms and expectations. Our racial-ethnic socialization shapes our attitudes, beliefs, and behavior, especially related to racial issues (Hughes et al., 2006).

Racial literacy: The historical and factual awareness of racial issues in the classroom and the emotional preparedness needed to discuss and engage with these issues (Stevenson, 2014).

Racial self-efficacy: The belief that one can cope with and manage racial-ethnic encounters in everyday life (Stevenson, 2014).

Raciolinguistic ideologies: Sets of ideas that draw on racism to shape dominant ideas about language (Flores & Rosa, 2015).

Racism: A system of prejudice and discrimination based on race that privileges individuals racialized as white and oppresses racially minoritized individuals.

RECAST framework: The Racial Encounter Coping Appraisal Socialization Theory, or RECAST, framework offers support to address racial stress and trauma and discuss racial topics in the classroom. The RECAST framework has three parts: (1) READ or becoming aware of racial stress and trauma; (2) RECAST or managing and coping with racial stress; and (3) RESOLVE or taking action against the root causes of racial tension (Stevenson, 2014).

Savior complex: Attitudes and actions where a person believes that they are responsible for "saving" or "rescuing" others by fixing their problems. The person acting as a "savior" often has a sense of superiority and takes action without the consent of those they are "helping," denying their agency.

Segregated settings: A term used by disability scholars to describe how self-contained classrooms often reproduce racial segregation because of the overrepresentation of racially marginalized students in these settings.

Self-contained classroom: An instructional model where students with disabilities are educated in a special education classroom rather than a general education classroom.

Self-efficacy: A belief in one's ability to accomplish a task or achieve a goal.

Sexism: A system of prejudice and discrimination based on gender and gender identity that privileges men and oppresses women, non-binary, and gender-fluid individuals.

Social justice: A view that wealth, opportunities, and privileges should be equitably distributed to all members of society.

Social-emotional learning: Learning skills and behaviors needed to develop healthy identities, manage emotions, and maintain healthy and supportive relationships (Collaborative for Academic, Social, and Emotional Learning, n.d.).

Social model of disability: A model that understands disability as diversity within minds and bodies, where individuals are disabled because of how society is built and organized.

Standard English: A socially constructed, idealized form of English that is not used by people in everyday life (Chang-Bacon, 2020; Flores & Rosa, 2015).

Structural oppression: Historically maintained structures and policies across institutions (e.g., the CS industry, education) that disadvantage certain groups and benefit others over time.

Syncretic: Combining different cultural, social, or religious beliefs and perspectives to create new practices.

Syncretic computational literacies: Merging literacies from students' homes and communities, different academic disciplines, and CS to create new types of literacies and conversations.

Technoableism: The belief that technology is a "solution" for disability and that disabled people can be "fixed" by technology (Shew, 2020).

Theory: A set of ideas based on scholarship and practice that are used to explain and interpret how society works.

Therapeutic practices: Practices that can improve quality of life by addressing and helping manage and resolve discomfort, emotional distress, pain, or stress.

Tokenism: Treating a single individual as representative of an entire group or allowing the presence of a few people with marginalized identities give an illusion of representation and inclusion.

Translanguaging design: Pedagogical designs that incorporate translanguaging practices into classroom activities in ways that allow students to use all of their language resources in learning.

Translanguaging pedagogy: A way of teaching that builds on students' diverse language backgrounds, supporting them to leverage existing resources in their language repertoires and to develop new ones.

Translanguaging shifts: In-the-moment moves and changes that teachers make to respond to students and allow them to use all of their language resources in learning.

Translanguaging stance: An orientation that frames language diversity across and within individuals as a resource, not a deficit.

Translanguaging theory: A theory of language that argues that people have one system of language features and practices that they draw on to make meaning, learn, and express themselves. These features and practices defy the named languages (like English and Spanish) that society has used to categorize language.

Transmisia/transphobia: Both terms describe a system of prejudice and discrimination against people who are transgender or non-binary and a fear or discomfort with people who are transgender or non-binary.

Transmisia emphasizes how prejudice and discrimination are linked to hatred, revulsion, and disgust rather than fear (KosmicKult, 2020). It is an alternative to ableist language connected with the word "phobia" (Planned Parenthood, n.d.)

Trigger: A topic or conversation that surfaces strong emotions or memories; triggers can motivate equitable action or reproduce inequitable patterns.

Underrepresentation: A group of people who are not represented within a context or setting proportionate to their overall representation within the general population.

Universal Design for Learning (UDL): An instructional planning and teaching approach that seeks to meet the needs of all learners by reducing barriers to learning. The three principles of UDL include providing learners with (1) multiple means of engagement, (2) multiple means of representation, and (3) multiple means of action and engagement (CAST, 2024).

Xenophobia: A system of prejudice and discrimination against foreigners.

REFERENCES

Baker-Bell, A. (2020). *Linguistic justice: Black language, literacy, identity, and pedagogy.* Routledge.

Bell, D. A. (2023). Who's afraid of critical race theory? In E. Taylor, D. Gillborn, & G. Ladson-Billings (Eds.), *Foundations of critical race theory in education* (3rd ed., pp. 30–41). Routledge. https://doi.org/10.4324/b23210-4

Bell, J. (2013). *The four "I's" of oppression.* Begin Within. https://beginwithin.info/articles-2/

Black, C., Cerdeña, J. P., & Spearman-McCarthy, E. V. (2023). I am not your minority. *Lancet Regional Health Americas, 19.* https://doi.org/10.1016/j.lana.2023.100464

Center for Applied Special Technology [CAST]. (2024). *The UDL guidelines.* https://udlguidelines.cast.org/

Chan, E. L., & Coney, L. (2020). Moving TESOL forward: Increasing educators' critical consciousness through a racial lens. *TESOL Journal, 11*(4), 1–13. https://doi.org/10.1002/tesj.550

Chang-Bacon, C. K. (2020). Monolingual language ideologies and the idealized speaker: The "new bilingualism" meets the "old" educational inequities. *Teachers College Record, 123*(1), 1–19. https://doi.org/10.1177/016146812112300106

Chinook Fund. (n.d.) *4 I's of oppression.* https://chinookfund.org/wp-content/uploads/2015/10/Supplemental-Information-for-Funding-Guidelines.pdf

Collaborative for Academic, Social, and Emotional Learning [CASEL]. (n.d.). What is the CASEL Framework? CASEL. https://casel.org/fundamentals-of-sel/what-is-the-casel-framework/#:~:text=High%2Dquality%20SEL%20instruction%20 has,Guide%20to%20Effective%20SEL%20Programs

Collins, P. H. (2019). *Intersectionality as critical social theory.* Duke University Press.

Combahee River Collective. (1977). *The Combahee River Collective statement.* BlackPast. https://www.blackpast.org/african-american-history/combahee-river-collective-statement-1977/

Crenshaw, K. (1991). Mapping the margins: Intersectionality, identity politics, and violence against women of color. *Stanford Law Review, 43*(6), 1241–1299.

Delgado, R., & Stefancic, J. (2023). *Critical race theory: An introduction* (4th ed.). NYU Press. https://doi.org/10.18574/nyu/9781479818297.001.0001

Eglash, R., Bennett, A., O'Donnell, C., Jennings, S., & Cintorino, M. (2006). Culturally situated design tools: Ethnocomputing from field site to classroom. *American Anthropologist, 108*(2), 347–362. https://doi.org/10.1525/aa.2006.108.2.347

Flores, N., & Rosa, J. (2015). Undoing appropriateness: Raciolinguistic ideologies and language diversity in education. *Harvard Educational Review, 85*(2), 149–171. https://doi.org/10.17763/0017-8055.85.2.149

González, N., Moll, L. C., & Amanti, C. (2005). *Funds of knowledge: Theorizing practices in households, communities, and classrooms.* Lawrence Erlbaum Associates.

Gutiérrez, K. D., Baquedano-López, P., & Tejeda, C. (1999). Rethinking diversity: Hybridity and hybrid language practices in the third space. *Mind, Culture, and Activity, 6*(4), 286–303.

Holdway, J., & Hitchcock, C. H. (2018). Exploring ideological becoming in professional development for teachers of multilingual learners: Perspectives on translanguaging in the classroom. *Teaching and Teacher Education, 75*, 60–70.

Hughes, D., Rodriguez, J., Smith, E. P., Johnson, D. J., Stevenson, H. C., & Spicer, P. (2006). Parents' ethnic-racial socialization practices: A review of research and directions for future study. *Developmental Psychology, 42*(5), 747.

Irvine, J.T., & Gal, S. (2000). Language ideologies and linguistic differentiation. In P. Kroskrity (Ed.), *Regimes of language: Ideologies, polities, and identities* (pp. 35–83). School of American Research Press.

Knuth, D. E. (1984). Literate programming. *The Computer Journal, 27*(2), 97–111.

KosmicKult. (2020, July 19). *Hate is NOT fear: Reframing homophobia, biphobia, and transphobia.* Medium. https://medium.com/@kosmickult/hate-is-not-fear-reframing-homophobia-biphobia-and-transphobia-beabec366dc6

Kuttner, P. J. (2016). Hip-hop citizens: Arts-based, culturally sustaining civic engagement pedagogy. *Harvard Educational Review, 86*(4), 527–555. https://doi.org/10.17763/1943-5045-86.4.527

Lachney, M., Babbitt, W., Bennett, A., & Eglash, R. (2019). Generative computing: African-American cosmetology as a link between computing education and community wealth. *Interactive Learning Environments*, 1–21. https://doi.org/10.1080/10494820.2019.1636087

Ladson-Billings, G. (1995). But that's just good teaching! The case for culturally relevant pedagogy. *Theory Into Practice, 34*(3), 159–165. https://doi.org/10.1080/00405849509543675

Ladson-Billings, G. (2021). *Culturally relevant pedagogy: Asking a different question.* Teachers College Press.

Ledesma, M. C., & Calderón, D. (2015). Critical race theory in education: A review of past literature and a look to the future. *Qualitative Inquiry, 21*(3), 206–222. https://doi.org/10.1177/1077800414557825

Louie, N., Adiredja, A. P., & Jessup, N. (2021). Teacher noticing from a sociopolitical perspective: the FAIR framework for anti-deficit noticing. *ZDM-Mathematics Education, 53.* (95–107). https://doi.org/10.1007/s11858-021-01229-2

Paris, D., & Alim, H. S. (2017). *Culturally sustaining pedagogies: Teaching and learning for justice in a changing world.* Teachers College Press.

Planned Parenthood. (n.d.). *What's transphobia, also called transmisia?* Planned Parenthood. https://www.plannedparenthood.org/learn/gender-identity/transgender/whats-transphobia

Sealey-Ruiz, Y. (2022). An archaeology of self for our times: Another talk to teachers. *English Journal, 111*(5), 21–26. https://doi.org/10.58680/ej202231819

Shew, A. (2020). Ableism, technoableism, and future AI. *IEEE Xplore, 39*(1), 40–85. https://doi.org/10.1109/MTS.2020.2967492

Steele, C. M. (2011). *Whistling Vivaldi: How stereotypes affect us and what we can do.* W. W. Norton & Company.

Stevenson, H. C. (2014). *Promoting racial literacy in schools: Differences that make a difference.* Teachers College Press.

U.S. Department of Education. (2004). Individuals with disabilities education act. Public Law 108–446. Individuals with Disabilities Education Act, 20 U.S.C. § 1400

Walker, D. L., & Saklofske, D. H. (2023). Development, factor structure, and psychometric validation of the impostor phenomenon assessment: A novel assessment of imposter phenomenon. *Assessment, 30*(7), 2162–2183. https://doi.org/10.1177/10731911221141870

SUGGESTIONS FOR FURTHER READING

The list below contains suggestions for further reading related to topics explored in this book.

Annamma, S. A., Ferri, B. A., & Connor, D. J. (2022). *DisCrit expanded: Reverberations, ruptures, and inquiries*. Teachers College Press.

Baker-Bell, A. (2020). *Linguistic justice: Black language, literacy, identity, and pedagogy*. Routledge. https://doi.org/10.4324/9781315147383

Benjamin, R. (2019). *Race after technology: Abolitionist tools for the new Jim code* (1st ed.). Polity. https://doi.org/10.1093/sf/soz162

Broussard, M. (2023). *More than a glitch: Confronting race, gender, and ability bias in tech*. MIT Press. https://doi.org/10.7551/mitpress/14234.001.0001

Buolamwini, J. (2023). *Unmasking AI: My mission to protect what is human in a world of machines* (1st ed.). Random House.

Connor, D. J., Ferri, B. A., & Annamma, S. A. (2015). *DisCrit: Disability studies and critical race theory in education*. Teachers College Press.

Costanza-Chock, S. (2020). *Design justice: Community-led practices to build the worlds we need*. MIT Press. https://doi.org/10.7551/mitpress/12255.001.0001

Delpit, L. D. (1988). *The silenced dialogue: Power and pedagogy in educating other people's children*. Harvard Educational Review, *58*(3), 280–299. https://doi.org/10.17763/haer.58.3.c43481778r528qw4

García, O., & Wei, L. (2015). Translanguaging: Language, bilingualism and education. In W. E. Wright, S. Boun, & O. García (Eds.), *The handbook of bilingual and multilingual education*, 223–240. Palgrave. https://doi.org/10.1002/9781118533406.ch13

González, N., Moll, L. C., & Amanti, C. (2005). *Funds of knowledge: Theorizing practices in households, communities, and classrooms*. Lawrence Erlbaum Associates.

Hammond, Z. L. (2015). *Culturally responsive teaching and the brain: Promoting authentic engagement and rigor among culturally and linguistically diverse students*. Corwin.

Kendi, I. X. (2019). *How to be an antiracist*. One World.

Ladau, E. (2021). *Demystifying disability: What to know, what to say, and how to be an ally*. Ten Speed Press.

Ladson-Billings, G. (1994). *The dreamkeepers: Successful teachers of African American children*. Jossey-Bass.

Ladson-Billings, G. (2021). *Culturally relevant pedagogy: Asking a different question*. Teachers College Press.

Love, B. L. (2019). *We want to do more than survive: Abolitionist teaching and the pursuit of educational freedom*. Beacon Press.

Margolis, J. (2017). *Stuck in the shallow end, updated edition: Education, race, and computing*. MIT Press.

Margolis, J., & Fisher, A. (2003). *Unlocking the clubhouse: Women in computing*. MIT Press.

Michael, A. (2015). *Raising race questions*. Teachers College Press.

Muhammad, G. (2020). *Cultivating genius: An equity framework for culturally and historically responsive literacy*. Scholastic.

Muhammad, G. (2023). *Unearthing joy: A guide to culturally and historically responsive curriculum and instruction*. Scholastic.

Nakamura, L. (2014). Indigenous circuits: Navajo Women and the racialization of early electronic manufacture. *American Quarterly, 66*(4), 919–941. https://doi.org/10.1353/aq.2014.0070

National Academies of Sciences, Engineering, and Medicine. (2021). *Cultivating interest and competencies in computing: Authentic experiences and design factors*. Washington, DC: National Academies Press. https://doi.org/10.17226/25912

National Academies of Sciences, Engineering, and Medicine. (2025). *Equity in K-12 STEM education: Framing decisions for the future*. Washington, DC: National Academies Press. https://doi.org/10.17226/26859.

Noble, S. U. (2018). *Algorithms of oppression*. New York University Press.

Paris, D., & Alim, H. S. (2017). *Culturally sustaining pedagogies: Teaching and learning for justice in a changing world*. Teachers College Press.

Price-Dennis, D., & Sealey-Ruiz, Y. (2021). *Advancing racial literacies in teacher education: Activism for equity in digital spaces*. Teachers College Press.

Ryoo, J. J., Margolis, J., & Charis, J. B. (2022). *Power on!* MIT Press. https://doi.org/10.7551/mitpress/14166.001.0001

Shew, A. (2024). *Against technoableism: Rethinking who needs improvement*. W. W. Norton & Company.

Stevenson, H. C. (2014). *Promoting racial literacy in schools: Differences that make a difference*. Teachers College Press.

Tozzi, C. (2017). *For fun and profit: A history of the free and open source software revolution*. MIT Press. https://doi.org/10.7551/mitpress/10803.001.0001

Valle, J. W., & Connor, D. J. (2019). *Rethinking disability: A disability studies approach to inclusive practices* (2nd ed.). Routledge. https://doi.org/10.4324/9781315111209

www.ingramcontent.com/pod-product-compliance
Lightning Source LLC
Chambersburg PA
CBHW081143230426
43664CB00018B/2784